Theories of Organizational Structure and Process

Theories of Organizational Structure and Process

John B. Miner
Georgia State University

SCHOOL OF
CALIFORNIA
PROFESSIONAL
PSYCHOLOGY
LOS ANGELES

The Dryden Press

Chicago   New York   Philadelphia   San Francisco   Montreal   Toronto
London   Sydney   Tokyo   Mexico City   Rio de Janeiro   Madrid

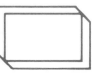
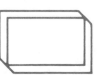

Acquisitions Editor: Anne Elizabeth Smith

Editing, design, and production:
Ligature Publishing Services, Inc.

Address orders to:
383 Madison Avenue
New York, New York 10017

Address editorial correspondence to:
901 North Elm Street
Hinsdale, Illinois 60521

Library of Congress Catalog Card Number: 81-67240
ISBN: 0-03-060532-6
Printed in the United States of America
234 038 987654321

CBS COLLEGE PUBLISHING
The Dryden Press
Holt, Rinehart and Winston
Saunders College Publishing

Dedication

To the major theorists who made this book possible—

Rensis Likert
Arnold S. Tannenbaum
Eric L. Trist
Chris Argyris
Warren G. Bennis
Ralph M. Stogdill
Daniel Katz
Robert L. Kahn
James D. Thompson
Joan Woodward
Tom Burns
G. M. Stalker

Charles Perrow
Paul R. Lawrence
Jay W. Lorsch
Alfred D. Chandler
Herbert A. Simon
James G. March
Richard M. Cyert
Henri Fayol
Max Weber
Peter M. Blau
Victor A. Thompson

—and the many who worked with them.

The Dryden Press Series in Management

Preface

Theories of Organizational Structure and Process is a sequel to *Theories of Organizational Behavior* published by Dryden Press in 1980. In fact the two were originally conceived as a single work. However, it soon became evident that the study of organization, even if restricted to its theoretical components, had become too large for one book, or even for one course. Thus a somewhat artificial division between organizational behavior (the micro level) and organizational structure and process (the macro level)—a distinction now widely accepted in the field—was introduced to differentiate the two books.

Organizational science is in reality one entity, and there is a constant interaction among ideas at the various levels of analysis. At certain points in this volume, reference is made to the theories considered in the earlier book. It may be useful to note at the outset what these theories are. In the motivational domain they include need hierarchy theory (Maslow, Alderfer), achievement motivation theory (McClelland, Atkinson, Weiner), motivation-hygiene theory (Herzberg), equity theory (Adams), expectancy theory (Georgopoulos, Vroom, Galbraith, Cummings, Porter, Lawler, Graen, Deci), goal-setting theory (Locke), behavior modification (Skinner, Hamner, Luthans, Goldstein, Sorcher), and job characteristics theory (Hackman). In the leadership domain are theory X and theory Y (McGregor, Miles), contingency theory (Fiedler), path-goal theory (House, Evans), decision-tree theory (Tannenbaum, Vroom), influence-power continuum theory (Heller), and the vertical dyad linkage model (Graen).

These organizational behavior theories focus on individual and small group functioning within the context of the organization. In contrast, theories of organizational structure and process relate primarily to intergroup relationships, organizationwide concepts, and organization-environment interactions. On occasion, however, these broader formulations incorporate concepts from the individual and small group levels, thus tying together the two major components of organizational science.

This book presupposes that readers have had some prior work in the fields of management, organizational study, behavioral science, human relations, and the like, as well as in statistics. Given a background of this kind, however, readers still should find little in this book that overlaps with their prior learning. The reason is that basic courses typically take a content- or problem-centered approach to planning, organizing, leadership, motivation, communication, and the like. In contrast, this book focuses on the important theories in the field and on the contributions of these theories to our understanding of organizations, as well as to applications and practice. Since much of what we know about organizations derives from theory, this approach is comprehensive in its coverage. It is also highly demanding of its readers, simply because good theories in the social sciences, as in the physical and biological sciences, often are quite complex. For these reasons the book is recommended for the more advanced, second-level student who has already had some exposure to the field.

Though *Theories of Organizational Behavior* and *Theories of Organizational Structure and Process* complement each other, each has been developed to be read and studied on its own. To this end, the first chapter of each book, deals with the scientific underpinnings of organizational study and remains essentially the same in both volumes. Those who have already read the first chapter in one book can skip the first chapter in the other book. Otherwise, the two books are distinct; it is not necessary to have read one to understand the other. On the other hand, if both are to be read, there is probably some advantage in considering organizational behavior first.

In the first part of this volume, theories with origins in human relations concepts and those with applications related to organization development have been grouped together. The authors of these human relations theories were originally trained in psychology or have subsequently become identified with that discipline. Next come the theories that have been developed by authors from diverse disciplines—sociology, political science, history, economics, management—but theories from sociology clearly predominate. The middle chapters focus on systems concepts and relationships between organization and environment, grading into strategy formulation and decision making. Classical management theory and the theory of bureaucracy have deliberately been placed last to avoid any implication that they are of interest only as straw men against which to pit human relations theories. On the other hand, readers who would follow a strict historical sequence should consider more classic theories first.

My major debt in preparing this volume is acknowledged in the dedication. Without the contributions of the various theorists of organizational structure and process, there would be nothing to write about. I am also indebted to those who have worked with me to move from the rough, handwritten manuscript to the final, published volume. In particular I want to thank Mary Blanton, Laura Anderson, Bethann Dunn, and my wife Barbara Miner.

J.B.M.
Atlanta, Georgia

Contents

1

Theory, Research, and Knowledge of Organizational Structure and Process

This book focuses on theories of organizational functioning at the so-called *macro* level to determine the usefulness of these theories to people who participate in organizations. We all participate in various organizations such as schools, companies, and hospitals throughout our lives, and we devote a large percentage of our time to such participation. Most people would like to function more effectively in organizations and to contribute to more effective functioning of the organizations themselves. It seems logical that the more we know about organizations and the way they operate, the better our chances of coping with them adequately and of achieving our own goals within them and for them.

For many people the term *theory* evokes images of a speculative, ivory-towered world, far removed from reality. Theories do not sound helpful in understanding the practical facts of organizational life. Yet one hears such statements as that of the eminent psychologist Kurt Lewin, who said that "nothing is so practical as a good theory." What Lewin means by a "good" theory, of course, is one that is validated by adequate research. To be truly useful, a theory must be intimately intertwined with research (Snizek and Fuhrman, 1980), and to the extent that it is, it has the potential for moving beyond philosophic speculation to become a sound basis for action.

It is important, then, to understand what scientific theory is and what it is not, as well as how theory relates to research and how research either supports or fails to support theory. These are the concerns of this chapter. The intent is to provide a basic understanding that can be drawn on as specific theories are discussed in the remainder of the book.

The Nature of Scientific Theory

This book is concerned with theories that can be tested through research, or scientific theories. Such theories are as potentially useful when applied to organizations as theories of physics and chemistry are when used in developing new manufacturing technologies and consumer products, or theories of biology are in advancing medical practice.

What Is Science?

Science has been defined as the enterprise by which a particular kind of ordered knowledge is obtained about natural phenomena by means of controlled observations and theoretical interpretations (Marx, 1963). The usually accepted goals of scientific effort are to increase understanding and to facilitate prediction (Dubin, 1969). At its best, science will achieve both of these goals. However, there are many instances in which prediction has been accomplished with considerable precision, even though true understanding of the underlying phenomena is minimal; this is characteristic of much of the forecasting that companies do as a basis for planning, for example. Similarly, understanding can be far advanced, even though prediction lags behind. For instance, we know a great deal about the various factors that influence the level of people's work performance (Miner, 1975), but we do not know enough about the interaction of these factors in specific instances to predict with high accuracy how well an individual will do in a particular job.

In an applied field the objectives of understanding and prediction are joined by a third objective—influencing or managing the future. An economic science that explained business cycles fully and predicted fluctuations precisely would represent a long step toward holding unemployment at a desired level. Similarly, knowledge of the dynamics of organizations and the capacity to predict the occurrence of particular structures and processes would seem to offer the possibility of engineering a situation to maximize organizational effectiveness. To the extent that limited unemployment or increased organizational effectiveness are desired, science then becomes a means to these goals. In fact much scientific work is undertaken to influence the world around us. To the extent applied science meets such objectives, it achieves a major goal.

The Role of Theory in Science

Scientific method evolves in ascending levels of abstraction (Brown, and Ghiselli, 1955). At the most basic level it portrays and retains experience in *symbols*. The symbols may be mathematical, but to date in organizational science they have been primarily linguistic.

Once converted to symbols, experience may be mentally manipulated, and relationships may be established.

Description utilizes symbols to classify, order, and correlate events. It remains at a low level of abstraction and is closely tied to observation and sensory experience. In essence it is a matter of ordering symbols to make them adequately portray events.

Explanation moves to a higher level of abstraction in that it attempts to establish meanings behind events. It attempts to identify causal, or at least concomitant, relationships so that observed phenomena make some logical sense.

At its maximal point, explanation becomes *theory*. Theory is a patterning of logical constructs, or interrelated symbolic concepts, into which the known facts regarding a phenomenon, or theoretical domain, may be fitted. A theory is a generalization, applicable within stated boundaries, that specifies the relationships between factors. Thus it is an attempt to make sense out of observations that in and of themselves do not contain any inherent and obvious logic (Dubin, 1976).

Scientific Assumptions

To operate at all, science must make certain assumptions about the world around us. These assumptions may not be factually true, and to the extent they are not, science will have little value. However, to the extent science operates on these assumptions and produces a degree of valid understanding, prediction, and influence, it becomes more worthwhile to utilize the assumptions. We are now at a point where this kind of expediency seems entirely justified.

We assume, first, that certain natural groupings of phenomena exist, so that classification can occur and generalization within a category is meaningful. For some years, for instance, the field of business policy, operating from its origins in the case method, assumed that each company is essentially unique. This assumption effectively blocked the development of scientific theory and research in the field. Now, increasingly the assumption of uniqueness is disappearing, and generalizations applicable to classes of organizations are emerging (Steiner and Miner, 1982). As a result, scientific theory and research are burgeoning in the policy field.

Second, we must assume some degree of constancy, or stability, or permanence in the world. Science cannot operate in a context of complete random variation; the goal of valid prediction is totally unattainable under such circumstances. Thus objects and events must retain some degree of similarity from one time to another. In a sense this is an extension of the first assumption, but now over time rather than across units. For instance, if organizational structures, once introduced, did not retain some stability, any scientific prediction of their impact on organizational performance would be impossible. Fortunately they do have some constancy, but not always as much as might be desired.

Third, science assumes that events are determined and that causes exist. This is the essence of explanation and theorizing. It may not be possible to prove a specific causation with absolute certainty, but evidence can be adduced to support certain causal explanations and reject others. In any event, if one does not assume some kind of causation, there is little point in scientific investigation; the assumption of determinism is what sparks scientific effort. If, for instance, one assumes that organizational role prescriptions do not influence individual performance, then the whole area of organizational design moves outside the realm of scientific inquiry. Organizational theory must assume some kind of causal impact of the organization on its members. It then becomes the task of science to determine the nature of this impact.

Finally, because science is firmly rooted in observation and experience, it is necessary to assume some degree of trustworthiness for the human processes of perceiving, remembering, and reasoning. This trustworthiness is always relative, but it must exist to some degree. The rules under which science operates are intended to increase the degree of reliability with which scientific observation and recording operate. The purpose is to achieve an objective, rational, replicable result, which will be convincing to those who are knowledgeable in the area of study.

The Rules of Scientific Inquiry

If the findings of research are to be replicated and the generalizations from research are to be valid, concepts must be clearly defined in terms of the procedures used to measure them. As we shall see, this has been a major problem in the field of organizational study. Often theoretical concepts are stated in such an ambiguous manner and the conditions for their measurement left so uncertain that the researcher is hard put to devise an adequate test of the theory.

Second, scientific observation must be controlled so that causation may be attributed correctly. The objective is to be certain that an outcome is in fact produced by what is believed to produce it and not by something else. Control of this kind is achieved through the use of various experimental designs, to be discussed later in this chapter, or through measurement and statistical adjustment. In the complex world of organizational functioning, establishing controls sufficient to pin down causation often has proved to be difficult.

Third, because science is concerned with generalization to contexts that extend far beyond a given experiment, it is essential that research utilize samples that are adequate in both size and conditions of their selection. One must have confidence that the results obtained are generalizable and can be put to use outside the research situation. The field of statistics becomes important for organizational study because of its potential for determining how much confidence can be placed in a particular research outcome.

Fourth, and this bears repeating, science requires that its propositions, hypotheses, and theories be stated in terms that can be tested empirically. This is where philosophy and science part company. Unfortunately, in the early years of its development, organizational study did not always clearly separate scientific from philosophic statements. The result has been considerable confusion, and on occasion effort has been wasted in attempts to test theories that are not really testable as stated.

Theory Building

A distinction is often made between deductive and inductive theory (Filley, House, and Kerr, 1976). In building a theory by deduction, one first establishes a set of premises. Then certain logical consequences of these premises are deduced and subsidiary concepts are established. The starting point is rational thought, and logical consistency is a major concern in development of the theory. Often such theories are stated in mathematical terms.

Inductive theory, in contrast, builds up from observation, often from research, rather than down from a set of premises. Essentially one puts together a theory that best seems to explain what is known in a given area at the present time. Then new tests of this theory, or of hypotheses derived from it, are carried out just as they would be if the theory were developed deductively.

A major pitfall in the use of the inductive approach, and we will consider instances of this in later chapters, is that the research from which the theory is induced may tend to become confused with an adequate test of the theory. Thus the same research is used twice for two different purposes, and a self-fulfilling prophecy results. In the case of truly deductive theories, this is not possible. When theories are developed inductively, it is crucial that they be tested on a new sample in a manner that is entirely independent of the pretheory research. If one goes back to the prior sample or to data used in developing the theory, anything unique and ungeneralizable (attributable to chance fluctuation) in that particular situation is very likely to be confirmed. As a result, a theory that is erroneous insofar as generalization and practical usefulness are concerned may well be accepted.

It is actually more useful to think of theories as falling at points along a deductive-inductive continuum than as falling into distinct categories. Probably no theory is completely devoid of some inductive input. On the other hand there are instances arising from entirely inductive processes. Such instances are often referred to as *dust-bowl empiricism*, implying that no theory is involved at all. However, the result may look very much like a theory, and it may not be entirely meaningful to reject the result as theory.

An example of dust-bowl empiricism would be a study in which a great many measures, say several hundred, are obtained on a sample of organizations. These data are then put into a computer, and closely related measures are identified through the use of correlation techniques, factor analysis, or some similar procedure. What emerges is a set of hypothesized relationships among variables—a set of statements very much like an inductively derived theory. This "theory" is then tested on a new sample of organizations, using the appropriate measures to make sure that it does not incorporate relationships that represent mere chance fluctuations associated with the particular sample from which the theory was induced.

It should be emphasized that any theory, irrespective of the method of its construction and the extent of current confirmation, is provisional in nature. Theories are constructed to be modified or replaced as new knowledge appears; this is the way science advances (MacKenzie and House, 1978). Furthermore, modification on the basis of research tends to be inductive rather than deductive. Findings emerge that do not quite fit the existing theory. Accordingly, the theory is changed so that these new data can be explained, and a test is then made of the revised theory. As a result of this kind of theoretical tinkering, even predominantly deductive theories may take on a strong inductive element over time; if they do not, they may well be replaced.

What Is a Good Theory?

The objective of this book is to look at the field of organizational study through the medium of its major theories. In the process we will evaluate these theories in terms of their current utility. To do this, we need some criteria for deciding whether a theory is good or not so good. It is evident from what has been said already that some explanatory statements may not meet the requirements of scientific theory at all, and that what was good theory at one time may be not-so-good theory some years later.

First, theories should contribute to the goals of science. They should aid understanding, permit prediction, and facilitate influence. The more they do these things, the better they are. A theory that is comprehensive in its coverage of the phenomena that it explains is preferable to one that is limited in scope. However, broad scope alone is not enough. Many so-called grand theories attempt too much and fail simply because they do not really explain the wide range of phenomena they attempt to consider (Pinder and Moore, 1980).

Second, there should be a clear delineation of the domain of the theory. The boundaries of application should be specified so that the theory is not utilized in situations for which it was never intended and is therefore useless. Definition of the coverage of a theory often has been neglected in the social sciences generally (Dubin, 1969), and the field of organizational science is no exception.

Third, theory should direct research efforts to important matters. The number of research studies that could be done in the world is almost infinite. Yet most of these studies, even if the time and effort to carry them out were available, would not yield significant results in a statistical sense, and many of those that did would be trivial in terms of their usefulness. Good theory helps us focus research efforts on salient variables, identify important relationships, and come up with truly *significant* findings in every sense of the word. Basically, then, good theory protects the researcher from wasting time.

Fourth, theories at their best yield a kind of added value to research efforts. If several hypotheses derived from a theory are confirmed by research, then the whole body of the theory becomes available for use. Thus theory-based research has the potential for yielding not just a few isolated facts, but powerful explanation and prediction across the whole domain of the theory. This aspect of good theory is one of its most practical consequences. Unfortunately many theories do not have this cumulative character.

Fifth, theories should be readily testable. It should be clear exactly what must be done to either confirm or disconfirm them. On occasion experimenters will carry out studies that they believe to be adequate tests of a theory, only to have the theorist say, "That is not what I meant." When theory is well formulated, this situation should rarely arise. Ideally the theorist will identify the variables of the theory in operational terms.

Sixth, good theory is not only confirmed by research derived from it, but is also logically consistent within itself and with other known facts. In the case of complex theories, it is entirely possible to develop propositions that would predict diametrically opposed outcomes in the same situation. This is particularly likely to happen when the theorist comes at the same subject matter from different directions, using different concepts and assumptions. Such internal, logical inconsistencies must be ironed out if the theory is to be of much use. Furthermore, theories do not exist in a vacuum; they are part of the total body of scientific knowledge. At any given time it may not be entirely clear how a particular theory fits into the larger scientific configuration, but a theory that from the outset quite obviously does not fit at all is to that degree deficient. Theories should build on what is known; they should not place us in the uneconomical situation of having to reinvent the wheel constantly.

Seventh, the best theory is the one that is simplest in statement. If a given set of phenomena can be explained parsimoniously with a few variables, that theory should be preferred over one that achieves the same level of explanation with a much more complex set of variables and relationships. Science does not value complexity in its own right; there is enough of that all around us in nature. Highly complex and involved theories are often very difficult to put into practice. Thus the ultimate objective must be to replace them with simpler explanations. Unfortunately the process of inductive theory modification often demands that new variables be added continually as unanticipated findings emerge and need to be explained. Under such circumstances a theory may fall of its own weight, for it is just too cumbersome to be useful.

Measurement and Research Design

In large part the value of a theory is inherent in the research it sparks and in the extent to which the theory is confirmed by this research. Research is only possible, however, to the extent that measures of the constructs of the theory are developed, that is, to the extent that the constructs are made operational. These twin topics of measurement and research concern us in this section. The objective is not to provide a detailed treatment. However, in later chapters we will be asking questions such as "Does this measure really effectively represent the constructs of the theory?" and "Does this research provide an appropriate test of the theory?" The answers to these questions will draw on some knowledge of both measurement procedures and research design, and the ensuing discussion is intended to provide that information.

Measuring Theoretical Constructs

Measures used in organizational research have often fallen far short of what might be desired (Price, 1972). In part this is a function of the newness of the field. In theories dealing with organizations the constructs emerging as most important have typically been far removed from those previously measured in the social sciences. Thus it has been necessary in many cases to develop reliable and valid measures of new constructs from scratch, which is a time-consuming process. Many organizational measures are still at a primitive stage of development. This situation can seriously hamper the interpretation of research results.

Reliability. A major concern in research is the reliability of measurement. Measures that are sufficiently stable and unambiguous will not produce sizable differences in score values when applied to the same phenomenon on separate occasions. The reliability of a measure is usually established by a correlation coefficient. Different approaches are used to determine this reliability coefficient, but all approaches approximate the ideal procedure, which utilizes parallel forms of the same measure. Parallel forms exist when two indexes of the same construct contain the same number of items of each type, concentrate equally on the various aspects of the construct, and produce the same average scores and distributions of scores through the range of possible values. Once such parallel measures have been developed, reliability is determined by administering both measures in the same sample and correlating the scores on the two measures.

The value of a reliability coefficient fluctuates to some extent, depending on whether the parallel form or some other approach is used. However, if one wishes to use a measure in an individual situation—to measure the work motivation of a *particular* person, for instance, or to compute the average span of control in a *certain* company—reliability coefficients above .90 are required. If, on the other hand, one is dealing with group data such as mean work motivation scores in two units of a company or average spans of control in relation to profitability in a number of companies, values down to about .70, and sometimes less, typically are acceptable.

The matter of reliability of measurement is important in research because it is impossible to interpret outcomes when unreliable measures are used and results are not statistically significant. The failure to obtain evidence of a relationship between two variables could be due to the fact that there is no relationship. But if one or both measures of the two variables are unreliable, a relationship may well exist that has not been discovered because of inadequate measures. The only satisfactory way to resolve this uncertainty is to develop and use measures of high reliability. Then if relationships are not found, they are not there.

Validity. In the discussion of the problems of theory construction, the need to create operational measures of the constructs of the theory was emphasized. This means that the measures must truly reflect the underlying constructs; they must provide valid data regarding the phenomena that they are supposed to represent. If they in fact measure constructs other than the ones they are intended to measure, the theory may well be assumed to be disconfirmed when it is actually correct. Worse still, a theory may be accepted when in fact its variables have been incorrectly stated.

The author once developed an index to measure conformity to organizational norms. Subsequent research revealed that the index was almost completely unrelated to any other measure of conformity that could be identified in the literature. However, moderate relationships were found with measures of intelligence. Apparently, if the measure did tap some tendency to conform, it was not the same construct that other researchers had in mind when they used the term. A much more likely interpretation was that we had developed a not particularly impressive measure of intelligence.

This example demonstrates how one goes about determining the validity of a construct measure. If the measure is what it purports to be, there are certain phenomena to which it should be related and certain other phenomena to which it should not be related. In the case of conformity, there were other indexes of the construct available. Often, when a new and highly innovative theory is under test, other measures are not available. Nevertheless it should be possible to identify certain relationships that would be expected to appear with a high degree of likelihood. In this process, however, it is important not to rely on *face validity* alone. The measure that looks to be appropriate as an index of a given variable on further investigation may or may not prove to tap that construct.

As we shall see later, establishing the validity of a particular construct measure is not easy. To some degree the answer is always inferential. Yet there are certain organizational measures in which one can have considerable faith, while there are others that, even after long years of use, leave considerable doubt as to their construct validity.

Designing Research

Research conducted to test theories characteristically investigates hypothesized relationships between variables. Such research is first concerned with whether a relationship exists at all and then with the causal path of that relationship. Research focused on the existence of a relationship is relatively easy to conduct; however, research into the causal problem is clearly much less tractable.

The study of causation typically requires the collection of data over time, on the premise that the cause must be shown to precede the effect. There are certain techniques, such as path analysis, that under appropriate circumstances can be used with data collected at one time to investigate causal hypotheses (Billings and Wroten, 1978). However, these techniques tend to require the collection of large amounts of data and often involve complex statistical analyses. The results are also difficult to interpret (James, 1980; Young, 1977). It is often much easier to reject certain alternatives as possible causes than to establish the true causes. Thus the use of concurrent approaches to the study of causation makes great demands on time, effort, and intellect, and does not fully eliminate the difficulties inherent in causal research.

A second factor that makes identification of causal relationships difficult is the necessity for establishing adequate controls. Control may be accomplished statistically through the use of procedures such as partial correlation and analysis of covariance to measure unwanted variables and then remove their effects from the relationships under study. However, these statistical techniques require that the data satisfy certain assumptions, and in many cases it is not at all clear that these assumptions can be met. The preferred alternative is to control variables through the original design of the study. That is not always easy.

Laboratory Experiments. Much of the research on causal relationships has been done in the laboratory. An extreme instance of this laboratory research is computer simulation in which no real subjects are involved. More frequently, the experiment is of the small group or group dynamics type; experimental variables are introduced among subjects, often college sophomores, and the results are measured under highly controlled conditions. Because the study is conducted outside the real world of ongoing organizations, it is easier to use longitudinal measures and to control unwanted variables. Yet even here major difficulties in maintaining controls have been noted (Evan, 1971). Furthermore, the results are very much a function of the variables considered (this is particularly true of computer simulations). If the real world is not effectively modeled in the laboratory, the results of laboratory experiments will not transfer. This means that any laboratory experimentation should be extended to ongoing organizations before the results are accepted. For example, some very significant results have emerged from studies of decision making in business games, but we do not know whether these games contain all of the ingredients of real organizations. Until this is determined, the results cannot be considered complete tests of organizational theory.

Field Experiments. The ideal situation, of course, is to take the techniques of sample selection, repetitive measurement, and variable control associated with laboratory research into the real world and conduct the same kind of research with ongoing organizations. In such a context the myriad variables that may be important do in fact operate, and any results obtained there can be expected to characterize the actual organizations to which any meaningful theory is addressed. The problem is that all the difficulties of designing and conducting good experiments that were so easily handled in the laboratory now become overwhelming. Real organizations have innumerable ways of resisting and undermining objective scientific research—not out of contrariness, but because the goals of the real world and the laboratory are different.

An Example of a Field Experiment. The difficulties of conducting causal research in organizations may be illustrated by a study by Belasco and Trice (1969) on the effects of a particular management development program. The study utilized 119 managers divided into four groups. Managers were assigned to each group on a random basis within sex, type of work supervised, and division groupings. In this manner as many factors as possible were held constant across the four groups to control for spurious factors that might contaminate the findings and make causal attribution difficult.

One group of managers was pretested, trained, and posttested on knowledge, attitudes, and behavior. The objective was to see if a change occurred.

A second group took the pretest, received no training, and then took the posttest. If this group changed as much as the first, clearly the training was not the cause of change. If this group did not change as much as the first, the training remained a strong contender as a cause.

A third group underwent no pretest, received training, and took the posttest. By comparing the posttest result for the third group with that for the first group, it was possible to identify any apparent change due to a sensitizing effect of the pretest (the groups were similar in all other respects). The problem addressed here is control for any effects the pretest may have had in alerting the managers to what they were supposed to learn later in training.

The fourth group received no pretest, no training, and only the posttest. This group, in comparison with the others, yields a measure of the effects of the passage of time only, and therefore isolates time from either repeated measurement or training as factors.

Clearly this kind of research requires a large number of subjects, the opportunity to assign them to groups as desired for research purposes, and extensive collaboration from the sponsoring organization throughout the study.   And, as elaborate as the research plan is, it could be argued that a fifth group, undergoing some training of a relatively neutral nature, should have been included to create a placebo situation and cancel out any so-called Hawthorne effect (receiving special attention). Thus even this very complex experiment cannot be said to have achieved the ideal in terms of control.

Patch-Up or Adaptive Designs. It is no accident that research of the kind Belasco and Trice conducted is not widespread in the literature. There are very few organizations that will permit the internal disruption that research of this kind requires. In particular there are likely to be problems with random assignments to conditions, sufficient sample sizes, and people being excluded from the training that was offered in the first place on the basis of some presumed potential value to the organization. Furthermore, there is the very real problem that organizations willing to go along with all this might not be typical, and therefore the results may lack generality.

It is quite evident that elegant research designs, with all the possible controls, are not likely to be implemented in ongoing organizations. Accordingly, certain variants are being proposed, such as patch-up (Evans, 1975) or adaptive (Lawler, 1977) designs. These designs represent major advances over the noncausal, correlational analyses, but no one such study answers all questions. Basically these studies utilize as many components of the ideal experimental design as possible, while recognizing that it is better to conduct some kind of research related to causes than to do nothing. Hopefully the relative relaxation of control requirements will be compensated for by the larger number of research investigations carried out. Accordingly, several interlocking investigations should develop the same level of knowledge as one very elegant study. On the other hand it is easy to relax scientific standards to the point where replication is not possible, and thus not obtain scientific knowledge that can be substantiated. Some recent trends in qualitative research on organizations show this tendency (Van Maanen, 1979). It is important to maintain a clear distinction between scientific research and personal narrative.

The State of Theoretical Knowledge of Organizations

In our analysis of theories of organizational structure and process, it may be useful to hold in mind certain historical facts about the field and about the scientists and practitioners within it. There has not always been a unity of opinion between scientist-researchers and practitioner-managers as to the most valuable theories of organizations. In fact there is, if anything, a slight negative correlation, with those theories espoused by one group tending to be rejected by the other. One might think that the practitioners would prefer the more hard-headed, practical theories, while the scientists would be guided more by the dictates of scientific values and theoretical sophistication. This, however, is not entirely the case.

Some very insightful quotes from Robert Dubin may help explain what has happened:

> We live in a highly secular world. The morality of the Judeo-Christian tradition is no longer the consensual boundary within which practical decisions are taken in the operation and management of work organizations. Secular man, even though he is an executive and decision maker, is very much in need of moral guidelines within which to make his decisions. . . . Today's rational organizational decision makers avidly seek moral justification for their actions and are only too ready to see the new morals in the scientific theories of the applied behavioral scientists. . . . Once this phenomenon is recognized, it becomes easier to understand how simple theories can often be widely accepted by practitioners at the very moment that they come under questioning and dispute among scientists (Dubin, 1976, p. 22).

As the Protestant Ethic has palled in significance for many managers, they seem to have turned to science for moral guidelines. In fulfilling this moral need, they have been particularly attracted by relatively simple theories with strong humanistic overtones that emphasize the perfectability of mankind—theories not unlike religion, but with the added sanctions of science. Unfortunately these managers often endorse theories that fail to meet scientific criteria, and in particular the tests of research evidence. Thus, as more and more practitioners learn about the theories and find them attractive, more and more scientists withdraw their original endorsements in response to additional research findings. Presumably such theories will ultimately fail to attract practitioner support as well. Or, as is entirely possible, the theories will establish themselves as social philosophies, which many of them often are, and continue to attract adherents without reference to the research findings and endorsements of the scientific world.

The high visibility of the humanistic philosophy-theories has led some writers to question whether organizational science possesses any theories at all (Tosi, 1975). This negative position has received further support from some individuals, a number of them scientists, who place very little stock in theory building in any event, preferring the slow but solid pace of unswerving empiricism. Yet there do appear to be some real scientific theories dealing with organizations, or at least explanations so advanced that not to call them theories is something of a quibble. This is not to say that these theories are necessarily and entirely valid; a number of them have not been fully tested. But they have contributed substantially to our knowledge of organizations.

The chapters that follow consider both philosophy-theories and theory-theories. Both types are tested equally against the criteria of good science and good scientific theory. The theories included in this book were nominated by recognized scholars in the field of organizational study. More than thirty-five individuals suggested theories for consideration. All theories on which most of the scholars agreed are discussed here. Several others, while nominated less often, are included because the author believes they extend our knowledge in new directions and/or make particularly important contributions. A number of newer theories that have stimulated very little research have been excluded, even though they are promising, because it is too early to reach even a preliminary judgment on them. Even without these newer theories, it is apparent that conflict is rife in the study of organizations at the present time (Roberts, Hulin, and Rousseau, 1978). Only objective, controlled, scientific research can separate the wheat from the chaff in theories of organizational structure and process in the years to come.

References

Belasco, James A., and Harrison M. Trice. *The Assessment of Change in Training and Therapy.* New York: McGraw-Hill, 1969.

Billings, Robert S., and Steve P. Wroten. "Use of Path Analysis in Industrial/Organizational Psychology: Criticisms and Suggestions," *Journal of Applied Psychology,* 63 (1978), 677–88.

Brown, C. W., and Edwin E. Ghiselli. *Scientific Method in Psychology.* New York: McGraw-Hill, 1955.

Dubin, Robert. *Theory Building.* New York: Free Press, 1969.

———. "Theory Building in Applied Areas." In Marvin D. Dunnette (ed.), *Handbook of Industrial and Organizational Psychology.* Chicago: Rand McNally, 1976, pp. 17–39.

Evan, William M. *Organizational Experiments: Laboratory and Field Research.* New York: Harper & Row, 1971.

Evans, Martin G. "Opportunistic Organizational Research: The Role of Patch-up Designs," *Academy of Management Journal,* 18 (1975), 98–108.

Filley, Alan C., Robert J. House, and Steven Kerr. *Managerial Process and Organizational Behavior.* Glenview, Ill.: Scott, Foresman, 1976.

James, Lawrence R. "The Unmeasured Variables Problem in Path Analysis," *Journal of Applied Psychology,* 65 (1980), 415–21.

Lawler, Edward E. "Adaptive Experiments: An Approach to Organizational Behavior Research," *Academy of Management Review,* 2 (1977), 576–85.

MacKenzie, Kenneth D., and Robert House. "Paradigm Development in the Social Sciences: A Proposed Research Strategy," *Academy of Management Review,* 3 (1978), 7–23.

Marx, Melvin H. *Theories in Contemporary Psychology.* New York: Macmillan, 1963.

Miner, John B. *The Challenge of Managing.* Philadelphia: W. B. Saunders, 1975.

Pinder, Craig C., and Larry F. Moore. *Middle Range Theory and the Study of Organizations.* Boston: Martinus Nijhoff, 1980.

Price, James L. *Handbook of Organizational Measurement.* Lexington, Mass.: D. C. Heath, 1972.

Roberts, Karlene H., Charles L. Hulin, and Denise M. Rousseau. *Developing an Interdisciplinary Science of Organizations.* San Francisco: Jossey-Bass, 1978.

Snizek, William E., and Ellsworth R. Fuhrman. "Theoretical Observations on Applied Behavioral Science," *Journal of Applied Behavioral Science,* 16 (1980), 93–103.

Steiner, George A., and John B. Miner. *Management Policy and Strategy.* New York: Macmillan, 1982.

Tosi, Henry L. *Theories of Organization.* Chicago: St. Clair, 1975.

Van Maanen, John. "Reclaiming Qualitative Methods for Organizational Research: A Preface," *Administrative Science Quarterly,* 24 (1979), 520–26.

Young, Jerald W. "The Function of Theory in a Dilemma of Path Analysis," *Journal of Applied Psychology,* 62 (1977), 108–10.

2

The Theory of System 4 and 4T

The theoretical formulations of Rensis Likert are among the best known in the behavioral humanist tradition. His constructs overlap in a number of respects with those of other participative management advocates, such as Maslow, McGregor, and Argyris, but there are important differences as well. In particular Likert's theory strongly emphasizes work groups and their interactions, as well as practical considerations of profit and loss. The major focus initially was on leadership within the group, but the theory quickly expanded to incorporate lateral and vertical intergroup relationships, organizational climates, and social systems. Ultimately it became a full-blown theory of organizational process and in certain respects of structure as well.

Likert's theoretical contributions evolved during his long career as director of the Institute for Social Research at the University of Michigan (Likert, 1978). This association started when Likert left his primarily wartime position directing survey research for the federal government in 1946. It ended on a formal basis when he retired from the University of Michigan in 1970. However, his continued activity in his professional career and his founding of Rensis Likert Associates in Ann Arbor after his retirement both contribute to Likert's strong identification with the University of Michigan up to now.

Likert's Theory of the Participative Organization

The theory to be considered in this chapter is set forth primarily in three books—*New Patterns of Management* (Likert, 1961), *The Human Organization* (Likert, 1967), and *New Ways of Managing Conflict* (Likert and Likert, 1976). These books have been supplemented by a number of journal articles. The program of research conducted by the Institute for Social Research has served as both an inductive source and an empirical testing ground for Likert's theoretical formulations. In fact this grounding in observation and research is so strong that Likert often writes as if he is describing established fact or presenting empirical elaborations, rather than formulating theory. Yet it remains advisable to scrutinize his views in the light of scientific theory in the same manner as the other conceptualizations are explored in this book. Certainly there are places in his writings where Likert clearly indicates that he is presenting theory.

New Patterns of Management

The first comprehensive statement of Likert's views (Likert, 1961) contained extensive discussions of research conducted by the staff of the Institute for Social Research during the late 1940s and the 1950s. Such sequencing might give the impression that the 1961 theory was an outgrowth of prior research and that this research cannot legitimately be viewed as a test of the theory. Yet Likert's earlier writings, extending back to the early 1940s (Likert and Willets, 1940–41), contain many statements that are analogous to those set forth more formally in the 1961 volume. Thus key concepts such as the principle of supportive relationships and the value of participative management appear to have guided the research of the University of Michigan group from the beginning. The concepts were clearly enunciated in external publications by the early 1950s (Likert, 1953; Mann and Likert, 1952). Though the early theory and research are not entirely free of "the chicken and the egg" problems, certain significant research specifically designed to test Likert's hypotheses was conducted in this period.

Principle of Supportive Relationships. The principle of supportive relationships is stated in somewhat varied forms in Likert's writings, but the meaning changes very little:

> The leadership and other processes of the organization must be such as to ensure a maximum probability that in all interactions and all relationships with the organization each member will, in the light of his background, values, and expectations, view the experience as supportive and one which builds and maintains his sense of personal worth and importance (Likert, 1961, p. 103).

Elsewhere Likert refers to such a statement as the "fundamental concept" and "general formula" of the theory (Likert, 1959). As a theoretical hypothesis, it should be prefaced with "If a high-producing organization is desired . . ."

This basic principle assumes an extremely important and influential role for leadership in the organization. Effective leaders are those who are employee-centered, in that they behave in ways that create a perception of supportiveness. At the same time, they transmit high-performance goals through a kind of "contagious enthusiasm" and possess the needed technical competence.

Highly Effective Groups and Linking Pins. The major source of supportive relationships lies in the work group. Thus a derivation from the basic principle states:

> Management will make full use of the potential capacities of its human resources only when each person in an organization is a member of one or more effectively functioning work groups that have a high degree of group loyalty, effective skills of interaction, and high performance goals. . . . an organization will function best when its

personnel function not as individuals but as members of highly effective work groups with high performance goals. Consequently, management should deliberately endeavor to build these effective groups, linking them into an overall organization by means of people who hold overlapping group membership. The superior in one group is a subordinate in the next group and so on through the organization (Likert, 1961, pp. 104–5).

Individuals who are in these positions of dual group membership ideally should exert influence in both groups—both upward and downward, as members and as leaders. In doing so they perform the linking pin function and open up channels of communication through the organization. Failure to perform the linking pin function effectively results in work group failure at the subordinate level. To the extent that there are many such failed groups and to the extent that groups of this kind exist toward the top of the hierarchy, the organization as a whole will function less effectively. Thus, open, two-way communication and influence are essential to organizational effectiveness. Group and intergroup meetings facilitate two-way communication and influence. Lateral or horizontal groupings and committees act as buffers against failures in the vertical linking pin system and are therefore recommended. The overall, overlapping group structure tends to bind group goals into those of the organization and creates unity of effort and a capacity to deal with conflict.

The key to an effective organization is an integrated system of overlapping groups. Therefore it becomes crucial to establish the conditions that make for effective group functioning. Likert (1961) notes twenty-four such characteristics, virtually all of which involve some application of the principle of supportive relationships.

1. Members are skilled in the roles required for interaction.

2. The group has existed long enough to have established stable, positive relationships.

3. The members and leader are attracted to the group and are loyal to each other.

4. There is high confidence and trust.

5. The group's values and goals adequately reflect those of individual members.

6. Individuals performing linking functions attempt to harmonize the values and goals of their groups.

7. Important group values have a high likelihood of member acceptance.

8. Members strive to contribute to group values and goals out of a desire to maintain a sense of personal worth.

9. Group activities occur in a supportive atmosphere.

10. The superior has considerable influence on the group atmosphere, making it supportive and cooperative.

11. The group fosters the development of members to their full potential.

12. Members accept the goals established by the group.

13. Group-set goals stretch members to the maximum.

14. There is considerable mutual help in achieving goals.

15. The atmosphere of the group fosters creativity.

16. The group fosters "constructive" conformity.

17. Open communication, especially of information that is important to the group, is facilitated.

18. The communication process is utilized in the interest of the group.

19. Members receive information from other group members and trust it.

20. There is a strong desire to influence other group members and to be receptive to influence.

21. Considerable influence is exerted by members on the leader, and needed information is transmitted to the leader.

22. In spite of the stability created by common goals and values, flexibility exists.

23. Appropriate individual decision making is facilitated by the common group goals and values.

24. Leaders are selected carefully, often through a peer nomination process.

Causal, Intervening, and End-Result Variables. Likert distinguishes three sets of variables that have major significance for organizational functioning. The variables and their interrelationships are given in Figure 2–1.

Likert particularly emphasizes the intervening variables and their measurement. He comes to this position via the following logic. There is often a sizable lag between a change in the causal variables and any resultant change in end-result variables. This lag, like that associated with technological innovation, may well be measured in years. Accordingly, to determine within a reasonable period of time what effects have been set in motion by a change and thus to establish a short feedback cycle, one must obtain measures of intervening variables. Effects may not show at the end-result point for years.

An important example of the need for a focus on intervening variables is provided by autocratic, production-oriented supervision. Such supervision can obtain results, but at the expense of squandering human assets, a process similar to liquidating physical assets. If the accounting system measures end-result variables only, these

22

Figure 2–1

Schematic Pattern of Relationships Between Causal, Intervening, and End-Result Variables Showing Measurements Yielding Prompt and Delayed Information

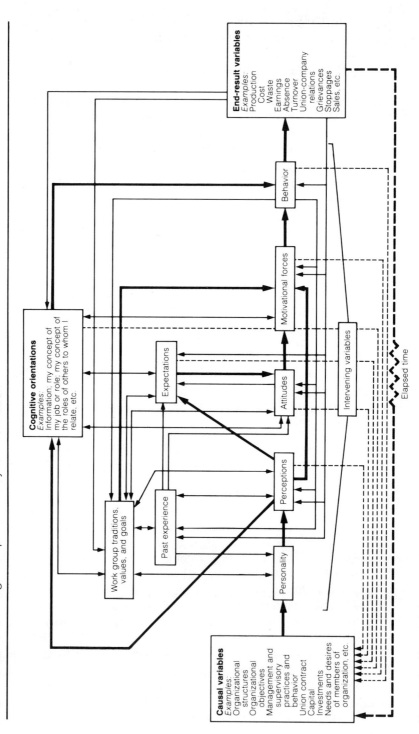

NOTE: Reprinted by permission of the publisher from Rensis Likert, *New Patterns of Management*. New York: McGraw-Hill, 1961. p. 201.

may be unaffected for some time, and the manager involved may be promoted to repeat the process before the consequences emerge. On the other hand an accounting system that deals with intervening variables will identify the nature and extent of the decline in human assets, and thus in the quality of the human organization, and will cost these changes against the productivity figures, making them look much less impressive (Likert, 1958). Consequently the manager who violates the principle of supportive relationships is less likely to be promoted, and the organization will benefit as a result.

Management Systems and the Principle of Participation. Though the principle of participation is emphasized as the best guide for managerial action throughout the 1961 book, Likert does not explicitly relate it to other alternative management systems until the next to the last chapter. Here he describes what he calls exploitive authoritative, benevolent authoritative, and consultative systems and sets them against the participative group system that embodies the principle of participation (see Table 2–1). The participative group system is said to operate toward the end of a single continuum on which the other systems also fall. Under the participative group system greater total influence is exerted in the organization as a whole, and consequently performance is more effective overall. However, "the amount and character of participation need to be geared to the values, skills, and expectations of the people involved if productive results are to be obtained. . . . Participation should not be thought of as a single process or activity, but rather as a whole range of processes and activities" (Likert, 1961, p. 242).

The Human Organization

The second of Likert's books (1967) covers much the same ground as the first, but a number of concepts are elaborated more fully, and there is a more pronounced emphasis on certain facets such as establishing high goals, organization structuring, and accounting for human assets.

Systems 1 through 4. Exploitive authoritative, benevolent authoritative, consultative, and participative group systems are now labeled systems 1, 2, 3, and 4 for the first time, and the list of characteristics of these systems presented in Table 2–1 is extended by the addition of those noted in Table 2–2. Furthermore, the total list, minus the performance items, is converted into a questionnaire that may be used to obtain reports on the current organization, past states of the organization, ideal circumstances, and so on. This "Profile of Organizational Characteristics" provides an index of how closely an organization approximates the theoretically superior system 4.

Table 2–1
Characteristics of Different Management Systems

Characteristic	Authoritative System		Participative System	
	Exploitive Authoritative	Benevolent Authoritative	Consultative	Participative Group
Motivational Forces				
Motives tapped	Security and status	Economic and ego	Economic, ego, and others	All motives, including group
Manner used	Mostly fear and punishment	Mostly rewards	Mostly rewards and some involvement	Participation and involvement
Attitudes developed	Hostile	Varied	Most favorable to organization	Strongly favorable to organization
Motivational conflicts	Marked	Frequent	Some	Rare
Felt responsibility	Decreases sharply from top to bottom	Mostly at managerial level	Substantial proportion	All personnel
Attitudes toward members	Subservient and hostile	Subservient and somewhat hostile	Generally cooperative	Favorable and cooperative
Satisfactions	Overall dissatisfaction	Some moderate satisfactions	Moderate satisfaction	High satisfaction
Communication				
Amount	Very little	Little	Quite a bit	Much
Direction	Downward	Mostly downward	Down and up	Down, up, and across
Downward				
Where initiated	At top	Primarily at top	Some at lower levels	All levels
Extent accepted	Great suspicion	Varies	Often accepted	Generally accepted
Upward				
Adequacy	Very little	Limited	Some	Great deal
Subordinate responsibility	None	Relatively little	Some	Considerable
Distorting forces	Powerful	Occasional	Relatively few	Virtually none
Accuracy	Inaccurate	Restricted	Limited	Accurate
Need to supplement	By spies or suggestion system	Suggestion system	Slight need	No need
Sideward communication	Usually poor	Fairly poor	Fair to good	Good to excellent
Superior-subordinate closeness	Far apart	Moderately close	Fairly close	Very close
Accurately perceived	Often in error	In error on some points	Moderately accurate	Quite accurate

Interaction–Influence				
Amount	Little	Little	Moderate	Extensive
Cooperative teamwork	None	Virtually none	Moderate	Substantial
Subordinate influence				
Superior perception	None	Virtually none	Moderate	A great deal
Subordinate perception	None	Little	Moderate	Substantial
Actual superior influence	Moderate	Moderate plus	May be substantial	Substantial but often indirect
Influence structure	Downward	Almost all downward	Largely downward	All directions
Decision Making				
Level	Top	Policy at top	Broad policy at top	All levels
Adequacy of information	Partial and inadequate	Moderately adequate	Reasonably adequate	Complete and accurate
Awareness of lower-level problems	Often unaware	Aware of some	Moderately aware	Quite well aware
Use of technical knowledge	Only if at higher levels	If at higher or middle levels	Much, at all levels	Most, anywhere
Made at best level				
For information	Too high	Often too high	Sometimes too high	Appropriate level
For motivation	Adverse motivation	Little contribution	Some contribution	Substantial contribution
Pattern	Person-to-person	Mostly person-to-person	Person-to-person and group	Largely group
Goal Setting				
Manner	Orders	Orders, possible comments	Goals set after discussion	Group participation
Commitment to high goals	Top only	Top only	Higher levels	All levels
Acceptance	Covertly resisted	Frequent covert resistance	Some covert resistance	Fully accepted
Control				
Level of concern	Top only	Largely at top	Some below top	All levels
Accuracy of information	Incomplete and inaccurate	Often incomplete and inaccurate	Moderately complete and accurate	Complete and accurate
Concentration	High in top management	Some delegation	Moderate delegation	Quite widespread
Opposing informal organization	Present and opposes	Less resistance	Varies	Informal and formal are one
Performance				
Productivity	Mediocre	Fair to good	Good	Excellent
Absenteeism and turnover	High	Moderately high	Moderate	Low
Scrap loss and waste	Relatively high	Moderately high	Moderate	At a minimum
Quality control	Necessary	Useful for policing	Useful as a check	Useful for self-guidance

SOURCE: Adapted from Rensis Likert, *New Patterns of Management*. New York: McGraw-Hill, 1961, pp. 223–33.

Table 2–2
Additional Characteristics of Different Management Systems (1967)

Characteristic	Authoritative System		Consultative	Participative System
	Exploitive Authoritative	Benevolent Authoritative		Participative Group
Leadership				
Trust in subordinates	None	Condescending	Substantial	Complete
Subordinates trust superiors	None	Subservient	Substantial	Complete
Subordinate freedom to discuss	Not free	Not very free	Rather free	Completely free
Use of subordinates' ideas	Seldom	Sometimes	Usually	Always
Communication				
Superiors share information	Minimum	Only what is felt to be needed	What needed and answers questions	All information wanted
Understanding of subordinate problems	None	Some	Quite good	Very good
Decision Making				
Subordinate involved	Not at all	Some consultation	Usually consulted	Fully involved
Control				
Data used for self-guidance	Policing only	Some guidance	Some self-guidance	Self-guidance and problem solving
Performance Goals and Training				
Level of goals	Average	High	Very high	Extremely high
Desired training provided	None	Some	Quite a bit	Great deal
Adequacy of training	Fairly good	Good	Very good	Excellen:

Source: Adapted from Rensis Likert, *The Human Organization*. New York: McGraw-Hill, 1967, pp. 197, 198, 201, 203, 207, 210, 211.

Shifts toward that system are expected to result in long-range improvements in productivity, labor relations, costs, and earnings.

On the other hand, shifts away from system 4, as occur in most cost reduction efforts, will set in motion strong negative influences on intervening variables, even though the immediate results may be favorable. These negative influences are related to a definite sequence of events that does not manifest itself fully in end-result variables for three or four years, or even longer. The human relations approach to management often is introduced at this point as a salve for the existing system 2 organization. Because it does not actually shift the organization toward system 4, however, it does not work. A shift can be achieved by teaching managers system 4 principles.

Changes in an organization toward a new system should be internally consistent. One cannot achieve the desired results by changing only certain aspects of the system, as when sensitivity training is introduced but everything else remains the same. The whole system needs to be shifted over a wide range of causal variables. The list of such variables in Likert's 1967 book is expanded considerably beyond those noted in the 1961 volume, as is the list of intervening variables (see Table 2–3). These variables should be measured periodically to monitor the progress and comprehensiveness of change.

Table 2–3
List of Organizational Variables to Measure

Causal Variables

Policies, philosophies, and values related in behavior

    Extent to which principle of supportive relationships permeates the company

    Extent to which the organization has high standards

    Extent of use of multiple, overlapping groups

    Extent of use of group decision making and methods of supervision

    Extent to which compensation system motivates goal-directed behavior

    Extent to which organizational variables are measured and used by units for self-guidance

    Extent to which elementary principles of organization are applied, i.e., clear roles, good planning, training

    Extent of use of advanced technology and R&D

    Extent to which the organization expects behavior consistent with its philosophy and values

    Extent to which there is stability of personnel assignment

    Extent to which adverse effects of size are minimized

Extent to which superiors are competent in technical matters, administrative know-how, and human interaction skills

Adequacy of the personnel selection process

Adequacy of training resources

Extent to which organization members possess cultural and personality characteristics needed for group decisions

Adequacy of capital and equipment

Table 2–3 (Continued)
Intervening Variables
Attitudinal, motivational, perceptual
  Extent of member loyalty to organization
  Extent to which members feel own and organizational goals are consistent
  Extent to which unit goals facilitate organizational goals
  Level of performance goals and motivation
  Extent to which the atmosphere is felt to be supportive
  Level of the expectations regarding various aspects of jobs and work
  Level of satisfaction with various aspects of job and company
  Extent of understanding of job role
  Character and cooperativeness of the interaction-influence system
  Extent to which economic needs are harnessed to organizational objectives
  Extent to which noneconomic needs harmonize with economic needs
  Extent to which unreasonable pressure to produce is felt
  Extent to which members seek high productivity or restrict it
  Extent to which good labor relations exist
  Level of mental health
  Effects of anxiety on health and functioning
  Level of shareholder confidence and loyalty
  Level of customer confidence
  Level of supplier confidence
Intervening behavioral variables
  Extent to which wide participation in decisions exists
  Extent to which members apply the principle of supportive relationships
  Extent to which members help their peers
  Extent of efforts to improve methods, technology, products
  Extent to which high performance standards and goals are encouraged and exist
  Extent to which control is disbursed
  Extent to which an effective interaction-influence system exists
  Level of cooperation toward organizational goals
  Extent to which turnover, absenteeism, manpower development, and firm growth rates
    are optimal
  Extent to which accidents and sickness are minimal

End-Result Variables (partial list)
Performance—productivity, quality, scrap, market share

Financial—costs, sales income, profits, compensation, reserves, value of investments
(physical, human organization, customers)

SOURCE: Adapted from Rensis Likert, *The Human Organization*. New York: McGraw-Hill, 1967, pp. 212–29.

Elsewhere Likert lists five "principles of effective management" that characterize the approach hypothesized to lead to favorable organizational outcomes:

1. The highest levels of productive and cooperative motivation are obtained when the noneconomic motives are made compatible with the economic motives.

2. High levels of cooperative motivation can be attained by applying the principle of supporting relationships.

3. High levels of cooperative motivation and the linking of such motivation to the goals of the common enterprise are achieved mainly through informal processes in face-to-face work groups.

4. The setting of goals and priorities and the assessment of accomplishments must be a continuing activity of the various groups.

5. In applying these ideas to a particular organization, management should take account of the unique problems, objectives, conditions, and traditions of the company (Likert and Seashore, 1963, p. 103).

Structural Considerations. Likert (1967) rejects the classical management view that an individual should have only one boss. He advocates horizontally overlapping groups with linking pins for many purposes and comprehensive group decision making for resolving any conflicts that may develop. Cross-function work groups that are product-related should be introduced at both higher and lower levels in the organization, as indicated in Figure 2–2. Geographic cross-function groups also may be introduced.

For effective coordination the whole organization must consist of multiple, overlapping groups that are skillful in group decision making. Such a structure is not consonant with systems such as 2, but is compatible with system 4. Product management and similar work forms can be introduced successfully by extremely able managers in systems other than 4, but these forms will produce much better results in their natural environment.

New Ways of Managing Conflict

Likert's most recent book dealing with system 4 theory (Likert and Likert, 1976) contains considerably less organization theory that is original than its predecessors. However, the systems 1 through 4 continuum is extended to cover a larger number of organizational forms. This elaboration generally follows some ideas developed earlier (Likert and Dowling, 1973).

System 0 covers permissive, laissez-faire organizations with little functional differentiation, large spans of control, and considerable confusion regarding roles. As might be expected from its position on the continuum, an organization of this kind is not hypothesized to be effective. On the other hand the system 5 organization of the future will be extremely effective. The authority of hierarchy will disappear, and authority will accrue entirely from group relationships and linking pin roles. Whereas system 4 organizations operate from an interplay of group and hierarchical forces, system 5 organizations will function almost entirely as overlapping groups.

Figure 2–2
Example of an Overlapping Group Structure with Vertical and Horizontal Linkages

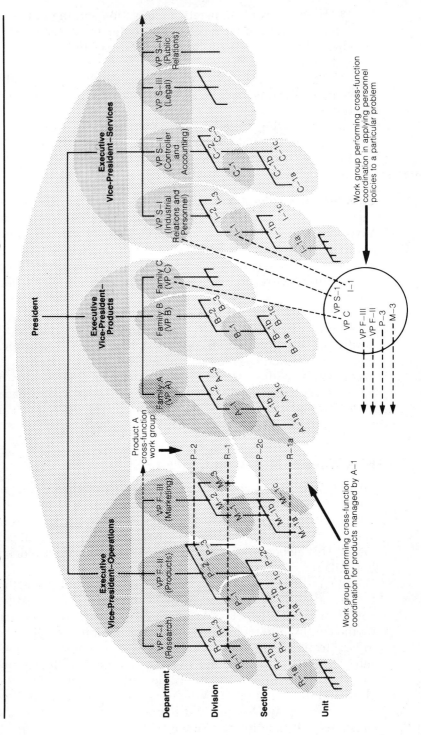

Note: Reprinted by permission of the publisher from Rensis Likert, *The Human Organization*. New York: McGraw-Hill, 1967, pp. 168–69.

The Theoretical Role of Conflict. The central thesis of the Likert and Likert book (1976) is that system 4 is the best method currently available for dealing with conflict, not only in the organizational context, but in other contexts as well. The essential propositions are that:

1. Conflict involves interactions among people or social units and occurs in a social system.

2. Conflict resolution depends on the effectiveness of the social system used.

3. The closer the social system is to system 4, the greater the probability of constructive conflict resolution.

4. System 4 can be used in every conflict situation by those who wish to achieve resolution. Applying system 4 to conflict situations requires an understanding of system 4 principles, skill in their use, and the passage of time.

Thus one would anticipate that a move to system 4 in an organization ultimately would not only improve productivity and profits (Likert says by 20 to 40 percent), but also cause a marked reduction in conflict.

System 4T. The designation T refers to *total.* The system 4T theory states that there are additional factors beyond position on the system 1 through 4 continuum that contribute to organizational effectiveness. Likert had previously mentioned a number of these factors without specifically incorporating them into his theory. The aspects of the human organization above and beyond the system continuum now include:

1. The levels of performance goals held by the leader and transmitted to subordinates.

2. The levels of knowledge and skill of the leader with regard to the technical field, administration, interaction processes, and problem solving.

3. The capacity and motivation of the leader to provide planning, resources, equipment, training, and help to subordinates.

4. The degree to which the structure provides for optimum differentiation and for sufficient linkages.

5. The extent to which stable working relationships exist within units.

With the addition of these variables the theory explicitly incorporates certain factors previously proposed by Bowers and Seashore (1966) in their four-factor theory of leadership (support, interaction facilitation, goal emphasis, and work facilitation). The theory as now stated is clearly much more than a theory of the effects of participation. In fact system 4 loses its preeminent role. Likert and Likert note that "If an organization, or a department, scores high on the system 1 to 4 scale and low on one or more of the other dimensions, such as technical competence or level of performance goals, the probabilities are great that it will not be highly effective in conflict management or performance" (1976, p. 50).

System 4T also introduces the concept of peer leadership and organizational climate. Peer leadership occurs when subordinate group members engage in leadership behavior. Such behavior tends to reflect the style of the leader. Under system 4T, peer leadership tends to strengthen the organization and has positive effects. In systems 1 or 2 it may well restrict output.

Organizational climate is defined as a composite state influenced by group member perceptions of the situation in the department, or some larger organizational entity, in which their group resides. It is influenced most by behavior toward the top of the organization and can severely constrain the type of management possible at lower levels. In system 4T, organizational climate is hypothesized to be a positive force.

General Principles. In essence Likert believes that there are general principles applicable to all managerial situations, though actual applications may vary with the particular culture involved. Bowers (1976), in interpreting Likert, states three reasons why management contains universal and transferable properties:

1. Human nature in its inherited essence is the same everywhere.
2. The scientific method is the same everywhere.
3. Culture, though it may influence the application of management principles, is not in itself a principle.

The implication is that the situational variations discussed by the contingency theorists, who are considered later in this book, are mere cultural variants in the application of basic principles (Likert and Dowling, 1973; Likert and Likert, 1976). It is not at all clear that this is what the contingency theorists mean, nor does Likert spell out in any specific detail what cultural variations would be expected to have what effects under what circumstances. As a result, any findings that fail to support Likert's may be attributed to cultural variations on an ad hoc basis.

Research Bearing on System 4 and 4T

In the early years almost all the research bearing on Likert's theory was conducted by staff members of the Institute for Social Research at the University of Michigan or by individuals closely associated with the institute. Though this organization has continued to be a major source of studies of the theory during the 1970s, a number of others have tested the theory, often utilizing instruments developed at Michigan. In addition, a sizable body of research dealing with participative management per se clearly has implications for system 4 theory.

The Classic Studies

Likert's books, particularly the 1961 and 1967 volumes, contain extensive reviews of research conducted in the early period by members of the Michigan group and those associated with them. The research, as presented, is almost universally favorable to the theory, though questions have been raised subsequently about some of the studies. Of these studies, a number have been cited and reprinted often enough to justify referring to them as classics (Zimmerman, 1978).

Comparisons of High- and Low-Producing Sections. A major research strategy in the early period was to enter organizations to identify high- and low-producing work groups and then administer extensive questionnaires to the members for the purpose of establishing leadership practices that differentiated the effective and ineffective groups (Likert, 1961). It is apparent that the questions used were developed with some idea of the value of the participative approach. Nevertheless, Likert's formal specification of concepts, such as the principle of supportive relationships, also appears to have been influenced by the results of the research. Thus the studies may be viewed as tests of the theory only in a general form.

Though the best known of these investigations were those conducted with clerical groups in an insurance company and with railroad section gangs, a summary of the results by Kahn and Katz (1960) includes other research. In high-producing groups it was found that leaders whose more differentiated role often included planning and interpersonal activities did not do the same things as their subordinates. High production also was associated with general rather than close supervision, with an employee-oriented, supportive approach, and with a high level of group involvement among members.

The data on which these conclusions are based vary considerably in the degree to which they differentiate the high and low groups. In several cases the support claimed for the conclusions is based on comparisons that are, at best, of marginal statistical significance. Furthermore, the concurrent, correlational nature of the research design makes causal interpretation inappropriate. All in all, this research appears now to have been of greater value for theory building than for theory testing.

The Harwood Research. The Harwood Company, a garment manufacturer, has been the site of significant behavioral science research
studies since the late 1930s (Marrow, 1972). One initial finding derived from a case study conducted at Harwood during World War
II was an outgrowth of ideas developed by Kurt Lewin (1952). Essentially the study demonstrated the use of participative decision
making in overcoming managerial resistance to hiring women over
the age of thirty during a labor shortage (Marrow and French, 1945).
This study was followed by a more sophisticated experiment dealing
with the use of participation in overcoming resistance to the introduction of new production processes (Coch and French, 1948).

For some time Harwood had suffered increases in turnover and
grievances, and decreases in production, whenever changes in job
activities were introduced. In the experiment job changes were undertaken among groups of eighteen hand pressers, thirteen pajama
folders, eight pajama examiners, seven pajama examiners, and two
sewing operators. The hand pressers, serving as a control group,
were merely told that certain job changes would be made. The pajama folders were persuaded that a change was needed and were
then asked to select their own representatives to undergo training.
These representatives subsequently trained the others. The remaining groups were treated essentially the same as the pajama folders,
but being smaller groups, all members underwent the initial training. The groups approved the plans for change by consensus, after
lengthy discussions of possible approaches.

Before the change, all groups had been producing at approximately sixty units per hour, the plant norm. All experienced the
usual drop in production after the change. The control group of hand
pressers never did recover, and stabilized at about fifty units. The
pajama folders whose representatives participated in initial training
recovered gradually and ultimately moved up to between sixty-five
and seventy units per hour. The remaining, full-participation groups
recovered more rapidly and stabilized at seventy to seventy-five
units. Data on aggressive acts toward management, grievances, and
turnover are generally in line with the production findings. In a
subsequent study the original control group of hand pressers was
broken up and after several months reconstituted (with only thirteen
members remaining). After changing to the new pressing procedures
introduced by means of the total participation approach, their production also rose to over seventy units per hour. Though no statistical tests are presented, the differences among the groups appear to
be sizable.

Though the results of this study seem clear enough, their interpretation is another matter. Zimmerman (1978) argues that the Harwood situation was atypical in a number of respects and that wide-

spread generalization of the findings is not warranted. Katzell and Yankelovich (1975) question whether a causal impact of participation on motivation can be assumed, given that no measures of motivation or of the effects of participation manipulations on the various groups were obtained. A number of other factors might account for the results, including differences in jobs and job changes, group sizes, methods of presenting the need for change, competition levels, quality of training, and knowledge of results (Gardner, 1977).

A subsequent study, conducted in Norway, which seemed to have eliminated a number of possible confounding effects and included a measure of how well the experimental manipulations "took," generally failed to yield significant findings (French, Israel, and Ås, 1960). The comparison of the United States and Norwegian results led Likert to conclude that participation must be culturally relevant if it is to work effectively. However, a subsequent attempt to replicate the Harwood study in the United States also failed to support the superiority of direct participation (Fleishman, 1965). These two studies suggest that generalization from the Harwood situation should be approached with considerable caution. Yet it is apparent that the Harwood results are not time bound. Findings similar to those of Coch and French (1948) were reported ten years later for a more extensive change in the production process at Harwood (French, Ross, Kirby, Nelson, and Smyth, 1958).

Pelz's Influence Hypothesis. The empirical basis for Likert's linking pin hypothesis appears to be certain research conducted by Pelz (1952). This research produced evidence that supervisors with considerable influence on their superiors who also "side with employees" and exhibit "social closeness to employees" elicit greater employee satisfaction than other supervisors. When the supervisor does not have much upward influence, behavior supportive of employees tends to make little difference, and in fact can have negative consequences because it raises false expectations.

The results on which these conclusions are based are not strong, but they are consistent. Furthermore, these results appear to be an outgrowth of ad hoc data analysis and thus require further independent study. In contrast to Likert, whose linking pin theory extends the role of two-way influence to all levels of the organization and to a wide range of end-result variables, Pelz is concerned only with first-level supervision and satisfaction with the supervisor. Yet, based on his findings, Pelz does advocate increasing the amount of influence given to these supervisors.

Morse and Reimer. The Morse and Reimer (1956) study was a true field experiment. Within a single department, decision making was shifted downward to increase employee participation considerably in two divisions and upward to emphasize top-level, hierarchical decisions in two other divisions. Pretests were administered prior to a six-month period during which the changes were introduced by means of training programs for supervisors. The divisions operated for a full year under the conditions thus created before the posttest was administered. There is considerable evidence, some of which is given in Table 2–4, that the experimental treatments did take.

In general there was an increase in satisfaction in the participative divisions and a decrease in satisfaction in the hierarchical divisions, though not all the changes were statistically significant. Productivity increased in both contexts, but the increase was significantly greater in the hierarchical groups. Job-related turnover was greater in the hierarchical divisions, but was relatively low in both situations.

The authors of the paper and subsequently Likert (1961) suggest that the greater productivity increases in the hierarchical groups

Table 2–4

Effects of Changes toward Greater Participation and Greater Hierarchical Control on Indexes of Satisfaction and Productivity

	Participative Groups		Hierarchical Groups	
	Before	After	Before	After
Treatment Effects				
Perceived decision-making allocation (on a nine-point scale from lower to upper levels)	(6.08	4.24)	(6.41	7.00)
Satisfaction Effects (on five-point scales from low to high satisfaction)				
Perceived self-actualization	(2.43	2.57)	(2.37	2.24)
Satisfaction in relations with supervision				
Immediate superior	3.71	3.80	3.64	3.48
One level up	(3.71	3.86)	(3.64	3.28)
Two levels up	(3.93	4.15)	(3.50	3.01)
Satisfaction with supervision as representatives of employees				
Immediate superior	(3.48	3.74)	3.59	3.43
One level up	(3.43	3.75)	(3.15	2.86)
Two levels up	(3.79	4.17)	(2.92	2.52)
Satisfaction with company	(4.01	4.18)	(4.15	3.88)
Job satisfaction	3.16	3.19	(3.13	3.00)
Productivity Effects (on scale of 100, with higher values indicating higher productivity)	(48.6	58.6)	(48.5	62.6)

( ) Difference statistically significant.

Source: Adapted from Nancy C. Morse and Everett Reimer, "The Experimental Change of a Major Organizational Variable," *Journal of Abnormal and Social Psychology*, 52 (1956), pp. 123–28.

would not be maintained over time. The Likert hypothesis is that higher productivity was achieved at the expense of squandering human assets, a practice that ultimately would result in decreased productivity, as well as the decline in satisfaction already noted. This hypothesis is, of course, post hoc, and the study neither supports nor refutes it. Clearly the productivity findings were not as expected, and questions have been raised about the use of a clerical cost index here, rather than a unit production measure (Zimmerman, 1978). Furthermore, the effects of interactions across divisions within the department are not known. Nevertheless, the study remains one of the most impressive yet on participative management, and data from a computer simulation study suggest that Likert is right about the time-lag effects (Brightman, 1975). At the end of five simulated years, democratic groups were more productive.

A later study, similar to that of Morse and Reimer, focused in much the same manner on introducing numerous aspects of the Likert theory (Seashore and Bowers, 1963). The results are open to question because the experimental and control groups were essentially self-selected, and hard data on absenteeism and productivity could not be interpreted. Nevertheless, there was evidence that the experimental treatments did take and that they contributed to greater satisfactions in many areas, as in the Morse and Reimer study.

The Weldon Research. The Weldon studies represent an extension of the earlier Harwood research. They compare changes made at Weldon where participative procedures were first introduced during a period subsequent to Weldon's acquisition by Harwood and at the main plant of Harwood where participation had been a way of life for some years (Marrow, Bowers, and Seashore, 1967; Marrow, 1972; Seashore and Bowers, 1970). The changes were carried out between 1962 and 1964; a follow-up analysis was conducted in 1969.

The results of the Weldon research are perplexing. On the Likert profile Weldon appears to have moved over the period of study from the borderline between systems 1 and 2 to early system 4. Yet in other respects the evidence that the workers perceived a major shift in their work is far from convincing. On balance, one cannot say with certainty to what extent the experimental manipulations as they relate to system 4 theory really took, yet very clearly something happened. The Likert profile results may have been a reaction to newly learned expectations, but a major increase in efficiency and productivity did occur, bringing Weldon very close to Harwood in these respects. Satisfaction increased with regard to the work done, but decreased insofar as immediate supervision was concerned; the overall pattern of motivational and attitudinal change was mixed and varied from measure to measure. In general the follow-up data closely matched the results obtained in 1964, after the changes had been completed.

Weldon was in serious difficulty at the time of its acquisition, and accordingly researchers had no time to introduce changes one at a time and study the effects of each separately. A whole battery of changes, extending well beyond the diversity of even system 4T, was introduced almost simultaneously. The researchers tried to isolate the effects of the various changes such as coaching low performers, terminating chronic low performers, introducing group problem-solving, and providing supervisory training. But the confounding of effects was so pronounced that this analysis must be considered very tentative. A major review concludes:

> The authors must be commended for trying to sort out the contribution of the various factors, but their estimates cannot be taken at face value, since their method of determining the various effects ignores such possibilities as delayed effects and interactions among the changes. While it seems almost certain that the sum total of the organizational changes made were responsible for the effects observed, isolating the precise degree of effect produced by each change is virtually impossible from the methodology employed. . . . Thus the title used for the book which summarized this project, *Management by Participation*, must be viewed as somewhat misleading at best (Locke and Schweiger, 1979, pp. 301–2).

Direct Tests of Likert's Formulations

The classic studies noted in the previous section remain the most widely cited with regard to Likert's theory. In addition, a wide range of investigations has been conducted to evaluate the participative approach to organizations. However, these studies often have been stimulated by other theories, or by no particular theory at all, and thus bear only tangentially on Likert's formulations. Actually the amount of published research carried out in recent years for the specific purpose of testing Likert's views is not large, and much of what has been done deals only with limited facets of the total theory.

Comprehensive Validation Research. A study conducted within the National Aeronautics and Space Administration validated various aspects of system 4 theory against criteria of unit effectiveness and also compared the theory with other theories of a similar nature (Mott, 1972). Questionnaire measures indicated good validity for the principle of supportive relationships and some validity for high performance goals, but group methods of supervision and participation were unrelated to effectiveness. Of the four theories considered, Likert's predicted the criteria least often.

Research conducted in development banks in Brazil using the "Profile of Organizational Characteristics" indicated that banks closer to system 4 were viewed as more effective by their employees and generally elicited higher levels of satisfaction (Butterfield and Farris, 1974). However, no relationships with external indexes of bank effectiveness were identified. On the other hand, a study comparing divisions within a single California company found system 4 conditions to be related positively not only to satisfaction, but also to objective measures of division performance (Roberts, Miles, and Blankenship, 1968). Similarly a comparison of ten high-performing plants in Yugoslavia with an equal number of less successful plants indicated that the high performers approximated system 4 more closely (Mozina, Jerovsek, Tannenbaum, and Likert, 1970).

Other research conducted by individuals associated with the Institute for Social Research has also tended to support the theory. Thus a comparison of the geographically dispersed departments of a nationwide company indicated that supportive behavior on the part of the supervisor, an overlapping group form of organization, and better use of group processes (including meetings) were associated with higher productivity (Likert, 1961). A similar study in the sales offices of an insurance company found that success was related to supportive behavior, high goals, group methods of supervision, peer-group loyalty, and an effective interaction-influence system (Likert, 1967). Likert and Likert (1976) describe a number of studies conducted in the United States and in other parts of the world that indicate a strong association between system 4 and productivity.

Table 2–5 contains composite results reported by Likert (1973) for data in the Institute for Social Research files at that time. The nature of the productive efficiency measure is not stated, but the correlation coefficients appear unusually high. Elsewhere, Likert and Bowers (1973) note that the productivity correlations reported were not obtained from the whole data base but from a single organization "where the performance measurements have a minimum of noise or error." A subsequent report by Bowers (1975) that does utilize the whole data base indicates a much lower level of correlation in analyses of hard data from the operating records of a number of firms. In these studies measures of causal and intervening variables are known to have been obtained from a single questionnaire index, a factor that would be expected to contribute to high method variance and inflated correlations among variables.

The results considered in this section are primarily concurrent in nature. This introduces two types of problems. One cannot establish, as the theory predicts, that system 4 conditions *caused* greater satisfaction and productivity; it might have been just the reverse. Furthermore, the theory incorporates a time-lag factor, and without some knowledge of temporal relationships one cannot say whether

Table 2–5

Correlations Among Theoretical Variables Found in University of Michigan Studies

Theoretical Variables	Organizational Climate	Peer Leadership	Group Process	Satisfaction	Productive Efficiency
Causal Variables					
Managerial leadership	.65	.48	.52	.70	.65
Organizational climate		.46	.58	.82	.66
Intervening Variables					
Peer leadership			.82	.50	.70
Group process satisfaction				.52	.69
End-Result Variables					
Total productive efficiency					.65

SOURCE: Adapted from Rensis Likert, "Human Resource Accounting: Building and Assessing Productive Organizations," *Personnel,* 50, no. 3 (1973), p. 12.

it is valid or not. A lack of significant findings may only mean that the time to achieve impact has not yet passed.

There is some evidence from predictive research to answer these criticisms. A comparative study of two General Motors plants in the Atlanta, Georgia, area showed a rapid movement toward system 4 in the experimental plant, followed a year or so later by improved productivity as well (Dowling, 1975). System 4 was introduced with intensive training. Though job enrichment was not involved and participation was, it is also true that the employees in the experimental plant acquired considerable job-related knowledge during the training, that an elaborate performance feedback system was introduced, and that certain staffing changes were made. Though these changes were all consistent with system 4T, their concomitant introduction makes it impossible to establish specific causes.

The Likert Profile of Organizational Characteristics. The basic measure of the systems 1 through 4 continuum has undergone considerable change over the years and often is used in something less than its entirety. Irrespective of these factors, however, it has consistently shown good construct validity. For instance, system 4 has shown a close association with the interpersonal process of informal helping within an organization (Burke and Weir, 1978) and with other measures of conceptually similar constructs (Hall, 1972). Likert profile scores tend to shift toward system 4 when individuals are exposed to sensitivity or laboratory training (Golembiewski and Munzenrider, 1973).

Likert (1967) reports split-half reliabilities for the profile that consistently fall in the .90s and usually in the high .90s. On the other hand, Butterfield and Farris (1974) report a test-retest value of .52 over a period averaging one year. This appears to indicate that if the instrument is as reliable as the internal consistency results suggest, it measures a phenomenon that typically shows considerable fluctuation over time.

The Linking Pin Concept. Research that takes its departure from the early work of Pelz (1952) dealing with the moderating effects of supervisory upward influence has yielded variable support for Likert's linking pin concept. The concept was not supported in one company studied, but was supported in another (House, Filley, and Gujarati, 1971). It is not entirely clear why these disparate results occur, though upward influence may only operate as a moderator when the employee is quite dependent on the immediate superior.

On the other hand, several other lines of investigation indicate that linking pin relationships can yield positive consequences. Research has emphasized consistently that two-way communication is more satisfying and more accurate than one-way, downward communication, but that it is also very time consuming (Miner, 1978). This may account in part for the long lag times associated with system 4 implementation. Research related to the vertical dyad linkage model (Miner, 1980) indicates that good linking pin relationships can be associated with a variety of positive outcomes, though the specific nature of these outcomes may vary from one situation to another (Graen, Cashman, Ginsburg, and Schiemann, 1977). Finally, Franklin (1975), using the Institute for Social Research data base, finds that the quality of group process at the superior level is related closely to organizational climate, managerial leadership, peer leadership, and group process at the subordinate level when measured roughly a year later. The data not only support the lag-time concept, but also show, as do the vertical dyad linkage results, that relationships at higher levels can have a strong influence on lower-level functioning. This is a necessary condition if linking pin structures are to enhance end-result variables.

The Value of Participation

With the introduction of such concepts as cross-functional teams, linking pins, and organizational climate, system 4 theory becomes a theory of the total organization, rather than merely a theory of the individual work group. However, the system 4 formulations do build up conceptually from the work group as a base. For this reason much of the very extensive research dealing with participation at the work group level has relevance for the theory, even though the studies were not conducted to test Likert's propositions. If participation turned out to have little value or, worse yet, a generally negative impact, system 4 theory would be shocked to its very foundations.

A number of reviews of the participation literature have been published. These present a strikingly consistent picture of the research results, even though the specific studies considered have varied somewhat as a function of the time and scope of the review:

1. . . . neither democratic nor autocratic supervision can be advocated as a method of increasing productivity, but member satisfaction is associated with a democratic style of supervision. Several studies suggest that satisfaction with supervision differs with the size and composition of the group. Satisfaction with democratic leadership tends to be highest in small interaction-oriented groups (Stogdill, 1974, p. 370). . . . group productivity does not vary consistently with directive and participative styles of leader behavior. There is a slight tendency for satisfaction to be related to participative leadership. Group cohesiveness tends to be related positively to participative styles of leader behavior. . . . Several studies indicate that supervisory and task characteristics interact to influence member satisfaction and group productivity (p. 392).

2. Work groups whose members have more of a say over the group's production goals, work, and working conditions usually have higher average job satisfaction than those having less control. There is some evidence that members of participative groups also have stronger work motivation. There are instances where increased work control was associated with reduced turnover or absenteeism, but in at least one case, absenteeism increased. Productivity is usually, but not always, higher in groups having more control. Even where it is higher, the dynamics are not always clear. . . . Work group participation appears to function better with people whose personalities "fit" that control pattern (Katzell and Yankelovich, 1975, pp. 233–35).

3. . . . participative leadership is often effective, as suggested by Proposition 3. ["Effective leaders are characterized by the exercise of participative decision making and supervision." (p. 222).] The fact that some studies have shown leader behavior to *result from* as well as *cause* subordinate satisfaction and performance does not negate this fact. However, in the strictest sense Proposition 3 cannot be said to be confirmed, because there is ample evidence that the effects of participative leadership are not omnipotent. Rather, for such leadership to be effective leaders must also have the

required skills, subordinates must have favorable attitudes toward participation, and the task must be complex, nonroutine, and require either a high quality decision or subordinate acceptance, or both. It therefore seems fair to say that the effects of participative leadership, like supportive leadership, are often positive but situational (Filley, House, and Kerr, 1976, p. 229).

4. . . . research findings yield equivocal support for the thesis that PDM ["participation in decision making"] necessarily leads to increased satisfaction and productivity, although the evidence for the former outcome is stronger than the evidence for the latter; the evidence indicates that the effectiveness of PDM depends upon numerous contextual factors; and PDM is not the only way to motivate employees. If the effects of PDM depend upon the context in which it is used, it follows that PDM might be not only ineffective in some circumstances, but might be actually harmful (Locke and Schweiger, 1979, p. 325).

It appears that participation is more likely to lead to increases in job satisfaction than in productivity and that the effects of participation are highly contingent upon situational or contextual factors. The way in which these contingency variables operate is not clear, but it appears that something more is involved than adapting participation to the situation or culture. On some occasions participation seems very unlikely to prove effective no matter how it is applied, and there are studies in which it has actually been shown to be harmful.

These conclusions regarding situational effects are consistent with the research findings generated from a number of leadership theories and from goal setting and management by objectives (Miner, 1980). A number of different moderator variables have been identified in the research, and it is not yet possible to specify a comprehensive list. Nor is it possible to specify the dynamics of their operation. One very important consideration appears to be the expertise and proficiency of the leader (Mulder, 1977). Where there are major differences in expertise and proficiency between leader and group members, attempted participation actually accentuates power distances within the group and increases the probability that the decision that emerges will be that of the leader. On the other hand, where expertise and skill are equally distributed, real participative decision making can occur, and the outcomes will reflect this fact.

Though Likert has tended to emphasize the widespread, if not universal, value of participation, there are data from the Institute for Social Research data bank itself that are at variance with such a view

(Bowers, 1975). Participation appears to be ineffective at the top of the organization, but effective in the middle and at the bottom; it is also ineffective in organizations whose purpose is to conduct research or to serve as administrative headquarters for a decentralized firm or both; and participation varies in effectiveness in other contexts. Bowers (1975) also found, as have others, that satisfaction was predicted more effectively than productivity and that prediction with a one-year lag produced better results than did a concurrent analysis.

Accounting Applications

Throughout his writings Likert expresses concern over the liquidation of the human organization to obtain short-term increases in productivity. His thinking in this regard appears to have been stimulated by the results of the Morse and Reimer (1956) study and by his experiences with hierarchically initiated cost reduction programs. Any attempt to demonstrate that certain approaches squander the human organization, while others preserve and develop it, requires that appropriate measures of the value, or at least of change in the value, of human assets be developed. By this logical route Likert became one of the very early proponents of so-called human resource or human asset accounting. Starting with a chapter in *The Human Organization* (1967), Likert has proposed a number of extensions to practice in this area.

The Likert Approach to Human Resource Valuation

Initially, Likert (1967) defined human assets in terms of "the value of the productive capacity of a firm's human organization and . . . the value of its customer goodwill." Goodwill was subsequently expanded to include shareholder and supplier loyalty, as well as reputation in both the financial and local communities (Likert and Bowers, 1969). However, at the level of application the focus has been primarily on internal, human organization variables.

A wide range of different approaches to the valuation of the human organization has been developed (Flamholtz, 1974). Though Likert emphasizes an approach grounded in his own theoretical views, he advocates the utilization of other approaches on the grounds that they provide different types of information. Two of these are specifically noted—one based on measuring the costs invested in the human organization for recruiting, selection, training, and the like, and the other based on estimating the replacement costs of the human investments (Likert and Bowers, 1973).

Measuring Causal and Intervening Variables. The essential and distinguishing aspect of Likert's own approach to human resource accounting is its heavy reliance on survey-type research using questionnaire measures. Two types of causal variables are stressed (Likert, 1973; Likert and Bowers, 1973):

1. Managerial behavior as reflected in support, team building, goal emphasis, and work facilitation (help with work).

2. Organizational climate as reflected in communication flow, decision-making practices, concern for persons, and influence on department, technological adequacy, and motivational conditions.

At the level of intervening variables, measures are obtained for:

1. Peer leadership as reflected in support, team building, goal emphasis, and work facilitation.

2. Group process as reflected in planning together, making good decisions, knowing jobs, sharing information, wanting to meet goals, member trust, and the meeting of unusual demands.

3. Satisfaction with fellow workers, superiors, jobs, the organization, pay, progress, and chances for getting ahead.

These causal and intervening variables are important because, according to theory, they determine the level of end-result variables in the future. Thus the future value of the human organization may be assessed by measuring causal and intervening conditions today.

Calculations. To determine increases or decreases in the value of the human organization, causal and intervening measures are taken at two points in time, and difference indexes are computed after the measures are standardized to eliminate differences in variability. These difference indexes are then multiplied by the correlation coefficient for the relationship between the particular causal or intervening variable and the end-result variable to give greater weight to changes in the variables that have greater causal impact. Finally, the estimate of performance change is converted into units of the performance measure, preferably dollars. Combined results may be obtained by utilizing multiple correlation techniques. What emerges is a statement of the consequences of various changes in the causal and intervening variables for productive efficiency. One can say what the consequences of a given change will be in terms of total cost decreases or increases for a given amount of production.

The information derived from these calculations may be used to determine whether a particular plant manager, for instance, is a human organization builder or liquidator. It may also be used to determine whether a shift toward system 4 is recommended as a means of offsetting a trend that anticipates declines in future productivity.

The Extent of Application

Though human resource accounting has considerable practical appeal, application of the Likert approach or any other approach has not been widespread (Rhode, Lawler, and Sundem, 1976). One inherent problem is the very diversity of approaches. It is difficult to determine which approach to introduce, and the cost of introducing several approaches may be too large to justify.

There are also measurement problems, especially in the Likert approach. Should measurements really be restricted to the variables of system 4 theory? Are the assumptions underlying the calculations justified, especially weighting the data according to the size of correlation coefficients? Is the measurement of change, as opposed to the measurement of absolute value, sufficient?

Without question, these considerations have contributed to the extremely slow rate with which human resource accounting has won acceptance. But a much more important factor is widespread skepticism over whether greater precision of measurement would really make any difference in the way organizations operate. What are the consequences of installing a human resource accounting system for organizational effectiveness and investment decisions? Is the Likert approach better or worse than others? For what purposes? These are research questions, but no such research has been conducted. The work to date has involved demonstration projects only. Managers need hard data on which to base decisions regarding the implementation of accounting approaches such as those Likert advocates. Until they receive such data, managers are likely to move very slowly, in spite of human resource accounting's inherent practical appeal and Likert's real creative contribution.

Organization Development Applications

Though the early change efforts at Harwood, Weldon, and several other companies might well qualify as organization development, there are certain other approaches identified with Rensis Likert and the Institute for Social Research that are even more clearly addressed to organization development. Two of these approaches seem to have originated in other contexts and to have been given only limited attention by Likert and his associates. The introduction of cross-functional teams, making extensive use of horizontal linking pins, is in fact closely allied with project management and the matrix structure and goes back at least fifty years (Miner, 1978). Likert (1975) views the cross-functional team approach as a means of moving toward system 4. He relates it closely to sociotechnical systems theory, as discussed in Chapter 4.

Another approach, management by group objectives (MBGO), had its origins in the MBO literature of the 1950s (Miner, 1980). The added element in MBGO is that objectives are set by the work group as a whole in problem-solving sessions (Likert and Fisher, 1977). The intent is to eliminate the tendency toward competition fostered by the more traditional type of management by objectives. There are several examples of the successful incorporation of MBGO in more comprehensive organization development efforts.

The Nature of the Survey Feedback Method

The primary approach in organization development introduced by Likert and his associates is the survey feedback method or, more broadly, survey-guided development. This approach has a long history at the Institute for Social Research, extending back to early work at the Detroit Edison Company (Mann, 1951; Mann and Likert, 1952). It is a natural outgrowth of the survey methodology that has characterized the work of the institute from its beginnings.

The Overall Process. The essential element of survey-guided development is the use of questionnaire data, aggregated both for work groups and for larger units, to induce change toward system 4. Since the data are fed back to the groups from which they were gathered for purposes of identifying problems and developing group solutions, the approach itself is system 4 in nature and therefore provides an experiential model for the type of management system desired as an end result. In early applications the questionnaire feedback moved down through the organization, level by level, like a waterfall. However, simultaneous feedback at all levels is now considered acceptable. The ideal appears to be a top-down approach, emphasizing overlapping group or linking pin relationships that nevertheless move the information rapidly.

The steps in the overall process are as follows:

1. Initial planning sessions involving key members of the outside consulting staff, plant management, and representatives from nonmanagerial personnel within the organization.

2. Administration of the questionnaires to all members of the organization.

3. Training for some members of the organization to act as internal resource persons in the feedback meetings.

4. Training for organizational members in basic concepts describing how organizations function.

5. The return of data to group supervisors.

6. Group feedback meetings.

7. The presentation of a systematic diagnosis.

8. The allocation of resources in accordance with needs indicated by the systematic diagnosis and feedback meetings.

9. Gathering, organizing, and evaluating intermediate feedback to monitor progress in the change activity.

10. A formal reassessment of the organization to examine progress (Bowers and Franklin, 1977, p. 117).

Thus questionnaires are administered in successive waves to provoke, monitor, and reassess change. This organization development process is set forth in detail in a manual by Hausser, Pecorella, and Wissler (1977) and in somewhat more general form in Nadler (1977). The training in organizational functioning noted in step 4 has a strong system 4 flavor and is described in Franklin, Wissler, and Spencer (1977).

The "Survey of Organizations." The questionnaire utilized almost exclusively in organization development efforts carried out with the assistance of the Institute for Social Research is the "Survey of Organizations." This instrument has gone through a number of revisions. Its basic measures are those for establishing the status of causal and intervening variables—managerial behavior or leadership, organizational climate, peer leadership, group process, and satisfaction. In addition, recent versions of the instrument contain questions dealing with supervisory needs, job challenge, extent of and aversion to bureaucracy, and goal integration. As a survey instrument, the "Survey of Organizations" appears to be well prepared and useful (Bowers, 1973; Hausser, Pecorella, and Wissler, 1977). Reported reliability coefficients range from .58 to .94 with a median of .86. However, it is clearly a special product of the converging influences of Likert's system 4 theory and Bowers and Seashore's (1966) four-factor theory of leadership. Thus, to the extent these theories are wrong, the instrument is less useful.

Research Evidence

Data bearing on the effectiveness of survey feedback as an intervention in organization development are not extensive. The major study, conducted by Bowers (1973), compares different organization development approaches used in twenty-three organizations on measures drawn from the "Survey of Organizations." Table 2–6 presents the findings for laboratory training, which appears to have a predominantly negative impact, and survey feedback, which yields positive changes with some consistency. Of the approaches considered, survey feedback produced the most positive changes. Subsequently, Bowers and Hausser (1977) have presented evidence that various organization development techniques have differential effects

Table 2–6

Changes on "Survey of Organizations" Variables over a One-Year Interval When Laboratory Training or Survey Feedback Intervenes

"Survey of Organizations" Variables	Intervening OD Treatment	
	Laboratory Training	Survey Feedback
Organizational Climate		
Concern for persons	(−.18)	(+.15)
Communications flow	(−.12)	(+.15)
Motivational conditions	(−.12)	+.01
Decision-making practices	(−.13)	(+.17)
Technological adequacy	(+.13)	+.05
Influence on department	(−.10)	+.01
Managerial Behavior		
Support	(−.11)	(+.18)
Team building	+.02	(+.36)
Goal emphasis	−.06	(+.17)
Work facilitation	−.08	(+.27)
Peer Leadership		
Support	(−.11)	+.06
Team building	−.04	(+.20)
Goal emphasis	.00	(+.14)
Work facilitation	+.03	(+.19)
Group Process	(+.27)	(+.21)
Satisfaction	(−.15)	+.09

( ) Change statistically significant over the one-year period.

SOURCE: Adapted from David G. Bowers, "OD Techniques and Their Results in 23 Organizations: The Michigan ICL Study," *Journal of Applied Behavioral Science,* 9 (1973), p. 32.

on different work groups, but that survey feedback has wide applicability.

The strength of the support for survey feedback emanating from this research must be tempered somewhat. No data on end-result variables are presented, and they are needed to reach a definite conclusion. The change in satisfaction following survey feedback does not achieve statistical significance. The data indicate that changes took place, but that the changes did not necessarily make a real difference. Furthermore, the fact that the change measures and the measure yielding the data that were fed back to and discussed in the groups were one and the same contaminates the results; only the survey feedback data were so contaminated. It would have been desirable to use as a pretest and posttest some measure other than the "Survey of Organizations."

A recent survey of the research on organization development fails to confirm the general superiority of survey feedback; laboratory training, however, appears to be relatively less effective (Porras and Berg, 1978). When survey feedback is related to various outcome variables and defined to include satisfaction and group behavior, as well as productive efficiency, significant positive results occur approximately half the time. In a recent study in a bank, survey feedback yielded positive consequences among tellers, but could not be shown to have caused changes noted among desk personnel (Nadler, Mirvis, and Cammann, 1976). All in all, survey feedback seems to work under some circumstances, but not others.

Conclusions

A theory that has had as widespread application as system 4 should be evaluated from the viewpoints of both the scientist and the manager. From the scientist's viewpoint the key questions relate to logical consistency of the theory, its value in advancing understanding, its validity as measured in an empirical test, and the like. The manager, on the other hand, is concerned with the usefulness of the theory in generating approaches that improve the effectiveness of the organization in achieving its goals. Since a manager must do *something* in any event, he should be satisfied with any approach that increases the likelihood of success and reduces risk. The manager does not have the option of waiting for a certain solution. In contrast, the scientist can and should adopt a conservative, wait-and-see stance until all the data are in. Obviously decision making in the two realms is not the same.

Scientific Goals

Many of the difficulties with system 4 theory relate to its origins in group dynamics. Basically it is a small group or work group theory extrapolated to the total organization. It often appears to extend beyond the domain to which it is most applicable. Almost all the research supporting the theory has come from the lower organizational levels. Survey research, based on the "Profile of Organizational Characteristics" and on the "Survey of Organizations," extends to higher levels, but the sheer weight of the data from lower levels tends to obscure results at higher levels where relatively fewer people are involved. When top-level data are analyzed separately, they tend not to support the theory (Bowers, 1975).

The major conceptual problem relates to the role of hierarchy. Under system 5, hierarchy is eliminated, but this system has not been elaborated fully, and accordingly it is inappropriate to assess the theory on the basis of system 5. However, the very nature of system 5 suggests why Likert is so unspecific about the role of hierarchy in system 4—he appears not to have really wanted it there either. Though Likert invokes the linking pin concept to explain how group goals are kept consonant with organizational goals, he gives little attention to the specific organizational processes involved. Furthermore, the research on upward influence and vertical linking pin relationships supports the theory only with regard to relatively circumscribed, dyadic interactions—again at the level of leadership and group dynamics, not organizational theory. We know nothing from the research about how failed groups at the top influence bottom-level groups, for instance.

A related difficulty with system 4 theory involves role conflict. Likert recognizes the need for clear definition of roles in an organization, but at the same time he advocates vertical and horizontal linking pin structures, cross-functional teams, and matrix designs that would be expected to increase uncertainty and conflict. The answer to this apparent paradox appears to lie in the implicit assumption that hierarchy is sufficiently weak and unimportant in system 4 to minimize its impact as a source of role conflict. Yet this whole area remains theoretically vague.

This same failure of Likert's theory to deal adequately with hierarchy increases competition from an alternative explanation of the research. Mulder (1977) has shown that participation provides fertile ground for the unilateral exercise of influence based on perceived expertise and proficiency. Given that the more competent individuals are selected for managerial roles and then provided with more training and information, the introduction of participation may only enhance the effective operation of hierarchy. This source of confounding permeates all the organizational research. Failure to explicate the role of hierarchy has led to inadequate concern for the nature and characteristics of managers in the organizational chain. As a consequence, the effects of managerial knowledge, information, training, and the like have not been controlled, and the effects of supportive supervision, participation, and so on, may well have been overestimated.

The problem of confounding in the research on system 4 theory in general is compounded by the way in which the theory itself is stated. System 4T incorporates not only supportiveness and participation, but also goal setting, technical knowledge and skill, resource availability, and structural differentiation. All these variables have been shown on occasion to relate to group or organizational effectiveness. But then what is the role of the original system 4 constructs? A theory to which more and more variables are added is more likely to violate the principle of parsimony. Are there some variables in system 4T theory that neither predict outcomes nor advance understanding? Is it possible that the system 4 variables are unnecessary? We do not know, primarily because the research results are so frequently open to alternative interpretation.

Likert tends to deal with disconfirming results by adding to his theory on an ad hoc basis, rather than thoroughly revising it. The results of this approach have been mixed. The hypothesis of lag from causal to intervening to end-result variables appears to have considerable validity, but the lack of specific time intervals provides an "escape hatch" when the theory appears not to have been confirmed—usually the elapsed time is said to have been too short.

A similar escape hatch is ascribing research failures to situational and cultural variables that were not specified prior to the conduct of the research. The theory is mute on when system 4 may be expected to be consonant or not consonant with situational demands and thus when the theory would be expected to work. To specify such circumstances would turn the theory into a contingency theory or perhaps a limited domain theory, rather than the general theory of organizational functioning to which Likert aspires. Yet without this specification of circumstances it is a much less powerful theory.

Actually there is enough research evidence to indicate that the effectiveness of system 4 type theories is contingent upon circumstances (Miner, 1980). The theory appears to work best at the level of the individual work group; this would seem to be its practical, if not its intended, domain. Within this domain a number of circumstances that can enhance or mitigate the effects of system 4 have been noted. Certainly neither theory nor research has charted this area adequately as yet. It seems possible, however, that many of the moderator or contingency variables now proposed may be reduced to the level of personality of work group members, i.e., for some types of people the group control and inducement approach of system 4 generates considerable satisfaction and energy output, while for others it does not. The more positive consequences would tend to occur when members want to interact with others and to do so effectively, like to have a sense of belonging to a group, have favorable attitudes toward peers generally, prefer collaboration to competition, and enjoy participating in the democratic process (Miner, 1980).

Goals of Application

A manager reading the literature on system 4 theory is likely to come away thoroughly confused. While Likert himself and many of those associated with him present a uniformly positive picture of the theory, many others exhibit various degrees of skepticism. The discrepancy appears to result from the research considered. Likert tends to focus on the research, and often on the publications, of the Institute for Social Research at the University of Michigan. In addition he refers to a number of sources intended primarily for the practitioner or the general public. He makes less use of scholarly, scientific sources, and when he does use them, it is often to illustrate a point made by the theory, rather than to test it. Reviews such as those of Stogdill (1974), Katzell and Yankelovich (1975), Filley, House, and Kerr (1976), and Locke and Schweiger (1979) draw on the scientific publications primarily and do so much more comprehensively.

Furthermore, Likert and those associated with him have cited the early studies at Harwood, Weldon, Detroit Edison, and so on, again and again; in fact that is why they are often considered classics. Yet the many methodological problems involved in these studies make interpretation difficult at best. By no means do all the early studies support system 4 theory in any event, and some are marred by difficulties with the direction of causation as well. The version of the theory tested in the early studies was very general; in fact many of the specifics of system 4 theory emerged from this research. As grounds for accepting the later versions of system 4 theory, the classic studies simply are not adequate.

The introduction of system 4 changes tends to be closely associated with the use of the "Profile of Organizational Characteristics" and the "Survey of Organizations." Since both of these self-report measures are highly subject to influence by conscious intent, it is well to be aware of the problems associated with both instruments as change measures. All the training, survey feedback, and other information used to introduce system 4 may well teach managers and employees alike how to respond on a second administration of the measures without changing their job behavior at all. Thus these measures should be supplemented with tests less subject to conscious manipulation, with behavioral indexes, and with end-result measures in the evaluation of the results of an organization development intervention.

In a sense system 4 theory discourages the use of end-result variables because of the lag times involved. These lag times present a real, practical problem. They appear to be a consequence of the use of the generally time-consuming participative process. Other change procedures can produce results much more rapidly, as Likert himself notes. Accordingly, if participation should turn out to be unnecessary in system 4T, this would be important to know. For the present, however, participation cannot be assumed to be unnecessary, and a manager changing to system 4T must be resigned to a long delay before results are achieved. In addition, there is no theoretical or empirical basis for determining when a true failure has occurred. If one waits just a little longer, success may be around the corner. This temporal uncertainty may well be too great for many managers to accept.

There are other risks involved in accepting system 4 or 4T and applying it. The complete lack of research on human resource accounting, coupled with the risk that attention might be diverted from other, possibly more crucial variables, argues for introduction on an experimental basis only. Survey feedback as an organization development technique appears to be subject to the same kinds of contingency effects as other participative approaches and thus to carry the same risks. It may work, but it may not; we are not certain when it will and will not; and there is some possibility of negative consequences (Locke and Schweiger, 1979).

One major source of negative consequences in any attempt to shift an organization toward system 4 is inherent in the group focus of the theory. Highly cohesive groups are generated. Though it is expected that the efforts of these groups will be directed toward organizational goals through linking pin relationships, little is known about how to accomplish this. Thus there is a risk that these groups will develop and work toward goals unrelated to or even inconsistent with those of a company. The goals could be those of each particular group, or those of a union, a social movement, or even a competitor.

System 4 approaches are often introduced during periods of prosperity and profit making. Very little is known about how such a system operates in a company coping with competitive pressures, decreasing market shares, and economic downturn. It may well fail to respond quickly enough or even respond effectively at all. There is some evidence that this problem is a real one. Management needs a great deal more information in this area.

With the rapid increase in the number of laws constraining corporate action, the number of legal actions against companies, and the size of the judgments rendered in recent years, the risks of autonomous functioning by either individuals or work groups can be sizable. Accordingly, many managers simply do not consider it advisable to shift control downward or even expand lower-level control for fear that the whole future of the firm will be jeopardized.

This whole matter of control within the organization is the major focus of the next chapter. The theory set forth there also emanates from the Institute for Social Research and is closely allied with that of Likert. Research related to it has some bearing on the validity of system 4 theory as well. Consequently it appears appropriate to suspend further consideration of Likert's theory until the data relating to control theory have been considered. It is important to recognize, however, that from a managerial perspective adoption of the major tenets of system 4 theory can involve high risk.

References

Bowers, David G. "OD Techniques and Their Results in 23 Organizations: The Michigan ICL Study," *Journal of Applied Behavioral Science*, 9 (1973), 21–43.

————. "Hierarchy, Function, and the Generalizability of Leadership Practices." In James G. Hunt and Lars L. Larson (eds.), *Leadership Frontiers*. Kent, Ohio: Kent State University Press, 1975, pp. 167–80.

————. *Systems of Organization*. Ann Arbor: University of Michigan Press, 1976.

Bowers, David G., and Jerome L. Franklin. *Survey Guided Development I: Data-Based Organizational Change*. La Jolla, Calif.: University Associates, 1977.

Bowers, David G., and Doris L. Hausser. "Work Group Types and Intervention Effects in Organizational Development," *Administrative Science Quarterly*, 22 (1977), 76–94.

Bowers, David G., and Stanley E. Seashore. "Predicting Organizational Effectiveness with a Four-Factor Theory of Leadership," *Administrative Science Quarterly*, 11 (1966), 238–63.

Brightman, Harvey J. "Leadership Style and Worker Interpersonal Orientation: A Computer Simulation Study," *Organizational Behavior and Human Performance*, 14 (1975), 91–122.

Burke, Ronald J., and Tamara Weir. "Organizational Climate and Informal Helping Processes in Work Settings," *Journal of Management*, 4, no. 2 (1978), 91–105.

Butterfield, D. Anthony, and George F. Farris. "The Likert Organizational Profile: Methodological Analysis and Test of System 4 Theory in Brazil," *Journal of Applied Psychology*, 59 (1974), 15–23.

Coch, Lester, and John R. P. French. "Overcoming Resistance to Change," *Human Relations*, 1 (1948), 512–32.

Dowling, William F. "At General Motors: System 4 Builds Performance and Profits," *Organizational Dynamics*, 3, no. 3 (1975), 23–38.

Filley, Alan C., Robert J. House, and Steven Kerr. *Managerial Process and Organizational Behavior*. Glenview, Ill.: Scott, Foresman, 1976.

Flamholtz, Eric. *Human Resource Accounting*. Encino, Calif.: Dickenson, 1974.

Fleishman, Edwin A. "Attitude Versus Skill Factors in Work Group Productivity," *Personnel Psychology*, 18 (1965), 253–66.

Franklin, Jerome L. "Down the Organization: Influence Processes across Levels of Hierarchy," *Administrative Science Quarterly*, 20 (1975), 153–64.

Franklin, Jerome L., Anne L. Wissler, and Gregory J. Spencer. *Survey Guided Development III: A Manual for Concepts Training*. La Jolla, Calif.: University Associates, 1977.

French, John R. P., Joachim Israel, and Dagfinn Ås. "An Experiment on Participation in a Norwegian Factory: Interpersonal Dimensions of Decision-Making," *Human Relations*, 13 (1960), 3–19.

French, John R. P., Ian C. Ross, S. Kirby, J. R. Nelson, and P. Smyth. "Employee Participation in a Program of Industrial Change," *Personnel*, 35, no. 6 (1958), 16–29.

Gardner, Godfrey. "Workers' Participation: A Critical Evaluation of Coch and French," *Human Relations*, 30 (1977), 1071–78.

Golembiewski, Robert T., and Robert Munzenrider. "Persistence and Change: A Note on the Long-Term Effects of an Organization Development Program," *Academy of Management Journal*, 16 (1973), 149–53.

Graen, George, James F. Cashman, Steven Ginsburg, and William Schiemann. "Effects of Linking-Pin Quality on the Quality of Working Life of Lower Participants," *Administrative Science Quarterly*, 22 (1977), 491–504.

Hall, John W. "A Comparison of Halpin and Croft's Organizational Climates and Likert and Likert's Organizational Systems," *Administrative Science Quarterly*, 17 (1972), 586–90.

Hausser, D. L., P. A. Pecorella, and A. L. Wissler. *Survey Guided Development II: A Manual for Consultants*. La Jolla, Calif.: University Associates, 1977.

House, Robert J., Alan C. Filley, and Damodar Gujarati. "Leadership Style, Hierarchical Influence, and the Satisfaction of Subordinate Role Expectations: A Test of Likert's Influence Proposition," *Journal of Applied Psychology*, 55 (1971), 422–32.

Kahn, Robert L., and Daniel Katz. "Leadership Practices in Relation to Productivity and Morale." In Dorwin Cartwright and Alvin Zander (eds.), *Group Dynamics: Research and Theory*. Evanston, Ill.: Row, Peterson, 1960, pp. 554–70.

Katzell, Raymond A., and Daniel Yankelovich. *Work, Productivity, and Job Satisfaction: An Evaluation of Policy-Related Research*. New York: Psychological Corporation, 1975.

Lewin, Kurt. "Group Decision and Social Change." In Guy E. Swanson, Theodore M. Newcomb, and Eugene L. Hartley (eds.), *Readings in Social Psychology*. New York: Henry Holt, 1952, pp. 459–73.

Likert, Rensis. "Motivation: The Core of Management," *American Management Association Personnel Series*, no. 155 (1953), 3–21.

———. "Measuring Organizational Performance," *Harvard Business Review*, 36, no. 2 (1958), 41–52.

———. "A Motivational Approach to a Modified Theory of Organization and Management." In Mason Haire (ed.), *Modern Organization Theory*. New York: Wiley, 1959, pp. 184–217

———. *New Patterns of Management*. New York: McGraw-Hill, 1961.

———. *The Human Organization: Its Management and Value*. New York: McGraw-Hill, 1967.

———. "Human Resource Accounting: Building and Assessing Productive Organizations," *Personnel*, 50, no. 3 (1973), 8–24.

———. "Improving Cost Performance with Cross-Functional Teams," *Conference Board Record*, 12, no. 9 (1975), 51–59.

———. "Managing an Interdisciplinary Research Institute: The Institute for Social Research." *Academy of Management Proceedings*, (1978), 384–88.

Likert, Rensis, and David G. Bowers. "Organization Theory and Human Resource Accounting," *American Psychologist*, 24 (1969), 585–92.

———. "Improving the Accuracy of P/L Reports by Estimating the Change in Dollar Value of the Human Organization," *Michigan Business Review*, 25 (March 1973), 15–24.

Likert, Rensis, and William F. Dowling. "Conversation with Rensis Likert," *Organizational Dynamics*, 2, no. 1 (1973), 33–49.

Likert, Rensis, and M. Scott Fisher. "MBGO: Putting Some Team Spirit into MBO," *Personnel*, 54, no. 1 (1977), 40–47.

Likert, Rensis, and Jane G. Likert. *New Ways of Managing Conflict*. New York; McGraw-Hill, 1976.

Likert, Rensis, and Stanley E. Seashore. "Making Cost Control Work," *Harvard Business Review*, 41, no. 6 (1963), 96–108.

Likert, Rensis, and J. M. Willets. *Morale and Agency Management*. Hartford, Conn.: Life Insurance Agency Management Association, 1940–41.

Locke, Edwin A., and David M. Schweiger. "Participation in Decision-Making: One More Look." In Barry M. Staw (ed.), *Research in Organizational Behavior*. Greenwich, Conn.: JAI Press, 1979, pp. 265–339.

Mann, Floyd C., and Rensis Likert. "The Need for Research on the Communication of Research Results," *Human Organization*, 11, no. 4 (1952), 15–19.

Marrow, Alfred J. *The Failure of Success*. New York: AMACOM, 1972.

Marrow, Alfred J., David G. Bowers, and Stanley E. Seashore. *Management by Participation*. New York: Harper & Row, 1967.

Marrow, Alfred J., and John R. P. French. "Changing a Stereotype in Industry," *Journal of Social Issues*, 1, no. 3 (1945), 33–37.

Miner, John B. *The Management Process: Theory, Research, and Practice.* New York: Macmillan, 1978.

———. "Limited Domain Theories of Organizational Energy." In C. C. Pinder and L. F. Moore (eds.), *Middle Range Theory and the Study of Organizations.* Boston: Martinus Nijhoff, 1980, pp. 273–86.

———. *Theories of Organizational Behavior.* Hinsdale, Ill.: Dryden, 1980.

Morse, Nancy C., and Everett Reimer. "The Experimental Change of a Major Organizational Variable," *Journal of Abnormal and Social Psychology*, 52 (1956), 120–29.

Mott, Paul E. *The Characteristics of Effective Organizations.* New York: Harper & Row, 1972.

Mozina, Stane, Janez Jerovsek, Arnold S. Tannenbaum, and Rensis Likert. "Testing a Management Style," *European Business*, 27 (Autumn 1970), 60–68.

Mulder, Mauk. *The Daily Power Game.* Leiden, the Netherlands: Martinus Nijhoff, 1977.

Nadler, David A. *Feedback and Organization Development: Using Data-Based Methods.* Reading, Mass.: Addison-Wesley, 1977.

Nadler, David A., Philip Mirvis, and Cortlandt Cammann. "The Ongoing Feedback System: Experimenting with a New Managerial Tool," *Organizational Dynamics*, 4, no. 4 (1976), 63–80.

Pelz, Donald C. "Influence: A Key to Effective Leadership in the First-Line Supervisor," *Personnel*, 29 (1952), 209–17.

Porras, Jerry I., and P. O. Berg. "The Impact of Organization Development," *Academy of Management Review*, 3 (1978), 249–66.

Rhode, John G., Edward E. Lawler, and Gary L. Sundem. "Human Resource Accounting: A Critical Assessment," *Industrial Relations*, 15 (1976), 13–25.

Roberts, Karlene, Raymond E. Miles, and L. Vaughn Blankenship. "Organizational Leadership, Satisfaction, and Productivity: A Comparative Analysis," *Academy of Management Journal*, 11 (1968), 401–14.

Seashore, Stanley E., and David G. Bowers. *Changing the Structure and Functioning of an Organization: Report of a Field Experiment.* Ann Arbor: Institute for Social Research, University of Michigan, 1963.

Seashore, Stanley E., and David G. Bowers. "Durability of Organizational Change," *American Psychologist*, 25 (1970), 227–33.

Stogdill, Ralph M. *Handbook of Leadership: A Survey of Theory and Research.* New York: Free Press, 1974.

Zimmerman, D. Kent. "Participative Management: A Reexamination of the Classics," *Academy of Management Review*, 3 (1978), 896–901.

3

Control Theory

Control theory had its origins in the same early studies conducted out of the Institute for Social Research at the University of Michigan as system 4 theory did. Certain aspects of control theory have been incorporated in Likert's formulations. But it was at the beginning and remains today the unique product of Arnold Tannenbaum, who has been at the University of Michigan throughout most of his professional career. He became associated with the Center for Group Dynamics when it moved from MIT to Syracuse University after Kurt Lewin's death. After completing his doctorate in psychology with Floyd Allport at Syracuse, Tannenbaum moved on with the Center for Group Dynamics to the Institute for Social Research at Michigan.

In Tannenbaum's (1956) own view, his theory emerged out of the early Michigan studies contrasting leadership behaviors in high- and low-producing work groups, out of the Morse and Reimer research in which he played an active role (Morse, Reimer, and Tannenbaum, 1951), and out of the early work on hierarchical influence done by Pelz (see Chapter 2). Tannenbaum interprets all these studies as analyses of the effects of variations in the amount and distribution of control. They are limited in scope, however, to the work group and to supervisory practices. Tannenbaum extended the framework of control to the total organization.

The Evolution of Tannenbaum's Control Theory

Much of Tannenbaum's thinking about the role of control in organizations was influenced by Allport's views on interpersonal control and dominance relationships. However, Tannenbaum was interested in theory at the organizational level from an early time (Morse, Reimer, and Tannenbaum, 1951). As a formal entity, control theory was created as a framework for a study of four local unions.

Control Theory As Articulated for the Union Research

The initial statements of control theory appear in several articles (Tannenbaum, 1968, Chapters 2, 3, and 19*; Tannenbaum and Kahn 1957), and a book (Tannenbaum and Kahn, 1968) dealing with the union research. Control is defined in a number of these publications as "the capacity to manipulate available means for the satisfaction of needs." It is concerned with the allocation of rewards and punishments in an organization, and for this reason differences in control systems strongly influence the way organizations function.

*The 1968 book contains edited versions of a number of journal articles published from 1956 on. Citations will be to this source by page or chapter, wherever possible.

Terms and Variables. Control may vary both in total amount within the organization, from whatever source, and in distribution. Characteristically distribution is considered in terms of groups at different levels in the organizational hierarchy. Within the union context high control at the rank-and-file level and low control at the officer level is associated with *democracy.* In contrast, high officer and low membership control reflects an *autocratic* or oligarchic system. In the *laissez-faire* or anarchic model, the amount of control in the organization is low at all levels; no one exercises much control. Where the amount of control in the organization is high for both officers and rank-and-file members, the system is *polyarchic.*

Several postulates describe the way control works.

1. There must be both a subject and an object, in that someone must control something. Controlling is the active aspect; being controlled, the passive.

2. Controlling must be motivated to occur. Thus there must be a perception of worthwhile rewards associated with the behavior.

3. Internal control within an organization and external control of the environment are closely related.

4. Control involves several phases of activity: the *legislative,* in which policies and courses of action are decided; the *administrative,* in which policies and courses of action are interpreted and implemented; the *sanctions,* in which rewards and punishments are given or withheld.

Hypotheses. Tannenbaum does not offer clear-cut statements of his hypotheses. Nevertheless, they can be gleaned from a close reading of his articles and books. In the union research, member control was hypothesized to be positively related to member participation, as reflected in such activities as attendance at meetings, for instance. A similar relationship was expected to exist for total amount of control.

The amount of control in the organization consistently plays a more important role in the theory than does the distribution. Thus the amount of control is hypothesized to relate positively to organizational power over the environment, competition and intraorganizational conflict, member loyalty, interorganizational conflict (with management, for instance), militancy, member conformity, and receipt of sanctions. Though total control is expected to exert a causal influence on these variables, reciprocal relationships are anticipated as well. A factor such as organizational power can contribute to total control, in addition to being caused by it.

Tannenbaum refers to the set of variables considered in this section as the *organizational power syndrome.* These variables are expected to yield increased order and uniformity in an organization. However, within this syndrome it is the total amount of control that matters. High total control is associated with a strong organization that is effective in the pursuit of its goals. However, a variety of distribution patterns can yield this same result. Even in discussing employee-centered leadership in this early period, Tannenbaum only goes so far as to state that this style fosters membership control and member participation; he does not extend the hypothesis to organizational effectiveness, as Likert has.

> In the typical evaluation of democracy in organizations and communities, great emphasis is put upon the *distribution* of control and all too little on the total *amount* of control exercised. . . . We should think less in terms of the autocratic-democratic dichotomy and more in terms of the basic dimensions of control, within which an infinite number of patterns can be found (Tannenbaum and Kahn, 1958, p. 237).

The specific hypotheses stated in relation to elevated member control and a democratic model involve member participation in union activities and a greater member interest in broad social goals, as opposed to bread-and-butter issues. In addition, the widely observed tendency for unions to become less democratic over time is attributed primarily to a relative decrease in member control in the later, more stable period.

Extensions During the 1960s

During the 1960s, control theory was increasingly extended from its original focus on local unions into the domain of organizations in general. These developments are documented in an early review article (Tannenbaum, 1962) and in *Control in Organizations* (Tannenbaum, 1968).

One major change introduced early in the decade was to relate increases in relative amounts of control at lower levels, and thus a particular control distribution, to organizational effectiveness. This was a step that Tannenbaum had not taken when the theoretical focus was on unions only. It puts him much more in line with Likert's views on the superiority of democratic (system 4) forms over more autocratic forms, and Tannenbaum (1968, p. 57) acknowledges his debt to Likert in this regard.

At the same time, the theory continues to stress the importance of the total amount of control. The relationship with effectiveness is reciprocal: greater control yields greater organizational effectiveness, and effectiveness contributes to greater control. The hypothesis is qualified as follows, however:

> . . . too much control may be as dysfunctional as too little, and a hypothesis more general than that offered above would specify an optimum level of control above or below which the

organization would function below its potential. We are not yet in a position to specify the optimum for specific organizations. We can safely assume, however, that many . . . are operating at a level considerably below it (Tannenbaum, 1968, p. 58).

Another new hypothesis states that "across areas of experience, satisfaction will be a positive function of control" (Tannenbaum, 1968, p. 241). On the average, people who have greater control over an aspect of their work will be more satisfied in that regard, though for some few individuals control may not have this significance.

The view that the total amount of control in an organization is not a fixed sum is elaborated on at some length, particularly with reference to how expansion may occur.

1. There may be an expansion into the organization's external environment, such that greater influence over competitors, governments, and the like occurs.

2. There may be certain kinds of internal changes—either in the structural factors that determine member interactions and influence, or in the motivational factors that cause members to exercise control and to become amenable to control.

Control may expand as a function of increased interpersonal exchange, greater personal inclusion in the organization, co-optation of new members, and the like. Participative approaches of the kind represented by system 4 are particularly likely to increase the amount of control in this manner. The "influence pie" is expanded from within, as more organizational members exert influence on each other.

Participation and Control

This matter of the nature of various types of participative systems and their relationships to the total influence pie has become of increasing concern for control theory in recent years.

> Participation is often thought to imply taking power from managers and giving it to subordinates, but in fact managers need not exercise less control where there is participation. A reduction in managerial power *may* occur, but it need not. . . . the participative organization may be one in which the *total amount of control* is higher than in the nonparticipative organization. . . . the success of participative approaches hinges not on reducing control, but on achieving a system of control that is more effective than that of other systems. In fact, many participative schemes are really designed implicitly, if not explicitly, to legitimize, if not enhance, the control exercised by managers (Tannenbaum, 1974, pp. 78–79).

As an outgrowth of this view, specific hypotheses have been formulated (Rosner, Kavcic, Tannenbaum, Vianello, and Wieser, 1973):

1. The degree of workers' participation in decision making is related positively to the amount of total control in the organization, and more specifically to the amount of control by the workers as a whole and by management.

2. The relationship between workers' participation in decision making and the amount of management control is mediated both by the frequency of communication between subordinates and superiors and by the amount of the workers' control.

3. A rise in the amount of workers' control increases trust in management, which in turn increases management control.

4. A rise in the amount of workers' control contributes to a sense of worker responsibility, which in turn increases management control.

According to these formulations, shifts in the direction of participative management would not be expected to eradicate hierarchy. Control would increase in the ranks of management also, though probably the *relative* amount there would be somewhat less than under a less participative system. For control theory, participation effects of this kind are not restricted to approaches such as system 4; they may occur under the impact of a socialist economy as well (Tannenbaum, Kavcic, Rosner, Vianello, and Wieser, 1974).

The Control Graph Method

Most research bearing on control theory has utilized a measurement procedure developed at the inception of the theory. The existence of the control graph method has been a boon to researchers. On the other hand, such extensive reliance on a single procedure for operationalizing theoretical variables raises questions about construct validity and the specificity of results to the particular measure used.

The Nature of the Method

The control graph method uses survey methodology. A questionnaire asks members of the organization to indicate how much control they believe individuals at various levels exert. Thus, in the union research, questions cast in the format "In general, how much do you think _____ has to say about how things are decided in this local?" were asked for the president, the executive board, the plant bargaining committee, and the membership (Tannenbaum and Kahn, 1958). Responses were given on a five-point scale, ranging from "a great deal of say" to "no say at all."

These scale values are averaged for all respondents to obtain scores reflecting control exercised at each organizational level. A graph is then constructed on which the amount of control reported for each level is plotted against the hierarchical level involved. Figure 3–1 illustrates various possible results. Curve 1 is positively sloped and reflects a democratic control structure. Curve 4 is negatively sloped and reflects an autocratic or centralized structure. Both curves indicate the same amount of control, but the control distributions vary dramatically.

Curve 3 reflects an essentially laissez-faire structure with very little control at any level. Curve 2 reflects a polyarchic system. A comparison of these two curves reveals sizable differences in the amount of control exercised in the organizations, even though the distributions are identical. The curves of Figure 3–1 have been selected to portray hypothetically pure cases. In actual practice the lines drawn to connect the various points on the hierarchical scale may yield a great variety of curves. Straight-line relationships occur only rarely.

Alternative Measures. Though control graphs typically are constructed to reflect control actually exerted (or active control), there are several alternative measures in the literature. One alternative is an index of passive control, which indicates the extent of control

Figure 3–1
Hypothetical Control Curves

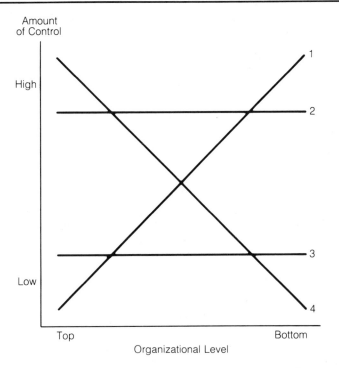

Amount of Control

High

Low

Top   Bottom

Organizational Level

over each hierarchical level (Tannenbaum, 1968, Chapter 3). The basic data derive from essentially the same questions used to measure active control. However, in this instance respondents rate on a five-point scale the amount of influence exerted by each level on all levels, including the level in question, as in Figure 3–2. The scores for the levels are then averaged in terms of influence *received* from all sources, and the points plotted just as with active control. In general these passive control curves tend to be flatter than active control curves: being controlled is more equally distributed across hierarchical levels. The data of Figure 3–2 also permit the construction of separate curves showing the amount of control exerted by each level on the various levels (top management, management below the top level, rank-and-file), though such a detailed approach is not commonly used.

Figure 3–2
Typical Set of Questions Used in Constructing Active and Passive Control Curves

1. In general, how much say or influence does top management have on what the following groups do in the company?

	Little or no influence	Some influence	Quite a bit of influence	A great deal of influence	A very great deal of influence
Top management	_____	_____	_____	_____	_____
Management below the top level	_____	_____	_____	_____	_____
The rank-and-file workers	_____	_____	_____	_____	_____

2. In general, how much say or influence does management below the top level have on what the following groups do in the company?

	Little or no influence	Some influence	Quite a bit of influence	A great deal of influence	A very great deal of influence
Top management	_____	_____	_____	_____	_____
Management below the top level	_____	_____	_____	_____	_____
The rank-and-file workers	_____	_____	_____	_____	_____

3. In general, how much say or influence do the rank-and-file workers have on what the following groups do in the company?

	Little or no influence	Some influence	Quite a bit of influence	A great deal of influence	A very great deal of influence
Top management	_____	_____	_____	_____	_____
Management below the top level	_____	_____	_____	_____	_____
The rank-and-file workers	_____	_____	_____	_____	_____

Another measure deals with ideal or desired control (Tannenbaum, 1968, Chapters 4 and 5). In this variant the word *should* is substituted for *does* in the questions (see Figure 3–2). Comparisons characteristically are made between actual and ideal curves. The ideal values tend to be higher than the actual, with the discrepancy being greatest at the lower levels.

On occasion, specific questions are asked about control in various areas (wages and salaries, hiring, pricing, investments, and so on) as a supplement to or replacement for the more global questions (Tannenbaum, 1968, Chapter 6). The responses to a number of specific questions may be summed to obtain a total measure. In this approach, as with the other measures discussed, question wording has not been completely standardized. There are variations from study to study, and it is not entirely clear what effects these variations may have on results. Also the verbal descriptors applied to the five points on the scale have not always been the same.

Reliability. Rather surprisingly, the reliability of the control graph method has received little attention. The use of large numbers of raters whose reports are averaged would tend to argue for good reliability; the use of a very limited number of questions to fix points on a curve suggests that reliability may not be as great as desired. Tannenbaum and Cooke (1979) note a lack of predicted correlations between the perceptions of various groups concerning the influence exerted by these groups. The problem is great enough to suggest low reliability in a measure that combines responses. In one study, judgments by the rank and file and by board members regarding the control of the president correlated .50, but the correlations for the control of the rank and file itself and of the board were .25 and .18, respectively (Tannenbaum, 1968, Chapter 4). Findings of this kind suggest that the composition of the sample used to determine control values may exert considerable influence on the results obtained.

Tannenbaum (1968, Chapter 10) also contains data on the split-half reliabilities (corrected for group size) of various control indexes. These range from .53 to .84, with a median of .67. Here, as elsewhere (Kavcic and Tannenbaum, 1979), the argument for reliability is predicated on the use of large numbers of respondents whose ratings are averaged. Ideally, however, data from repeat administrations would be used to determine reliabilities. Such data do not exist in the published literature. Furthermore, other investigators have reported split-half reliabilities well below .67 (Pennings, 1976).

Criticism of the Method

The authors of the control graph method themselves raised certain questions at an early point regarding the approach (Tannenbaum and Kahn, 1957):

1. There is no provision for scaling the hierarchical level and amount of control dimensions to achieve equal units of measurement. As a result, unknown biases may be introduced into the findings.

2. The theory assumes a measure of actual control in organizations, while the measure is a perceptual one. The measures may not be analogous with the theory's constructs.

3. The control graph does not deal with the means through which control is exercised and thus may be insufficient.

4. It may be more appropriate to deal with specific areas in which control is exercised, rather than to use a global index.

5. The roles of passive and ideal control curves need to be explored further.

Among these points, matters of construct validity and difficulties in global measurement have received the most attention. In addition, certain aspects of the reliability problem, which Tannenbaum tends to de-emphasize, have been given consideration.

Construct Validity. The question of whether actual control, as opposed to mere perception of control, is represented in the control graph has been the subject of considerable research. Tannenbaum (1968, Chapters 13 and 14) presents evidence that, though individual perceptions influence the results obtained, group or structural factors also tend to operate. The latter are interpreted as specific structural effects of actual control, with the following qualification:

> It must be noted, however, that this particular interpretation does not follow necessarily from the logic of our analysis. It is possible, for example, that our measures have tapped some cultural stereotype common to the office as a whole, rather than the actual behaviors assumed to be associated with control and bases of power (Tannenbaum, 1968, p. 222).

Overall, the results from this line of research are consistent with the idea that a sizable amount of variance in control graph measures is attributable to actual control, but they do not extend to the point of certain proof.

One problem with the control graph method is that respondents are free to interpret "say or influence" in their own way. Thus what is said to be influence at one level may not be the same thing as influence at another. There is evidence that this is the case:

> . . . influence is specific as to hierarchic level. This indicates that the levels not only are perceived to have a different degree of influence, but that there is also a qualitative difference. . . . the questions measure influence in three dimensions, one for each hierarchical level. This means that it is not possible to draw a control curve as this requires

unidimensional variables (Gundelach and Tetzschner, 1976, pp. 59–60).

Conclusions such as these appear somewhat extreme, based on the data; at the very least, one can utilize measures of slope and total control to test the theory, whether or not a graph actually is constructed. Yet questions as to what the control graph measures mean are raised by this type of analysis—questions that are given further credence by the fact that, in the measurement of control, different hierarchical groups often yield different outcomes. It appears that control under one circumstance is not the same as control under another, and that the control graph method lacks the capacity to differentiate.

Kavcic and Tannenbaum (1979) have recently constructed a questionnaire to determine whether respondents are interpreting control in the manner they intend. The results given in Table 3–1 make it clear that a sizable number of individuals are not providing answers that are consistent with control theory constructs.

Yet a majority of individuals taking the questionnaire are responding in a theoretically appropriate manner, and attempts to correlate control graph measures with other measures that appear to tap the same constructs have produced favorable results. Thus the distribution measures do correlate (averaging in the .50s) with other indexes of centralization (Tannenbaum, 1968, Chapter 20), and both slope and total control show the expected relationships with independent measures of participation (Tannenbaum et al., 1974). All in all, it appears that the global questions yield only very rough measures of actual control, and do so with considerable "noise," and

Table 3–1

Percent of Respondents Defining Control in a Manner Consistent with the Theory (N = 3,000)

Statement for Which a True Response Is Consistent with the Theory	Percent Giving True Response
A director has great influence if others always follow his suggestions.	75
Only persons who make decisions have influence; others carry out decisions.	65
A person has influence if he can change the attitude of others.	63
Sometimes it is possible that subordinates have greater influence than their supervisors.	60
A subordinate has influence on a superior if a superior follows the suggestion of a subordinate.	58
A person at a high level has little or no influence if no one does what this person wishes them to do.	38

Table 3–1 (Continued)

Statements for Which a False Response Is Consistent with the Theory	Percent Giving False Response
A person has influence if he makes decisions even if no one carries out the decision.	70
A supervisor can never have greater influence than his subordinates.	64
Only those who formally make decisions can have influence.	63
A person can have influence only if he is feared.	63
If a director has great influence, he will never take into account the suggestions of others.	59
A person has influence on others only if they like him.	<u>43</u>
Average percent consistent with theory	60

Source: Adapted from Bogdan Kavcic and Arnold S. Tannenbaum, "A Longitudinal Study of the Distribution of Control in Yugoslav Organizations as Perceived by Members," 1979 (unpublished).

that the underlying constructs tapped by given measures may vary considerably, depending on the specific question, the respondent sample, the organization, and other circumstances.

Global vs. Specific Measurement. Many problems currently associated with the control graph method might be solved by substituting a series of questions about influence in specific decision areas for the global questions. This approach should establish constructs with greater precision and at the same time increase reliability, because scores are based on a greater number of items. Yet, as indicated in Table 3–2, when one gets down to the matter of predicting criteria, there appears to be no difference between the standard global measure and an index based on eight specific items. The latter is more reliable, and results are not significant on all criteria for either measure, but the data do not support an outright rejection of the global measure for the more specific index.

Degree of Concordance. It has been noted that the control curves produced by representatives of different hierarchical levels often do not agree—there is a lack of agreement or integration within the organization. Tannenbaum gave this phenomenon little attention. Subsequent research indicates that organizations can differ considerably in the degree of concordance between the control curves that emanate from different levels. Furthermore, variations in concordance can be good predictors of outcome criteria, especially criteria emanating from employees rather than managers (McMahon and Perritt, 1973; McMahon and Ivancevich, 1976).

Table 3–2

Correlations Between Global and Index (Based on Eight Specific Items) Measures of Control and Various Morale and Performance Criteria

Criteria	Control Measures	
	Global	Index
Absences	.24	.03
Lateness	.35	.20
Satisfaction with foreman	(.66)	(.65)
Satisfaction with company	(.54)	(.42)
Turnover	−.22	(−.28)
Willingness to transfer	(−.39)	−.04
Performance-quantity	.07	−.04

( ) Correlation statistically significant.

SOURCE: Adapted from Martin Patchen, "Alternative Questionnaire Approaches to the Measurement of Influence in Organizations," *American Journal of Sociology,* 69 (1963), p. 50.

This matter of concordance or agreement between the control ratings of various levels is not a direct derivative of control theory. In fact for that theory, concordance is an index of measurement error or unreliability. Nevertheless, the fact that variations in concordance do exist among organizations and may have significant consequences has implications for control theory. In one sense the fact that such a measure derives from theoretical concepts supports the usefulness of control theory. In another sense the fact that the measure is not explicated by the theory and in fact is considered to reflect error indicates limitations in the power of the theory. As will be seen in later chapters, certain organizational theories that utilize integration as a control construct explain the concordance results better than does control theory.

Tests of Hypotheses

Most of the research on control theory has been conducted by Tannenbaum and his associates. This research often has been international in character, with particular focus on the socialist economic system in Yugoslavia. However, a number of studies, both domestic and international, have been conducted without any involvement of the author of the theory.

The Union Research

Questionnaire data, including control graph measures, were obtained from rank-and-file members of four union locals in Michigan.

The number of respondents per local varied from 163 to 223 (Tannenbaum and Kahn, 1958). In general the control curves sloped positively toward greater control in the membership and bargaining committee than in the president and executive board, though there were sizable variations from local to local. The more democratic the local (the greater the member control), the more member participation as reflected in attendance at meetings. As hypothesized, a similar relationship held for total control. The greater the positive slope of the control curve for the local, the more likely members were to endorse broad social goals. However, this finding did not apply to political action and appeared to reflect primarily a desire for expanded organizing activity.

Analyses dealing with the organizational power syndrome produced consistently supportive results. Total control proved to be related to union power, union-management conflict, intralocal conflict, loyalty, conformity, and participation in union affairs. High total control was associated with uniformity in a wide range of areas.

Overall, these results support control theory, but in several respects the union research must be viewed as a pilot study. The findings are presented as comparisons between ranks for four organizations, too few for appropriate statistical testing. Furthermore, the data are concurrent and do not yield evidence to support the causal hypotheses of the theory. Though the authors advance suggestions as to the relative effectiveness of the locals, they report no direct tests of hypotheses related to effectiveness and control in the original study.

Predicting Organizational Effectiveness

Among the theory's hypotheses, those dealing with the prediction of organizational effectiveness have received the greatest research attention subsequent to the union studies. Researchers have focused on the view that the total amount of control in an organization contributes in an important way to an effective organization. However, a number of studies also have dealt with the hypothesis that a more positive, or at least a less negative, control curve and thus a more democratic system is a source of success.

The Pattern of Results. Total amount of control has been found to correlate positively with independent measures of organizational effectiveness in a wide range of situations. A review and reanalysis of early University of Michigan studies reports a significant relationship for five out of six studies (Smith, 1966). Similarly a report on early research conducted in Yugoslavia indicates consistently positive results with the total control index, though measures of control distribution did not produce the hypothesized relationship in any instance (Rus, 1970).

A recent review by Tannenbaum and Cooke (1979) of many more studies yielded essentially the same conclusions. Over twenty studies are considered, many of them unpublished. Only a small fraction of the studies failed to yield some evidence of a significant positive relationship between total control and organizational effectiveness. The results given in Table 3–3 are typical. Negative relationships between total control and several effectiveness indexes were found in one study (McMahon and Ivancevich, 1976). However, this research differed from most other studies in that the control measures were obtained from management personnel and the effectiveness measures from operating employees. An analysis, apparently based on a largely overlapping sample and utilizing effectiveness measures derived from first-level managers, produced results much more consistent with the literature as a whole (McMahon and Perritt, 1973).

Research dealing with the distribution of control, or slope of the control curve, has not produced the same consistent results as total amount of control. Often the correlations never attain statistical significance. When they do, it may be that the more democratic systems are more effective, as with the League of Women Voters (see Table 3–3), but this is by no means always true. On the evidence Tannenbaum's early hesitation in endorsing democratic control structures seems justified. He would have done well to hold to this position after the union research.

Tannenbaum summarizes the findings presented in *Control in Organizations:*

> 1. Organizations with influential rank-and-file members *can be* as effective as organizations with relatively uninfluential members (contrary to the traditional view).

Table 3–3

Correlations Between Control Measures and Effectiveness in Two Studies

Samples and Effectiveness Criteria	Amount of Total Control As Indicated by Members	Degree of Positive Slope As Indicated by Members
112 leagues of a voluntary association		
Expert ratings of effectiveness	(.29)	(.31)
32 stations of a delivery company		
Company time standard records	(.43)	.14

( ) Correlation statistically significant.

Source: Adapted from Arnold Tannenbaum, *Control in Organizations.* New York: McGraw-Hill, 1968, p. 83.

2. Organizations with powerful officers *can be* as effective as organizations in which the officers are less influential (contrary to most participative views).

3. Organizations with influential rank-and-file memberships are likely to be more effective than those with uninfluential memberships *provided* the officers are not less influential (contrary to the traditional views).

4. Organizations with powerful officers are likely to be more effective than those with less powerful officers *provided* the memberships are not less influential (contrary to most participative views).

5. Organizations with influential leaders *and* members are likely to be more effective than organizations with less influential members and/or leaders (contrary to both traditional and participative views).

6. Differences in power between persons of different rank are *not* likely to be associated with criteria of performance. This statement sharply contradicts some arguments for participative organization to the extent that these arguments identify participation with "power equalization" (Tannenbaum, 1968, pp. 309–10).

Causation. Control theory hypothesizes not only a relationship between amount of control and effectiveness, but also a causal relationship. Increased control should produce greater effectiveness; yet, at the same time, greater effectiveness should increase control. Studies dealing with causation are few in number, but they do exist. In one instance measures of the amount of control taken in one year correlated significantly with a number of performance criteria obtained a year later. Criteria obtained at the same time as the control data yielded much lower and generally nonsignificant results (Tannenbaum, 1968, Chapter 8). In this particular study significant predictions from performance to control level were not obtained.

A longitudinal study conducted by Farris (1969), on the other hand, yields evidence of a stronger effect of performance on control than of control on performance. The generally low correlations in this instance, however, make interpretation difficult.

One of the few laboratory studies dealing with control theory further supports the view that greater control can contribute to greater effectiveness (Levine, 1973). The control levels in three-person problem-solving groups were experimentally manipulated. Groups with a high total amount of control performed consistently better and were more satisfied. Accordingly, it seems appropriate to conclude that high levels of control can be a source of effectiveness. The reverse is probably true as well, but the data are too sparse at this time to be sure.

Control and Satisfaction

The Tannenbaum and Cooke (1979) review covers a number of studies in which total amount of control was positively related to measures of satisfaction, loyalty, morale, and the like. Positive slope, or its approximation, also tends to be related to variables of this kind, but not to the degree that amount of control is. Unlike the analyses involving organizational effectiveness criteria, however, those utilizing satisfaction criteria typically risk contamination due to common method variance, since the same questionnaire was used to measure both the control variables and the criteria. Correlations as high as .90 between total amount of control and satisfaction suggest that common method variance may well be a problem, given the relatively low reliability of control measures (Ivancevich, 1970).

In any event, though control theory anticipates a positive overall relationship between amount of control and satisfaction, it further hypothesizes that individuals will experience greater satisfaction in areas where their control is greater. In general this appears to be true (Tannenbaum, 1968, Chapter 16). Workers tend to report greater satisfaction in areas in which, on independent evidence, they would be expected to exert greater control. In one instance where control was expanded in certain areas and not others, the changes in control correlated .46 with increases in satisfaction.

Participation and the Expandable Influence Pie

Control theory posits that increases in control at lower levels through the introduction of participative procedures can, and frequently do, result in increases in control at upper levels also, thus expanding the total amount of control in the organization considerably. As a consequence, a resort to participative management would not be expected to eliminate hierarchy, though the degree of negative slope in the control curve might be reduced somewhat.

Concurrent Research. An early study cited by Likert (1961) compared control curves for departments that varied in the extent to which participative procedures were applied in them. Differences in control at the worker level reflected the participation differences. Furthermore, the same rank ordering was maintained at the higher management level. Participative approaches were correlated with a greater amount of control in general, as the theory would anticipate, and with greater productivity as well. All the control curves exhibited a negative slope, irrespective of the level of participation.

This and other concurrent evidence tends to substantiate the expandable pie concept (Tannenbaum and Cooke, 1974). Studies of industrial organizations, now extending to thirteen countries, consistently indicate that hierarchical control systems predominate even in socialized societies such as Yugoslavia and in the kibbutzim of Israel (Tannenbaum et al., 1974; Tannenbaum, 1979). Exceptions, involving positive slopes, appear to occur in voluntary organizations and local unions where the departure from bureaucratic organization is sizable. There is also some basis for anticipating a less hierarchical curve in professional organizations (Farris and Butterfield, 1972).

Measures of participation tend to correlate positively with the total amount of control in the organization (Tannenbaum et al., 1974). Yet the reverse also may be true in some cases:

> Data from the international study also show that coercion as a "basis of power" for the supervisor tends to be negatively correlated with the total amount of control in organizations. However, these correlations are not always large, and an exception occurs in 10 Yugoslav plants where, for reasons that we do not understand, a high level of control is associated with coercive leadership practices (Tannenbaum and Cooke, 1974, p. 40).

Furthermore, the international research finds that the greater total control in participative systems is primarily a function of differences at lower levels, not all levels:

> The major contribution to the enhanced influence in the participative, compared to the nonparticipative, plants appears to result from the greater influence of workers. . . . This power equalization, however, does not mean a reduction in the control exercised by managers—managers, on the average, hold their own (Rosner et al., 1973, p. 207).

Though this outcome is not entirely consistent with theoretical predictions and the earlier Likert (1961) data, other hypotheses regarding participation are supported in this study. Frequency of superior-subordinate communication and amount of worker control tend to mediate the relationship between worker participation and management influence in a positive manner. Similarly, trust in management and a sense of worker responsibility (and thus presumably a lack of worker-management conflict) mediate the relationship between worker and manager control.

Predictive Research. The studies considered to this point do not indicate that increasing participation at lower levels will *cause* an expansion of total control, though the results generally are consistent with such an interpretation. To answer the causal questions, longitudinal research to observe the effects of expanded participation over time is needed.

An effort to obtain longitudinal data of this kind was incorporated in the Harwood and Weldon research discussed in Chapter 2. Control graphs, obtained at Weldon in 1962, 1963, and 1964, during the period of a concentrated effort to increase participation, indicate that very little change in actual control occurred. If anything, there was a diminution of control at higher levels and an increase at lower levels; no expansion of the influence pie occurred. Data from Harwood over the same period indicated that an increase in total control did occur there, which was in evidence at all levels (Marrow, Bowers, and Seashore, 1967). However, Harwood had already shifted to a participative system by 1962, and the Harwood measures taken from 1962 to 1964 were intended as controls for those at Weldon.

This suggests that delayed response may be characteristic of increases in control, and indeed the data collected at Weldon in 1969 indicate an increase in total control over the earlier period (Seashore and Bowers, 1970). The change was most pronounced at the highest level and quite minimal at the employee level. Thus the role played by participation in the 1969 results becomes problematic. As indicated in Chapter 2, the findings from the Weldon research as a whole are subject to multiple interpretations; this appears to be no less true of the control graph findings.

Other attempts at longitudinal analyses carried out in conjunction with early University of Michigan studies also fail to yield the anticipated results. In one instance comparisons of data collected in 1958 and in 1961 during a period of intensive efforts to introduce participative procedures in experimental groups produced only very weak evidence of an increase in total control. The increases that were found occurred entirely at the upper levels; actual employee control did not increase, though the results for desired control were consistent with expectations for a program to increase employee participation (Tannenbaum, 1968, Chapter 11).

A study by Kavcic and Tannenbaum (1979) compared control graphs over a five-year period, using 3,000 persons in 100 Yugoslav organizations. Since "the law had moved progressively in the direction of defining the Yugoslav enterprise as a highly participative social entity," sizable increases in the amount of control were anticipated over the period of the study. Once again the changes in actual total control were minimal, though positive, and primarily attributable to increases in control at the top of the organizations. At the same time, desired control increased more substantially, especially at the worker level. In this case the time spans involved appear broad enough to have captured any lag effects that might have been present.

Table 3–4 contains data from a study in which control graphs were constructed from the responses of all personnel in branch offices of an insurance company to questionnaires administered before and three months after a management development program for branch managers was carried out (Baum, Sorensen, and Place, 1970). The program was human relations oriented and stressed power equalization. This emphasis is clearly evident in the scores on desired control, which shifted sharply in a power-equalized direction in the experimental branches where the managers received the training and failed to shift in the control branches where managers did not receive the training.

Nonetheless, total actual control did not increase after training, and though control at lower levels shifted upward, the control exercised by the branch managers decreased. These effects are still in evidence after the control group data are used to correct for apparent regressions toward the mean. In this instance no expansion in the influence pie occurred—what the workers won, the managers lost.

Interpretations. The pattern of a high positive correlation between participative approaches and total control in concurrent studies, combined with little evidence that participation causes increased

Table 3–4

Changes in Control Measures Before and After a Management Development Program in an Insurance Company

Control Measure	Before	After	Change
Actual Control			
Branch Managers			
Experimental group	4.65	4.04	(−.61)
Control group	4.52	4.30	−.22
Adjusters			
Experimental group	2.76	2.62	−.14
Control group	2.63	2.60	−.03
Clerical personnel			
Experimental group	1.85	2.35	(+.50)
Control group	1.93	2.05	+.12
Desired Control			
Branch managers			
Experimental group	4.61	3.50	(−1.11)
Control group	4.16	4.11	−.05
Adjusters			
Experimental group	2.85	2.52	−.33
Control group	2.75	2.69	−.06
Clerical personnel			
Experimental group	1.67	2.18	(+.51)
Control group	1.74	2.12	+.38

( ) Change statistically significant.

Source: Adapted from Bernard H. Baum, Peter F. Sorensen, and William S. Place, "The Effect of Managerial Training on Organizational Control: An Experimental Study," *Organizational Behavior and Human Performance*, 5 (1970), pp. 176–78.

control, suggests that high levels of control may contribute to a resort to participation. This would seem particularly feasible if control contributes to organizational effectiveness (as it apparently does) and in organizations where there is considerable control at high levels. The high-level manager who exerts a sizable influence on his organization and who is well entrenched by virtue of managing a very effective organization may simply be in the best position to risk introducing participative procedures.

It has been suggested also that the expandable influence pie concept will hold only where intraorganizational conflict (as, for instance, between management and workers) is at a minimum. In the presence of conflict, what one level wins, the other loses, as in the insurance firm (Gundelach and Tetzschner, 1976). In the absence of conflict, trust, responsibility, two-way communication, and the like can operate to permit greater control at all levels. Data presented by Smith (1966) indicate that in bureaucratic systems such as industrial organizations, high levels of conflict are likely to be associated with low levels of overall control, with the result that the level of laissez-faire (or anarchy) is approached. In contrast, less conflict is associated with greater overall control. Here, also, we cannot identify cause-and-effect relationships, but since the expandable pie hypothesis is not always valid, it seems reasonable to posit internal conflict as a moderator.

In describing such a conflict-laden situation where the results do not fit the theory, Tannenbaum notes:

> . . . democratic control (i.e., positive slope) does not have the predicted effect. . . . While the pattern of control may lead to high rank-and-file morale, it does not appear to promote basic identification with organizational objectives and practices or motivated action leading to high performance. It appears that in this organization, high rank-and-file control relative to the leaders may have the effect of members acting simply in terms of their own self-interests and not accepting the contributions of leaders. . . . In the absence of shared organizational norms and a system of high mutual influence (i.e., high total control) to regulate and coordinate member action with respect to these norms, it is not surprising that democratic control is not conducive to high organizational performance (1968, p. 163).

Conclusions

Scientific Goals

The discussion in the preceding chapter led to the conclusion that system 4 theory had not been successful in developing a conceptually sound method of dealing with hierarchy. Because the roots of the theory were in group dynamics, the whole matter of hierarchical relationships was not well integrated with other constructs. In many respects control theory may be viewed as an attempt to fill this gap in the system 4 theory. Control theory focuses primarily on hierarchy and attempts to integrate it with participative management.

Control theory has been only partially successful in integrating hierarchy with participative management. The difficulties have been in handling participation. The simplest hypothesis is that the concept of slope can be used to represent participation and that the more positive or less negative the slope, the more democratic and effective the organization. Support for this hypothesis was obtained only rarely and then typically not in business firms.

The more complex hypothesis dealing with participation left hierarchy intact (and the negative slope that goes with it), while tying participation into the finding that total control consistently was related to effectiveness. Here, too, however, the participation part of the hypothesis runs into difficulty. Attempts to introduce participative approaches have the expected impact on levels of desired control, but not on other aspects of the control graph. If anything, the data appear to be explained best by the following hypothesis: where considerable control in an absolute sense exists above the worker level, there is a greater willingness to expand worker control, and the total amount of organizational control is likely to expand only in those instances where conflict between workers and management is at a minimum.

In spite of its failures (or very limited success) in dealing with the concept of participation, control theory has made a sizable contribution to the understanding of organizational functioning. The finding that satisfaction tends to be greater in areas where the individual experiences greater control provides new insights into job enrichment research (Miner, 1980). Knowing that organizations can vary in total amount of control—that control is not a fixed sum and that therefore control gained by some members need not be control lost by others—is valuable in understanding both organization-member and organization-environment relationships.

However, the most important contribution of control theory is the hypothesis (now soundly grounded in research) that a greater amount of control, or at least the perception of greater control on the part of lower-level participants, contributes to a more effective organization. This finding has emerged from study after study in spite of major imperfections in the questionnaire used. Because most imperfections such as unreliability of measurement would tend to void the finding of any significant results, the underlying phenomenon in this case must be very powerful indeed. The only report of results opposite to those hypothesized above occurred when the control measures were obtained at the managerial level exclusively (McMahon and Ivancevich, 1976). In other studies the emphasis on the shared perceptions among worker respondents (and their concordance with perceptions at higher levels, as well) that the organization exercises considerable control may be the key construct. Presumably these perceptions of organizational control would have some validity.

Control theory thus provides a basis for understanding how organizational effectiveness is obtained. Effectiveness appears to be a product of control processes that produce uniformity and coordinate effort behind goals. The result is a type of conformity. However, the pressures toward conformity need not come only from the top for the organization to be effective; ideally, control comes from all directions.

Tannenbaum once suggested that the relationship between control and effectiveness might be curvilinear. Yet tests of the theory have continued to treat the hypothesis as linear, and that is the hypothesis the research supports. It seems reasonable that an organization might experience too much control, but the theory lacks specificity in this area and relevant research is nonexistent.

Goals of Application

Control theory has not generated any applications that are uniquely its own. However, the theory clearly implies that anything that can be done to increase the amount of organizational control and/or the perception of it at lower levels will contribute to a more effective organization. Though guidelines for accomplishing this have not been developed and the introduction of participative management seems insufficient, several recommendations can be made.

For one thing, control in the sense that Tannenbaum uses the term is not the same as managerial control in the traditional literature. Newman (1975) defines managerial control as "the series of steps a manager takes to assure that actual performance conforms as nearly as practical to plan." Control of this kind invariably involves evaluation and feedback. In contrast, Tannenbaum is concerned with a much broader concept, which encompasses managerial control, as well as other types of influence. Accordingly, increasing the total amount of control should not be equated with introducing an expanded array of managerial control systems. This may be part of the process, but it is certainly not all that Tannenbaum intended or that the research supports.

Furthermore, expanding control may well require increasing control at the lower levels—that is, not only the receipt of control, but also its exercise. As Tannenbaum (1966) notes, managers may resist this on the strength of a fixed-pie assumption. If conflict is rampant in the organization, the managers' assumption that their own control will suffer may be correct. Accordingly, it may be necessary to develop mutual trust and a sense of responsibility before expanding control levels.

Control theory does not concern itself with how to increase organizational control, and this is one of its major deficiencies from the viewpoint of the practicing manager. On the other hand, the theory has produced one conclusion that has tremendous practical significance: Organizations do need to be well controlled, and this does not have to be accomplished through centralization and a steep slope of hierarchy.

References

Baum, Bernard H., Peter F. Sorensen, and William S. Place. "The Effect of Managerial Training on Organizational Control: An Experimental Study," *Organizational Behavior and Human Performance*, 5 (1970), 170–82.

Farris, George F. "Organizational Factors and Individual Performance: A Longitudinal Study," *Journal of Applied Psychology*, 53 (1969), 87–92.

Farris, George F., and D. Anthony Butterfield. "Control Theory in Brazilian Organizations," *Administrative Science Quarterly*, 17 (1972), 574–85.

Gundelach, Peter, and Helge Tetzschner. "Measurement of Influence in Organizations—Critique of the Control-Graph Method," *Acta Sociologica*, 19 (1976), 49–63.

Ivancevich, John M. "An Analysis of Control, Bases of Control, and Satisfaction in an Organizational Setting," *Academy of Management Journal*, 13 (1970), 427–36.

Kavcic, Bogdan, and Arnold S. Tannenbaum. "A Longitudinal Study of the Distribution of Control in Yugoslav Organizations, as Perceived by Members," 1979 (unpublished).

Levine, Edward L. "Problems of Organizational Control in Microcosm: Group Performance and Group Member Satisfaction as a Function of Differences in Control Structure," *Journal of Applied Psychology*, 58 (1973), 186–96.

Likert, Rensis. *New Patterns of Management*. New York: McGraw-Hill, 1961.

Marrow, Alfred J., David G. Bowers, and Stanley E. Seashore. *Management by Participation*, New York: Harper & Row, 1967.

McMahon, J. Timothy, and John M. Ivancevich. "A Study of Control in a Manufacturing Organization: Managers and Non-Managers," *Administrative Science Quarterly*, 21 (1976), 66–83.

McMahon, J. Timothy, and G. W. Perritt. "Toward a Contingency Theory of Organizational Control," *Academy of Management Journal*, 16 (1973), 624–35.

Miner, John B. *Theories of Organizational Behavior*. Hinsdale, Ill.: Dryden, 1980.

Morse, Nancy C., Everett Reimer, and Arnold S. Tannenbaum. "Regulation and Control in Hierarchic Organizations," *Journal of Social Issues*, 7, no. 3 (1951), 41–48.

Newman, William H. *Constructive Control: Design and Use of Control Systems*. Englewood Cliffs, N.J.: Prentice-Hall, 1975.

Patchen, Martin. "Alternative Questionnaire Approaches to the Measurement of Influence in Organizations," *American Journal of Sociology*, 69 (1963), 41–52.

Pennings, Johannes M. "Dimensions of Organizational Influence and Their Effectiveness Correlates," *Administrative Science Quarterly*, 21 (1976), 688–99.

Rosner, Menachem, Bogdan Kavcic, Arnold S. Tannenbaum, Mino Vianello, and Georg Wieser. "Worker Participation and Influence in Five Countries," *Industrial Relations*, 12 (1973), 200–212.

Rus, Veljko. "Influence Structure in Yugoslav Enterprise," *Industrial Relations*, 9 (1970), 148–60.

Seashore, Stanley E., and David G. Bowers. "Durability of Organizational Change," *American Psychologist*, 25 (1970), 227–33.

Smith, Clagett G. "A Comparative Analysis of Some Conditions and Consequences of Intra-Organizational Conflict," *Administrative Science Quarterly*, 10 (1966), 504–29.

Tannenbaum, Arnold S. "The Concept of Organizational Control," *Journal of Social Issues*, 12, no. 2 (1956), 50–60.

———. "Control in Organizations: Individual Adjustments and Organizational Performance," *Administrative Science Quarterly*, 7 (1962), 236–57.

———. *Social Psychology of the Work Organization*. Belmont, Calif.: Wadsworth, 1966.

———. *Control in Organizations*. New York: McGraw-Hill, 1968.

———. "Systems of Formal Participation." In George Strauss et al. (eds.), *Organizational Behavior: Research and Issues*. Madison, Wis.: Industrial Relations Research Association, 1974, pp. 77–105.

———. "Organizational Psychology." In Harry C. Triandis and Richard W. Brislin (eds.), *Handbook of Cross Cultural Psychology: Social Psychology*. Boston: Allyn & Bacon, 1980, pp. 281–334.

Tannenbaum, Arnold S., and Robert A. Cooke, "Control and Participation," *Journal of Contemporary Business*, 3, no. 4 (1974), 35–46.

———. "Organizational Control: A Review of Studies Employing the Control Graph Method." In C. J. Lammers and D. Hickson (eds.), *Organizations Alike and Unlike*. London: Routledge & Kegan Paul, 1979.

Tannenbaum, Arnold S., Bogdan Kavcic, Menachem Rosner, Mino Vianello, and Georg Wieser. *Hierarchy in Organizations: An International Comparison*. San Francisco: Jossey-Bass, 1974.

Tannenbaum, Arnold S., and Robert L. Kahn. "Organizational Control Structures: A General Descriptive Technique as Applied to Four Local Unions," *Human Relations*, 10 (1957), 127–39.

———. *Participation in Union Locals*. Evanston, Ill.: Row, Peterson, 1958.

4

Sociotechnical Systems Theory

In many respects sociotechnical systems theory is the European counterpart of system 4 theory. It has been associated closely from its beginnings with the Tavistock Institute of Human Relations in London, just as system 4 theory has been with the Institute for Social Research at the University of Michigan. Collaboration between these two organizations has been considerable over the years, including joint editorial responsibility for the journal *Human Relations.*

The Tavistock Institute was an outgrowth of the Tavistock Clinic formed in 1920 to provide psychotherapy to those who could not otherwise afford it. The institute emerged as a separate, incorporated entity when the clinic entered the British national health service after World War II (Dicks, 1970). One major figure in the institute and its chairman for many years was Eric Trist, who is the primary author of sociotechnical systems theory. Trist was joined in his theoretical efforts and in his research by others, who were either employed by the institute or strongly influenced by it. Thus in many respects sociotechnical systems theory is a product of the same kind of group interaction on which the theory itself focuses.

Trist remains the prime contributor to the theory, even though he left the institute after some twenty years. He served on the faculties of the University of California at Los Angeles and subsequently at the University of Pennsylvania, from which he has now retired. He was originally trained as a psychologist.

Statements of the Theory

Sociotechnical systems theory dates from the description of the change from a system of coal mining that emphasized autonomous work groups to a more mechanized system extrapolated from factory procedures (Trist and Bamforth, 1951). It is the thesis of Trist and of Bamforth, who had been a miner himself, that the introduction of the new longwall methods broke up the existing sociotechnical whole and created an imbalance:

> . . . a qualitative change will have to be effected in the general character of the method so that a social as well as a technological whole can come into existence. Only if this is achieved can the relationships of the cycle work-group be successfully integrated and a new social balance be created.
> . . . it is difficult to see how these problems can be solved effectively without restoring responsible autonomy to primary groups throughout the system and ensuring that each of these groups has a satisfying sub-whole as its work task, and some scope for flexibility in work-pace. . . . It is likely that any attempts in this direction would require to take advantage of the recent trend of training face-workers for more than one

role, so that interchangeability of tasks would be possible within work teams (Trist and Bamforth, 1951, p. 38).

Open Systems and the Causal Textures of Environments

Sociotechnical systems theory began with the idea that there must be a best match, or joint optimization, between the task or technical environment and the social system. The theory at this stage operated at the work-group level primarily and gave little attention to the functioning of the organization as a whole. However, at least as early as 1959, the theory was extended through the introduction of open systems concepts (Trist, 1969).

An enterprise is an open system that engages in continuing exchanges with other enterprises, institutions, and individuals in its external environment. Its sociotechnical system must permit it to maintain a steady state in which work can be done in the face of changing environmental circumstances. This open systems approach contrasts with that of closed systems, which regard the enterprise as "sufficiently independent to allow most of its problems to be analyzed with reference to its internal structure and without reference to its external environment" (Trist, 1969, p. 270).

With the introduction of open systems concepts, sociotechnical theory became concerned with the total organization, including top management. Its authors also began creating a typology of environments that organizations (or segments of organizations) might face. The typology focuses on the different causal textures of environments—"the extent and manner in which the variables relevant to the constituent systems and their inter-relations are, independently of any particular system, causally related or interwoven with each other" (Emery and Trist, 1973, p. 41). Four ideal types of environments are described in various publications (Emery and Trist, 1965, 1973; Emery, 1967; Trist, 1976a, 1977).

Placid Random Environments. In the placid random environment the interconnectedness of elements is at a minimum, and change is slow, if it occurs at all. Factors that may help or hinder goal achievement are randomly distributed, so that the optimal strategy is simply trying to do the best one can on a local basis; planning in any real sense is not possible. Learning occurs, but only at the level of simple conditioning.

Placid random environments are said to typify preagricultural, primitive societies and to occur only in certain specialized subsystems of modern societies—certain types of small job shops, surviving general stores, typing pools, and assembly lines. Other examples of a placid random environment are "an old-fashioned mad-house" and a concentration camp, where the prediction of events is almost impossible. In discussing such environments, the theorists treat the organizational context surrounding an individual or work unit and the environmental context surrounding an enterprise or organization as interchangeable concepts.

Placid Clustered Environments. Though placid clustered environments, too, change slowly, the grouping of factors within them follows some logic. As a result, goal achievement is either helped or hindered, and strategies to deal with the environment may be developed. Organizations in such environments can develop environmental knowledge and use that knowledge to position themselves effectively. Traditional agricultural and business societies were of this type. Firms of limited size that possess a distinctive competence and fill a stable market demand have placid clustered environments in the present business structure. Such firms tend to be highly specialized and relatively invulnerable to economic cycles.

Disturbed Reactive Environments. With the advent of industrialism, environmental change accelerated and large-scale bureaucracies emerged to cope with this change. The disturbed reactive context is characterized by competitive challenge, and organizations in such environments must develop strategies to deal with other organizations of the same kind having the same goals. Each firm in an industry must counteract power moves by other firms in the industry at the same time it is establishing its own strategies. As a result, organizations in such an environment are continually engaged in a complex set of reactions to each other.

Turbulent Fields. Disturbed reactive environments are said to have reached their peak after World War II. The predominant form since then increasingly has been the turbulent field. Though definitions of the other three environments are not always as precise as might be desired, from a theoretical perspective only the turbulent environment is of central significance to the theory. The other types are posited primarily for purposes of contrast. Unlike the placid environments, and like the disturbed reactive environments, change is rampant in turbulent fields. But this change arises "not simply from the interaction of the component organizations, but also from the field. . . . The 'ground' is in motion" (Emery and Trist, 1965, p. 26).

Turbulent fields have emerged as a consequence of the development of huge organizations that exert effects beyond their industries, the increasing significance of public and governmental actions for economic organizations, the rapid change occasioned by increased research and development, and the expanded scope and speed of communication. Such fields introduce so much greater uncertainty than their predecessors that individual organizations can no longer cope with it through their own independent efforts. Strategic planning, as it was utilized in other environments, is inadequate when change is rampant.

Just as system 4 theory introduced a possible fifth system without elaborating on it, so sociotechnical theory merely touches on a fifth type of environment in a footnote:

> Any attempt to conceptualize a higher order of environmental complexity would probably involve us in notions similar to vortical processes. We have not pursued this because we cannot conceive of adaptation occurring in such fields. . . . In case there may be something to the hunch that a type V environment has the dynamics of a vortex, it is worthwhile noting that vortices develop at system boundaries when one system is moving or evolving very fast relative to the other (Emery and Trist, 1973, p. 41).

Postindustrial society

Emery and Trist contend that society is still utilizing an organizational structure appropriate to disturbed reactive environments in coping with the more complex turbulent environments of the present. This cannot possibly work, because turbulent environments are too fast-changing, complex, interdependent, and uncertain for the essentially rigid and uncreative bureaucratic form. This theme is elaborated from a variety of viewpoints (Emery, 1967, 1974; Emery and Trist, 1965, 1973; Trist, 1973, 1975a, 1976a, 1976b, 1977). A key concept of bureaucracy is redundancy of parts, whereby the work is broken down to the simplest and least costly elements possible. Individuals who perform such work are easily trained and replaced, but reliable control systems (requiring additional redundancy) are needed to make the system operate effectively. Such systems are so cumbersome, they are unresponsive to turbulent environments.

Organizations by their nature require redundancy to minimize error in the face of environmental change. However, an alternative design to redundancy of parts is redundancy of functions among individuals and units that have wide repertoires of activities and are self-regulating. "Only organizations based on the redundancy of functions have the flexibility and innovative potential to give the possibility of adaptation to turbulent conditions" (Trist, 1977, p. 273).

In addition, turbulent environments require a set of simplifying values, much like systems of professional ethics, to foster intraorganizational and interorganizational collaboration rather than competition. Organizations, accordingly, become institutionalized and act in accord with the needs of the larger society. Hierarchy is reduced, if not eliminated, and alternatives such as composite, autonomous groups, matrices, and networks are fostered (Herbst, 1976). Because organizational design principles imply certain values, the movement toward these nonhierarchical forms and toward redundancy of functions can only occur within a value system that stresses the worth of individuals and of democratic processes.

Moving toward a postindustrial society capable of coping with a turbulent world requires active intervention:

1. The *object of intervention* is to increase the probability of securing the advent of one of the more rather than one of the less desirable of the "alternative futures" which seem to be open.

2. The *instrument of intervention* is "adaptive planning"—the working out with all concerned of plans subject to continuous and progressive modification which are what have to be made when what has to be done cannot be decided on the basis of previous experience.

3. The *agency of intervention* is government—but in collaboration with other key institutional groups—for adaptive planning will require the active participation as well as the free consent of the governed (Emery and Trist, 1973, p. 124).

As a result of this planned intervention, the changes noted in Table 4–1 will occur. A new set of values, congruent with postindustrialism, will replace the Protestant Ethic values of industrialism. "The core relevant values involved are those associated with organizational democracy" (Trist, 1976a, p. 18).

Autonomous Work Groups

Much of the preceding argument for organizational democracy must be considered social philosophy rather than testable scientific theory, but at the level of organizational design, sociotechnical theory contends that a turbulent world has already arrived and that democratic alternatives to hierarchy will be more effective than bureaucracy. Here, hypotheses of a scientific nature are indeed advanced, and they indicate a very specific type of democratic organization.

The Emery and Thorsrud Hypotheses. In writing about sociotechnical systems theory as applied to work groups, Trist typically credits certain hypotheses developed by Emery (Trist, 1973, 1975a). Though formulated much earlier, these hypotheses were first published in Emery and Thorsrud (1976). They state how a sociotechnical system

Table 4–1
Changes Associated with the Move Toward a Postindustrial Society

Cultural Value Changes
1. From achievement to self-actualization
2. From self-control to self-expression
3. From independence to interdependence
4. From endurance of distress to capacity for joy

Changing Organizational Philosophies
1. From mechanistic to organic forms
2. From competitive to collaborative relations
3. From separate to linked objectives
4. From a view of one's resources as owned absolutely to a view of one's resources as shared with society

Changing Ecological Strategies
1. From responsive to crisis to crisis-anticipation strategies
2. From specific to comprehensive measures
3. From requiring consent to requiring participation
4. From damping conflict to confronting conflict
5. From short to long planning horizons
6. From detailed central control to generalized control
7. From small local government to large area government
8. From standardized to innovative administration
9. From separate to coordinated services

SOURCE: Adapted from Fred E. Emery and Eric L. Trist, *Toward a Social Ecology*, London: Plenum, 1973, pp. 174, 182, 186.

should be organized and operated to produce positive outcomes in the modern world.

In this context the primary task of management is to cope with the environment across the boundary of the organization. To the extent management must "coordinate internal variances in the organization," it will be less effective. Organization members must be given considerable autonomy and selective independence if the enterprise is to achieve the steady state it needs for effectiveness in its environment.

This inevitable theoretical commitment to autonomous work groups appears inconsistent with the contingency concepts of sociotechnical theory. The explanation given is as follows:

> It seemed that there was "The Myth of the Machine." The organization theory opposing ours was not "a machine theory of organization" but a general theory of bureaucracy. . . . In the first and older perspective our task was to prove for each technology that organizational choice was possible; as each new technology emerged our task was on again. In the second perspective, the relevance of our approach could be

established by asking a single question: Is management necessary to the organization? If the answer is yes, then, regardless of technology, some degree of self-management of groups of members is possible. Sociotechnical theory does not thereby go out of the door. To go from what is organizationally possible to what is viable one must answer such critical questions as "what groups should be formed around what tasks"; how semi-autonomous; "what degree of multiskilling is necessary." These questions can be answered only by some form of socio-technical analysis in each practical instance (Emery and Thorsrud, 1976, p. 7).

At best this view assigns the theory's sociotechnical aspects a role secondary to environmental determinism and antibureaucracy.

Much of the theory deals with job enrichment—challenging job content, opportunity to learn, individual decision making, recognition in the work place, the opportunity to relate work to social life, and a sense that the job leads to a desirable future. In a more specific sense this means task variety, tasks forming meaningful wholes, optimum length of work cycle, individual goal setting coupled with feedback, inclusion of auxiliary and preparatory tasks, inclusion of tasks worthy of community respect, and the perception of a contribution to product utility. These hypotheses for positive outcomes are not unlike those of other job enrichment views (Miner, 1980).

But "the redesigning of jobs leads beyond the individual job to the organization of groups of workers and beyond into the revision of our notions about supervision and the organization of support services. . . . the implications were even wider . . . a challenge to traditional management style and philosophy" (Emery and Thorsrud, 1976, p. 17). At the group level this calls for interlocking tasks, job rotation, or physical proximity where there is task interdependence or stress, or where individual jobs do not create a perception of contribution to product utility. Multiskilling of operators, according to the principle of redundancy of functions, is necessary for job rotation and a key concept of the theory. Information for self-control should be made immediately available to the operators themselves. Meetings and contacts that foster group formation should be institutionalized. Foremen should be trained to deal with groups rather than individuals. Incentives should be of a group nature. The group must monitor and control individual contributions and assign tasks. In essence the system is one of group rather than hierarchical control, and effort is induced by group processes rather than superior managers. Thus group productivity is fostered by:

1. Communicating quickly, directly, and openly the needs for coordination arising from task or individual variability.

2. Allocating tasks and other rewards and punishments to control what they consider to be a fair contribution by members (Emery and Thorsrud, 1976, p. 163).

Though the term *autonomous work group* is typically used to describe this type of organization, the groups are in fact only semiautonomous, since they are dependent on the company for resources, and the company remains responsible for compliance with legal constraints. The degree of autonomy will vary with the circumstances. At a minimum the group will decide on working methods and work allocation. Beyond this the members may control changes in the composition of the group, the equipment and tools used, maintenance, planning, quality standards, and at the highest level the defining of work goals. Thus much of the traditional supervisory task is taken over by the group. What remains to supervision is not the exercise of power over individuals, but the coordination of the group with the resources and objectives of the larger organization.

The Herbst Hypotheses. Herbst (1976) has extended the theoretical treatment of nonbureaucratic structures designed to cope with turbulent environments. His *composite autonomous group* comes closest to what has been discussed previously. In such a context all members can perform all tasks. Consequently there is no special leadership function, and members can adopt whatever work structures and procedures seem desirable. Because of complete multiskilling, group size must remain small, though sets of autonomous groups linked by rotation of membership are possible.

The *matrix group* contains members who have a primary specialist function, but some overlapping competencies with other members. The lack of complete multiskilling introduces some structural constraints, but permits much larger group sizes. Such groups may produce a variety of products and may choose their own procedures and even input needs. Generally, members work in small subsets, with those subsets "directively correlated" toward specified goals.

A *network group* tends to be widely dispersed. Long-term, directive correlations that are accepted by members focus their efforts on particular aims; correlations of this kind exist in the professions. Network groups typically find ways to go beyond what is already established. Members are maximally autonomous, but build on and extend each other's work. In principle, such groups are temporary systems set up to achieve particular goals; competencies are overlapping, and size is limited.

To deal with larger organizational structures, the theory posits linked, composite, autonomous groups; networks of networks; and matrices of organizational units. All these nonbureaucratic structures are hypothesized to be superior to the bureaucratic hierarchy.

However, Herbst makes the following statement:

> ... there are conditions, especially in the field of public administration, where bureaucratic organizations function well. ... relevant conditions for this are:
>   1. That the task be decomposed into independent parts.
>   2. Both the nature and requirements for task performance are stable over fairly long periods of time.
>   3. Sufficient areas of discretion and responsible autonomy with respect to task performance exist at all levels so that even the lowest level provides the opportunity for the performance of a relatively autonomous professional role.
>
> At the present time these conditions are decreasingly met (1976, p. 19).

Such a theoretical statement appears consistent with the contingency aspects of sociotechnical theory, but inconsistent with the Emery and Thorsrud (1976) statements of the inevitable superiority of autonomous work groups over bureaucracy. One could avoid the contradiction by reference to alternative types of environments, but Herbst does not do this. Indeed, if government is to be the key source of interventions for adaptive planning and changes to cope with turbulent environments, it would be hard to argue that government itself does not face such an environment.

Alternative and Elaborated Positions

The scientists concerned with sociotechnical systems theory constitute a network group, as described by Herbst. The individuals whose ideas have been considered to this point constitute the core of the group, but there are others whose contributions either extend the theory or, in a few instances, provide alternative explanations. The status of these contributions relative to the basic theory is not clear. In some cases the core group seems to have granted its stamp of approval, as when Trist endorses a book in its foreword (Kingdon, 1973; Susman, 1976), but even then agreement on all points is not certain.

Alternative and elaborated positions have developed and extended sociotechnical theory as it relates to the causal textures of environments and to the turbulent field in particular. Among others, Terreberry (1968), Metcalfe (1974), and Mileti and Gillespie (1976) have made contributions in this area. The latter set forth a number of formal propositions dealing with organization-environment relationships. These and other statements appear to be aimed at greater theoretical specificity than earlier statements by Emery and Trist.

This same specificity of theoretical statements appears to be the objective in a number of contributions dealing with autonomous work groups—in particular the contributions of Cummings and Srivastva (1977), Davis (1977), and Susman (1976). Kingdon (1973) devotes particular attention to the matrix group and to organizations that incorporate this structure. Miller and Rice (1967) extend the theory to ways in which commitment can be achieved in sociotechnical systems and to the importance of group and organizational boundary definitions. These alternative and elaborated positions are of too great a range to deal with in any detail here, and it is not clear in all cases that the contributions would warrant such attention in any event. However, it is important to note the scope of the sociotechnical systems theory network.

Sociotechnical Research

The research generated by sociotechnical systems theory has involved, almost without exception, either the introduction of autonomous work groups in situations where they did not previously exist or the study of such groups after they emerged spontaneously. Most of these studies have come from Europe and the United States, though some are from India and other parts of the world. Unfortunately many of these investigations are better classified as case studies or demonstration projects than as scientific research studies, since systematic measurement and controls are lacking. (These studies are considered as examples of applications in the next section.) The following discussion focuses on research that can be considered legitimate tests of the theory.

Coal Mining Studies

Though the original work on the mining of coal in England was essentially descriptive (Trist and Bamforth, 1951), subsequent investigations in the same context were more scientific.

Conventional and Composite Group Comparisons. In one instance comparisons were made between two groups of approximately forty workers. One group utilized the then conventional longwall method of mining that was technology-dominated, highly specialized, and segmented. The other group—a more sociotechnically balanced, composite, autonomous group—used the same technology (Trist, 1969; Trist, Higgin, Murray, and Pollock, 1963). The composite, autonomous group was characterized by (1) multiskilling so that task continuity could be maintained from shift to shift; (2) self-selected teams that allocated tasks among themselves; (3) payment based on a bonus allocated by the group in equal shares; and (4) a generally high degree of group autonomy and self-regulation. None of these factors was present in the conventional group. An attempt was made to match the coal panels mined by the two groups so that only differences in work organization would be reflected in the results.

Though the findings as given in Table 4–2 were not subject to statistical test, the pattern for the sociotechnical system was clearly superior.

Comparison of Degrees of Compositeness. A second study compared two groups, organized to varying degrees according to composite autonomous principles (Trist, Higgin, Murray, and Pollock, 1963). Here, the differentiation was less pronounced than in the previous study, but the matching of coal panels to eliminate differences attributable to the difficulty of the work was good. The more autonomous group was found to be more productive, even though the comparison group exercised a degree of autonomy. A factor in this result appears to be the greater creativity in dealing with work problems exhibited by the more autonomous group.

In interpreting the results of this and the preceding research it is important to recognize that an autonomous group approach had been characteristic in the industry prior to the introduction of the longwall technology. In fact the early sociotechnical systems theory hypotheses derived from this source. Many miners had had long experience with this approach and tended to revert to it in some situations, even after the longwall technology was introduced. Accordingly, the experimental groups were more emergent than contrived and appear to be particularly congruent with sociotechnical concepts. The authors note: "In pits where there is no composite tradition resistance to the introduction of composite working is likely to be considerable" (Trist, Higgin, Murray, and Pollock, 1963, pp. 292–93). Given this situation, the extent to which the early coal mining findings can be generalized is left in doubt.

The Rushton Research. More recent research with the Rushton Mining Company in Pennsylvania deals directly with this problem (Goodman, 1979). Autonomous group procedures were introduced in some sections and not in others. Furthermore, the procedures were introduced in the various sections with a time lag to further facilitate control comparisons. There was no previous history of autonomous group functioning in this situation. The experimental procedures were introduced by a research team headed by Eric Trist and were generally comparable to those of the early British studies (Trist, Susman, and Brown, 1977; Susman, 1976).

The initial reports appear to have been favorable (Mills, 1976). However, comprehensive comparisons of experimental and control

Table 4–2

Comparisons of Conventional and Composite Group Systems of Coal Mining

	Conventional Longwall System	Composite, Autonomous Group System
Productivity as a percent of estimated face potential	78	95
Percent of shifts lagging behind established production cycle	69	5
Absenteeism without reason as a percent of possible shifts	4.3	.4
Absenteeism because of sickness or other reasons as a percent of possible shifts	8.9	4.6
Absenteeism because of accidents as a percent of possible shifts	6.8	3.2

SOURCE: Adapted from Eric L. Trist, G. W. Higgin, H. Murray, and A. B. Pollock. *Organizational Choice: Capabilities of Groups at the Coal Face Under Changing Technologies.* London: Tavistock, 1963, pp. 123, 125.

sections prior to and during the first seventeen months of the study are mixed:

1. *Productivity.* The experiment did not significantly increase productivity.

2. *Safety.* The experiment did not significantly affect accident rates. There were significant reductions in the number of violations of . . . mining regulations. Safety practices and attitudes toward better safety practices improved. . . .

3. *Job Skills.* Miners in the experimental section reported that the programme had substantially increased their job skills.

4. *Job Attitudes.* Greater feelings of responsibility, more interest in work, more positive feelings about one's work group seem to be attributable to the experiment.

5. *Communication.* There was much more communication both vertically and horizontally, whereas previously communication had been primarily from top to bottom.

6. *Managerial Stress.* The programme increased stress for the supervisors of the experimental crew and some middle managers.

7. *Labour-Management Relations.* There were no changes in traditional indicators of labour-management relations such as the number or content of grievances (Goodman and Lawler, 1979).

Two additional points are important. The top wage was introduced in experimental sections for all members, consistent with the concept of multiskilling. Because of a variable wage scale, significant earnings differences existed in the control sections. This fact appears to have been a source of some conflict within the mine, but also may have fostered more positive attitudes in the autonomous groups. In addition, it is apparent that without a historical background favorable to the approach, sociotechnical systems procedures may be resisted. There were several votes against installing autonomous groups and other evidence of resistance from certain quarters, including some members of management (Trist, Susman, and Brown, 1977).

Indian Textile Mill Studies

In addition to the early British coal-mining studies, probably the best known investigation emanating from the Tavistock group is an analysis of the introduction of autonomous work groups into two textile mills in India. Since the beginning of the research in 1953, the Ahmedabad Manufacturing and Calico Printing Company has been involved in several studies, and data now are available for a seventeen-year period (Rice, 1958, 1963; Miller, 1975). Because production figures were obtained for a period prior to the creation of the experimental groups and because certain comparisons are made both between autonomous and nonautonomous groups within the company and between the company and the industry as a whole, this research seems to qualify as an experiment.

In the two years after the autonomous groups were formed there was an increase in productivity from approximately 80 percent to 95 percent of potential, a change that is attributed to the sociotechnical procedures on the basis of control comparisons. At the same time, the quality of work improved significantly, by a factor of 59 percent. Follow-up data through 1960 indicate that the company assumed a position of considerable competitive advantage over other leading mills after the introduction of the autonomous groups.

Ten years later one group formed on an autonomous basis was still functioning in that manner and maintaining its high performance (Miller, 1975). However, other autonomous groups were not doing as well. Furthermore, these groups appear to have backed away from the sociotechnical procedures over the years under the pressures of environmental change (a result not predicted by the theory because autonomous groups should be ideally suited to cope with change and uncertainty). In one group it now seemed that the experimental induction never really took at all, except briefly to impress the researchers. Unfortunately there were no measures to determine exactly how autonomous various groups were at different times; data on this point are essentially impressionistic.

Interpretations of this research tend to vary widely. Katz and Kahn (1978, p. 709) indicate that, "By and large the history of the effects of the experimental plan is an amazing success story." Many others have taken a similar position, though characteristically without considering Miller's (1975) follow-up data. Of particular interest are Miller's comments on the use of experimental and control comparisons within the company:

> Comparisons of performance data need to be treated with a good deal of caution. It is virtually impossible to make precise comparisons between different types of looms weaving different types of cloth. Before and after comparisons on the same looms weaving a similar type of cloth are more reliable (Miller, 1975, p. 356).

Yet, even in this instance, variations in the quality of yarn and supplies and in the criteria of measurement cloud the attribution of change over time to worker performance.

This matter of what caused the changes has been a major source of concern. Roy (1969) argues that a key factor may well have been the sizable pay increases instituted with the introduction of the sociotechnical system. He presents evidence from his own research supporting this interpretation. Certainly a confounding of experimental changes and pay increases has characterized sociotechnical research. However, it is not possible to account for the *continued* high performance of the one autonomous group on this basis, given changes in the payment system that occurred over the years (Miller, 1975).

Research Further Removed from Theoretical Origins

The coal mining studies and the textile mill research in India all had close ties to the Tavistock origins of sociotechnical systems theory. Though research further removed from these origins has not been extensive, it is important.

Studies in Norway and Sweden. Sociotechnical theory was next extended beyond the early British and Indian applications to studies in Norway and subsequently in Sweden. Here, the applications were widespread, facilitated by positive government interventions and a friendly social climate. Yet the emphasis was on demonstration projects and case applications, rather than on scientific studies. There was a tendency to assume that industrial democracy was good and then move on to problems of dissemination, rather than to question basic theoretical hypotheses.

One exception to this generalization involved a study conducted within the Swedish Tobacco Company (Agervold, 1975). As the data of Table 4–3 indicate, comparisons of an autonomous group with a similar nonautonomous group in another factory tended to support the hypothesis of more positive attitudes in the sociotechnical context. However, it is apparent that plant differences per se account for part of the differential, and the experimental effects must be discounted proportionately. Because the results of statistical tests are not provided, it is difficult to evaluate these attitudinal findings, but it would appear that the impact of introducing autonomous work groups was not pronounced. Data on productivity changes indicate a 14 percent increase at the very least in the experimental group, but it is difficult to evaluate this because control figures are not given.

In studies such as this the question of the extent to which the dictates of sociotechnical systems theory really were followed is important. If the experimental interventions did not take or were somewhat less than what the theory would anticipate, any failure to achieve hypothesized results would be expected. A first attempt at dealing with this measurement problem was proposed by Gulowsen (1972).

Table 4–3

Experimental and Control Data for Two Plants of the Swedish Tobacco Company

	Experimental (Autonomous) Group, Plant 1	Controls		
		Controls, Plant 2	All Workers, Plant 1	All Workers, Plant 2
Satisfaction with the company	4.1	2.9	4.0	3.5
Evaluation of own work	3.4	2.0	3.0	2.6
Stress in work	2.5	3.0	2.8	2.8
Solidarity and good fellowship	4.2	3.4	3.8	3.5
Influence experienced in own work	2.1	2.0	2.1	2.2
Influence experienced in own working conditions	2.0	1.5	1.6	1.7
Group influence experienced	2.2	2.1	1.7	1.8

NOTE: Higher scores indicate more of the variable.

SOURCE: Adapted from Mogens Agervold, "Swedish Experiments in Industrial Democracy." In Louis E. Davis and Albert B. Cherns (eds.), *Cases and Commentary*, vol. 2, The Quality of Working Life. New York: Free Press, 1975, p. 52.

Figure 4–1

Gulowsen's Group Autonomy Scale

Most autonomous	The group can influence the formulation of its qualitative goals.
	The group can influence the formulation of its quantitative goals.
	The group decides whether it wants a leader for the purpose of regulating boundary conditions, and if so, who.
	The group can govern its own performance above and beyond where and when to work.
	The group can decide when to work.
	The group makes decisions in connection with the choice of production methods.
	The group determines the internal distribution of tasks.
	The group decides on its own membership.
	The group decides whether it wants a leader with respect to internal questions, and if so, who.
Least autonomous	The group determines how work operations will be performed.

Figure 4–1 shows a scale of items indicating the degree to which a group is autonomous. The scale has been applied to eight different work groups, and based on these data, it appears to be unidimensional or cumulative, thus meeting the requirements for Guttman scaling; i.e., a positive response to a higher-level item implies a positive response to all lower-level items. Unfortunately scales such as this have not been used widely in research on sociotechnical systems theory. As a result, unfavorable findings often are explained post hoc as incomplete experimental induction, and no solid evidence is offered of the degree to which an autonomous system was in fact created.

Findings in the United States. Pasmore (1978) carried out one of the few studies comparing alternative approaches to organizational change in two parallel units of a food processing firm. One unit was first surveyed, then fed the results of the survey in accordance with the approach discussed in Chapter 2, then redesigned along sociotechnical lines, and then surveyed again. During this same period the second unit experienced the same survey interventions, but did not shift to a sociotechnical form. Subsequently, both units had the second survey results fed back to them, and the second unit then experienced a sizable amount of job enrichment, though not enjoying other benefits of the autonomous group approach. Finally, both units were surveyed again.

Significant improvements in employee attitudes were found, but they could not be attributed to any particular intervention technique; all three procedures produced positive results. In terms of productivity and cost savings, however, the autonomous group procedure is clearly superior. In particular there was a sizable savings in labor costs due to a 19 percent reduction in personnel required to operate the unit.

Research reported by Cummings and Srivastva (1977) produced much less positive results. In one instance sociotechnical procedures were introduced into the estimating and die engineering components of an aluminum forging plant. Control comparisons were made with data obtained from the personnel, engineering, and information systems groups in the same plant. The overall effects of the autonomous group procedure appear to have been a significant negative shift in attitudes, a decrease in productivity, at least as experienced by those involved, and a generally more negative evaluation of the experimental groups by outside departments using their services. The experiment was terminated by management after six months.

A second study in the same company compared a wheel line production unit organized on a sociotechnical basis with another unit not so organized (Cummings and Srivastva, 1977). There was little attitudinal change, other than a greater amount of insecurity in the experimental group. Absenteeism was higher in the autonomous groups, and the members of these groups perceived their performance as poorer. Their supervisors rated their performance higher than the supervisors of the control subjects, but these measures appear to be considerably biased.

Though the overall results of the second study were perceived more positively by the company's management, neither set of findings supports sociotechnical theory. Cummings and Srivastva (1977) attribute these results to the failure of sociotechnical interventions to take fully under the impact of individual resistance and the economic crisis position of the company at the time of the study. Though the authors used no comprehensive measure of experimental take such as Gulowsen's (1972), there is some evidence to support their contentions. On the other hand, the theory would not have predicted the results obtained. If anything, sociotechnically organized groups should ultimately emerge as more effective, not less effective, in coping with turbulent environmental circumstances.

In any event, research conducted in a more favorable economic milieu does yield more positive outcomes. The initial results, obtained when autonomous groups were introduced in one of the company's plants, appear to be very favorable, though control data were not available (Bramlette, Jewell, and Mescon, 1977). Subsequently, two sociotechnically organized plants in the company were compared with plants of a more traditional nature (Beldt, 1978). The data indicate that the experimental plants were distinctly superior in terms of absenteeism, production volume per worker hour, labor costs per unit of output, and employee satisfaction.

On the other hand, it is not entirely clear what caused these outcome differences. The sociotechnical plants had younger workers who were somewhat better educated, and one plant utilized an exceptionally advanced technology. Furthermore, as indicated in Table 4–4, the workers in the experimental plants did not exhibit the value structures one might anticipate. Such factors as trust, cooperation, autonomy, creativity, and equality were not more highly valued in the autonomous group; compassion, tolerance, individuality, and risk actually were valued less. But skill and success were valued highly, and the few managers required in these plants were strongly motivated individuals. It may be that for some reason the experimental plants attracted people more motivated toward and more capable of outstanding productivity.

Table 4–4

Differences in Mean Value Scores of Workers and Motives of Managers in Sociotechnical and Traditional Plants

	Sociotechnical Plants	Traditional Plants
Worker Values		
Compassion	(15	31)
Skill	(67	48)
Trust	58	54
Cooperation	62	55
Tolerance	(12	30)
Autonomy	40	28
Individuality	(29	45)
Creativity	27	35
Success	(60	41)
Equality	59	55
Risk	(18	34)
Managerial Motivation		
Total score	(9.0	3.0)
Favorable attitude toward authority	(1.1	0.0)
Competitiveness	(2.3	1.3)

( ) Difference statistically significant.

SOURCE: Adapted from Sandra F. Beldt, "An Analysis of Values in Traditional Organizations and Nontraditional Organizations Structured Using Socio-Technical Systems Design." Ph.D. dissertation, Georgia State University, 1978, pp. 106, 108, 109, 115, 116, 117.

Demonstrations and Applications

Interpreting the results of research conducted to test sociotechnical theory is not easy, even when the researcher makes a serious effort to utilize adequate scientific controls. In the projects considered in this section, however, interpretation is practically impossible. The projects are important because they demonstrate the nature of and sometimes the pitfalls associated with sociotechnical systems design, and not because they contribute to evaluation of the underlying theory. In this respect the term *experiment* as applied to these projects is often inappropriate and misleading.

Principles of Sociotechnical Systems Design

Among individuals presenting guidelines or principles for undertaking sociotechnical interventions are some of the original theorists, for example, Emery and Trist (1978), Trist (1975b), and Herbst (1976). Cummings and Srivastva (1977) describe a systematic procedure for implementing sociotechnical systems, and Walton (1975) analyzes why even apparently successful projects often do not diffuse beyond the original experimental site. The principles presented by Cherns are indicative of what has been done in this regard:

1. *Comparability.* The means to design must be consistent with the end to be achieved. If people in the organization are to share in decision making, they must share in the design.
2. *Minimal Critical Specification.* At each stage of the design what is critical should be identified and only that should be specified. . . . Precision about what has to be done may be necessary, but rarely precision about how it is to be done. . . . if you specify more than you need, you foreclose options that should be kept open.
3. *Variance Control.* If variances cannot be eliminated, they should be dealt with as near to their point of origin as possible. A variance is an unprogrammed event. . . . Applying the principle of variance control would lead us to incorporate inspection with production, allowing people whenever possible to inspect their own work.
4. *Multifunction.* Design the organization so that it can achieve its objectives in more than one way. Allow each unit a repertoire of performance . . . redundancy of functions.
5. *Boundary Location.* Roles that require shared access to knowledge or experience should be within the same departmental boundaries.
6. *Information Flow.* Information systems should be designed to provide information to the organizational unit

that will take action on the basis of the information. . . . sophisticated information systems can supply a work team with exactly the right kind and amount of feedback, thus enabling the team to learn to control the variances that occur in its spheres of responsibility.

7. *Support Congruence.* The system of social support should be designed to reinforce the behaviors that the organization structure is designed to elicit. If an organization is designed on the basis of group or team operations with team responsibility, a payment system based on individual performance would be incongruent.

8. *Design and Human Values.* A prime objective of organizational design should be to provide a high quality of working life to its members.

9. *Transitional Organization.* There is a changeover period from old to new that requires a transitional organization. . . . what is required is a careful rehearsal of the roles that have to be performed during the changeover, especially the continuing training role of the supervisor.

10. *Completion.* Design is an iterative process. The closure of options opens new ones. . . . the multifunctional, multilevel, multidisciplinary team required for the original design is also needed for its evaluation and review (1977, pp. 55–63).

A wide range of applications based on such principles have been reported in the literature, including a number in compilations on the subject (Davis and Cherns, 1975; International Labour Office, 1979a, 1979b; Pasmore and Sherwood, 1978). The examples that follow are among the most widely discussed.

The Norwegian Industrial Democracy Program

The Norwegian projects are unusual in that they represent a concerted effort on the part of industry, unions, and eventually government to change a whole society. The first four projects considered here were undertaken in the early 1960s with active assistance from the Tavistock group (Emery and Thorsrud, 1976). Subsequent diffusion has been slow within Norway, and the massive social change originally envisaged has not occurred (Thorsrud, Sorensen, and Gustavsen, 1976). Yet there have been other applications, some of the most interesting being in the shipping industry (Herbst, 1974).

Christiana Spigerverk. The first project, undertaken in the wire drawing department of a steel mill, met with considerable resistance at the shop floor level initially and had continuing problems with union manning requirements throughout. Except for two weeks in the middle of the project when conditions were optimal, little success was in evidence. A major problem was that multiskilling and the introduction of a group bonus system brought earnings of the autonomous groups to a level that disrupted the overall factory pay structure. As a result, strong pressures against "rate busting" were exerted on the groups, pressures to which they responded. In this first effort the groups seemed unable to cope with strong environmental forces.

Hunsfos Pulp and Paper. Autonomous groups were introduced among about thirty operators in the chemical pulp department and considerably later in a paper machines department. Overall, the project appears to have been a qualified success. Major improvements occurred in the initial period, but there was a subsequent loss of momentum. "Considerable resistance occurred among foremen and production management and among some operators who previously held protected, high status jobs" (Thorsrud, Sorensen, and Gustavsen, 1976, p. 434). However, a degree of management acceptance did develop, and efforts to expand the project into other areas were undertaken. It is not entirely clear from the published reports what the long-term consequences for the Hunsfos firm were.

NOBO Factories. Initial changes were introduced in a small NOBO plant in a rural location, and within that plant in a new department producing electric panel heaters. The project was apparently a major success:

> The company management were well experienced in making these sorts of measures of worker productivity and well aware of the sorts of allowances that have to be made, often intuitively, for the effects of equipment change. They believed the observed changes were real and were significant. Their calculations also led them to believe that quality standards had improved and maintenance costs dropped (Emery and Thorsrud, 1976, p. 96).

When the production process was transferred to a new location and expanded, the autonomous group procedures went with it and have continued in use. Diffusion to the main company did not occur, however.

Norsk Hydro. The Norsk Hydro project initially involved the introduction of sociotechnical approaches throughout a new fertilizer plant. The plant was manned at a level sharply below comparable plants without autonomous work groups, at sizable cost savings. These savings existed even though compensation levels rose with multiskilling and bonus payments. Yet, in spite of the generally favorable evaluation of the fertilizer plant results, diffusions to other existing plants did not progress on schedule. Management resistance to revised roles has been considerable. In one instance a plant that had initiated autonomous groups was shut down because of market factors. There have been union sources of resistance as well. All in all, the results, though favorable, did not achieve the breadth of application originally envisaged.

Swedish Extensions

Diffusion in Norway, though it has continued, has been slow; in Sweden, on the other hand, diffusion has been rapid (Peterson, 1976). Apparently the idea of industrial democracy on the shop floor is particularly consonant with Swedish culture. Furthermore, it is in Sweden that some of the most dramatic shifts away from assembly line technology have occurred.

Saab-Scania. The initial pilot project at Saab-Scania was undertaken in 1969 in units of a truck plant. The results of this effort were then utilized in 1972 to start up an engine manufacturing plant organized on a sociotechnical basis. In this latter instance there was no assembly line in the conventional sense; the plant was designed to permit parallel groups to assemble complete engines at their own pace. The results of the pilot project were generally favorable. It is difficult to evaluate the total plant project and difficult as well to turn back from the sociotechnical commitment embodied in the design of the plant itself.

> By the conventional criteria of management, the system is a success. Quantity of production is within the expectation (worker minutes per engine) of conventional assembly methods. Absence and turnover, which were special problems in the assembly operation, are now no higher than in other worker categories. . . . Changes of this kind require investment, in many senses of that word. The system of parallel workshops requires more space than the conventional assembly line. The method of conveying engines and materials was more costly to install. To these costs must be added the time of the committees that labored to invent and create the system (Katz and Kahn, 1978, pp. 726, 728).

The Volvo Plant at Kalmar. The Volvo project is very similar to Saab-Scania, except that its scale is larger. Again, a new factory is involved, but in this case a total automobile is the product. The assembly process is broken down into a series of group operations, with inspections built into each group (Gyllenhammar, 1977). The Kalmar plant appears to have been somewhat more expensive to build than conventional plants and about as efficient. However, a major objective was to deal with the company's labor supply problems and that has been accomplished. Also fewer supervisors are needed, and the technology permits greater flexibility in introducing new models (International Labour Office, 1979a). The company clearly is satisfied with the results, and the sociotechnical approach has diffused to other operations.

General Foods at Topeka

The Topeka project was carried out in a new plant of small size. It was generally considered to be a success from the beginning (Walton, 1972). As in many such projects, staffing could be maintained at a low level due to multiskilling. Costs were consistently low, though the extent to which this was a function of the new equipment is unknown.

Subsequent events at the Topeka plant have not followed as positive a course (Walton, 1977). Commitment to the sociotechnical approach within the work force has been cyclical, but some erosion is in evidence overall. Problems with the payment system have continued, particularly problems with the group-based allocations of rewards. Plantwide issues have not been dealt with as effectively as they could be. Though opposition from within has grown, the autonomous groups have remained solidly in place. Furthermore, production costs continue to be low, absenteeism and turnover rates acceptable, and overall job satisfaction high.

Some of these effects might be accounted for by the high visibility of the project in the national press. On the other hand, the climate within General Foods has been distinctly mixed. "Few dispute the success of the plant, but there has been a considerable amount of speculation about the reasons for [success]. . . . It remains to be seen whether this particular approach is transferable to other parts of the organization and other organizations" (Goodman and Lawler, 1979, p. 159).

Though the Topeka project has been perhaps the most widely publicized, many other such efforts have been undertaken in the United States and elsewhere. While the sociotechnical approach antedates the concept of organization development, the two have tended to merge in recent years so that autonomous work groups are now often introduced as organization development interventions, just as survey feedback is. Apparently organization development is not a single phenomenon; it can take a great many forms.

Conclusions

Much of what was said in the concluding section of Chapter 2 about system 4 theory is equally applicable to sociotechnical systems theory. Both originated at the work group level and work best at that level. In larger organizational and environmental contexts they become much less effective. Furthermore, the research related to both theories has been conducted almost entirely at lower levels, primarily with production groups.

Scientific Goals

The theory, as it deals with causal textures of environments, has been the subject of considerable criticism. Metcalfe (1974) considers it excessively vague and lacking in rigor. In part for this reason, no research has focused directly on the environmental aspects of the theory. Rhenman takes issue with several of the theory's basic propositions in the environmental area:

1. All environments contain some random elements, some clustering, some risk of reaction, and a certain amount of structural change.
2. The four classes of environment suggested by Emery and Trist leave no room for distinguishing between different types of value environments.
3. Structural change in the environment need not always be a disadvantage. For organizations that can dominate their environment in particular, such changes can be of positive value. In this context I question Emery and Trist's claim that some sort of matrix organization is needed to deal with the turbulent environment (Rhenman, 1973, p. 190).

There is in fact little evidence that bureaucratic organizations are inherently incapable of coping with turbulent environments and that sociotechnical organizations are particularly adept in this regard. Stinchcombe (1974) argues that, through appropriate adjustment of line-staff relationships, bureaucracies can function as a major source of innovation, and he presents evidence to support this view. The position that bureaucracies are inevitably too rigid and bound by tradition to cope with rapid change through innovation is not supported by the evidence. The complex relationships involved will be treated in detail in Chapter 5. Furthermore, there is no logical reason why the processes and procedures generated by autonomous groups cannot become equally entrenched over time, and it remains to be demonstrated that autonomous groups are necessarily inherently creative. In fact there is reason to believe from the research on decision making that, as normally constituted, they may act to limit creativity (Steiner and Miner, 1982). In line with this view is the finding that autonomous work groups often are vulnerable to turbulent forces and changing conditions in their environments, not only in the start-up phase, but also after they are established. Evidence to this effect comes from Cummings and Srivastva (1977), Miller (1975), and Walton (1977).

The role of management in a sociotechnical system presents certain problems. There appears to be no place in the theory for the manager who coordinates internal variances in the organization. Theoretically this should be done closer to the variances themselves, by the workers. Seemingly this argues for a positively sloped control curve and flies directly in the face of much evidence generated by control theory, as discussed in Chapter 2. The theory's hypotheses about management have never been tested adequately. Rice (1963) devotes considerable attention to changes at this level but does not make them a subject of research investigation.

The introduction of autonomous groups tends to generate considerable managerial stress, presumably as a result of the role ambiguity that results (Walton and Schlesinger, 1979). In one apparently most successful application, plant managers were found to be those who usually perform very well in bureaucratic settings (Beldt, 1978). Though government is considered to be the intervention agent of choice, top management has in fact filled that role much more frequently and apparently with greater success. These and other considerations related to the role of management are not handled in a logically consistent manner by sociotechnical systems theory, if they are handled at all.

The original emphasis on organizational designs that are contingent on an optimal social-technical fit seems inconsistent with the subsequent advocacy of autonomous work groups as the one best (and bureaucracy as the one worst) design. As Herbst (1976) suggests, there must be situations where bureaucracy is appropriate, given the technological context. Working up from a kind of technological determinism does not necessarily produce the same result as working down from a corresponding kind of environmental determinism. The inconsistencies that may result are, at least in part, a function of the theory's network form of authorship, but they are real, nevertheless.

The foregoing discussion yields a rather dismal picture for sociotechnical systems theory. However, when one moves to the workgroup level where the theory began, the picture brightens. This is the level at which the research has been done, and the results often are positive. It is hard to predict whether the outcome will be greater output, better quality, less absenteeism, reduced turnover, fewer accidents, greater job satisfaction, or what, but the introduction of autonomous work groups is often associated with improvements (Cummings and Molloy, 1977).

It is difficult to understand why a particular outcome such as increased productivity occurs in one study and not another, and why on some occasions nothing improves. Sociotechnical systems theory is of little help in explaining these variations. Furthermore, what actually causes the changes when they do occur is not known. It is tempting to assert that change is caused by industrial democracy per se, but the sociotechnical approach calls for making so many changes at once that it is almost impossible to judge the value of the individual variables, including those of industrial democracy. Increased pay, self-selection of work situation, multiskilling with its resultant job enrichment, and decreased contact with authority almost invariably occur in autonomous work group studies. The compounding of experimental variables makes interpretation very hazardous (Locke and Schweiger, 1979). ⌐

Even among work groups, sociotechnical theory has faced its share of criticism, primarily on grounds of incompleteness. Thus, Hackman contends:

1. The theory does not specify the attributes of group tasks that are required for creation of effective autonomous work groups. . . . because key task attributes are not specified, it is not possible to devise measures of those attributes for use in theory guided diagnoses of work systems prior to change, in evaluations of the effects of changes on the work, or in tests of the conceptual adequacy of the theory itself.

2. Individual differences among people are not explicitly dealt with in the sociotechnical approach. . . . the theory does not deal with the fact that social needs vary in strength among people. Such differences may affect whether individuals seek to participate in an autonomous group.

3. The theory does not address the internal dynamics that occur among members of work groups. . . . The assumption apparently is that members of autonomous work groups will develop on their own satisfactory ways of working together. . . . Given the substantial evidence about ways that groups can go "sour," the validity of that assumption must be considered questionable (1978, p. 64). ⌐

Certainly sociotechnical theory has suffered as a consequence of inattention to measurement. Except for an instrument developed very recently by Oliver (1981), little has been done to follow up on Gulowsen's (1972) initial work, and there are no reports of any subsequent use of his measure. Accordingly, it is often impossible to determine whether an appropriate test of the theory has actually been carried out.

Hackman's second point about individual differences is equally well taken. Apparently, autonomous work groups are not for all, just as bureaucratic authority systems seem not to be for all. Many may view the forced social interaction with distaste and rebel against the tyranny of group decision. Theoretical extension and research into individual differences seem curiously lacking, given the clinical background of the original Tavistock unit.

Hackman's final point, though largely correct, cannot be considered a valid criticism of the theory. It is hypothesized that, to the extent they are left alone, groups will develop effective solutions; they may need some training and structuring initially, but not in the continuing work situation. That such groups may go sour is not necessarily attributable to failures of internal group dynamics. The theory would attribute such phenomena largely to external forces that limit autonomy, to inappropriate sociotechnical fit, and the like. Such hypotheses should certainly be viewed as theoretically justified. Whether they are valid is a matter for research.

Goals of Application

The basic question of application is whether autonomous groups should be introduced. That the theory itself has run into difficulties is of little managerial significance. The theory has spawned an approach that may well be justified in its own right. If anything, the techniques of sociotechnical application appear to have outdistanced the theory, much as psychoanalytic therapy has moved beyond psychoanalytic theory in another domain.

It seems safe to assume that there are circumstances under which sociotechnical concepts are more likely to work than others. According to Walton (1974), these are:

1. A small-town environment.
2. A relatively small work force (less than 100).
3. A new factory; a start-up situation.
4. Geographic separation from the rest of the company.
5. The use of outside consultants.
6. Long lead times to allow for planning and training.
7. The absence of a union or a favorable climate in this regard.

There is reason also to believe that past experience with autonomous work groups, as in the early coalfield research, or a favorable cultural climate, as in Sweden, can be helpful. Presumably both factors make available larger numbers of individuals who possess the personal characteristics such as social motivation needed in successful autonomous work groups.

Sociotechnical innovations can produce resistance, not only among management, but also within part of the work force itself.

This is why the start-up situation with self-selection of those involved is particularly attractive. Yet sociotechnical innovations can work, and there are very few instances of truly negative consequences. Given this situation, the approach is to be recommended where there is a reasonable chance of success and where the company faces a basic problem that sociotechnical concepts can reasonably be calculated to solve, as in the instance of Volvo's labor force difficulties. This is not to say that autonomous work groups are an all-purpose solution. At present at least, autonomous work groups are best advised as a solution to special problems, except in such countries as Sweden where there is extensive cultural support (Walton, 1975). In other contexts there is a real risk that too widespread application will exhaust the resources needed for success and undermine the whole endeavor. Success has occurred consistently where the scale is small and the context is isolated enough to permit social pressures to operate uncontested, or where social pressures are supported by external forces, as in Sweden.

Management should consider two additional factors. Sociotechnical systems in the United States often have operated as nonunion enclaves in unionized companies. Even prolabor advocates admit the resilience of autonomous work groups in the face of organizing attempts (Cherns, 1975). Whether this is good or bad depends on one's point of view, but introducing autonomous work groups does seem to eliminate or at least temporarily reduce pressures from a union. Whether the approach is worth the investment depends on the relative costs involved.

Second, the sociotechnical approach appears to reduce manpower needs. Because of multiskilling, more flexible work organization, and the assumption of managerial tasks by the work group, fewer people are needed. Thus, even though each person is typically paid more, total costs tend to be reduced. This is a major managerial advantage, but for unions it means fewer potential dues-paying members and for the society as a whole it may mean increased unemployment. Under conditions of substantial business growth, neither of these considerations should represent a problem. But without growth, adoption of sociotechnical approaches on a major scale could raise a whole new set of problems, no matter how streamlined and efficient the resulting organization might be.

We end with a generally favorable vote for the sociotechnical approach, given the right circumstances and the right people, though it is not necessarily a favorable vote for sociotechnical theory and the reasons it espouses for introducing autonomous work groups. Even more, the apparent success of applications of the sociotechnical approach calls for expanded research. The number of unanswered questions is staggering.

References

Agervold, Mogens. "Swedish Experiments in Industrial Democracy." In Louis E. Davis and Albert B. Cherns (eds.), *Cases and Commentary*, vol. 2, The Quality of Working Life. New York: Free Press, 1975, pp. 46–65.

Beldt, Sandra F. "An Analysis of Values in Traditional Organizations and Nontraditional Organizations Structured Using Socio-Technical Systems Design." Ph.D. dissertation, Georgia State University, 1978.

Bramlette, Carl A., Donald O. Jewell, and Michael H. Mescon. "Designing for Organizational Effectiveness: A Better Way; How It Works," *Atlanta Economic Review*, 27, (1977), no. 5, 35–41; no. 6, 10–15.

Cherns, Albert R. "Perspectives on the Quality of Working Life," *Journal of Occupational Psychology*, 48 (1975), 155–67.

––––––. "Can Behavioral Science Help Design Organizations?" *Organizational Dynamics*, 5, no. 4 (1977), 44–64.

Cummings, Thomas G., and Edmond S. Molloy. *Strategies for Improving Productivity and the Quality of Work Life*. New York: Praeger, 1977.

Cummings, Thomas G., and Suresh Srivastva. *Management of Work: A Socio-Technical Systems Approach*. Kent, Ohio: Kent State University Press, 1977.

Davis, Louis E. "Evolving Alternative Organizational Designs: Their Sociotechnical Bases," *Human Relations*, 30 (1977), 261–73.

Davis, Louis E., and Albert B. Cherns. *Cases and Commentary*, vol. 2, The Quality of Working Life. New York: Free Press, 1975.

Dicks, Henry V. *Fifty Years of the Tavistock Clinic*. London: Routledge & Kegan Paul, 1970.

Emery, Fred E. "The Next Thirty Years: Concepts, Methods and Anticipations," *Human Relations*, 20 (1967), 199–237.

––––––. "Bureaucracy and Beyond," *Organizational Dynamics*, 2, no. 3 (1974), 3–13.

Emery, Fred E., and Einar Thorsrud. *Democracy at Work*. Leiden, the Netherlands: Martinus Nijhoff, 1976.

Emery, Fred E., and Eric L. Trist. "The Causal Texture of Organizational Environments," *Human Relations*, 18 (1965), 21–32.

––––––. *Toward a Social Ecology*. London: Plenum, 1973.

––––––. "Analytical Model for Sociotechnical Systems." In William A. Pasmore and John J. Sherwood (eds.), *Sociotechnical Systems: A Sourcebook*. La Jolla, Calif.: University Associates, 1978, pp. 120–31.

Goodman, Paul S. *Assessing Organizational Change: The Rushton Quality of Work Experiment*. New York: Wiley, 1979.

Goodman, Paul S., and Edward E. Lawler. "United States." In *New Forms of Work Organisation 1*. Geneva, Switzerland: International Labour Office, 1979, pp. 141–73.

Gulowsen, Jon. "A Measure of Work Group Autonomy." In Louis E. Davis and James C. Taylor (eds.), *Design of Jobs*. Baltimore, Md.: Penguin, 1972, pp. 374–90.

Gyllenhammar, Pehr G. "How Volvo Adapts Work to People," *Harvard Business Review*, 55, no. 4 (1977), 102–13.

Hackman, J. Richard. "The Design of Self-Managing Work Groups." In Bert King, Siegfried Streufert, and Fred E. Fiedler (eds.), *Managerial Control and Organizational Democracy*. New York: Wiley, 1978, pp. 61–91.

Herbst, P. G. *Sociotechnical Design: Strategies in Multidisciplinary Research*. London: Tavistock, 1974.

––––––. *Alternatives to Hierarchies*. Leiden, the Netherlands: Martinus Nijhoff, 1976.

International Labour Office. *New Forms of Work Organization 1*. Geneva, Switzerland: ILO, 1979a.

————. *New Forms of Work Organization 2.* Geneva, Switzerland: ILO, 1979b.

Katz, Daniel, and Robert L. Kahn. *The Social Psychology of Organizations.* New York: Wiley, 1978.

Kingdon, Donald R. *Matrix Organization: Managing Information Technologies.* London: Tavistock, 1973.

Locke, Edwin A., and David M. Schweiger. "Participation in Decision-Making: One More Look." In Barry M. Staw (ed.), *Research in Organizational Behavior.* Greenwich, Conn.: JAI Press, 1979, pp. 265–339.

Metcalfe, J. L. "Systems Models, Economic Models and the Causal Texture of Organizational Environments: An Approach to Macro-Organization Theory," *Human Relations,* 27 (1974), 639–63.

Mileti, Dennis S., and David F. Gillespie. "An Integrated Formulation of Organization-Environment Interdependencies," *Human Relations,* 29 (1976), 85–100.

Miller, Eric J. "Socio-Technical Systems in Weaving, 1953–1970: A Follow-up Study," *Human Relations,* 28 (1975), 349–86.

Miller, Eric J., and A. K. Rice. *Systems of Organization: The Control of Task and Sentient Boundaries.* London: Tavistock, 1967.

Mills, Ted. "Altering the Social Structure in Coal Mining: A Case Study," *Monthly Labor Review,* 99, no. 10 (1976), 3–10.

Miner, John B. *Theories of Organizational Behavior.* Hinsdale, Ill.: Dryden, 1980.

Oliver, John E. *Scoring Guide for the Oliver Organization Description Questionnaire.* Atlanta, Ga.: Organizational Measurement Systems Press, 1981.

Pasmore, William A. "The Comparative Impacts of Sociotechnical Systems, Job-Redesign, and Survey-Feedback Interventions." In William A. Pasmore and John J. Sherwood (eds.), *Sociotechnical Systems: A Sourcebook.* La Jolla, Calif.: University Associates, 1978, pp. 291–301.

Pasmore, William A., and John J. Sherwood, eds. *Sociotechnical Systems: A Sourcebook.* La Jolla, Calif.: University Associates, 1978.

Peterson, Richard B. "Swedish Experiments in Job Reform." *Business Horizons,* 19, no. 3 (1976), 13–22.

Rhenman, Eric. *Organization Theory for Long-Range Planning.* London: Wiley, 1973.

Rice, A. K. *Productivity and Social Organization: The Ahmedabad Experiment.* London: Tavistock, 1958.

————. *The Enterprise and Its Environment.* London: Tavistock, 1963.

Roy, S. K. "A Re-examination of the Methodology of A. K. Rice's Indian Textile Mill Work Reorganisation," *Indian Journal of Industrial Relations,* 5, no. 2 (1969), 170–91.

Steiner, George A., and John B. Miner. *Management Policy and Strategy.* New York: Macmillan, 1982.

Stinchcombe, Arthur L. *Creating Efficient Industrial Administrations.* New York: Academic Press, 1974.

Susman, Gerald I. *Autonomy at Work: A Sociotechnical Analysis of Participative Management.* New York: Praeger, 1976.

Terreberry, Shirley. "The Evolution of Organizational Environments," *Administrative Science Quarterly,* 12 (1968), 590–613.

Thorsrud, Einar, Bjorg A. Sorensen, and Bjorn Gustavsen. "Sociotechnical Approach to Industrial Democracy in Norway." In Robert Dubin (ed.), *Handbook of Work, Organization, and Society.* Chicago: Rand McNally, 1976, pp. 421–64.

Trist, Eric L. "On Socio-Technical Systems." In Warren G. Bennis, Kenneth D. Benne, and Robert Chin (eds.), *The Planning of Change.* New York: Holt, Rinehart & Winston, 1969, pp. 269–82.

————. "A Socio-Technical Critique of Scientific Management." In D. O. Edge and J. W. Wolfe (eds.), *Meaning and Control.* London: Tavistock, 1973, pp. 95–119.

――――. "The New Work Ethic in Europe and America." In Carl A. Bramlette and Michael H. Mescon (eds.), *Man and the Future of Organizations*, vol. 4. Atlanta, Ga.: Department of Management, Georgia State University, 1975a, pp. 45–64.

――――. "Planning the First Steps toward Quality of Working Life in a Developing Country." In Louis E. Davis and Albert B. Cherns (eds.). *Problems, Prospects and the State of the Art*, vol. 1, The Quality of Working Life. New York: Free Press, 1975b, pp. 78–85.

――――. *A Concept of Organizational Ecology*. Philadelphia: Management and Behavioral Science Center, University of Pennsylvania, 1976a.

――――. "Action Research and Adaptive Planning." In A. W. Clark (ed.), *Experimenting with Organizational Life*. London: Plenum, 1976b, pp. 223–36.

――――. "Collaboration in Work Settings: A Personal Perspective," *Journal of Applied Behavioral Science*, 13 (1977), 268–78.

Trist, Eric L., and K. W. Bamforth. "Some Social and Psychological Consequences of the Longwall Method of Coal-Getting," *Human Relations*, 4 (1951), 3–38.

Trist, Eric L., G. W. Higgin, H. Murray, and A. B. Pollock. *Organizational Choice: Capabilities of Groups at the Coal Face Under Changing Technologies*. London: Tavistock, 1963.

Trist, Eric L., Gerald I. Susman, and Grant R. Brown. "An Experiment in Autonomous Working in an American Underground Coal Mine," *Human Relations*, 30 (1977), 201–36.

Walton, Richard E. "How to Counter Alienation in the Plant," *Harvard Business Review*, 50, no. 6 (1972), 70–81.

――――. "Innovative Restructuring of Work." In Jerome M. Rosow (ed.), *The Worker and the Job: Coping with Change*. Englewood Cliffs, N.J.: Prentice-Hall, 1974, pp. 146–76.

――――. "The Diffusion of New Work Structures: Explaining Why Success Didn't Take," *Organizational Dynamics*, 3, no. 3 (1975), 2–22.

――――. "Work Innovations at Topeka: After Six Years," *Journal of Applied Behavioral Science*, 13 (1977), 422–33.

Walton, Richard E., and Leonard A. Schlesinger. "Do Supervisors Thrive in Participative Work Systems?" *Organizational Dynamics*, 7, no. 3 (1979), 25–38.

5

Goal Congruence Theory and the Route to Organization Development

Chapters 2 and 4 considered certain applications typically classified under the broad umbrella of organization development. In this chapter two additional theories that have grown out of organization development approaches are considered. In both instances the theorists' ideas led them, first, to embrace laboratory training as a method of interpersonal skill development, and subsequently to expand into the broader arena of organization development.

Goal congruence theory is the creation of Chris Argyris who developed his views initially while serving on the faculty at Yale University. He is now at Harvard. During the 1950s, when his ideas were crystallizing, Argyris was strongly influenced by the thinking of E. Wight Bakke (1950, 1959) with whom he worked at the Yale Labor and Management Center.

The second theorist considered in this chapter is Warren Bennis who was at Massachusetts Institute of Technology for many years before moving into university administration, first at the State University of New York at Buffalo and later at the University of Cincinnati. He resigned as president of the latter school in 1977 to write and is currently at the University of Southern California. A major influence on Bennis at MIT, not only in his theory development but also in his conceptions regarding laboratory training and organization development, was Douglas McGregor. In fact Bennis helped edit two posthumous volumes of McGregor's (1966, 1967) writings after McGregor's death in 1964.

Argyris's Goal Congruence Theory

Though Argyris has written extensively, three major statements appear to represent milestones in his thinking. The first is *Personality and Organization* (Argyris, 1957), the second, *Integrating the Individual and the Organization* (Argyris, 1964), and the third, an article in *Administrative Science Quarterly* entitled "Personality and Organization Theory Revisited" (Argyris, 1973). These three publications provide the framework around which the hypotheses of goal congruence theory may be developed.

Personality and Organization

Argyris's investigation into the effects of budgets on managers reveals the issues with which he was concerned in his early theorizing and the direction of his thinking. Argyris reached the following conclusions after extensive, unstructured interviews with financial and operating managers in four manufacturing plants:

1. Budget pressure tends to unite the employees against management, and tends to place the factory supervisor under tension. This tension may lead to inefficiency, aggression and perhaps a complete breakdown on the part of the supervisor.

2. The finance staff can obtain feelings of success only by finding fault with factory people. The feelings of failure among factory supervisors lead to many human relations problems.

3. The use of budgets as "needlers" by top management tends to make the factory supervisors see only the problems of their own department. . . . They are not "plant-centered" in outlook (Argyris, 1952, p. 25).

In building a theory to deal with such problems, Argyris first followed Bakke (1950) very closely (Argyris, 1954). Subsequently, however, though retaining many of his earlier concepts, he developed goal congruence theory as a distinct entity in its own right (Argyris, 1957).

The Mature, Healthy, Self-Actualizing Personality. A basic concept of Argyris's theory is that of the healthy adult personality, as distinguished from the personality of an infant or small child. Table 5–1 shows the dimensions of personality that are relevant; "the individual's plotted scores (or profile)" along these dimensions are equated with self-actualization. This is a much more specific formulation of the self-actualization construct than other theorists have offered (Miner, 1980). Individuals develop or progress to varying degrees along these dimensions. Various forces within society, including organizations, and within the individuals themselves inhibit this process.

Sources of Organizational Incongruence. The second theoretical building block in Argyris's goal congruence theory is the concept of organization as epitomized in classical management theory. The

Table 5–1
Developmental Trends to a Mature, Healthy, Self-Actualizing
Personality

From (as infants)	**To** (as adults)
1. A state of passivity	A state of increasing activity
2. A state of dependence on others	A state of relative independence
3. Being capable of behaving in only a few ways	Being capable of behaving in many ways
4. Having erratic, casual, shallow, quickly dropped interests	Having deeper interests
5. Having a short time perspective (primarily in the present)	Having a much larger time perspective (extending into the past and future)
6. A lack of awareness of self	An awareness and control over oneself

SOURCE: Adapted from Chris Argyris, *Personality and Organization.* New York: Harper & Row, 1957, p. 50.

principles of that theory are accepted as given because "to date no one has defined a more useful set of formal organization principles" (Argyris, 1957, p. 58). Included are the principles of task specialization, chain of command, unity of direction, and span of control.

Such a formal organization is viewed as incongruent with development to a healthy, mature state as set forth in Table 5–1; it operates to inhibit members, forcing them back toward an infantile state. The potential incongruency between the developmental needs of individuals and the requirements of formal organization is exaggerated to the extent that:

1. employees are more mature than the organization assumes.
2. the organization structure follows classical principles closely.
3. one moves downward in the organization.
4. the jobs approach an assembly line character.

As a result of the incongruency, healthy employees often become passive, dependent, and submissive over time. In the process they experience the kinds of problems Argyris noted in his analysis of the effects of budgets. Frustration, conflict, failure, and a short time perspective prevail. Among other reactions the employee may leave the organization (only to face the same problems elsewhere), attempt to move to high levels in the organization (though there are few such positions), adapt by resorting to emotional defense mechanisms such as escape from reality and psychosomatic illness, or become apathetic and uninvolved. The employee may also express aggression in the context of the informal work group by restricting output.

In reaction to the high turnover and absenteeism, low productivity, and lack of organizational identification thus produced, management often introduces more controls and becomes more directive. As a result, the undesired behavior is increased.

Basic Propositions. These processes are summarized in a set of ten theoretical propositions.

    1. There is a lack of congruency between the needs of healthy individuals and the demands of the formal organization. . . . An administrator, therefore, is always faced with an inherent tendency toward continual disturbance.

    2. The resultants of this disturbance are frustration, failure, short-time perspective, and conflict.

    3. Under certain conditions the degree of frustration, failure, short-time perspective and conflict will tend to increase (among these conditions are those previously noted— greater employee maturity, structure follows classical principles, etc.).

    4. The nature of the formal principles of organization cause the subordinate, at any given level, to experience competition, rivalry, inter-subordinate hostility, and to develop a focus toward the parts rather than the whole.

    5. The employee adaptive behavior maintains self-integration and impedes integration with the formal organization.

    6. The adaptive behavior of the employees has a cumulative effect, feedbacks into the organization, and reinforces itself.

    7. Certain management reactions tend to increase the antagonisms underlying the adaptive behavior. . . . These actions tend to be: (1) Increasing the degree of directive leadership. (2) Increasing the degree of management controls. (3) Increasing the number of pseudo human relations programs.

    8. Other management actions can decrease the degree of incongruency between the individual and formal organization. . . . One way is to use a new input of individuals who do not aspire to be healthy, mature adults. A second way is to change the nature of the formal organizational structure, directive leadership, and management controls. . . . job and/or role enlargement is one effective method to change the organization structure. . . . employee-centered leadership is one possible way to modify the directive leadership.

    9. Job or role enlargement and employee-centered leadership will not tend to work to the extent that the

adaptive behavior has become embedded in the original culture and the self-concept of the individuals.

10. The difficulties involved in proposition 9 may be minimized by the use of reality-oriented leadership (i.e., the leader ought to first diagnose what *is* reality and then use the appropriate leadership pattern) (Argyris, 1957, pp. 233–37).

Integrating the Individual and the Organization

Following the publication of his 1957 volume, Argyris expanded and modified his theory. Though this process appears to have been gradual, the outcome was a new, comprehensive, theoretical statement (Argyris, 1964).

Psychological Energy and Success. Argyris (1964) replaces his maturity or infant-adult dimension with certain formulations regarding psychological energy. Argyris maintains that psychological energy exists in all people, cannot be blocked permanently, and varies with the state of mind of the individual. Furthermore:

> The *potential energy* an individual has available to him will be a function of the degree of self-esteem: the higher the self-esteem the greater the *potential energy*. The *actual* energy an individual has will be a function of the degree to which he can experience psychological success. Psychological success (and its derivatives of self-esteem, etc.) is therefore defined as the conditions for creating the proper state of mind (p. 29).

Among other factors a climate of trust serves to enhance opportunities for psychological success.

In restating his first theoretical proposition on the sources of incongruency, Argyris now substitutes "individuals aspiring for psychological success" for the former "healthy individuals." He no longer uses the specific statements given in Table 5–1. Not everyone desires psychological success, and it is the incongruency between individual needs and organizational form that causes disturbance and unintended consequences (such as passivity, aggression, etc.). This incongruency may result as much from placing a person who does not aspire to psychological success in a context where aspirations of this type are required, as from placing a person who does desire psychological success in the typical pyramidal organization. In any event, wherever such incongruencies exist, people will consume energy producing unintended consequences of the organizational form and thus divert energy from organizational goals.

Dropping the maturity dimension set forth in Table 5–1 creates a problem in defining self-actualization, which is retained in the theory. The solution is to view self-actualization as having no specific content. People have a need to actualize themselves that can be identified from their behavior. "The actualization can be in the direction of maturity. . . . However, in this scheme, the actualization could be toward apathy and alienation" (Argyris, 1964, p. 142). This shift to a view of self-actualization as having no set content actually appeared several years earlier and was reflected in a procedure developed for scoring self-actualization as revealed in interviews (Argyris 1959, 1960a).

The Mix Model. Argyris (1964) proposes that problems associated with incongruency are best overcome by modifying pyramidal organizations to provide more meaningful challenges and opportunities for psychological success. At the same time, individuals must be changed to make them less fearful of the opportunity for psychological success. These and other changes must be made to reduce disturbances and unintended consequences. The mix model presents a set of six hypotheses about how organizations should be changed to achieve these ends and make them "axiologically good," to use Argyris's term.

1. The direction of core activities such as achieving objectives, internal maintenance, and environmental adaptations should be spread in an interrelated manner throughout the organization, rather than concentrated in a single component such as top management.

2. The members of the organization should be aware of the organization as a totality in all its patterned interrelationships, rather than as a random set of parts.

3. The objectives that guide the organization should be those of the whole, rather than of individual components.

4. The organization should be able to influence goal attainment and internal maintenance in accordance with its own desires, rather than lacking influence in these respects.

5. The organization should be able to influence its externally oriented activities in its environment in accordance with its own desires, rather than lacking influence in this respect.

6. The nature of the organization's core activities should be influenced by considerations extending into both the past and the future, rather than being determined only by the present.

These hypotheses for integrating organizational and individual goals appear to have much in common with the hypotheses regarding individual development toward health and maturity set forth in Table 5–1. This relationship is in fact made explicit in an earlier statement:

As long as complex organizations use people, it may be possible that they will tend to obtain greater commitment, flexibility, responsibility, and openness and thereby enhance their chances for survival and growth if they strive to create conditions wherein the individual is able to actualize his potential as much as possible. . . . a first step toward integrating the individual and the organization is for both to aspire toward the conditions represented by the axiologically good organization (Argyris, 1962a, p. 76).

The Mix Model and Organizational Structure. The mix model is a statement of conditions for organizational effectiveness. However, the theory anticipates that the degree to which the organization's structure should fully match these conditions depends on the kinds of decisions to be made. Argyris's statements on organizational structures are given in Table 5–2. He indicates a clear need for varying structures in accordance with decision types:

If one asks the individual in the organization of the future to see the company organizational chart, he will be asked, "For what type of decision?" In order to accomplish this, "decision rules" will have to be defined to guide our choice of the proper structure.

But the power to choose among structures remains democratic:

. . . the task of defining the decision rules to tell the participants which organization structure should be used under a given set of conditions will be assigned to as many participants as possible. . . . If autocracy is to be used, the use of it will be defined under participative conditions (Structure IV) (Argyris, 1964, pp. 211–12).

Table 5–2 represents Argyris's initial effort to provide guidelines for the participative selection of structures.

The Theory Revisited

In its earliest version goal congruence theory carried a message that was distinctly anti-formal organization. Subsequently, this message was muted somewhat, though it remained in evidence. In the third version (Argyris, 1973, 1974a) there is some return to a more militant organizational position.

Actually, by 1972 Argyris had revived the infant-adult dimensions of Table 5–1. While infant individuals in adult organizations and adult individuals in infant organizations both yield incongruence, the latter circumstances represent "the predominant conditions in 'real' life." Congruence between person and organization was presumed to be rare (Argyris, 1972).

Table 5–2

Conditions for the Use of Structures Having Varying Degrees of
Axiological Goodness

Degree of Axiological Goodness	Type of Organizational Structure	Condition for Use
Low	I. Pyramidal	1. When time is important and subordinate acceptance is assured 2. When decisions are routine and the use of authority is legitimized 3. When the decision does not affect the distribution of power, reward, controls, work specialization, or the centralization of information 4. When a large number of people are involved and it is difficult to bring them together 5. When the individuals do not desire psychological success
	II. Overlapping groups (Likert)	1. When the decision is not routine, but does not affect the distribution of power, control, information, and the specialization of work 2. When time is important 3. When the decision to make a change cannot be delegated to all
	III. Power according to functional contribution	Anywhere there are differences in competence. Individuals receive their power according to the perception that other members have of their potential contribution.
	IV. Power according to inevitable organizational responsibilities (each individual has equal power)	1. When decisions involve high responsibility and are basic to the organization 2. When the decision affects the distribution of power, control, information, and the specialization of work 3. When the decision defines rules for the conditions under which a particular structure would be used
High		

Source: Adapted from Chris Argyris, *Integrating the Individual and the Organization.* New York: Wiley, 1964, pp. 198–210.

In this later, more formal restatement of the theory, the seven infant-adult dimensions of Table 5–1 are reduced to four. These new dimensions are not entirely consistent with those stated previously, especially with regard to the development of abilities. Thus:

Infants begin as—
    dependent and submissive
    having few abilities
    having shallow abilities
    having a short time perspective

While adults strive toward—
    independence, autonomy, and control over the immediate world
    developing many abilities
    developing a few abilities in depth
    developing a longer time perspective
    (Argyris, 1973, p. 142)

Pyramidal organizations now are characterized by specialized and fractionalized work, established production rates and speed of work, order giving, performance evaluation, the use of rewards, and perpetuated membership. These are associated with bureaucracy and scientific management, rather than with classical management theory, as previously stated. The consequences of incongruence for organization members are fighting the organization, leaving it, apathy and indifference, or becoming market- (or pay-) oriented in dealing with the organization. References to upward mobility as a response have been consistently ignored after the first theoretical statements. In tone the revisited theory is not a great deal different from the original version. However, there are specific variations that require somewhat different empirical tests. In particular the future of formal organizations is viewed more negatively:

> . . . none of the theories discussed (primarily those of bureaucracy and rational systems), with the exception of personality and organization theory and those similar . . . would predict the single most important trend about public and private organizations, namely, their increasing internal deterioration and lack of effectiveness in producing services or products (Argyris, 1973, p. 159).

Research on Goal Congruence Theory

Rather surprisingly, there has been little research undertaken as a direct test of Argyris's theoretical hypotheses. Argyris has marshaled a considerable amount of research, the results of which could be predicted or explained by goal congruence theory (Argyris, 1957,

1964, 1972, 1973). At first reading, these findings appear convincing; the studies cited consistently support the theory. Yet the use of ad hoc explanation, selective coverage of relevant research, and the fact that alternative theories might also predict and explain the same results raise a note of caution. In reality only research that is directly focused on theoretical hypotheses can establish the validity of the theory.

Argyris's Interview-Based Studies

In the 1950s and early 1960s Argyris conducted several studies to test his views. Since that time, however, he has become decidedly pessimistic regarding traditional scientific research and has focused primarily on various types of organizational change programs.

The Attack on Research. Essentially, Argyris (1968) believes that scientific research has an authoritarian bias analogous to the effects of pyramidal organizations. Subjects react to experimental controls as they would to organizational controls, and the findings are distorted accordingly. His solution for this situation also derives from his theory—"to reduce the researcher's control over the subject . . . to provide the subject with greater influence, with longer time perspective regarding, and greater internal involvement in, the research project . . . having worker representative groups (in organizations) and student representative groups (in universities) to help in the design and execution of research" (Argyris, 1968, p. 193).

These ideas are intriguing. Yet certain assumptions are inherent in Argyris's position. First, he assumes the validity of goal congruence theory. If employees do not react to organizational controls as hypothesized, then the extension to experimental controls is not likely to be valid either, following Argyris's own logic. Second, he assumes that certain apparent similarities between the two situations make the theoretical extension from organization to research warranted. Both of these assumptions require evidence. On the latter there is almost no evidence. We do not know whether goal congruence theory works within the domain of scientific research because no one, including Argyris, has tested it there, with or without subject participation in the research design. It remains, however, to determine whether the theory is valid in its organizational context.

The Bank Study. In an early study, members of various departments of a bank were interviewed to determine the degree of fusion or goal congruence they experienced in their jobs and to relate this index to other factors in accordance with the theory (Argyris, 1954). Though this study precedes Argyris's (1957) first formal statement of goal congruence theory, it tests certain hypotheses that are part of that theory.

Measures of the degree to which individual members actualize themselves in the organization and of the degree to which the organization appeared to express itself were obtained. When both indexes were high, as they were in three departments, the departments appeared to be effective; when the indexes were lower, as they were in one instance, the department exhibited more conflict and less organizational commitment. There was some evidence that low personal actualization scores were predictive of voluntary turnover. The reliability of the coding of interview data to obtain this personal actualization score was satisfactory, but the organizational measure yielded marginal reliability at best.

The Plant Studies. In subsequent research Argyris concerned himself less with the congruence of goals than with personal actualization. The emphases in the reports on these studies, which were carried out in two plants of a manufacturing firm, are somewhat different from one publication to another (Argyris, 1958, 1959, 1960a, 1960b).

In this instance the coding reliability of the self-actualization index was rather low (roughly 70 percent agreement). Nevertheless, this score did operate as hypothesized, with high scores characterizing the more effective plant. In addition the self-actualization data support a number of theory-based predictions regarding differences between the two plants and between components within them.

In the less effective plant, employees report more widespread pressure, and though the foremen do not exhibit the same pattern, those who experience pressure, experience it more intensely. The foremen also place greater emphasis on promotion and pay, in accordance with the theory, but neither plant has much turnover at the foreman level. Among employees there is less concern with quality, less friendliness, and more prounion sentiment in the less effective plant. These are, of course, concurrent findings; they do not establish cause and effect.

Research by Others

In his reviews of research Argyris (1964, 1973) notes several studies that directly support the goal congruence hypotheses, though not with total consistency. In particular, positive consequences are likely to accrue from fusion or goal congruence. Unfortunately most of these studies have not been published in the regular professional literature and cannot be evaluated adequately on the basis of Argyris's descriptions. Those studies noted by Argyris that have been published are considered next.

Some Specific Studies. Bonjean and Vance (1968) developed a questionnaire measure of self-actualization that correlated .61 and .72 with Argyris's index in two separate samples. Those individuals who were found to experience low self-actualization reported getting angry with supervisors more, making more errors in their work, thinking more about earning money, feeling less satisfied with their jobs, and thinking more about seeking other work. All these findings are consistent with goal congruence theory predictions. Yet high and low self-actualization subjects did not differ with regard to restriction of output, aggression toward co-workers, and lack of interest in work.

Pennings (1976) related measures of organizational autonomy and participation to various criterion indexes in forty offices of a brokerage firm to test certain hypotheses set forth by Argyris. As noted in Table 5–3, the results generally support the theory. The only major departure is that "good" organizational structures were not associated with reduced anxiety levels; in fact additional analyses indicate a significantly higher level of anxiety under participative conditions, a finding inconsistent with an expectation of greater mental health.

A somewhat similar study by Dewar and Werbel (1979) was conducted in thirteen consumer reporting agencies. As goal congruence theory would predict, high levels of formalization and routinization of the technology were associated with reduced job satisfaction, and neither formalization nor routinization showed any relationship to the amount of conflict. On the other hand, extensive surveillance and rule enforcement were related to conflict. The implication is that conflict arises not so much out of specific organizational struc-

Table 5–3

Correlations Between Organizational and Personal Factors Across Forty Brokerage Firm Offices

	Organizational Factors	
Personal Factors	Autonomy of the Office	Participation in the Office
Total production	(.45)	.23
Production change over three years	.19	(.50)
Loss due to errors	−.28	−.11
Morale	(.45)	(.38)
Anxiety level	.16	.09

( ) Correlation statistically significant.

SOURCE: Adapted from Johannes M. Pennings, "Dimensions of Organizational Influence and Their Effectiveness Correlates," *Administrative Science Quarterly*, 21 (1976), p. 695.

tures as from directive leadership. However, it may well be that the presence of conflict elicited the directive leadership rather than the leadership eliciting the conflict.

Goal congruence theory hypothesizes that the tendency to oppose bureaucratic procedures increases at each lower organizational level. However, Rossel (1971) found that such negative orientations are most pronounced just below top management; they are much less in evidence at the top, but also at levels down into first-level supervision. These findings appear to be related to opportunities for promotion, a topic that Argyris considered in his early theories, but subsequently dropped.

Finally, a study by Burke and Weir (1978) indicates that the "good" organization in Argyris's sense creates a climate where members not only help each other more, but are more likely to solicit help from each other. However, this mutual helping operates more with regard to personal than to work-related problems, which suggests that direct impact on work outcomes such as the quantity and quality of production may be minimal.

Evidence from Reviews of Related Literature. In reviewing tangentially related literatures, Argyris consistently comes to positive conclusions. In many instances he reinterprets studies that were carried out without reference to his theories. It seems appropriate here to look at the conclusions reached by others who have reviewed the same literature.

James and Jones (1976) note a paucity of research dealing with relationships between organizational structure and the individual. However, they conclude that structural factors may influence attitudes and behavior, as Argyris anticipates. Yet the evidence does not seem to support the view that formal organization has a direct linear impact on attitudes and behavior:

> . . . a high degree of formalization and standardization was found to be positively related to satisfaction and behavior because it reduced role ambiguity in one set of studies. However, formalization and specialization were described as deleterious to satisfaction and behavior when important task characteristics were deleted from jobs. . . . nonlinear relationships exist between formalization, specialization, standardization and behavior and attitudes where a certain level of structure is conducive to positive attitudes and behavior, but too much or too little structure has a negative connotation (James and Jones, 1976).

Much the same conclusion emerges from a review by Bryman (1976). He points to considerable evidence that many people desire and prosper under a far greater degree of structure than Argyris would advocate. Structure provides stability and order, with the result that uncertainty and anxiety are reduced. There is no basis for concluding that individuals with needs of this kind are necessarily immature and emotionally unhealthy, nor that they constitute a small minority.

A recent review of the self-esteem literature supports the view that the nature of work roles can serve to influence self-esteem, and presumably its correlate psychological success (Tharenou, 1979). However, there is little evidence bearing on Argyris's hypotheses regarding the specific effects of formal organizational structure. At the level of the individual job it appears that greater standardization and routinization often are associated with lower self-esteem. However, the correlations are consistently low and in some studies not significant at all. Again, high structure seems appropriate for certain individuals, and self-esteem by no means suffers under such circumstances.

Bennis's Theory of Bureaucratic Demise

The theoretical contributions of Warren Bennis are less fully developed than those of Argyris, but they have had a considerable impact, and their influence on the emergence of organization development as it is currently practiced is at least equal to that of Argyris. Building on certain earlier views, Bennis first formally presented his theory in a speech to the American Psychological Association in 1964 and followed this with a number of publications on the subject that frequently overlapped (Bennis 1966a, 1966b, 1966c, 1966d, 1967, 1969a, 1969b; Bennis and Slater, 1968).

Problems with Bureaucracy

Like the sociotechnical theorists, Bennis considers bureaucracy unsuited to the demands of the times. As a structural solution to the problems of human organization, it fails to deal effectively with its own internal realities or with factors in the current external environment. Therefore, through a process comparable to natural selection, bureaucracy will ultimately become extinct. "Within the next twenty-five to fifty years, we should all be witness to, and participate in, the end of bureaucracy and the rise of new social systems better able to cope with twentieth-century demands" (Bennis, 1966c, p. 4).

Internal and External Problems. For Bennis, bureaucracy means essentially the same thing as it did for Argyris—division of labor along functional lines, hierarchy, rules, impersonality, a system of procedures, and promotion based on technical competence. In rating bureaucracy's internal inadequacies, Bennis draws on Argyris's views, but adds other considerations as well:

Bureaucracy does not adequately allow for personal growth and the development of mature personalities.

It develops conformity and "group-think."

It does not take into account the "informal organization" and the emergent and unanticipated problems.

Its systems of control and authority are hopelessly outdated.

It has no adequate judicial process.

It does not possess adequate means for resolving differences and conflicts among ranks and, most particularly, among functional groups.

Communication (and innovative ideas) are thwarted or distorted because of hierarchical divisions.

The full human resources of bureaucracy are not being utilized because of mistrust, fear of reprisals, etc.

It cannot assimilate the influx of new technology or scientists entering the organization.

It will modify the personality structure such that man will become and reflect the dull, gray, conditioned "organization man" (Bennis, 1966c, p. 6).

Though these inadequacies are viewed as real and important, they can be handled, at least in part, through the emergence of a pervasive ethic of productivity. Thus the key problems causing the demise of bureaucracy are environmental.

The environmental changes that concern Bennis are the rapid growth of science, the growth of intellectual technology, and the growth of research and development. Building on the turbulent field concepts of the sociotechnical theorists, he points to the "scientific and technological revolution" as the major threat to bureaucracy. Adapting to such rapid environmental change is beyond the innovative capacity of that structure.

Bureaucratic Vulnerability. Elsewhere, Bennis (1967) and Bennis and Slater (1968) formulate the problems of bureaucracy somewhat differently, citing four basic sources of vulnerability. Again the emphasis is on change and complexity and on the difficulty bureaucracy has in coping with them. First, there is the knowledge and population explosion and the concept of bureaucracy as efficient only in dealing with the routine and predictable. Second, the growth in organizational size and international scope, while not necessarily sounding a death knell for bureaucracy, "is leading to a neo-Jeffersonian approach" (Bennis, 1969b, p. 21). Third, the need for diverse, specialized competencies, often of a professional nature, has increased, bringing into the labor force individuals who are not easily absorbed by bureaucratic structures.

Finally, Bennis describes a philosophic shift in management itself that is essentially antithetical to bureaucratic precepts:

A new concept of man based on increased knowledge of his complex and shifting needs, which replaces an oversimplified, innocent, push-button idea of man.

A new concept of power, based on collaboration and reason, which replaces a model of power based on coercion and threat.

A new concept of organizational values, based on humanistic-democratic ideals, which replaces the depersonalized, mechanistic value system of bureaucracy. (Bennis, 1969b, p. 22).

These changes in philosophy are hypothesized to result from a need for religious experience coupled with the secularization of religion. The position taken here is very similar to that subsequently utilized by Dubin (1976) to explain the widespread appeal the various humanistic philosophy theories have for practicing managers (see Chapter 1).

Dealing with Core Problems. Bennis hypothesized first five (1966b), and then six, core problem areas for organizations. The solutions utilized by bureaucracies and the "new twentieth-century conditions" that organizations of the future will face point up further deficiencies of the bureaucratic form. This line of argument is set forth in Table 5–4.

Organizations of the Future

Seemingly influenced by his long association with the Massachusetts Institute of Technology, Bennis's analysis of bureaucracy's inadequacies focuses heavily on its inability to adapt to accelerating scientific and technological change. In proposing solutions that are more in tune with the "new twentieth-century conditions," he turns to the world of science and research and couples this scientific orientation with a strong commitment to organizational democracy.

The Professional Model. In projecting the type of organization that will function effectively in the world of the future, Bennis draws heavily on the professional model as reflected in universities, hospitals, research and development organizations, and the like. Given that the major problem is to cope with technological change, more and more professionals will enter all kinds of organizations. However, professionals are committed to their professions and to professional organizations, not to the employing organization per se. Thus their very presence tends to foster structures other than those of a bureaucratic nature.

Table 5–4

Core Problem Areas for Organizations, Bureaucratic Solutions, and Future Conditions

Core Problem Areas	Bureaucratic Solutions	New Twentieth-Century Conditions
1. *Integrating* individual and organization goals	No solution—the tension involved is disregarded	Scientific understanding of man's complexity Rising aspirations Humanistic ethos
2. Distributing *social influence* and the sources of power and authority	Explicit reliance on rational, legal power Implicit use of coercive power	Separation of management and ownership Rise of trade unions and educational level Negative effects of authoritarian rule
3. Producing mechanisms for the control of conflict—*collaboration*	Resolving conflicts through vertical hierarchy and horizontal coordination Use of loyalty	Professionalization creates need for interdependence Leadership too complex for one-man rule
4. *Adapting* to environmental change	Environment stable and tasks routine Adapting haphazard, with many unanticipated consequences	Turbulent environment Rapid technological change
5. Dealing with growth and decay—*revitalization*	Assumption of future similar to past	Rapid changes make constant attention to revisions imperative
6. Achieving *identity* through commitment to organizational goals (added subsequently)	Primary goal clear, simple, and stable	Increased goal complexity due to diversity and multiple capabilities Creates role conflict and ambiguity

Source: Adapted from Warren G. Bennis, *Organization Development: Its Nature, Origins, and Prospects.* Reading, Mass.: Addison-Wesley, 1969, pp. 26–27.

With regard to the labor force of the future the following distribution of employment is projected:

40% of the work force will have positions in problem-solving organizations, most of them technologically based.

40% will be social change agents, that is, individuals working on revitalization of our institutions or with those

problems people feel in times of transition, including
moral and ethical problems.

20%, to my despair, will do the remaining unprogrammed,
low-level jobs of the society. . . . perhaps there are
enough people with physical or mental handicaps, or
people with low aspirations, to do them. It's difficult to
think about . . . (Bennis, 1969a, p. 237).

Thus some 80 percent will be either professionals or employed in
professional organizations. The reduction in nonprofessional employment will be made possible by automation and computeriza-
tion; intellectual power will be substituted for muscle power. In the
1960s Bennis appeared to vascillate between predicting the virtual
elimination of the nonprofessional component in society and ignoring this component as irrelevant to his theorizing.

Temporary Systems. In describing the organizational structures
suited to our times, Bennis drew heavily on his knowledge of the
project structures that had become widespread in research and development organizations:

1. The key will be "temporary": there will be adaptive,
rapidly changing *temporary systems.*
2. These will be organized around *problems-to-be-solved.*
3. The problems will be solved by groups of relative
strangers who represent a set of diverse professional skills.
4. The groups will be conducted on *organic* rather than
mechanical models; they will evolve in response to the
problem rather than programmed role expectations.
5. The function of the "executive" thus becomes
coordinator, or "linking pin" between various project groups.
He must be a man who can speak the diverse languages of
research and who can relay information and mediate among
the groups.
6. People will be differentiated not vertically according to
rank and role but flexibly according to skill and professional
training (Bennis, 1966c, p. 12).

This structure, which is labeled *organic-adaptive,* is presumed to
operate within a society that is also characterized by relationships
of a largely temporary nature (Bennis and Slater, 1968). Motivation
is fostered as individual-professional and organizational goals come
closer together. Commitment to work groups will be at a minimum
with temporary systems, thus reducing one manifestation of indi-
vidual-organizational goal incongruence.

The hypotheses for the "good organization" set forth by Bennis
lack the diversity of Argyris's mix model. They differ in a number

of respects from the autonomous group concepts of the sociotechnical theorists (Chapter 4) and from system 4 (Chapter 2). What is in fact distinctive about Bennis's views is his emphasis on the professional and on professional forms of organization.

Revisions in the 1970s

Just as Douglas McGregor came to modify some of his views on theory X and theory Y after serving as a university president (Miner, 1980), so Bennis changed his theories after similar administrative experiences:

> The 1964 paper I mentioned earlier was written within the liberal-democratic framework, and it contained many of the inherent problems and advantages of that perspective. . . . I feel far less certainty and closure at this time than I did five years ago (Bennis, 1970, p. 597).

> Bureaucracy is the inevitable—and therefore necessary—form for governing large and complex organizations (Bennis, 1973, p. 144–45).

> The temporary system has its place, but it's not going to occupy a paramount or pervasive position. There will always be a bureaucracy; the sun will never set on bureaucracies (Bennis, 1974, p. 57).

At first glance the author would appear to be totally rejecting his own theory. However, a closer reading of many of his statements during the 1970s suggests a more appropriate interpretation: Bennis considered it necessary to limit the domain of his theory, and thus to shift it from organizations in general to a particular type of essentially professional organization.

Yet Bennis has not accepted this more limited role for his theory with consistency either. The following statement is clearly at variance with those quoted previously:

> Ten years ago, I predicted that in the next twenty-five to fifty years we will participate in the end of bureaucracy as we know it and the rise of new systems better suited to twentieth century demands of industrialization. . . . I have no reason to believe differently today. On the contrary I realize now that my prediction is already a distinct reality so that the prediction is foreshadowed by practice. By "bureaucracy," I mean the typical organizational structure that coordinates the business of most every human organization we know of (Bennis, 1975, p. 330).

On the evidence one must conclude that the domain of the theory is uncertain at the present time.

The Research Evidence

Bennis's theory of bureaucratic demise has not generated a great deal of research, in part because of its sizable infusion of philosophy, in part because of uncertainty over the true meaning of certain hypotheses, in part because certain hypotheses can be fully tested only at some point in the future, and in part because of a lack of measures of key variables. Bennis himself has neither contributed measures of his own nor carried out studies related to his theory, though he did do earlier research on the effects of the laboratory training carried out under the National Training Laboratories program at Bethel, Maine, on participant self-perceptions (Burke and Bennis, 1961). However, there are some findings that bear on the theory.

Innovation Generation and Adoption. A central theme in the theory of bureaucratic demise is that bureaucracies cannot mobilize innovative strategies to cope with rapid environmental changes such as those produced by modern scientific and technological developments. This view is espoused by both Argyris and Bennis and has been argued from somewhat different premises by others such as Thompson (1969). However, the facts are not entirely consistent with the hypothesis.

The research indicates that the decentralized, participative, *organic-adaptive* structures that Bennis advocates are well suited to the *generation* of innovations, but within such structures *adoption*, or the actually putting of the innovation into effect, appears to be much more difficult (Pierce and Delbecq, 1977; Zaltman and Duncan, 1977). Organic-adaptive structures, especially when staffed with professionals, tend to foster a search for ideas and to create a positive intellectual climate, but often nothing happens after that, or in some cases the implementation that does occur represents a highly distorted version of the original idea. For purposes of effective implementation a more formalized system is needed.

Twenty theater productions (temporary systems) were studied in which role boundaries were deliberately blurred early in the study. The greater the blurring (i.e., the more organic-adaptive), the greater the professional growth and the better the utilization of individual skills involved, as the Bennis theory would predict. However, "In the second stage, the members would primarily perform their traditional roles . . . the actors would act, the directors direct, the designer design. . . . The second stage, then, would be instrumental for task accomplishment because of the emphasis on role-clarity" (Goodman and Goodman, 1976, pp. 500–501).

Conditions for Innovation. There is also evidence that bureaucracies, even highly formalized ones, can be innovative under certain conditions. In fact under current circumstances, they appear to have somewhat greater total innovative potential than other organizational forms. A national interview study of over 3,000 employed men concluded:

> There is a small but consistent tendency for men who work in bureaucratic organizations to be more intellectually flexible, more open to new experience, and more self-directed in their values than are men who work in nonbureaucratic organizations. This may in part result from bureaucracies' drawing on a more educated work force. In large part, though, it appears to be a consequence of occupational conditions attendant on bureaucratization—notably, far greater protections, somewhat higher income, and substantively more complex work (Kohn, 1971, p. 461).

One problem with the nonbureaucratic forms of the Bennis theory is that they tend to elicit considerable anxiety and tension in many people (Bryman, 1976). This anxiety, if sufficiently high, can block creativity; it can also so inhibit action that innovative ideas are not implemented. The greater predictability and protection against arbitrary action provided by truly bureaucratic organizations should reduce anxiety levels for many people and, at least for them, foster innovation.

In any event, formalized bureaucracies clearly can be highly innovative and challenging under certain circumstances (Payne, Pheysey, and Pugh, 1971). One factor that can contribute to this result is a value system supporting innovation operating in the organization, especially in the leadership group. At least in professional organizations, innovative values can override structural considerations almost completely (Hage and Dewar, 1973). Thus, if values favoring innovation exist at the top, innovations are likely to occur even in highly formalized systems.

Another related factor appears to be freedom from the demands of direct supervision and thus the structuring of jobs specifically for purposes of innovation. Stinchcombe (1974) found in his studies in South America that time spent in innovation was considerably greater for bureaucratic managers than for entrepreneurs and that, within bureaucracies, time spent in innovation was greater at the top of the organization than at lower levels where supervisory demands were more pressing. The most energy devoted to innovation, however, came from those in highly paid staff positions within bureaucracies where there were few supervisory requirements.

One can conclude that a number of considerations determine whether or not an organization will adapt to environmental change in an innovative and effective manner and that a resort to bureaucratic determinism to explain organizational demise represents a gross oversimplification at best.

From Laboratory Training to Organization Development

The theoretical views of both Argyris and Bennis call for a movement to organizational forms that are less formalized, pyramidal, and bureaucratic. Though both advocate various methods for achieving this objective, both made their first major contributions in the area of laboratory (or T-group, or sensitivity) training and subsequently in organization development. Because they have developed influential theories that provide a rationale for change efforts involving laboratory training and organization development, both authors have had a major impact on practice. Certainly many others have had a role in the growth of laboratory training and its conversion to organization development, but the underpinnings for the use of this particular strategy in organization development typically are found in goal congruence theory and in the theory of bureaucratic demise at the level of the organization, as well as in McGregor's theory X and theory Y at the level of the leadership process (see Miner, 1980).

Argyris's Contributions to Organizational Change Practices

Laboratory Training. In his early use of laboratory training, Argyris hypothesized that if executives could become more authentic, could increase their interpersonal competence, could change their values, and ultimately change their behavior, their organizations would shift to forms more appropriate than the pyramidal form. The objectives of training then are to increase:

1. Giving and receiving nonevaluative descriptive feedback.
2. Owning and helping others to own to their values, attitudes, ideas, and feelings.
3. Openness to new values, attitudes, and feelings as well as helping others to develop their degree of openness.
4. Experimenting (and helping others to do the same) with new values, attitudes, ideas, and feelings.
5. Taking risks with new values, attitudes, ideas, and feelings (Argyris, 1962b, p. 26).

Shifts in accordance with the objectives did occur among eleven top-level executives from the same division of a major company who trained together under Argyris. Changes in values and interpersonal competence were achieved. However, there also was evidence that the managers had considerable difficulty applying the new values and skills at work and that they experienced some fadeout. The impact at the organizational level appears not to have been great (Argyris, 1962b). A second application study with members of a board of directors also suggests that individual changes occurred; these changes appear to have carried over from the laboratory sessions to the regular board meetings (Argyris, 1965).

In spite of his initial enthusiasm for the laboratory approach, Argyris (1978) has come to have serious doubts about it. The back-home, on-the-job effects often are not great, and disenchantment has set in; current interest in the business world is not high, as Argyris notes.

Organization Development. As Argyris presents it, organization development focuses more directly on organizational problems and change than does laboratory training. The basic cycle moves from the collection of information, to making an organizational decision, and finally to developing a commitment to that decision. The role of the interventionist is a relatively active one:

> The interventionist should attempt to create norms of
> individuality, concern, and trust. He should attempt to draw
> out conflict, threat, or confusion so that they may be dealt
> with openly. . . . the interventionist should intervene so that
> the clients may experience psychological success (Argyris,
> 1970, p. 221).

Clearly, even where laboratory training is not used in the traditional manner, the commitment to its values and to goal congruence theory remains strong. In many cases Argyris (1971) advocates the use of confrontation meetings in which important organizational problems of an interpersonal nature are faced openly. His reported examples deal almost exclusively with top management groups. This pattern is particularly evident in a book dealing with an organization development project carried out with the staff of a major newspaper:

> The first step in the study was to conduct a diagnosis of the
> client system. This produced a map of the living system
> which identified some major internal factors causing
> organizational ineffectiveness. The factors were fed back to
> top management. . . . After obtaining valid information about
> the client system the next step was for the executives to

decide if they wanted to take action to begin to correct the problems identified. . . . After the top executives chose to attempt to correct some of the problems, they faced the task of becoming internally committed to the actions implicit in the decision. The first step was to agree to attend a learning seminar (Argyris, 1974b, pp. 276–77).

In this approach to organization development Argyris clearly views interpersonal change as a necessary prelude to organizational change. Furthermore, much of the original laboratory training is retained in the learning seminars. In the particular instance of the newspaper, this approach did not eventuate in basic organizational changes, and at least in a relative sense, the change program was a failure.

Learning Seminars and Double-Loop Learning. In recent years Argyris has developed an expanded theoretical underpinning for the learning seminars (Argyris, 1976; Argyris and Schön, 1974) and for organizational learning as a whole (Argyris and Schön, 1978). Though the theoretical terms are new, the basic concerns are not—authenticity, openness, confrontation, and the like remain central. A key concept is double-loop learning:

> In organizational single-loop learning, the criterion of success is effectiveness. Individuals respond to error by modifying strategies and assumptions within constant organizational norms. In double-loop learning, response to detected error takes the form of joint inquiry into organizational norms themselves. . . . In both cases, organizational learning consists of restructuring organizational theory of action (Argyris and Schön, 1978, p. 29).

As an example:

> When the plant managers and marketing people were detecting and attempting to correct error in order to manufacture Product X, that was single loop learning. When they began to confront the question of whether Product X should be manufactured, that was double loop learning, because they were now questioning underlying organization policies and objectives (Argyris, 1977, p. 116).

As in prior approaches, Argyris once again emphasizes questioning basic premises, cutting through defensiveness, getting at the realities for the individual and for the organization. In this sense his concept of the role of the change agent has changed little over the years.

Bennis's Contributions to Organization Development

Laboratory Training. Bennis's concern with changing organizations and with laboratory training preceded his formal statement of the theory of bureaucratic demise (Bennis, Benne, and Chin, 1961; Burke and Bennis, 1961). Thus his recommendations for practice were not so much an outgrowth of his organizational theory as a development parallel with it. In the early period he appeared to be interested in laboratory training primarily as a means to individual and group change, rather than organizational change. His focus is on internal group processes, group development, trainer behavior, and the like; the T-group is concerned with what is happening now within the group itself, not with the outside world (Bennis, 1964). Accordingly, learning is based on experience.

Yet the stated values underlying the training are clearly consistent with an unfreezing of commitment to current structures and a shift to nonbureaucratic forms of organization (Schein and Bennis, 1965):

Values of science
  Spirit of inquiry
  Expanded consciousness and choice
  Authenticity in interpersonal relations
Values of democracy
  Collaboration
  Conflict resolution through rational means

Laboratory groups are temporary systems in the fullest sense of that concept. Thus laboratory training represents an ideal method of moving to the type of organization Bennis advocated.

Not surprisingly, Bennis (1966c) came to a position much like that of Argyris in which laboratory training of "family groups" within organizations was favored as a method of planned organizational change. This commitment to laboratory training as a component of organizational change programs has remained strong, but Bennis recognizes that it is not appropriate under all circumstances.

In undertaking any planned social change using lab training, the core of the target system's values must not be too different from the lab training values. . . . legitimacy for the change must be gained by obtaining the support of the key people. . . . voluntary commitment of the participants may be a crucial factor in the success of the program. . . . the state of cultural readiness must be assessed (Bennis, 1977, pp. 211–15).

Organization Development. Bennis (1969) lists a number of characteristics of organization development, as he views it:

1. An educational strategy intended to produce organizational change that focuses on "people" variables such as values and interpersonal relationships.

2. The changes desired are associated with specific organizational problems such as growth, member satisfactions, and effectiveness.

3. An educational strategy such as laboratory training, confrontation meetings, or learning seminars, which stresses experienced behavior.

4. A change agent, usually external, who is in a collaborative relationship with the organization and who holds values of a kind that will lead to a less bureaucratic and more humane and democratic system.

5. Objectives of the change effort that are congruent with the change agent values and that include:

    a. improved interpersonal competence.

    b. changed values that emphasize human factors and feelings.

    c. increased understanding within and across groups with reduced tensions resulting.

    d. development of effective team management.

    e. more open and rational forms of conflict resolution.

    f. more organic systems characterized by mutual trust and shared responsibility.

In spite of his belief that the T-group is far from universally appropriate, Bennis (1969, p. 78) notes "the T-group coloration that almost all organization development programs take on." Given this coloration, he outlines several problems that seriously limit the applicability of organization development:

1. The organization development consultant tends to use the truth-love model when it may be inappropriate and has no alternative model to guide his practice under conditions of distrust, violence, and conflict. Essentially this means that in pluralistic power situations, in situations which are not easily controlled, organization development practice may not reach its desired goals (Bennis, 1969, p. 78).

2. Organization development pays lip service only to structural (or technological) changes while relying only on a change in organizational "climate. . . ." The organization development literature is filled with vague promises about "restructuring" or "organizational design" but with some exceptions few outcomes are actually demonstrated. . . . Far more has to be done in bridging an engineering design approach with organizational development change strategies (Bennis, 1969, p. 80).

Given conclusions such as these, it becomes important to look into the actual results obtained with organization development programs grounded in laboratory training or, to use Bennis's words, those having a "T-group coloration."

The Effectiveness of OD in the Argyris-Bennis Mode

Organization development (OD) comes in many colors. The concern here is with the approaches utilized by Argyris and Bennis. Other approaches have been considered in Chapters 2 and 4, though they by no means exhaust all the alternatives. In the field of organization development, practice has frequently outstripped theory (Burke, 1977), and a book such as this that takes theory as its starting point inevitably fails to cover the full range of techniques.

Researchers in organization development do not always fully describe the particular techniques they used. Accordingly, it often is difficult to determine whether they are considering the Argyris-Bennis mode or not. Furthermore, reviewers do not always differentiate among the various theories, making it difficult to determine whether their conclusions apply to the approaches we are considering. Within these limitations, however, we can reach some conclusions about the effectiveness of organization development rooted in laboratory training.

Multistudy Analyses. Though it is widely assumed that research on organization development is virtually nonexistent, this is clearly not the case. However, the publications are unusually scattered (Pate, Nielsen, and Bacon, 1976; Porras and Berg, 1978a). The quality of the research is relatively high for field investigations, and it is improving. Roughly 75 percent of the OD studies utilize procedures related to laboratory training as part of the overall process. Within this category the use of pure laboratory training focused on internal group processes as the major intervention form appears to be declining, while the inclusion of external organizational tasks is on the increase.

In Chapter 2 reference was made to an analysis by Bowers (1973) of data from OD programs carried out in twenty-three organizations. As indicated in Table 2–6, laboratory training had a predominantly negative impact, using the "Survey of Organizations" variables. Related approaches yield somewhat more positive results, or at least somewhat less negative, but the overall conclusions are not favorable to the type of organization development championed by Argyris and Bennis. On the other hand, all these studies were carried out in conjunction with the Survey Research Center at the University of Michigan and relied entirely on a single change measure dealing primarily with climate.

Analyses that cast a wider net tend to yield somewhat more favorable results. Alderfer (1977) considers a still limited range of studies and finds evidence for changes in work attitudes, production rates, quality of production, turnover, and absenteeism—all in an organizationally positive direction. The results of a much more extensive research survey by Porras and Berg (1978b) are outlined in Table 5–5. Their most striking finding is the high frequency of change in performance indexes as contrasted with factors such as individual job satisfaction. Though these results do not allow us to isolate the effects of procedures based on laboratory training only, the results cannot be entirely independent of laboratory training procedures simply because some 75 percent of the studies used them. On the other hand, when traditional laboratory training was the dominant intervention, the percentage of significant results obtained was the lowest among the five approaches considered, and a more task-focused version of laboratory training was only slightly superior. Overall, the data suggest that positive results can be anticipated approximately half the time and that organizationally significant factors such as profits, performance, and output are most likely to be affected.

Table 5–5

Changes Resulting from Organization Development Interventions in Thirty-Five Studies

Type of Measure	Proportion of Studies Where a Type of Measure Was Used Yielding Significant Changes
All studies*	
Individual satisfaction	38
Group performance	63
Organizational economic performance	65
Turnover and absenteeism	50
People-oriented process variables (i.e., motivation)	46
Task-oriented process variables (i.e., goal emphasis)	45
Individual process variables (i.e., openness)	62
By type of dominant intervention	
Laboratory training	
Outcome variables (satisfaction, performance, etc.)	44
Process variables (motivation, goal emphasis, etc.)	44
Task-focused laboratory training-team building	
Outcome variables	53
Process variables	45

* Approximately three-quarters of these studies utilized some form of laboratory training.

Source: Adapted from Jerry I. Porras and P.O. Berg, "The Impact of Organization Development," *Academy of Management Review*, 3 (1978), 254–59.

An additional review by Smith (1975), which focuses on the effects of laboratory training as well as its use in organization development, concludes:

> Of the studies reviewed in this article, 100 permit the drawing of a conclusion as to whether or not an effect of training was obtained. Of these studies, 78 did show an increase in one or more scores after training which was significantly greater than any change the controls may have shown. . . . Only 31 studies permitted the drawing of a conclusion as to persistence of change at follow-up. Of these 21 did show persistence of change (Smith, 1975, p. 615).

In the organization development context, changes of some kind were found with even greater frequency, but not always in total alignment with the trainers' intentions:

> The use of sensitivity training within organizational development can frequently achieve effects. These effects have not always been the intended ones, but the existing studies do not make it possible to formulate any hypotheses as to what differentiates the projects which fail to achieve their purpose. More intuitive data would suggest a wealth of historical and cultural factors with which organizational change agents need to contend (Smith, 1975, p. 615).

In short the approaches pioneered by Argyris and Bennis can work—but it is hard to predict either the exact nature of the impact or when an impact will occur.

The Automobile Assembly Plant Study. A good example of what can and cannot be accomplished with organization development is provided by a longitudinal study conducted among managers in a plant where automobiles were assembled (Kimberly and Nielsen, 1975; Pate, Nielsen, and Mowday, 1977). The formal organization development effort extended over a year and three months in the following sequence:

1. Diagnosis through the use of individual and group interviews with a sample of managers.
2. Team skills training through the use of experimental exercises in a workshop setting.
3. Collection of questionnaire data on organizational health and effectiveness and on the behavior of immediate superiors.
4. Confrontation with the questionnaire results in the context of the work group.
5. Development of action plans for change by the groups.
6. Team building requiring natural work groups to identify blocks to effectiveness and to develop plans to overcome them.

7. Intergroup building involving meetings between interdependent work groups to establish mutual understanding and enhance collaboration.

The results obtained when various preintervention measures are compared with postintervention measures are given in Table 5–6. Given the number of significant changes, these results appear most impressive. However, control group data are not provided in Table 5–6. To compensate for this deficiency, the authors sought for possible alternative explanations for the changes in various company and industry statistics. Not infrequently they found them.

The organizational climate and supervisory behavior changes may or may not have been a consequence of the organization development program, though the climate changes appear to be, on the basis of a study conducted elsewhere in the corporation that used a control group. The production rate changes before and after were not significant, but there was a sizable drop during the OD program, and then a partial recovery. This overall pattern, however, seems to reflect industry market fluctuations.

The quality data seem to indicate sizable improvements as a result of the OD effort. Yet design changes in the plant became increasingly less severe over time, and the cars to be assembled were inherently simpler. These engineering factors, rather than the OD interventions, appear to account for most of the quality improvements. The increase in profitability also may reflect these market and design factors, though the issue is not addressed directly by the authors.

The grievance rate unexpectedly increased rather than decreased. However, this pattern antedates the study by many months; so while the OD program apparently did not cause the increase in grievance

Table 5–6

Changes Associated with an Extensive Organization Development Program in an Automobile Plant

Nature of Measure	Before Measure	After Measure
Organizational climate		
Trust	(3.7	4.8)
Support	(3.8	4.4)
Open communications	(3.0	4.6)
Understanding of objectives	(4.5	5.3)
Commitment to objectives	(4.4	5.2)
Handling of conflict	(3.8	4.9)
Utilization of member resources	(3.8	4.8)
Self-direction	(3.2	4.8)
Supportive environment	(3.2	4.6)

Table 5–6 (Continued)

Supervisory behavior

Listening	(3.5	4.5)
Expressing ideas	(4.1	5.1)
Influence	(2.9	4.1)
Decision making	(3.4	4.4)
Relations with others	(2.9	3.9)
Task orientation	(4.2	4.9)
Handling of conflict	(3.7	4.3)
Willingness to change	(4.3	5.0)
Problem solving	(3.3	4.3)
Self-development	(3.2	4.0)

Production rates

Number of cars per month

Day shift	14,039	13,442
Night shift	13,706	13,371

Quality of work

Number of acceptable cars per month

Day shift	(10,133	12,494)
Night shift	(9,539	12,362)

Average percentage of cars acceptable per day	(69	90)

Profitability

Average monthly profit or loss	(−$116,995	+$19,983)

Grievances

Average daily grievances	(4.9	7.1)
Average daily grievances per 100 employees	(.21	.33)

Absenteeism

Average percentage absent per day	(9.9	7.9)

( ) Difference statistically significant.

SOURCE: Adapted from John R. Kimberly and Warren R. Nielsen, "Organization Development and Change in Organizational Performance," *Administrative Science Quarterly*, 20 (1975), pp. 196–201. Larry E. Pate, Warren R. Nielsen, and Richart T. Mowday, "A Longitudinal Assessment of the Impact of Organization Development on Absenteeism, Grievance Rates, and Product Quality," *Academy of Management Proceedings*, 1977, p. 354.

rate, it did not have a dampening effect on it either. Certainly these data are not evidence for the efficacy of the program. The best evidence for the impact of OD comes from the absenteeism statistics. There are no known alternative explanations for the improvements on this variable.

This study demonstrates the need for incorporating control groups in research designs. With considerable ingenuity the authors were able to compensate partially for the lack of controls, only to find that many changes potentially attributable to the organization development effort evaporated. However, the program probably did have an impact—on absenteeism almost certainly, and possibly on profitability, climate, and supervisory behavior. On these measures there do not appear to be offsetting negative consequences.

Conclusions

The theories considered in this chapter and the applications associated with them have proved controversial. The theorists have been accused both of leaning too far to the left and of offering token solutions to organizational problems while covertly supporting the industrial status quo to an unwarranted degree. These matters are more philosophic than scientific or practical and are unlikely to be resolved here. Even the veiled (and sometimes not-so-veiled) implications that these theorists have personal problems with authority or are engaged in an unwarranted imposition of their professional values on others are not really important. All of us generate our theories out of personal experiences and values. The crucial questions are whether theories are right or wrong and whether their applications are useful or not, not how the theorists arrived at their views. It is possible to develop very right theories out of very wrong (bad) motivations.

Scientific Goals

It would appear that Argyris and Bennis have used bureaucratic and classical management forms as straw men for their alternative structures. From the evidence bureaucracy need not be as rigid, uncreative, oppressive, and incapable of environmental adaptation as these theorists contend. It does not lead to organizational degeneration and failure any more than any other form. It seems unlikely to disappear from the face of the earth in the immediate future, largely because it is the only structure that has adequately dealt with the kinds of problems and decisions that occur at the upper levels of large organizations.

Surely there are bureaucracies that deserve all the criticisms Argyris and Bennis heap on them; many have withered and died, as a review of the Fortune 500 firms over the years will clearly indicate. However, these failures appear to be more a function of a wide range of managerial errors than a function of the inadequacies inherent in bureaucratic structure. A number of firms that have effectively utilized bureaucracy for many years have remained high on the list of corporate performers throughout their existence. Whether bureaucracies cope effectively and prosper seems to depend largely on such factors as the values of the leadership group, individual member capabilities, and adequate incorporation of staff-level positions.

Contrary to the original Bennis view, bureaucracies handle conflicts within the realm of legitimate hierarchical authority (which functions in much the same manner as the judicial process), and they have adjusted in many cases to sizable infusions of professionals and professional structures under an overall bureaucratic umbrella (Miner, 1974).

The Argyris and Bennis theories may also be faulted for a lack of internal consistency, which makes testing them difficult. The authors both tend to introduce new concepts over time in response to new influences on their thinking without indicating exactly how these concepts relate to prior theory. Alternative hypotheses are sometimes left standing side by side without any theoretical integration. Thus, Bennis now appears to be both limiting his theory to the domain of professional structures and retaining his original grand theory of organizational change. Similarly, Argyris has hypothesized two different types of self-actualization constructs, both of which he still seems to treat as viable. In the same manner he has retained both the infant-adult and psychological energy-success constructs to explain the hypothesized effects of organization on individual personality. The types of empirical tests required by these two formulations differ sharply.

Since goal congruence theory has been developed in more detail over a longer period of time, its inconsistencies and limitations tend to show up more clearly. It has been widely criticized for dealing only with individual-organization relationships and ignoring the effects of organizational environment. One could superimpose the theory of bureaucratic demise on the goal congruence theory, as Bennis has done, and treat both as one theory. Nevertheless, good theory should be written to apply within a specific domain, and Argyris is certainly justified in establishing theoretical boundaries for his constructs.

Even within its domain, however, goal congruence theory faces many conceptual and empirical difficulties. A basic problem is the contention that bureaucracy *causes* emotional illness, infantile behavior, dependent personalities, and the like. The concept of human maturity set forth in Table 5–1 would appear to be valid. However, many personality theorists, including the writer, would add to the list a capacity to deal with authority relationships effectively, so that overreactions, either positive or negative, are minimized. In this view, then, learning to function in a bureaucratic system and to delay immediate gratification for future reward is a sign of maturity, not infantilism.

There is evidence that bureaucratic organizations tend to attract emotionally disturbed individuals at the lower levels, presumably because these people can function effectively in such positions and not at higher levels (Miner and Anderson, 1958). But this does not mean the organization *caused* the pathology. It seems probable that Argyris, observing organization members within a limited time span and noting the contiguity of pathology and formal structure, incorrectly attributed direct causation to the structure, when in fact it was often the ambiguity- and anxiety-reducing structure itself that permitted particular individuals to function in an organizational setting at all.

Actually, Argyris is not consistent as to whether immature people (those lacking psychological success) are created by formal organizations and thus can mature in an alternative structure, or whether they are of a personality type that functions well only in congruent systems (bureaucracies); he says both at different points. Obviously the implications for organizational design differ considerably in the two instances. Possibly both processes occur in different individuals, but then the theory should deal clearly with methods of identifying the two classes of people, which it does not.

A special problem arises with goal congruence theory in regard to the relationship between bureaucratic authority and dependency. The theory appears to confuse objective and subjective (personality-based) dependency. Hierarchical systems do create objective dependency relationships to varying degrees for most, if not all, members. But because one individual is dependent on another for rewards does not mean that that person constantly craves the support, help, approval, instruction, and domination of others, and becomes angry when they are not received, in the manner of the dependent personality. Certainly, bureaucratic systems do attract dependent personalities; they may well create some dependent personalities under certain circumstances; but they clearly attract a great many nondependent people, even though all work under a degree of objective dependency.

In his earliest theoretical statements Argyris did consider alternative responses to formal structure other than regression into passive dependency, including upward mobility in the organizational hierarchy. The theory did not specify how to identify these people, however, or mention alternative responses of this kind later.

Lichtman and Hunt (1971) have criticized Argyris for neglecting individual differences and offering a "one best way" prescription analogous to scientific management. Argyris (1973) disputed this, and indeed such concepts as his reality-centered leadership and mix model do require contingent hypotheses. However, these contingent hypotheses are given relatively little attention, have not been tested empirically, and at times are completely ignored. Often they are treated more as escape valves than as formal parts of the theory. To be useful, these contingency variables and hypotheses need to be much more clearly stated—where, when, and how various structures and leadership behaviors are to be used should be spelled out.

Individual personalities come in a great variety of forms. Some fit well and thrive in one type of organization, generating considerable energy for movement toward organizational goals, while others fit in another type. Some personalities may not fit any known organization. A society that is to use its human talent effectively must generate a variety of organizational forms. The mix model approaches this problem, but goal congruence theory as a whole tends to bypass it. Bureaucratic demise theory first failed to recognize the need for organizational variety at all, and then confronted it face to face later on.

Many readers may consider this review of the Argyris and Bennis theories excessively critical. However, it should be understood that this is criticism from the 1980s. These theories appeared during a period of rapid growth in the service and professional occupations and during major shifts in the balance of personality types within the population, primarily away from those types that fit bureaucracies best (Miner, 1974). The theories, especially Bennis's, fostered the development and expansion of professional structures at a time when they were greatly needed. The theories also contributed, as did the system 4 and sociotechnical theories, to organizational changes of other kinds that appear to have been consonant with shifting personality constellations. In this sense the Argyris and Bennis theories once performed an extremely useful societal function, whatever their long-term scientific imperfections. Probably they should now be credited with their past contributions and left alone, in favor of more currently promising approaches. Indeed this is exactly what their authors appear to have done since the mid-1970s.

The foregoing recommendation requires two qualifications. The essence of goal congruence theory is that when individual members and organizations fit each other—when their goals are congruent—organizational effectiveness will be fostered because members will devote their efforts to organizational goal achievement. This is an integration hypothesis, and it is consistently supported by the research of Argyris and of others cited in this chapter. Similar integration formulations are reinforced by the findings on concordance cited in Chapter 3 and by findings noted in later chapters of this book. Goal congruence theory emphasized, if it did not create, one of the most important concepts in organizational theory at an early time.

Bennis's views on temporary systems, the professional model, and the like appear to be useful within the limited domain that he has more recently assigned them (Bennis, 1970). As part of a theory of professional organizational structures, his formulations appear to have considerable validity.

Goals of Application

Bennis has raised two issues that he feels are special problems for OD. One is the inability of truth-love formulations to cope effectively with violent conflict, opposing constituencies, and power fights—especially under conditions of free-lying power. In essence he is establishing the boundaries for practice as he has done in other instances. Incongruent organizational values and cultural contexts also indicate that laboratory training and organization development based on it may not prove effective, or may achieve only short-lived results.

Perhaps the factors that Bennis notes as antithetical to the effective use of OD explain the practice's roughly 50 percent "hit rate." Unfortunately research studies typically have not considered such matters as preexisting conflict levels and organizational value systems, and related these to experimental outcomes. Clearly there are boundaries within which OD that is rooted in laboratory training will work and outside of which it either fails to work or, in the case of traditional laboratory approaches, even backfires.

Bennis's second point is that few organization development efforts actually bring about the kind of structural changes the goal congruence and bureaucratic demise theories would hypothesize. In this respect OD approaches emanating from sociotechnical systems theory are very different. Under appropriate circumstances the Argyris-Bennis approach tends to influence people directly, change organizational climates and processess, and yield performance effects. But it typically achieves these results while leaving structures surprisingly unaffected. Either structural change is not as important as it was thought to be, or the effects now being attained represent only a small portion of potential effects. Without research into OD efforts that move beyond team building into organizational restructuring, this type of question simply cannot be answered.

At the present time approaches utilizing traditional laboratory training seem to risk contributing to organizationally undesirable outcomes. Accordingly, more task-oriented forms are to be preferred. If one is reasonably sure that the milieu is "right" for OD, and that is not easy to establish, then the somewhat newer approaches such as the kind used in the automobile plant offer promise. However, it is not possible to predict exactly what kinds of changes will occur. Furthermore, it is questionable whether the approaches considered in this chapter will likely yield greater improvements than alternative procedures, including even a well-thought-out, hierarchy-based reorganization. In areas in which theory has not even kept up with practice, let alone extended beyond it, decisions will inevitably be made with a high degree of uncertainty for some time to come.

References

Alderfer, Clayton P. "Organization Development," *Annual Review of Psychology*, 28 (1977), 197–223.

Argyris, Chris. *The Impact of Budgets on People*. New York: Controllership Foundation, 1952.

——. *Organization of a Bank: A Study of the Nature of Organization and the Fusion Process*. New Haven, Conn.: Labor and Management Center, Yale University, 1954.

——. *Personality and Organization*. New York: Harper & Row, 1957.

——. "The Organization: What Makes It Healthy," *Harvard Business Review*, 36, no. 6 (1958), 107–16.

——. "Understanding Human Behavior in Organizations: One Viewpoint." In Mason Haire (ed.), *Modern Organization Theory*. New York: Wiley, 1959, pp. 115–54.

——. *Understanding Organizational Behavior*. Homewood, Ill.: Dorsey, 1960a.

——. "Organizational Effectiveness Under Stress," *Harvard Business Review*, 38, no. 3 (1960b), 137–46.

——. "The Integration of the Individual and the Organization." In George B. Strother (ed.), *Social Science Approaches to Business Behavior*. Homewood, Ill.: Irwin, 1962a, pp. 57–98.

——. *Interpersonal Competence and Organizational Effectiveness*. Homewood, Ill.: Irwin, 1962b.

——. *Integrating the Individual and the Organization*. New York: Wiley, 1964.

——. *Organization and Innovation*. Homewood, Ill.: Irwin, 1965.

——. "Some Unintended Consequences of Rigorous Research," *Psychological Bulletin*, 70 (1968), 185–97.

——. *Intervention Theory and Method: A Behavioral Science View*. Reading, Mass.: Addison-Wesley, 1970.

——. *Management and Organizational Development: The Path from XA to YB*. New York: McGraw-Hill, 1971.

——. *The Applicability of Organizational Sociology*. Cambridge, England: Cambridge University Press, 1972.

——. "Personality and Organization Theory Revisited," *Administrative Science Quarterly*, 18 (1973), 141–67.

——. "Personality vs. Organization," *Organizational Dynamics*, 3, no. 2 (1974a), 3–17.

——. *Behind the Front Page: Organizational Self-Renewal in a Metropolitan Newspaper*. San Francisco: Jossey-Bass, 1974b.

——. *Increasing Leadership Effectiveness*. New York: Wiley, 1976.

——. "Double Loop Learning in Organizations," *Harvard Business Review*, 55, no. 5 (1977), 115–25.

——. "Reflecting on Laboratory Education from a Theory of Action Perspective," 1978 (unpublished).

Argyris, Chris, and Donald A. Schön. *Theory in Practice: Increasing Professional Effectiveness*. San Francisco: Jossey-Bass, 1974.

——. *Organizational Learning: A Theory of Action Perspective*. Reading, Mass.: Addison-Wesley, 1978.

Bakke, E. Wight. *Bonds of Organization*. New York: Harper, 1950.

——. "Concept of the Social Organization." In Mason Haire (ed.), *Modern Organization Theory*. New York: Wiley, 1959, pp. 16–75.

Bennis, Warren G. "Patterns and Vicissitudes in T-Group Development." In Leland P. Bradford, Jack R. Gibb, and Kenneth D. Benne (eds.), *T-Group Theory and Laboratory Method*. New York: Wiley, 1964, pp. 248–78.

——. "Organizational Developments and the Fate of Bureaucracy," *Industrial Management Review*, 7 (1966a), 41–55.

————. "Changing Organizations," *Journal of Applied Behavioral Science*, 2, no. 3 (1966b), 247–63.

————. *Changing Organizations*. New York: McGraw-Hill, 1966c.

————. "Organizational Revitalization," *California Management Review*, 9, no. 1 (1966d), 51–60.

————. "Organizations of the Future," *Personnel Administration*, 30, no. 5 (1967), 6–19.

————. "The Temporary Society," *Journal of Creative Behavior*, 3, no. 4 (1969a), 223–41.

————. *Organization Development: Its Nature, Origins, and Prospects*. Reading, Mass.: Addison-Wesley, 1969b.

————. "A Funny Thing Happened on the Way to the Future," *American Psychologist*, 25 (1970), 595–608.

————. *The Leaning Ivory Tower*. San Francisco: Jossey-Bass, 1973.

————. "Conversation with Warren Bennis," *Organizational Dynamics*, 2, no. 3 (1974), 51–66.

————. "The Problem: Integrating the Organization and the Individual." In William G. Monahan (ed.), *Theoretical Dimensions of Educational Administration*. New York: Macmillan, 1975, pp. 317–46.

————. "Bureaucracy and Social Change: An Anatomy of a Training Failure." In Philip H. Mirvis and David N. Berg (eds.), *Failures in Organization Development and Change: Cases and Essays for Learning*. New York: Wiley, 1977, pp. 191–215.

Bennis, Warren G., Kenneth D. Benne, and Robert Chin. *The Planning of Change*. New York: Holt, Rinehart & Winston, 1961.

Bennis, Warren G., and Philip E. Slater. *The Temporary Society*. New York: Harper & Row, 1968.

Bonjean, Charles M., and Gary G. Vance. "A Short-Form Measure of Self-Actualization," *Journal of Applied Behavioral Science*, 4 (1968), 299–312.

Bowers, David G. "OD Techniques and Their Results in 23 Organizations: The Michigan ICL Study," *Journal of Applied Behavioral Science*, 9 (1973), 21–43.

Bryman, Alan. "Structure in Organizations: A Reconsideration," *Journal of Occupational Psychology*, 49 (1976), 1–9.

Burke, Richard L., and Warren G. Bennis. "Changes in Perception of Self and Others During Human Relations Training," *Human Relations*, 14 (1961), 165–82.

Burke, Ronald J., and Tamara Weir. "Organizational Climate and Informal Helping Processes in Work Settings," *Journal of Management*, 4, no. 2 (1978), 91–105.

Burke, W. Warner. *Current Issues and Strategies in Organization Development*. New York: Human Sciences Press, 1977.

Dewar, Robert, and James Werbel. "Universalistic and Contingency Predictions of Employee Satisfaction and Conflict," *Administrative Science Quarterly*, 24 (1979), 426–48.

Dubin, Robert. "Theory Building in Applied Areas." In Marvin D. Dunnette (ed.), *Handbook of Industrial and Organizational Psychology*. Chicago: Rand McNally, 1976, pp. 17–39.

Goodman, Richard A., and Lawrence P. Goodman. "Some Management Issues in Temporary Systems: A Study of Professional Development and Manpower—The Theater Case," *Administrative Science Quarterly*, 21 (1976), 494–501.

Hage, Jerald, and Robert Dewar. "Elite Values Versus Organizational Structure in Predicting Innovation," *Administrative Science Quarterly*, 18 (1973), 279–90.

James, Lawrence R., and Allan P. Jones. "Organizational Structure: A Review of Structural Dimensions and Their Conceptual Relationships with Individual Attitudes and Behavior," *Organizational Behavior and Human Performance*, 16 (1976), 74–113.

Kimberly, John R., and Warren R. Nielsen. "Organization Development and Change in Organizational Performance," *Administrative Science Quarterly*, 20 (1975), 191–206.

Kohn, Melvin L. "Bureaucratic Man: A Portrait and an Interpretation," *American Sociological Review*, 36 (1971), 461–74.

Lichtman, Cary M., and Raymond G. Hunt. "Personality and Organization Theory: A Review of Some Conceptual Literature," *Psychological Bulletin*, 76 (1971), 271–94.

McGregor, Douglas. *Leadership and Motivation*. Cambridge, Mass.: MIT Press, 1966.

———. *The Professional Manager*. New York: McGraw-Hill, 1967.

Miner, John B. *The Human Constraint*. Washington, D.C.: BNA Books, 1974.

———. *Theories of Organizational Behavior*. Hinsdale, Ill.: Dryden, 1980.

Miner, John B., and James K. Anderson. "The Postwar Occupational Adjustment of Emotionally Disturbed Soldiers," *Journal of Applied Psychology*, 42 (1958), 317–22.

Pate, Larry E., Warren R. Nielsen, and Paula C. Bacon. "Advances in Research on Organization Development: Toward a Beginning," *Academy of Management Proceedings*, 1976, pp. 389–94.

Pate, Larry E., Warren R. Nielsen, and Richard T. Mowday. "A Longitudinal Assessment of the Impact of Organization Development on Absenteeism, Grievance Rates, and Product Quality," *Academy of Management Proceedings*, 1977, pp. 353–57.

Payne, Roy L., Diana C. Pheysey, and D. S. Pugh. "Organizational Structure, Organizational Climate, and Group Structure: An Exploratory Study of Their Relationships in Two British Manufacturing Companies," *Occupational Psychology*, 45 (1971), 45–55.

Pennings, Johannes M. "Dimensions of Organizational Influence and Their Effectiveness Correlates," *Administrative Science Quarterly*, 21 (1976), 688–99.

Pierce, Jon L., and André L. Delbecq. "Organizational Structure, Individual Attitudes and Innovation," *Academy of Management Review*, 2 (1977), 27–37.

Porras, Jerry I., and Per O. Berg. "Evaluation Methodology in Organization Development: An Analysis and Critique," *Journal of Applied Behavioral Science*, 14, (1978a), 151–73.

———. "The Impact of Organization Development," *Academy of Management Review*, 3 (1978b), 249–66.

Rossel, Robert D. "Autonomy in Bureaucracies," *Administrative Science Quarterly*, 16 (1971), 308–14.

Schein, Edgar H., and Warren G. Bennis. *Personal and Organizational Change through Group Methods: The Laboratory Approach*. New York: Wiley, 1965.

Smith, Peter B. "Controlled Studies of the Outcome of Sensitivity Training," *Psychological Bulletin*, 82 (1975), 597–622.

Stinchcombe, Arthur L. *Creating Efficient Industrial Administrations*. New York: Academic Press, 1974.

Tharenou, Phyllis. "Employee Self-Esteem: A Review of the Literature," *Journal of Vocational Behavior*, 15 (1979), 316–46.

Thompson, Victor A. *Bureaucracy and Innovation*. University, Ala.: University of Alabama Press, 1969.

Zaltman, Gerald, and Robert Duncan. *Strategies for Planned Change*. New York: Wiley, 1977.

Psychological Open Systems Theory

The two theories considered in this chapter represent something of an enigma in that their authors write as psychologists while acknowledging major debts to the sociologist Talcott Parsons (1951). Certainly there is considerable blurring of disciplinary boundaries in all theories drawing on systems concepts, including sociotechnical systems theory (Chapter 4) and other theories considered in subsequent chapters of this book, as well as in the two theories treated here. However, the formulations of Ralph Stogdill, as originally set forth in *Individual Behavior and Group Achievement* (1959), and of Daniel Katz and Robert Kahn in *The Social Psychology of Organizations* (1966) contain a degree of emphasis on individual, psychological variables not found in the more sociological approaches discussed later.

Stodgill, Katz, and Kahn received their degrees in psychology. Stogdill not only received his professional training at Ohio State University, but spent most of his career there as well. He retired from the university in 1975 and died in 1978. Katz earned his doctorate at Syracuse University and has been associated with the Institute for Social Research at the University of Michigan for many years, as has Kahn, who obtained his degree at the University of Michigan.

Stogdill's Group-Focused Systems Theory

Stogdill (1959) opens his book with the statement, "It is the purpose of this book to develop a theory of organization achievement." He then writes for more than a hundred pages about groups and group members, with little reference to organizations. Basically the theory represents a direct extrapolation from the group to the organization. The only difference is that "an organization is a group in which the positions in the system are differentiated relative to function and status. . . . it is found convenient to differentiate organizations from groups only in terms of degree of structure, since both must be regarded as groups" (Stogdill, 1959, p. 125). As a consequence, the variables of the theory tend to be drawn to a considerable degree from individual psychology and group dynamics; the reader must substitute the word *organization* for *group* at numerous points.

A second caution with regard to terminology: Stogdill tends to define his terms with an admirable degree of precision, but his definitions are not always in line with common usage among either lay or professional readers. As a result, it becomes important to pay close attention to Stogdill's definitions. In addition, Stogdill's whole theory is not easy to comprehend.

Individual Behavior and Group Achievement (1959)

Stogdill (1959) describes three major theoretical variables and hypothesizes relationships among them. As is common with systems concepts, the three variable types are *inputs, mediating variables* or *mediators,* and *outputs.* Inputs are associated with individuals as members; outputs, with the group (organization). Mediating variables are structures or processes within the group. The group itself is defined as an "*open interaction system* in which actions determine the *structure* of the system and successive interactions exert coequal effects upon the *identity* of the system. . . ."

> By *interaction* is meant that, in a system composed of two members, A reacts to B and B reacts to A in such a manner that the response of each is a reaction to the behavior of the other. By *open system* is meant that, within limits necessary to maintain interaction, members may leave or enter the system without destroying the identity of the system. By *structure* is meant that the system is so differentiated or ordered that member A is not identical with member B, and the reaction of A to B is not identical with the reaction of B to A. By *identity* is meant the continuity of interaction which permits the system to be recognized as the same group during successive periods of observation (Stogdill, 1959, pp. 18–19).

In a group of minimum structure, where members successively exchange positions while still maintaining system identity, individual freedom of action is limited to staying in the system or leaving it. Similarly freedom of action is hypothesized to be highly constrained under conditions of maximum structure; in between is an optimum degree of structure that maximizes freedom.

Member Inputs. There are three types of member inputs—*performances, interactions,* and *expectations.* A performance is perceived by members of a group as an act that identifies an individual as a participant in the group's operations. The performances of members taken together describe the task being carried out by the group. These individual performances, as well as interaction behaviors, are inputs under the theory; so, too, are expectations—defined as readiness for reinforcement.

The expectations of members form the basis of group purpose. Members are prepared or unprepared to experience various possible outcomes. They have ideas about both the probability of occurrence and the desirability of these outcomes. Values represent a special type of expectation.

A personal *value system* may be defined as a highly generalized set of expectations in which desirability estimates are mutually confirmed with little reference to probability estimates, and which serve as a referent or criterion for evaluating the desirability of alternative outcomes. . . . these value systems . . . are reinforced by satisfying as well as unsatisfying outcomes, and are little diminished by the failure of outcomes to confirm their validity (Stogdill, 1959, pp. 72–73).

Groups tend to exert strong influences on the expectations of members. The goals and norms of the group serve as counterparts to individual value systems. Such group structures of expectation are highly stable over time. Member interactions tend to reinforce these expectations, with the result that considerable singleness of purpose in pursuit of valued outcomes tends to emerge within the group.

Mediating Variables: Formal and Role Structures. *Formal structure* within the group differentiates positions in such a way that members exhibit predictable patterns of performance and response. Positions have *status* and *function*.

The *status* of a position defines the degree of freedom granted its occupant in initiating and maintaining the goal direction and structure of the system in which the position is located. . . . The *function* of a position defines the general nature of the contribution that its occupant is expected to make toward the accomplishment of the group purpose (Stogdill, 1959, p. 123).

Role structures, in contrast to formal structures, attach to the person rather than to the position. They represent a set of expectations conditioned in part by the status and function of the position occupied, but also by the demands made on the individual by other members and by the members' view of the individual as a person. Role structures involve *authority* and *responsibility*.

Authority may be defined as the degree of freedom that the occupant of a position is expected to exercise in initiating performance and interaction within a formally acknowledged structure. *Responsibility* may be defined as the specific set or range of performances that a member is expected to exhibit by virtue of the operational demands made upon his position in a formally acknowledged structure (Stogdill, 1959, p. 129).

Because roles are not always clearly defined and role expectations may vary among members of a group, role confusion and conflict represent distinct possibilities. The result is a diminution of the power of the group. The group's power is dependent not only on unity of purpose, strength of effort, and coordination of operations, but also on integration of its structure.

Group Outputs. Outputs, in contrast to inputs, are group achievements, not individual behaviors. The three output types are productivity, integration, and morale.

> Group *productivity* is defined as the degree of change in expectancy values created by the group operations. Group *integration* is defined as the extent to which structures and operations are capable of being maintained under stress. Group *morale* is defined as degrees of freedom from restraint in action toward a goal (Stogdill, 1959, p. 198).

The three types of group outputs can vary simultaneously, but only when there are comparable variations in inputs. When inputs are held constant, an increase in one output must occur at a cost to one or both of the other outputs. Productivity is hypothesized to be high when function and status are clearly defined, when group structure and goal direction are maintained, and when responsibility and authority are enlarged to the degree permitted by the need to control operations. Under these circumstances mediator variables contribute the most to the utilization of inputs.

Integration is analogous to group cohesion, but the definition is behavioral, not subjective. Integration requires a clearly defined role structure and is influenced by the level of member satisfaction, though integration is not identical with satisfaction. Integration tends to be high when:

1. Members are loyal to the group, support it, and are closely agreed on group goals and methods of obtaining them.

2. Subgroups support the structure and goals of the larger group, and their activities are coordinated with these goals.

3. The structure and operations of the larger group (organization) are supported by both individual members and subgroups.

In many respects integration for Stogdill is comparable to goal congruence in the Argyris theory (Chapter 5).

Morale also is defined behaviorally, in terms of freedom of action, rather than subjectively, in terms of feelings. Morale can be either too high or too low for the group's own welfare. Morale, like freedom of action, is a curvilinear function of the degree of group structure. Thus bureaucracies can become so rigid that they restrict individual freedom of action, group morale, and adaptive initiative. Success also can contribute to high morale. Operations control, like structure, is hypothesized to stand in a curvilinear relationship to morale.

When freedom to act and morale are high, motivation will be high also, but when morale is low, action can be so constrained that motivation is not manifested in behavior.

Four hypotheses regarding group outputs are stated:

1. Productivity and morale are positively related.
2. Morale can be related either positively or negatively to integration.
3. Integration and productivity are negatively related.
4. Morale, productivity, and integration may be positively related when the group is strongly motivated in striving toward goal achievement or when motivation is very low (Stogdill, 1959, p. 222).

Hypothesis 4 assumes changes in member inputs; the first three hypotheses do not. The final theoretical model, devoid of hypothesized relationships among variables, is given in Figure 6–1. The model is said to portray an open system exchanging members and values with its environment, though Stogdill devotes relatively little attention to exchanges between the system and the environment.

Intragroup-Intergroup Theory (1962)

Since 1959, Stogdill has elaborated on his theory in several respects. One early development is described in Figure 6–2 (Stogdill, 1962). The model attempts to account for individual accomplishments and individual and group reputation as outputs, in addition to the group achievements of productivity, integration, and morale. Performances, interactions, and expectations are inputs common to all mediators and outputs. The primary direction of effects is from inputs through mediators to outputs, but there are also feedback effects. There is considerable mixing across the individual attributes, interpersonal relations, and group attributes due to their common input pool. A secondary set of effects runs from reference groups to norms to group purposes and from personality to role structure to formal structure.

In the same publication (1962) Stogdill considers the matter of intergroup relations, setting forth a partial model for this purpose. This model specifies certain environmental and cultural factors (resources, institutions, mores, social classes, philosophy, science, technology, coalitions, alliances) that influence the relations between groups. The variables of Figure 6–2 are assumed to interact as they operate within the two groups and to produce intergroup outcomes. The extent of the involvement between groups is a function of the type of group involvement (total groups, subgroups, or

Figure 6–1

The Structure of the Theory of Organization Achievement

Member Inputs	Mediating Variables		Group Outputs
Behaviors	Formal Structure	Role Structure	Achievement
Performances	Functions	Responsibility	Productivity
Interactions	Status	Authority	Morale
Expectations	(Purpose, Norms)	(Operations)	Integration
Group Structure and Operations			Effects

NOTE: Reprinted by permission of the publisher from Ralph M. Stogdill, *Individual Behavior and Group Achievement.* New York: Oxford University Press, 1959, p. 13.

Figure 6–2

Model for a Person, Interperson, and Group System

Inputs	Mediating Variables	Outputs
Performances	Individual Attributes	
	1. Individual's reference groups 2. Individual personality, values	Individual accomplishments
Interactions	Interpersonal Relations	

	1. Group norms
	 2. Role structure
	    Responsibility
	    Authority
		Individual and group reputation

Expectations	Group Attributes	

	1. Group purposes, goals
	 2. Formal structure
	    Functions
	    Status
		Group achievements
		 Productivity
		 Integration
		 Morale

SOURCE: Adapted from Ralph M. Stogdill, "Intragroup-Intergroup Theory and Research." In Muzafer Sherif (ed.), *Intergroup Relations and Leadership.* New York: Wiley, 1962, p. 52.

individuals), the formality of the contact, and whether the contact is authorized, unauthorized, or accidental. This intergroup model, as contrasted with the basic group model, admittedly is incomplete and lacks hypotheses regarding relationships among variables.

Dimensions of Organization Theory (1966)

In a later statement Stogdill (1966) deals primarily with the scope of organization theory. Here he is clearly more concerned with organizations than with groups, but at the same time dynamic relationships are treated as secondary to variable listings. The group-organization differentiation becomes much more pronounced:

> We may define a group as a social interaction system with minimum structure. We shall regard an organization as a social interaction system in which the differentiation of expectations defines the structure of positions and roles in the system. Most of the groups and subgroups with which we shall be concerned will exhibit characteristics of organization (Stogdill, 1966, p. 13).

The basic model is stated as follows:

The input and output variables are now essentially the same, but there is a concern with *measured* inputs, both human (skill, effort, expectation, time, knowledge, motivation) and material (money, materials, facilities). Furthermore, the specific hypotheses regarding output relationships are stated somewhat more generally:

> In view of the number of variables and the complexity of the interrelationships among the variables that affect the output, it is difficult to formulate any all-inclusive statements of relationships among the output variables. If inputs are held constant and operations become stabilized over a given period of time, it would appear that an increase in one output must necessarily be accomplished at the expense of one or both of the other outputs (Stogdill, 1966, p. 39).

The number of mediating variables is expanded to include operations (individual task performance, technical processes), interpersonnel (interaction, intercommunication, interexpectation, interpersonal affect, intersocial comparisons), and structure (purpose and policies, positions, roles, communication nets, work group structures and norms, and other subgroup structures and norms). Though extensions of this kind do increase the inclusiveness of the theory, they also confuse inputs and mediators somewhat, while raising questions regarding the parsimoniousness of theoretical statement. Though precise definitions were invariably given in earlier explications, this no longer holds in the 1966 statement.

Stogdill's move to an open systems perspective is increasingly in evidence in 1966. External, environmental constraints are listed as climate and material resources, folk mores and religious norms, common law and political philosophy, governmental and legal regulations, economic institutions and norms, professional and craft norms, fraternal and philanthropic norms, and family and community norms. Stogdill lists a number of survival mechanisms for coping with these environmental factors, though without adequate explication. Stogdill is clearly trying to combine a number of approaches to organization theory, particularly including the classical management and behavior concepts. It is also apparent that integrating them is not easy.

Basic Concepts (1967)

Certain variables in the Stogdill statement of 1966 did not survive in the next version, while some new variables were added (Stogdill, 1967a). Furthermore, some variables are renamed, though the definitions remain much the same. The model now includes specific feedback loops from mediators to inputs and from outputs to mediators and inputs, as well as the major progression from inputs to mediators to outputs.

Inputs are actions (performances), interactions, and expectations, plus *task materials*; outputs are product (productivity), drive (morale), and cohesiveness (integration). The differentiation of mediators into operations, interpersonnel, and structure is retained from the 1966 version, but within these categories there are major changes. Operations are divided into human performances and technical processes; structures into the familiar positions (status and function) and roles (responsibility, authority, plus *delegation*), to which are added *formal* and *informal subsystems* and *departmentation*. New structural variables are added and other variables are dropped without explanation.

The greatest changes, however, occur in the area of interpersonnel, which covers "a large complex of behaviors and relationships that account for exchanges between member and member, and between member and organization" (Stogdill, 1967a, p. B671). The components of this category are completely recast to include the following:

Interpersonal relations (superior, subordinate, peer)
Personal-organizational exchange relations
Reinforcement, satisfactions, and dissatisfactions
Internal-external relations (reference groups)
Subgroup norms and pressures
Subsystem interrelations

Finally, the original hypotheses regarding output relationships are reinstated. One condition for a positive relationship between morale and integration is external threat to the group; this relationship can be negative when the group is divided into cliques and when there are differences in loyalties.

Behavioral Model of Organization (1974)

In speeches given at the American Psychological Association meetings in 1969 and the Eastern Academy of Management meetings in 1973, Stogdill attempted to reformulate his theory in mathematical terms. The resulting paper represents the most sophisticated of his theoretical statements (Stogdill, 1974). For this purpose he used finer categories of analysis in restating the input variables. He also formally incorporated the concept of *satisfaction* in the theory:

> Satisfaction, although a characteristic of individuals, is not an input. It varies as a result of reinforcement or nonreinforcement, and should be regarded as a subtype of mediating variable that can feed back as an input as the group progresses in its activities (Stogdill, 1974, p. 8).

The subcategories introduced are listed in Table 6–1.

Formulas for the major mediating and output variables are set forth in Figure 6–3. In these formulas specific outputs are tied directly to specific types of mediators. The concept of drive (morale) also is delineated somewhat more fully than it had been in the past:

> Drive is defined as degree of group arousal. Mutually reinforced expectations define an area of freedom for the group and determine to a large degree the objective or objectives toward which drive will be directed. Under conditions of high commitment to group goals and freedom from restraint, drive is likely to be expended in effort toward goal achievement. However, under high restraint, drive may become directed toward the reduction of restraint as a secondary objective (Stogdill, 1974, p. 12).

As in the early formulation of the theory, the influences of environmental factors are recognized, but no attempt is made to incorporate them directly in the mathematical statements.

Research Bearing on the Theory

Like a number of systems theories of organization, Stogdill's group-focused approach has generated little research. In many of its early forms the theory produced more static models and lists of variables than testable hypotheses, though there were some of the latter, too.

Table 6–1
Subcategories Under Member Inputs and the Mediating Variable of Satisfaction

Performances
Nontask
Task
Specialized

Interactions
Mutual (reciprocated)
Nontask-related
Task-related
Bypassing immediate superiors

Expectations (regarding)
Contributions to be made
Freedom to act and decide
Goal (outcome) values
Freedom to interact
Discontinuity of membership
Mutual liking
Nontask performances
Task specialization
Returns from the organization
Task performance
Task urgency
Reference group support

Satisfaction (with)
Status
Contributions to organization
Freedom of action
Organization and supervision
Returns from the organization

SOURCE: Adapted from Ralph M. Stogdill, "A Behavioral Model of Organization." Unpublished manuscript, Ohio State University, 1974, p. 7.

The later mathematical formulations were never formally published and are not widely known. So, though they constitute highly testable hypotheses, no evidence bearing on them exists.

Related Literature. Stogdill's 1959 volume contains extensive reviews of research related to the theory. However, it is clear that this research was the base from which the theory was generated. Stogdill, like Argyris (Chapter 5), tends to extrapolate from and reinterpret studies originally conducted to test hypotheses differing considerably from those of his own theory. Given this background, research conducted before 1959 cannot be used as evidence for the theory.

In a later review of relationships among the output variables, Stogdill (1972) cites studies carried out prior to 1959 and later studies not typically intended as direct tests of the group-focused theory. Six of the more recent studies related productivity to drive (morale) and three of these reported positive correlations as hypothesized.

Figure 6–3
Mathematical Relationships Between Mediating Variables and Outputs in Group-Focused Systems Theory

$$\textbf{Operations} = \text{Task performances} \times \text{Expectations regarding task performance} \times \frac{\text{Task-related interactions}}{\text{Mutual interactions}}$$

$$\textbf{Interpersonnel} = \text{Nontask performances} \times \text{Expectations regarding nontask performances} \times \text{Nontask-related interactions}$$

$$\textbf{Structure} = \text{Specialized performances} \times \text{Expectations regarding task specialization} \times \frac{\text{Mutual interactions}}{\text{Interactions bypassing immediate superiors}}$$

$$\textbf{Productivity} = \text{Operations} \times \left(\text{Expectations regarding goal values} + \text{Expectations regarding contributions to be made}\right) \times \frac{\text{Expectations regarding task urgency} + \text{Expectations regarding discontinuity of membership}}{\text{Satisfaction with status} + \text{Satisfaction with contributions to organization}}$$

$$\textbf{Cohesiveness (Integration)} = \text{Structure} \times \left(\text{Satisfaction with status} + \text{Expectations regarding mutual liking}\right) \times \frac{\text{Expectations regarding reference group support} + \text{Satisfaction with organization and supervision}}{\text{Expectations regarding task urgency} + \text{Expectations regarding discontinuity of membership}}$$

$$\textbf{Drive (Morale)} = \text{Interpersonnel} \times \left(\text{Expectations regarding freedom to act and decide} + \text{Expectations regarding task urgency} + \text{Satisfaction with freedom of action}\right) \times \frac{\text{Expectations regarding contributions to be made} + \text{Expectations regarding returns from the organization}}{\text{Satisfaction with contributions to organization} + \text{Satisfaction with returns from the organization}}$$

Fourteen correlations from nine studies since 1959 bear on the association between productivity and cohesiveness (integration). Five of the correlations were negative (as hypothesized), but another five were positive, and four were not significantly different from zero. Research on the drive-cohesiveness relationship was practically nonexistent in the more recent period, but when the earlier studies were subdivided, they indicated a negative relationship under conditions of threat, a finding that appears inconsistent with the 1967 statement of the theory.

Stogdill's Research. Stogdill (1965) carried out extensive research in twenty-seven organizational units using rating and questionnaire measures of mediator and output variables (but not inputs). The measures were developed with the constructs of the theory in mind and are of satisfactory reliability. The organizational units were taken from metals, chemical, aircraft, textile, and retailing firms, and state government. Stogdill's own statement of the findings from factor analyses as they relate to the group-focused theory is as follows:

> The theory predicts the following findings in the present research:
>
> 1. Group productivity and cohesiveness are negatively related in several types of organizations.
>
> 2. Employee satisfaction is more highly related to group cohesiveness than to group productivity.
>
> The theory did not predict the following findings:
>
> 1. Supervisory leadership is more highly related to employee satisfaction than to group performance.
>
> 2. One aspect of employee attitudes (satisfaction with freedom on the job) is related to group drive.
>
> 3. Group drive and group cohesiveness are more highly related than was previously thought to be true (Stogdill, 1965, pp. 292–93).

Mediators such as responsibility and authority generally showed little relationship to output variables.

A subsequent correlational analysis of the output measures utilized in this research (Stogdill, 1972) produced significant negative relationships between productivity and cohesiveness (integration) in 38 percent of the units; there were no significant positive correlations. However, the expected positive correlation between productivity and drive (morale) occurred only 15 percent of the time, and there was one significant negative value. Drive and cohesiveness did not exhibit a consistent pattern, as hypothesized, though 58 percent of the correlations were positive in direction; only three values were significant, and these varied in sign.

In another study conducted within a single company, Stogdill (1967b) found varied levels of support and nonsupport for the output relationship hypotheses, depending on the particular measures of output variables utilized. Since many different measures of the same construct were used in the different studies considered in Stogdill's (1959, 1972) literature reviews, measurement factors may well account for the extremely variable results noted there. On the other hand, these findings do raise questions about construct validity. Either the constructs of the theory lack sufficient precision of definition or Stogdill has fitted measures to them too loosely.

In a final study Stogdill (1966) hypothesizes that under conditions of increased inputs, rather than the stable input states assumed (but not actually measured) in preceding studies, output variables may be positively intercorrelated. The study covered six football games and related coach's ratings of morale and integration and yards lost or gained (productivity) to each other. Morale, integration, and productivity were highly positively correlated on offense. Under game conditions, when major investments of effort (performances) and expectations can be anticipated over short periods of time, this result would be expected. However, this study, like all others, did not actually measure inputs.

Applications

As Stogdill (1959) noted originally, a theory need not define an applied technology, and indeed his has not done so. On the other hand, there is inherent in the theory a prescription that productivity should not be overemphasized—that a delicate balance between outputs is necessary to an effective organization. About obtaining this optimum balance between productivity, morale, and integration, Stogdill (1972, p. 40) says, "The methods for accomplishing this desirable state of affairs on a rational basis are yet to be developed. The most effective managers appear to obtain the balance intuitively." This would suggest that a technology might be developed by studying effective and ineffective managers as defined by their capacity to approximate the theoretical ideal.

Katz and Kahn's Open Systems Theory

Both Daniel Katz and Robert Kahn have been actively involved in the research of the Institute for Social Research at the University of Michigan from an early time (see Chapters 2 and 3). They acknowledge a clear debt to Rensis Likert. Yet in many respects their theorizing represents an alternative to system 4 theory (which is not really a systems theory), while maintaining a very similar value orientation.

The Social Psychology of Organizations (1966)

The book that first presents psychological open systems theory is in part a theoretical statement and in part a review of organizational literature in certain areas (Katz and Kahn, 1966). The theory is covered largely in the first seven chapters and reviewed in the last, though several important theoretical statements occur in the intervening chapters on power and authority and on leadership.

The Systems Concept. The basic model involves energic inputs, the transformation of these inputs within the system, and an output that recycles or returns as energic input to keep the system going. In many cases outcomes are converted to money, which in turn provides the needed input. The defining characteristics of such open systems are:

1. The importation of *energic inputs* from the social environment.

2. Transformation of available energy as *throughput*, so that work is done within the system.

3. The exportation of a product or *output* into the environment.

4. A *cycle of events* in which the product exported to the environment provides the energy for repetition of the cycle.

5. The development of *negative entropy* whereby more energy is imported from the environment than is expended in work, thus counteracting the entropic imperative, which inevitably tends toward disorganization and death.

6. The existence of *information inputs* or signals about how the environment and the system are functioning; *negative feedback* from internal functioning, which provides information to correct deviations from course; and a *coding* process that simplifies energic and information inputs and permits their selective reception.

7. A *steady state* that preserves the character of the system and is marked by a stable ratio of energy exchanges and relations between the parts.

8. Movement in the direction of increasing *differentiation*, elaboration, or specialization.

9. The operation of the principle of *equifinality* under which a system can achieve the same final state from different initial conditions and by various paths.

Defining Characteristics and Structures. Energic inputs are differentiated as *maintenance* inputs that sustain the system and *production* inputs that are processed and yield productive outputs. System integration is achieved through the operation of *roles*, or standardized patterns of behavior required of all who perform a function or set of tasks; *norms*, or expectations of role incumbents that serve to verbalize and sanction role requirements; and *values* that are even more general ideological justifications and aspirations.

The theory posits five basic types of subsystems:

1. *Production* or technical—concerned with the throughput and the work done.

2. *Supportive*—concerned with procurement of inputs, disposal of outputs, and institutional functions related to the environment.

3. *Maintenance*—concerned with tying people to their roles, either through selection of personnel or through rewards and sanctions, thus preserving the system.

4. *Adaptive*—concerned with adaptive change to environmental variations.

5. *Managerial*—concerned with direction, coordination, and control of other subsystems and activities. This system operates through the use of regulatory mechanisms that utilize feedback about output as related to input, and through authority structures that legitimize directives in some manner.

A number of other constructs and processes are proposed, the most theoretically relevant of which are system *boundaries*—those barriers between system and environment that determine degrees of openness for the system—and *leading* systems—those that exert greater influence over the inputs of other component systems, and thus control interactions.

The authors describe the developmental process in organizations as follows:

> At Stage 1 certain characteristics of a human population and some common environmental problem interact to generate task demands and a primitive production structure to fulfill them. At Stage 2 devices for formulating and enforcing rules appear. An authority structure emerges and becomes the basis for managerial and maintenance subsystems. Stage 3 sees the further elaboration of supportive structures at the organizational boundaries—structures for procurement, disposal, and institutional relations (Katz and Kahn, 1966, p. 109).

As set forth in Table 6–2, the consequence of this evolution is a set of structures, each with its own dynamic, or common motivation for the group, and mechanisms for achieving this dynamic. Within the managerial structure a maximization principle is hypothesized, which as a dynamic often tends to override the maintenance of a steady state. This is so because:

1. The proficiency dynamic leads to an increase in organizational capabilities.

2. Expansion is the simplest method of dealing with problems of internal strain.

3. Expansion is also the most direct solution in coping with problems of a changing social environment.

4. Bureaucratic role systems in their nature permit of ready elaboration.

5. Organizational ideology encourages growth aspirations (Katz and Kahn, 1966, pp. 99–100).

Organizational Typology and Effectiveness. Organizations fall into four major types, based on the functions they perform for society. Productive (economic) organizations create wealth, manufacture goods, and provide services. Maintenance organizations socialize people for their roles in society, including other organizations.

Table 6–2

The Dynamics and Mechanisms of Subsystem Structures

Subsystem Structure	Dynamic (Common Motivation)	Mechanisms
Production	Technical proficiency	Division of labor Job specifications and standards
Supportive (Boundary) 　Procurement and disposal	Focused manipulation of environment	Control of sources of supply Creation of image
Institutional	Social manipulation and integration	Contributing to community Influencing social structure
Maintenance	Maintaining steady state; predictability	Standard legitimized procedures System rewards Socialization
Adaptive	Pressing for change	Recommending changes to management
Managerial 　Conflict resolution within hierarchy	Control	Sanctions of authority
Coordinating functional structures	Compromise vs. integration	Alternative concessions Adjudication machinery
Coordinating external requirements with resources and needs	Long-term survival Optimization Improving resource use Increasing capabilities	Increasing business volume Adding functions Controlling environment Organization planning

Source: Adapted from Daniel Katz and Robert L. Kahn, *The Social Psychology of Organizations*. New York: Wiley, 1966, p. 86.

Adaptive organizations create knowledge and often apply it as well. Managerial (political) organizations adjudicate, coordinate, and control resources and people.

In addition, organizations may be classified in terms of many secondary characteristics. Among these are throughput as it relates to products or to people; maintenance through intrinsic or extrinsic rewards; degree of permeability of organizational boundaries; extent of structural elaboration; and steady state or maximization as the dominant dynamic.

A condition for organizational survival is negative entropy whereby more energy is brought into the organization than emerges as output. Some energy is consumed by the organization in creating and maintaining itself. If this amount is large, the organization is inefficient; thus, efficiency is defined in terms of the ratio of energic output to energic input.

Organizational effectiveness, on the other hand, is defined as the maximization of energic return to the organization by all means. To the extent economic and technical means are employed for energic return, efficiency is affected as well. But maximization by political means is also possible and often is of considerable significance. Here the maximization typically occurs at some cost to the environment, either in the form of other organizations (such as competitors) or individuals. However, the authors also define as political certain processes carried out within the organization's boundaries, such as paying lower wages than other firms. As they themselves indicate, their distinction between efficiency and political effectiveness as components of organizational effectiveness is somewhat arbitrary.

Organizational Roles. Katz and Kahn (1966) define an organization as an open system of roles, thus emphasizing a view of organizations as contrived in nature and consisting of a structure of acts or events. This role-related component of the theory was first proposed and defined at an earlier date (Kahn, Wolfe, Quinn, Snoek, and Rosenthal, 1964), as were other concepts and constructs.

Roles are made up of certain recurrent activities within the total, interrelated pattern that yields the organizational output. Specifically, roles are those activities existing within a single subsystem and a single office. An *office* is a point within organizational space consisting of one or more roles to be performed by individuals. Individuals are surrounded by others, including superiors and subordinates, who operate as role senders to them. This process of role sending and receiving is described in Figure 6–4. *Role conflict* occurs when compliance with role sendings of one type would make it difficult or impossible to comply with role sendings of another type. *Role ambiguity* arises from a lack of role-related information or inadequacies in the communication of such information. In an

Figure 6–4
Model of the Role Episode

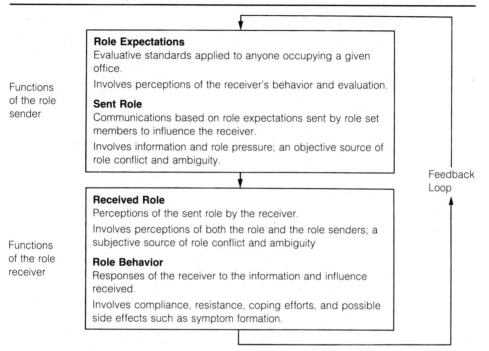

Functions
of the role
sender

Role Expectations
Evaluative standards applied to anyone occupying a given
office.
Involves perceptions of the receiver's behavior and evaluation.

Sent Role
Communications based on role expectations sent by role set
members to influence the receiver.
Involves information and role pressure; an objective source of
role conflict and ambiguity.

Feedback
Loop

Functions
of the role
receiver

Received Role
Perceptions of the sent role by the receiver.
Involves perceptions of both the role and the role senders; a
subjective source of role conflict and ambiguity

Role Behavior
Responses of the receiver to the information and influence
received.
Involves compliance, resistance, coping efforts, and possible
side effects such as symptom formation.

Source: Adapted from Robert L. Kahn, et al., *Organizational Stress: Studies in Role Conflict and Ambiguity*. New York: Wiley, 1964, p. 26. Daniel Katz and Robert Kahn, *The Social Psychology of Organizations*. New York: Wiley, 1966, p. 182.

ongoing organization the simplicity of Figure 6–4 is often disturbed
when one role involves many activities, when multiple roles exist
in a single office, or when one person occupies several offices.

Though Katz and Kahn tend to deemphasize hypothesis formulation, they offer four statements that they call interesting speculations or predictions about organizational roles:

1. The more activities contained within a role, the more
likely it is to be varied and satisfying, the more likely it is to
involve coordination among the activities it comprises, and
the less immediate will be the necessity for coordination with
other roles and offices.

2. The more interrole coordination an organization requires,
the more the achievement of coordination is assigned to
offices high in the organizational structure.

3. The more coordinative demands concentrated in a given
office, the more the incumbent seeks a generalized,
programmed solution. . . . Such a programmed solution is

sought because it can be set up to hold for a considerable period of time, thus relieving the incumbent of the continuing press of certain types of decisions.

4. The greater the programming of inter-job coordination, the greater will be the use of organizational authority and sanctions (Katz and Kahn, 1966, pp. 181–82).

Hierarchical and Democratic Systems. One other area in which specific hypotheses are formulated with regard to organizational process and structure is that of hierarchical versus democratic organization. Hierarchical systems are said to survive longer and to be more efficient:

1. When the tasks do not require creativity and when identification with organizational goals is not essential.

2. When environmental demands are clear and obvious so that information about them is redundant and multiple processors of this information are not needed.

3. When rapid decision making is necessary.

4. When the environment is such that it requires little adaptive change, thus approximating the conditions of a closed system.

Essentially the opposite set of conditions argue for a democratic organizational structure. With regard to formal, hierarchical structure the authors conclude:

It is an instrument of great effectiveness; it offers great economies over unorganized effort; it achieves great unity and compliance. We must face up to its deficiencies, however. These include great waste of human potential for innovation and creativity and great psychological cost to the members. . . . The modification of hierarchical organization to meet these criticisms is one of the great needs of human life (Katz and Kahn, 1966, p. 222).

Hierarchical Position and Leadership. Leadership theory rarely considers position in a hierarchical organization a variable of major importance (Miner, 1980). The work of Katz and Kahn (1966) is one exception. Effective leaders are differentiated by position level and by the types of relationships and role expectations associated with that level. These leadership requirements are outlined in Table 6–3. Presumably an organization staffed to meet these requirements at each level would be more effective than one not so staffed.

The Social Psychology of Organizations (1978)

The theory set forth in the 1978 edition of Katz and Kahn's original book is essentially unchanged, though there are many embellish-

Table 6–3
Leadership Requirements at Different Hierarchical Levels

Hierarchical Level	First-Level Supervision	Middle Management	Top Management
Nature of leadership required	Administration—the use of existing structure	Interpolation—supplementing and piecing out the structure	Origination—change, creation, and elimination of structure
Required cognitive abilities and skills	Technical knowledge Understanding of rules	Subsystem perspective—two-way orientation of leader	Systemic perspective—external and internal
Required emotional abilities and skills	Equity and fairness in applying rules and using sanctions	Integration of the immediate work group with the larger system (good human relations)	Charisma

SOURCE: Adapted from Daniel Katz and Robert L. Kahn, *The Social Psychology of Organizations.* New York: Wiley, 1966, p. 312.

ments and expanded examples. The book has grown by over 60 percent, but the additions are primarily nontheoretical.

The Principle of Integration. One change in the 1978 edition of Katz and Kahn's book is the explicit inclusion of integration as a characteristic of open systems. Thus the list of nine defining characteristics of open systems is extended to include *integration* and *coordination*. These characteristics counter differentiation and unify the system. Integration may be achieved through shared norms and values. Unification through coordination involves fixed control arrangements such as setting the speed of an assembly line.

As organizational structures grow, there is a tendency toward increased differentiation or specialization, followed by a complementary tendency toward increased integration or coordination. As the structure divides, integration is increasingly needed. Both differentiation and integration can be pushed beyond the point of maximum system return, however. An optimum point, and thus a curvilinear relation to efficiency, is posited. In particular the use of fixed coordination devices is questioned when they are applied at high levels across many units of the system. Making decisions at lower levels, where they can apply to a smaller slice of the organization, is considered preferable.

The Environment. Katz and Kahn's 1978 treatment devotes considerably more attention to the environment and to organizational methods of coping with it than did their 1966 version, thus countering a potential source of criticism for an open systems theory. Though much of the discussion draws heavily on the theory and research of others, some original theory is included.

Five environmental sectors within which organizations function are identified:

1. The value patterns of the cultural environment.
2. The political structure or pattern of legal norms and statutes.
3. The economic environment of competitive markets and inputs.
4. The informational and technological environment.
5. The natural or physical or ecological environment, including geography, natural resources, and climate.

Each of these sectors may vary along four dimensions drawn largely from sociotechnical systems theory (Chapter 4): stable to turbulent, homogeneous to diverse, random to clustered, and scarce to munificent. Thus an organization may have a stable natural environment and a turbulent economic one, and so on. Generally, Katz and Kahn do not hypothesize about relationships among dimensions across sectors, but instead stress the need for measurement and empirical study. However, the sectors are thought to reflect a hierarchy of complexity, especially with regard to turbulence. As a lower-level sector such as the natural environment fails to provide stability, each higher-level sector is mobilized for that purpose. If all else fails, including political stabilization, turbulence may be reduced by a resort to common cultural values in the manner advocated by sociotechnical systems theory.

Organizational response in coping with environments may be summarized as follows:

> The lack of assurance of sustained inputs and continuing markets for outputs leads to various forms of organizational response to reduce uncertainty. The first attempt is to control the environment directly and to incorporate it within the system. Then come efforts at indirect control through influencing other systems by means of political manipulation or economic bargaining. Or the organization may move to change its own structure to accord with environmental change. The concept of the temporary society can be considered in this context for it calls for adaptive, problem-solving task forces (Katz and Kahn, 1978, p. 141).

Research on Open Systems Theory and the Application Void

Research on the basic open systems formulations of Katz and Kahn is limited. A number of studies such as Pfeffer's (1972) investigation of mergers take their lead from open systems concepts. But such studies typically cite several related theoretical positions at once. The most that can be said about the theory from this type of research is that environmental factors are important for organizations and that organizations attempt to cope with these factors. There is nothing, other than general support for an open systems concept, that bears specifically on the constructs and hypotheses of the Katz and Kahn (1966, 1978) theory as distinct from similar theories, some of which precede by a number of years the first Katz and Kahn statement. The problem appears to be that psychological open systems theory is stated abstractly without any indication of how to measure the variables operationally. Such circumstances almost invariably stifle research on a theory, because researchers cannot be sure they are really testing the theory.

A rare instance of research that appears to relate specifically to the theory is a study by Staw and Szwajkowski (1975). This study tests the general proposition that organizations must import resources from the environment to survive and that in less munificent environments organizations will exert greater effort to obtain these resources. The specific hypothesis tested was that in scarce environments companies will be more likely to engage in unfair market practices or restraint of trade to procure added resources. This hypothesis represented an extrapolation from the Katz and Kahn (1966) statements. The research was subsequently used in Katz and Kahn (1978) in the formulation of more specific statements on the effects of environmental scarcity or munificence.

Staw and Szwajkowski (1975) found that companies involved in litigation over practices such as price fixing, illegal merger, refusal to deal, and the like had not only been less profitable over the preceding five years, but also came from industries that were equally low in profitability. The data are given in Table 6–4. Though they do not unequivocally support a causal interpretation running from environmental scarcity to increased effort to secure inputs, they certainly are highly consistent with such a hypothesis.

Role-Related Research

Because of the segmented nature of the Katz and Kahn theory, it is possible to test parts of the theory without saying much about the remainder. This is particularly true of the formulations about organizational roles that antedated the major theoretical statement by two years. Actually the role-related concepts have been the subject of considerable research, which often has supported the theory.

The Original Organizational Stress Studies. Kahn, Wolfe, Quinn, Snoek, and Rosenthal (1964) studied role processes associated with fifty-three offices in the managerial subsystems of seven firms. They conducted standardized interviews with role receivers to get at role perceptions and responses and with role senders for each receiver to get at role expectations and pressures. In addition, a nationwide survey dealing with role conflict and ambiguity was used to determine the generalizability of the intensive study results. This survey involved 725 employed individuals.

The findings indicate widespread role conflict and ambiguity. Both phenomena have negative consequences for the individual, including reduced job satisfaction, low confidence, and tension, as well as a tendency to withdraw from the sources of tension. Role conflict tends to be high in boundary-spanning positions, those extending both outside the company and outside the department, in innovative problem-solving positions, and in management positions. Individuals differ not only in the degree of objective role conflict they elicit from senders, but also in the degree of role stress they actually experience.

Though organizational performance was not measured in this research, the authors argue strongly for the desirability of reducing role stress. This need appears to increase as organizations grow in size, up to about 5,000 persons; beyond that point the stress curve levels off. The increase with size is attributed to burgeoning coordination devices, which in turn increase the potential for role conflict. The solution recommended is giving each work group as much autonomy as possible. When the principle of coordinative economy is followed, the organization is "decentralized, flat, and lean, a federated rather than a lofty structure" (Katz et al., 1964, p. 395). Whether such organizations are more effective is, of course, an empirical question, extending well beyond the bounds of the research into roles actually conducted.

Table 6–4

Comparisons of Financial Performance of Fortune 500 Firms Cited for Illegal Acts, All Firms in Their Industries, and All Fortune 500 Firms

	Mean Performance		
	Cited Firms	Industries of Cited Firms	All Fortune 500 Firms
Return on equity	(9.6	9.8)	11.5
Return on sales	(5.4	5.1)	6.0

( ) Figures differ significantly, *not* from each other, but from those for all Fortune 500 firms.

Source: Adapted from Barry M. Staw and Eugene Szwajkowski, "The Scarcity-Munificence Component of Organizational Environments and the Commission of Illegal Acts," *Administrative Science Quarterly*, 20 (1975), p. 349.

Later Research. The finding that negative consequences for both the individual and the organization are associated with role conflict and ambiguity is one of the best substantiated in the organizational theory literature (Greene, 1972; Posner and Butterfield, 1978; Rizzo, House, and Lirtzman, 1970). In this respect the Katz and Kahn theory receives strong support. Some positive evidence antedated the theory and may well have influenced its formulation. However, enough research has been conducted since to allay any concerns about post hoc theorizing. There are studies that do not support the theory, but these are few in number, and the negative results usually can be accounted for by special aspects of the particular study.

A major factor contributing to the large amount of role-related research appears to be the development of adequate measuring instruments (Rizzo, House, and Lirtzman, 1970). With such instruments it has been possible to establish relationships with indexes of organizational effectiveness, thus extending the scope of the findings beyond that of the original research (Kahn et al., 1964). In one study, for example, a significant correlation of .37 was obtained between a role clarity measure and the effectiveness of twenty regional offices of an insurance company (Posner and Butterfield, 1978).

Reformulations at the Subsystem Level. A series of publications (Doll, 1977a, 1977b; Doll and Melcher, 1976) report on attempts to operationalize certain constructs of the Katz and Kahn theory and relate the constructs to behavior. In this research the independent variables are role expectations, norms, and values as measured by questionnaire items. The dependent variables are commitment to membership, dependability of role performance, and the degree of extra-role performance that spontaneously supports organizational goals; these three contribute to an overall index of individual behavior. Independent and dependent variables seem to have been measured within the same questionnaire. Reliabilities are said to be satisfactory, but are not reported.

In operationalizing variables, this research often moves beyond the Katz and Kahn (1966) statements. In addition, new hypotheses are occasionally derived from the theory. These procedures are justified on the grounds that the original theory is too loosely stated to be tested. However, one wonders if the Katz and Kahn theory or some other explanation was in fact tested. On the other hand, this research indicates how useful the theoretical constructs and variables may be as building blocks in the development of more precise and sophisticated theories.

Table 6–5 shows the correlations between certain aspects of production and maintenance subsystems and overall individual behavior. Subjects were 226 individuals occupying various roles in twenty-five organizations. As hypothesized, the increasing complexity of the production subsystem that accompanies increasing size is associated with less efficient behavior. The only departure from this pattern is the lack of a significant relationship between unpredictable role behavior and overall behavior. Within the maintenance subsystem the hypothesized relationships consistently occurred, but role expectations regarding intrinsic satisfactions in the work appear to be most important. Overall, the data clearly support the reformulated theory. Similar results were obtained when communication processes were studied (Doll, 1977b).

The Hierarchical Concepts

A most striking aspect of the Katz and Kahn theory is its segmented nature. With many theories, verification of one hypothesis leads to the assumption of truth for other logically related hypotheses. This often cannot be done with Katz and Kahn's formulations. The role-

Table 6–5
Correlations Between Aspects of Production and Maintenance Subsystems and Overall Behavior

Independent Variables	Dependent Variable: Overall Behavior
Production subsystem	
Complexity of the role set	(− .35)
Degree to which functional specialization is extensive (many role restrictions)	(− .41)
Unpredictability of role behavior	.09
Degree to which role expectations regarding task demands are high	(− .32)
Maintenance subsystem	
Degree to which role expectations relate extrinsic rewards to performance and seniority	(.23)
Degree to which role expectations associating intrinsic satisfactions with role performance are extensive	(.51)
Degree to which role expectations associate undesirable behavior with institutionalized rather than capricious punishments	(.28)
Degree to which values and norms are explicit	(.36)

( ) Correlations statistically significant.

SOURCE: Adapted from William J. Doll and Arlyn S. Melcher, "The Production Subsystem of the Katz and Kahn Framework—A Reformulation and Empirical Evaluation," *Midwest Division of the Academy of Management Proceedings*, 1976, p. 292. William J. Doll, "The Maintenance Subsystem of the Katz and Kahn Framework," *Midwest Division of the Academy of Management Proceedings*, 1977, p. 340.

related concepts have no necessary relationships to open systems concepts; they could be embedded in a quite different theoretical milieu and still operate in the same manner. Similarly, the theoretical statements regarding hierarchical versus democratic systems and the hierarchical concept of leadership have no necessary relationships to the rest of the theory. Accordingly, the research evidence that follows must be considered applicable only within very narrow limits.

The Use of Rules. Hierarchical systems hypothetically function best when creativity is not required, environments are obvious, rapid decisions are needed, and closed system conditions apply. Baum (1978) tested the effects of a strongly rules-oriented procedure for handling absenteeisms under circumstances he interpreted as hierarchically ideal. The objective was to compare the effects on chronic absentees of hierarchically controlled procedures and preestablished punishments with decentralized, flexible control conditions. The results clearly support the hierarchical approach under the circumstances specified. Absenteeism was reduced substantially more under experimental conditions than under control conditions.

The above findings support the Katz and Kahn theory as long as one assumes that conditions appropriate for a hierarchical approach existed. In a previous study that compared the effects of a similar legalistic approach on classroom attendance with a laissez-faire approach, the results were similar. Both attendance and performance improved under the standardized attendance rules (Baum and Youngblood, 1975). The two studies combined suggest that preestablished, hierarchical approaches with high legitimacy may be effective, irrespective of circumstances. It is not at all certain that a classroom environment meets the theoretical requirements for a hierarchical system, though some might contend that an intermediate accounting class of the kind used in this research does.

The Three-Pattern Approach to Leadership. The hierarchical approach to leadership has stimulated very little research, though there is reason to believe hierarchy makes some difference, as noted in Chapter 2. A recent review of the related literature, while crediting Katz and Kahn with an important theoretical contribution, cites little evidence to support or contradict their views (Kmetz, 1978).

One exception is a study contrasting various leadership theories (Mott, 1972). Measures of the required cognitive and emotional abilities and skills other than charisma, as set forth in Table 6–3, were developed specifically for the study. These were related to effectiveness measures obtained at the division and branch levels of an organization. Matching the two levels of management to the three levels specified by the theory presents a problem. Presumably, however, the branch managers were either first-level supervisors or middle managers and the division managers either middle- or top-level leaders.

None of the measures was related to branch effectiveness, so the theory fails to gain support there in any event. Furthermore, technical skill and fairness were significantly related to division effectiveness, which they should not have been according to the theory. Significant relationships were also obtained at the division level for subsystem perspective and integration. These correlations were in accord with the theory and were the highest obtained in the study. Systemic perspective did not achieve a satisfactory level of significance. Overall, the data indicate that the variables of the Katz and Kahn theory are related to organizational effectiveness, but not necessarily in the exact manner specified by the theory.

The Application Void

Like Stogdill's version, Katz and Kahn's version of systems theory has not been a source of specific, new applications. However, the authors do discuss applications, and certain potential uses are inherent in some of their other work.

Applications Derived from Other Sources. In their writing about open systems theory the authors endorse certain applications, particularly some change procedures (Katz and Georgopoulos, 1971; Katz and Kahn, 1966, 1978). They note the general need for an enlargement of adaptive subsystems to cope with changing environments and new social inputs.

In this connection Katz and Kahn advocate a much greater application of democratic principles. They recommend the use of project teams that combine service and production functions, sensitivity training, and organization development programs of various kinds. The objective is to move toward a system with broader, more flexible roles and more open subsystem boundaries—in short, debureaucratization. At the same time, value changes are needed:

> The task for the adaptive processes of an organization is one of the creative adaptation of central values to changing inputs. . . . Adaptation through genuine participation and active involvement based upon democratic principles and processes can still be successful. The great need of our time is a reformulation of social values that would make possible a higher level of integration for all social systems (Katz and Georgopoulos, 1971, pp. 365–66).

With regard to legislated placement of worker representatives on corporate boards as a step toward representative democracy along lines that have become commonplace in Europe, the authors have this to say:

> The movement toward legislated worker representation in the conduct of enterprise is both a significant force for future organizational change and a reflection of changes that have already occurred at the organizational level. An employing organization is a system that exists in a larger social context, and that context includes both labor unions and legislative bodies. Organizational change can be extended or contained, accelerated or retarded, demanded or denied by these contextual agencies (Katz and Kahn, 1978, p. 746).

These endorsements of democratization within organization do not represent a necessary logical outgrowth of open systems theory, even though they are stated in the terminology of the theory. In fact the attendance control system developed by Baum (1978), which appears to be a logical development from the theory, clearly moves in the direction of hierarchical rather than democratic processes. Other theories considered in this volume contain inherent rationales for the generally democratizing change procedures they have either generated or embraced. The theories may be wrong, but if they are right, the applications proposed follow logically. This is much less true of the psychological open systems theories that are essentially neutral in the hierarchy-democracy debate. Given this situation, it is difficult to understand why Katz and Kahn recommend democratization, except as a value as opposed to a scientific conclusion.

Possible Uses in Working Theory. Since psychological open systems theory was first published, its constructs often have been used to interpret organizational phenomena and the results of research studies. In these instances the theory has not been tested, but rather used as a framework for explaining organizational processes.

Thus, Katz and Golomb (1974–1975) used the concepts of integration (role expectations, norms, and values), effectiveness, and adaptive value modification at the individual, systemic, and societal levels to analyze the kibbutzim communities in Israel. The authors also used their constructs of boundary transactions and environmental feedback systems as a framework for a study of the reactions of recipients of government services to their "bureaucratic encounters" (Kahn, Katz, and Gutek, 1976; Katz, Gutek, Kahn, and Barton, 1975) and for an analysis of feedback as it operates in social systems in general and in governmental program evaluation in particular (Katz, 1975). Similarly, Smith and King (1975) utilized open systems concepts in their study of the effectiveness of different mental hospitals. Rosen (1970) did not originally formulate his study of the effects of rotating foremen across work groups in open systems theory terms, but he found the theory useful in developing an ad hoc interpretation of the results.

These examples suggest that the theory, or at least certain constructs of the theory, might be useful to practitioners in developing working theories to cope with day-to-day decisions in ongoing organizations. Managers in particular need such working theories to filter and organize the information that comes to them. Inevitably they will develop some theories, and the Katz and Kahn framework offers some promise for this purpose. However, if the theory is to be widely applied in this way, it will have to be restated and transmitted with this purpose in mind, either in published form or through management development programs. To date, neither the authors nor anyone else has undertaken such an effort.

Conclusions

Systems theory has had a broad impact on thinking in a number of fields. For organization theory it was a whole new way of looking at organizations and their environments. Its arrival was widely heralded, and many predicted that it would be the source of new and important breakthroughs in knowledge. For some time now, however, even some of its strongest advocates have evidenced a degree of disenchantment (Scott, 1974). The breakthroughs have not come, or at least not on the scale anticipated. The problems seem to lie in the theory's extremely wide-ranging and highly abstract constructs and in its inability to spawn a significant body of research. In psychological systems theory at least, these factors are closely related.

Scientific Goals

To some extent the problems are inherent in the basic nature of systems theory:

> In some respects open-system theory is not a theory at all; it does not pretend to the specific sequences of cause and effect, the specific hypotheses and tests of hypotheses which are the basic elements of theory. Open-system theory is rather a framework, a meta-theory, a model in the broadest sense of that overused term. Open-system theory is an approach and a conceptual language for understanding and describing many kinds and levels of phenomena (Katz and Kahn, 1966, p. 452; 1978, p. 752).

Much the same kind of statement appears in Stinchcombe's critique of the Stogdill theory:

> The intellectual purpose . . . is the same as that of an outline
> for a textbook on organizations. It is a list of general topics,
> under which one can discuss the identification of crucial
> phenomena, their explanation, and the general generating
> mechanisms that might explain them. One cannot say of an
> outline for a book that it is true or false, logically consistent
> or inconsistent, economical or prolix, powerful or weak.
> These are criteria that apply to explanatory theories (Goldner
> and Stinchcombe, 1967, p. B678).

A general principle in systems theory is that everything relates to everything else. In practice, at least for psychological systems theories, this has meant that causal hypotheses are minimized; the theories tend to be static rather than dynamic. Though both the Stogdill and Katz and Kahn theories state hypotheses, as often as not these hypotheses lack a clear tie to the basic open system model. They are not logically embedded in the model, and thus their research confirmation provides no value added insofar as the larger theory is concerned. This problem exists less for Stogdill, and not at all in his more recent mathematical statement of the theory; it is a major difficulty with the Katz and Kahn formulations.

The failure to generate research is in part a consequence of the lack of hypotheses to test and in part a consequence of the highly abstract and general nature of those hypotheses that do emerge. Many of the theoretical variables are presented without reference to operationalization at all. As a result, the researcher must guess at what would be an appropriate measure and, having done so, like Doll (1977a), be faced with the real possibility of not having tested the original theory at all. Another consequence of the very general nature of the systems theory formulations is illustrated by Stogdill's output variables. Here the problem is that a wide range of measures, many of them having little empirical relationship to each other, are accepted as measures of the constructs. Stogdill (1965) himself offers multiple measures having low correlations with each other. Again there is a construct validity problem, and it rests in the extremely broad, abstract way in which variables are defined.

In general, psychologists and those with a psychological orientation to the organizational theory field have viewed Stogdill's formulations quite favorably (Filley and House, 1975; Jacobs, 1971; Schriesheim and Bird, 1979). The solid base of research evidence underlying the construction of the theory makes it extremely attractive and leads one to forget the sparcity of posttheory tests. The same use of extensive literature reviews characterized the original presentation of the Katz and Kahn (1966) views and is even more evident in their 1978 statement. To some degree, the undeniable excellence of the authors' underlying scholarship may have fostered uncritical acceptance of their theories. In any event it is apparent that sociologists have been much less impressed (Goldner and Stinchcombe, 1967; Silverman, 1970).

Stogdill struggled with these and other problems with his theory for over twenty years. He revised it constantly. The original statement assumed a close parallel between group and organization that does not now appear warranted, and it neglected the environment. Like many psychologists, Stogdill was apparently more comfortable theorizing about individuals and groups than about large organizations. He tried to work up through an intergroup model, but that effort was admittedly incomplete. Then he began listing variables at the organization and environment levels with the prospect of moving from this to a full-blown theory. The result was confusing. It was not clear how the old and new variables related to each other, and true theoretical hypotheses never were developed. The problems of measurement became even more acute.

Ultimately, Stogdill appears to have recognized that the broad, abstract definitions of variables in the early theory were unlikely to produce confirming research evidence—the gap from theory to research was too great. So he attempted to develop precise hypotheses in mathematical form, using variables of much more limited scope. He broke down the original constructs into smaller units and, accordingly, was able to bridge the gap between model construction and theory building. Such an effort runs a high risk of being wrong; the hypotheses really can be tested. Stogdill did not publish this version of the theory, though he did write it out in a working paper. No research has been done on it, though it has enough logical coherence and related evidence to justify a research investment in it.

Certainly, Stogdill's final theory is the most promising. Earlier versions, insofar as they have been tested, still lack research support. The most extensive work has been done on the hypothesized relationships among output variables. The data do not consistently support these hypotheses. However, the hypotheses are predicated on the stability of inputs. Since input measures have not been devised, it is impossible to know whether the inputs might have varied in any given study. Accordingly, the research that has been conducted cannot be considered an adequate test of the theory. Satisfactory tests of Stogdill's theory are simply too sparse to justify conclusions. As a scientist, one must keep an open mind and say "I don't know."

The Katz and Kahn formulations are a special problem because they are so highly segmented. Even within theoretical segments, integrating hypotheses often are lacking. Thus we do not know how organizational subsystems would be expected to affect each other or how specific role expectations, norms, and values contribute to integration. As the authors themselves note, they have created some models and provided generalized definitions of constructs. In given areas they formulate hypotheses, but not always. Thus it becomes necessary to evaluate the theory in its separate parts.

The strongest support for Katz and Kahn's formulations is found in role theory, especially in the role episode concepts set forth in Figure 6–4. The evidence on the effects of role conflict and ambiguity is very convincing. Yet even in the role area, certain hypotheses, such as those regarding role size and the use of programmed solutions, remain untested.

The evidence also is insufficient or inadequate for other Katz and Kahn hypotheses such as their recently formulated statements about the environment and those dealing with the negative effects of increasing coordination and control procedures in response to organizational growth. The hypotheses related to hierarchy face major data problems. As discussed in Chapter 5, the relationship between hierarchy and adaptive innovation is complex, but the hypothesis of a simple, negative relationship does not fit the evidence. Katz and Kahn state their hypotheses about hierarchical versus democratic systems and about leadership abilities in contingent terms, but the research does not support the contingency variables proposed.

In many areas of the Katz and Kahn theory there is either no research or the research that has been done, such as Doll's (1977a, 1977b) and Baum's (1978), is not conclusive. In the literature one encounters frequent references to the Katz and Kahn formulations, but they are more often cited for conceptual clarification than for research hypotheses. When the theory is considered in formulating hypotheses, it tends to be used at such a high level of abstraction that it cannot be differentiated from a number of similar theories. Often the concepts are stated so broadly they contribute very little to prediction and understanding.

Goals of Application

Neither the Stogdill nor the Katz and Kahn theory is yet ready for application; there is some question whether either one ever will be ready. Stogdill mentions the need for a manager to maintain a balance of outputs. Others question this need (Goldner and Stinchcombe, 1967), and the research data on output relationships do not warrant any conclusion on this point at present.

The models and concepts of open systems theory seem to be helpful to many people in thinking about organizational phenomena. For this reason a reformulation of the theory to permit its use by managers was suggested. Very little has been done along these lines. There have been some attempts in certain areas, such as Miner's (1969) model for the personnel function, but they remain limited in scope and incomplete.

Katz and Kahn (1978) and Katz and Georgopoulos (1971) do recommend a number of democratic applications. However, these applications do not derive logically from their theory, and certain other theories considered in preceding chapters provide a much better rationale for industrial democracy. As we have noted, psychological systems theory covers a broad range at a typically high level of abstraction. As a result, it applies equally well to hierarchical and democratic systems, a consideration that some reviewers consider a major advantage (Filley and House, 1975).

In discussing theory only, Katz and Kahn (1966, 1978), like Stogdill (1959), exhibit considerable balance in a manner consistent with their theoretical constructs. Sometimes, as they follow the logic of their theory, they come to hierarchical solutions, as in the case of the attendance control procedures studied by Baum (1978). Other times they arrive at democratic solutions, as in the case of the tendency to increase systemwide coordination with growth. It is only when they move on to applications per se that their statements become inappropriately one-sided and more value- than science-based. They may be right, but not because of their theory. Psychological systems theory in and of itself is neutral on the hierarchy-democracy question in organizations. In this regard it differs sharply from the theories considered in preceding chapters.

References

Baum, John F. "Effectiveness of an Attendance Control Policy in Reducing Chronic Absenteeism," *Personnel Psychology*, 31 (1978), 71–81.

Baum, John F., and Stuart A. Youngblood. "Impact of an Organizational Control Policy on Absenteeism, Performance, and Satisfaction," *Journal of Applied Psychology*, 60 (1975), 688–94.

Doll, William J. "The Maintenance Subsystem of the Katz and Kahn Framework," *Midwest Division of the Academy of Management Proceedings*, 1977a, pp. 334–45.

———. "The Regulatory Mechanisms of the Katz and Kahn Framework," *Academy of Management Proceedings*, 1977b, pp. 188–97.

Doll, William J., and Arlyn S. Melcher. "The Production Subsystem of the Katz and Kahn Framework—A Reformulation and Empirical Evaluation," *Midwest Division of the Academy of Management Proceedings*, 1976, pp. 285–96.

Filley, Alan C., and Robert J. House. "A Summary of Stogdill's Theory of Individual Behavior and Group Achievement." In Henry L. Tosi (ed.), *Theories of Organization*. Chicago: St. Clair, 1975, pp. 139–52.

Goldner, Fred H., and Arthur L. Stinchcombe. "Critique of: Basic Concepts for a Theory of Organization," *Management Science*, 13 (1967), B677–80.

Greene, Charles N. "Relationships among Role Accuracy, Compliance, Performance Evaluation, and Satisfaction within Managerial Dyads," *Academy of Management Journal*, 15 (1972), 205–15.

Jacobs, T. O. *Leadership and Exchange in Formal Organizations*. Alexandria, Va.: Human Resources Research Organization, 1971.

Kahn, Robert L., Daniel Katz, and Barbara Gutek. "Bureaucratic Encounters—An Evaluation of Government Services," *Journal of Applied Behavioral Science*, 12, (1976), 178–98.

Kahn, Robert L., Donald M. Wolfe, Robert P. Quinn, J. Diedrick Snoek, and Robert A. Rosenthal. *Organizational Stress: Studies in Role Conflict and Ambiguity*. New York: Wiley, 1964.

Katz, Daniel. "Feedback in Social Systems: Operational and Systemic Research on Production, Maintenance, Control, and Adaptive Functions." In C. A. Bennett and A. A. Lumsdaine (eds.), *Evaluation and Experiment: Some Critical Issues in Assessing Social Programs*. New York: Academic Press, 1975.

Katz, Daniel, and Basil S. Georgopoulos. "Organizations in a Changing World," *Journal of Applied Behavioral Science*, 7 (1971), 342–70.

Katz, Daniel, and Naphtali Golomb. "Integration, Effectiveness and Adaptation in Social Systems: A Comparative Analysis of Kibbutzim Communities," *Administration and Society*, 6 (1974–75), 283–315, 389–421.

Katz, Daniel, Barbara A. Gutek, Robert L. Kahn, and Eugenia Barton. *Bureaucratic Encounters: A Pilot Study in the Evaluation of Government Services*. Ann Arbor, Mich.: Institute for Social Research, University of Michigan, 1975.

Katz, Daniel, and Robert L. Kahn. *The Social Psychology of Organizations*. New York: Wiley, 1966, 1978.

Kmetz, John L. "Leadership and Organizational Structure: A Critique and an Argument for Synthesis." Paper presented at the Conference on the Functioning of Complex Organizations, West Berlin, Germany, 1978.

Miner, John B. "An Input-Output Model for Personnel Strategies," *Business Horizons*, 12, no. 3 (1969), 71–78.

———. *Theories of Organizational Behavior*. Hinsdale, Ill.: Dryden, 1980.

Mott, Paul E. *The Characteristics of Effective Organizations*. New York: Harper & Row, 1972.

Parsons, Talcott. *The Social System*. Glencoe, Ill.: Free Press, 1951.

Pfeffer, Jeffrey. "Merger as a Response to Organizational Interdependence," *Administrative Science Quarterly*, 17 (1972), 382–94.

Posner, Barry Z., and D. Anthony Butterfield. "Role Clarity and Organizational Level," *Journal of Management*, 4, no. 2 (1978), 81–90.

Rizzo, John R., Robert J. House, and Sidney I. Lirtzman. "Role Conflict and Ambiguity in Complex Organizations," *Administrative Science Quarterly*, 15 (1970), 150–63.

Rosen, Ned A. "Open Systems Theory in an Organizational Sub-system: A Field Experiment," *Organizational Behavior and Human Performance*, 5 (1970), 245–65.

Schriesheim, Chester A., and Barbara J. Bird. "Contributions of the Ohio State Studies to the Field of Leadership," *Journal of Management*, 5 (1979), 135–45.

Scott, William G. "Organization Theory: A Reassessment," *Academy of Management Journal*, 17 (1974), 242–54.

Silverman, David. *The Theory of Organisations*. New York: Basic Books, 1970.

Smith, Clagett G., and James A. King. *Mental Hospitals: A Study in Organizational Effectiveness.* Lexington, Mass.: Heath, 1975.

Staw, Barry M., and Eugene Szwajkowski. "The Scarcity-Munificence Component of Organizational Environments and the Commission of Illegal Acts," *Administrative Science Quarterly,* 20 (1975), 345–54.

Stogdill, Ralph M. *Individual Behavior and Group Achievement.* New York: Oxford University Press, 1959.

————. "Intragroup-Intergroup Theory and Research." In Muzafer Sherif (ed.), *Intergroup Relations and Leadership.* New York: Wiley, 1962, pp. 48–65.

————. *Managers, Employees, Organizations.* Columbus, Ohio: Bureau of Business Research, Ohio State University, 1965.

————. "Dimensions of Organization Theory." In James D. Thompson (ed.), *Approaches to Organizational Design.* Pittsburgh, Pa.: University of Pittsburgh Press, 1966, pp. 3–56.

————. "Basic Concepts for a Theory of Organization," *Management Science,* 13 (1967a), B665–76.

————. "The Structure of Organization Behavior," *Multivariate Behavioral Research,* 2 (1967b), 47–61.

————. "Group Productivity, Drive, and Cohesiveness," *Organizational Behavior and Human Performance,* 8 (1972), 26–43.

————. "A Behavioral Model of Organization." Unpublished manuscript, Ohio State University, 1974.

7

Sociological Open Systems Theory

Though the field of sociology has spawned more than one theory of organizational functioning and structure that utilizes systems concepts (see Tosi, 1975), the work of James Thompson is more centrally focused on the open systems approach than are the others. Thompson's theory is tied closely to the theories considered in Chapter 6. In its concern with technological variables it also is related to the theories discussed in Chapter 8; in its concern with decision making it has much in common with the theories treated in Chapter 11. Above all else, it is an open systems theory dealing with organization-environment relationships and their effects.

Thompson obtained his sociology degree from the University of North Carolina and became one of the first behavioral scientists to join a business school faculty (at Cornell). He subsequently held business school appointments at the University of Pittsburgh and Indiana University, before returning to a sociology department at Vanderbilt. He died in 1973.

Throughout most of his career, Thompson was a conceptualizer and theorist rather than a researcher, though he did conduct some original organizational research at an early point (Thompson, 1956). His later research derived form secondary sources and was not focused on the major hypotheses of his theory (McNeil and Thompson, 1971). He wrote sparingly and succinctly. Two books contain practically all his theoretical writings, and those who read these books typically find themselves going back over sentences again and again to glean their full meaning.

The Theoretical Propositions of James Thompson

Thompson presented many of his ideas initially in various essay-type articles. These ideas subsequently were polished and extensively supplemented in his major work, *Organizations in Action* (Thompson, 1967). He published a textbook dealing with the behavioral sciences in general (Thompson and Van Houten, 1970), and after his death, editors prepared a volume containing the papers that led up to *Organizations in Action*, selections from that book, and certain subsequent contributions, not all of which are focused on organizational issues (Rushing and Zald, 1976).

Thompson's primary approach to theory construction was the conceptual inventory—a series of parallel propositions, usually stated in somewhat abstract terms, conceptually derived rather than drawn from an extensive perusal of existing research. This conceptual emphasis distinguishes Thompson from March and Simon (1958) and Berelson and Steiner (1964) whose approaches to proposition formulation involved much greater empirical generalization.

The theoretical variables are not tightly interrelated logically, however; the propositions do not derive from a common set of postulates and assumptions, as is the case with the most rigorous deductive theories. Rather, sets of propositions are developed to deal with various areas of major concern in the study of organizations.

Early Papers

Though we will rely on Thompson (1967) for a formal statement of the theory, knowledge of the variables considered in prior publications should facilitate understanding. Early on, Thompson established propositions based on such variables as the abstractness of the organization's goal as reflected in its product, the ease of utilizing the technology for new purposes, and the degree of mechanization as opposed to professionalization of the technology (Thompson and Bates, 1957).

Decision Making and Conflict. Subsequently, Thompson and McEwen (1958) analyzed organizational decision making in the goal-setting context. Organizations must gain support from their environments in setting goals, and this is accomplished by using the strategies of *competition* (rivalry between two or more organizations for the exchange of goods and services), *co-optation* (absorbing outsiders into the policy-making structure of the organization to avert threat), and *coalition*, (combining organizations for a common purpose). As one moves up the scale from competition to coalition, environmental conditioning becomes increasingly costly, with coalition being the most extreme strategy.

Thompson and Tuden (1959) look at the internal processes of organizational decision, utilizing the proposition that the role of administration is often to manage the decision process as well as make the decisions. The key variables are the degree of agreement or disagreement among decision makers in their beliefs about the causation of alternative actions and in their preferences for possible outcomes. When agreement is high on both dimensions, decisions are made by specialists' *computations* and the appropriate structure is *bureaucracy*. When agreement about causation is lacking, decisions are made by majority *judgment* (voting) and the appropriate structure is a *collegium*. When agreement about outcomes is lacking, decisions are made by bargaining and *compromise* within a *representative body*. When disagreement rules on both dimensions, an *inspirational* decision, perhaps made by a charismatic leader, is needed, and the ideal structure involves the randomness and disorganization of *anomie*. Again, organizational costs associated with decision making increase as one moves from computation, through judgment and compromise, to inspiration.

Conflict in organizations is in part a function of the differentiations and interactions required by their technologies, but organizations also can exercise some control over these processes and thus have a degree of discretion in handling conflict (Thompson, 1960). In addition to technology, the labor force and the heterogeneity of the task environment (the part of the environment that is not indifferent to the organization) can be sources of conflict. Technology produces conflict based on administrative allocations, and defense against conflict is achieved through varying organizational structures. The labor force produces conflict because employees bring latent roles to the job, as with nepotism and patronage; defense is achieved by limiting diversity through recruitment and selection. The task environment yields conflict as a result of competing pressures, and the defense against this is manipulating the exposure of members to these pressures.

Systems Formulations. The preceding statements do not utilize systems concepts explicitly, though they certainly imply them. However, in 1962 Thompson wrote a paper in which he focused on output roles and the nature of boundary-spanning transactions. The major variables considered were the degree to which the output role incumbent was armed with set routines for dealing with individuals in the environment, such as customers, and the degree to which these nonmembers were compelled to participate in a relationship with the output role occupant. Thompson and Hawkes (1962) also utilize the open system concept explicitly in discussing reactions to community disaster.

By 1964 Thompson had begun to incorporate these systems formulations into his propositions on organizational functioning:

1. Variations in environmental conditions will bring about changes in decision strategies for input and output components of the firm.

2. Variations in environmental conditions can penetrate the input and output "buffers" and cause changes in the technical core of the organization (thus violating the ideal isolation of the technical core in its mediating role).

3. Variations in environmental conditions will alter the dependence of input, technical core, and output components relative to one another.

4. When input or output components transfer uncertainty rather than absorb it, there will be conflict among input, technical core and output components (Thompson, 1964, pp. 341–42).

At this point what had been a series of segmented theories of decision making, conflict, boundary roles, and the like was beginning to fuse into a more comprehensive statement under the open systems rubric.

Organizations in Action

Thompson's (1967) theory spans a wide organizational domain, but it does not include voluntary organizations. The organizations covered operate as open systems facing uncertainty, but at the same time they need certainty; it is in this latter sense that they are said to be subject to criteria of rationality. Both the environment and technology are sources of uncertainty.

Rationality. Organizations engage in input activities. To be rational they strive to make their core technologies function as well as possible, and to accomplish this they seek to seal off these technologies from environmental influences—thus approximating closed system conditions.

Buffering on both the input and output sides is one way to stabilize the environment of the technical core. Examples of input buffering are stockpiling of raw materials and preventive maintenance; an example of output buffering would be using warehoused product inventories to deal with market fluctuations.

To the extent buffering is insufficient, *smoothing* or leveling activities are invoked to reduce environmental fluctuations. Reduced late-night airline fares and the scheduling of nonemergency operations for low-use periods by hospitals represent attempts to smooth input and output transactions.

When smoothing activities are inadequate, organizations resort to *forecasting* to anticipate fluctuations and adapt the technical core to them. Peak load periods are thus known in advance and may be treated as constraints. Staffing or other input levels can be increased to anticipate needs and an essentially closed-system logic can be maintained.

Finally, should all else fail, organizations must resort to *rationing*, whereby services or products are provided on some preestablished basis. Major environmental fluctuations, as for instance a community disaster facing a hospital or a sudden fad facing a manufacturer, can necessitate rationing. This strategy is less than ideal because the organization must forego opportunities.

Domains of Organized Action. Organizations typically stake out a domain within which certain goods and/or services are provided. When this domain is recognized by those in the task environment who can provide needed support for the organization, a degree of domain consensus exists. Thus organizations develop dependencies on components of their environment, which vary with the degree of need (for a raw material, for instance) and the number of alternative sources of supply. For the organization, dependence and power relative to various environmental components are inversely related.

Under a competitive strategy, organizations seek to establish and hold power by maintaining multiple alternatives, by seeking prestige, and by focusing their efforts to achieve power on those components of the task environment that otherwise are most likely to place them in a dependent position. As noted previously, support from the environment, or power over it, may also be obtained by bargaining, co-optation, and coalition.

To the extent an organization is constrained from action in the various sectors of its environment, it will seek increasing degrees of power over those sectors in which it remains free to act. Thus a firm operating in an impoverished market will seek to exercise power over sources of raw materials and labor to adjust them to market demand for the product. To the extent such efforts fail, there is likely to be an attempt to enlarge the task environment, for instance, by involving previously uninvolved governmental units or by resorting to the courts.

Design. Organizations may deal with environmental problems by placing their boundaries around activities that could be performed by other task environment components. In organizations where the technology is *long-linked*, as with an assembly line, domains tend to expand through vertical integration, perhaps expanding backward into raw material production or forward into direct marketing. Organizations in which the technology is *mediating*, as with commercial banks that mediate between depositors and borrowers, expand their domains by increasing the populations served. Intensive technologies that draw on a variety of techniques to achieve a change in a person (as in a general hospital) or an object (as in the construction industry) require that the domain be expanded by incorporating the person or object involved. Intensive technology yields a custom-made output, and problems are reduced to the extent the client can be controlled.

These types of growth often yield a lack of balance in that capacities vary considerably from one component to another. To deal with such situations:

1. Multicomponent organizations subject to rationality norms will seek to grow until the least reducible component is approximately fully occupied.

2. Organizations with capacity in excess of what the task environment supports will seek to enlarge their domains (Thompson, 1967, p. 46).

Technology and Structure. Components within an organization may be interdependent in various ways. Under *pooled* interdependence each part makes a separate contribution to the whole and is in turn supported by the whole, as with branch sales offices. Under *sequential* interdependence one part must act before another can, as in the relationship of production to marketing. Under *reciprocal* interdependence, the interdependence is two-way and thus symmetrical. Operations and maintenance units are reciprocally interdependent in that maintaining equipment in good repair is an input to operations, while equipment needing repair is an input to maintenance. As one moves from pooled to sequential to reciprocal interdependence, coordination becomes more difficult and costly. The appropriate approach for pooled interdependence is *standardization*; for sequential interdependence, *planning* and scheduling; and for reciprocal interdependence, coordination by *mutual adjustment*.

Because coordination is costly, the ideal is to use standardization if possible, then planning, and finally mutual adjustment only if absolutely necessary. Components also are grouped to minimize coordination costs. Thus reciprocally interdependent units are placed together in small, relatively autonomous, local groups. If only sequential interdependence is involved, then these units are so grouped. With only pooled interdependence, positions are grouped homogeneously to facilitate the use of standardization.

Problems of reciprocal interdependence, if present, are dealt with at the lowest organizational levels possible. Groups higher up are developed to deal with sequential interdependence, and finally toward the top, homogeneous units are created to facilitate standardization among components having pooled interdependence, as in a divisionalized structure. As a result of these priorities, similar positions may not be grouped together, and standardized rules must be used to blanket homogeneous positions across divisions. Liaison positions with staff designations are created to link the rule-making agency with these positions. When departments cannot handle all sequential interdependence, committees tend to be invoked to deal with the remaining coordination, and when departments cannot encompass all reciprocal interdependence, project teams are created.

Rationality and Structure. The logic of organizational design based on technology must be supplemented by a concern with environmental characteristics. To the extent that the task environment is heterogeneous, an attempt will be made to identify homogeneous segments and create boundary-spanning units to deal with each. These units are further subdivided if the amount of interaction across the boundary requires it.

Organizations will rely heavily on standardized rules in coping with stable environments and with environments in which the range of variation is known. If the range of variation is very large or unknown, localized boundary-spanning units are needed to monitor and plan effectively.

Thompson specifies environments in terms of their homogeneity-heterogeneity and stability-variability, and he indicates organizational forms for boundary-spanning units to match these different environments:

Homogeneous-stable—a few functional divisions utilizing standardized rules for adaptation.

Heterogeneous-stable—a variety of functional divisions matched to homogeneous segments of the task environment and utilizing rules extensively.

Homogeneous-variable—geographic, decentralized divisions concerned with planning responses to change.

Heterogeneous-variable—divisions functionally differentiated to match segments of the task environment and decentralized to monitor and plan.

What has been said about the effects of technology and environment on structure requires some integration. Propositions dealing with the joint effects of the two forces are as follows:

1. When technical-core and boundary-spanning activities can be isolated from one another except for scheduling, organizations under norms of rationality will be centralized with an overarching layer composed of functional divisions.

2. Under conditions of complexity, when the major components of an organization are reciprocally interdependent, these components will be segmented and arranged in self-sufficient clusters, each cluster having its own domain (. . . a product division or a profit center, or it may in general usage be known as a decentralized division) (Thompson, 1967, pp. 75–76).

Assessment. Sociological systems theory is more concerned than most theories about how organizations assess themselves and are assessed by others. One proposition states that assessments based on *efficiency* tests involving input-output calculations are most preferred, followed by *instrumental* tests (whether a desired state of affairs is achieved), and finally *social* tests involving the judgments of reference groups. Often efficiency tests cannot be applied due to insufficient knowledge and ambiguous standards.

Other hypotheses dealing with the assessment process have been proposed. Given stable task environments, organizations seek to demonstrate historical improvement; in dynamic environments they seek to demonstrate success relative to comparable organizations.

Generally the demonstration of improvement along dimensions of particular concern to sectors of the environment on which the organization is most dependent is considered to be of greatest value.

In evaluating internal units, organizations are guided by the unit's method of coordinating interdependence. Accordingly, those units using standardized rules are assessed in terms of degree of adherence to those rules; those units following plans and schedules are assessed in terms of filling the previously established quotas; and units relying on mutual adjustment are assessed in terms of the expressed confidence of reciprocally dependent units.

The Variable Human. Thompson (1967) devotes considerable attention to the inducement-contribution bargain, whereby organizational members either explicitly or implicitly agree to contribute effort in various forms and amounts in return for inducements such as pay. This bargain is determined through power processes. Where the technology is routine, collective bargaining is the method of choice. In intensive technologies, whether one achieves the occupational ceiling early or late is important. Those in early-ceiling occupations seek leverage to upgrade the occupation through collective action. Under late-ceiling conditions such as those obtaining in the professions the key element in bargaining is the person's visibility among occupational colleagues. Within management the bargain is strongly influenced by the individual's reputation for having scarce abilities to solve organizational problems. In roles that are boundary-spanning the bargain is determined by the power of the environmental segment on which the organization depends and by the person's ability to handle this dependence effectively.

Discretion. The exercise of discretion in organizations is not always viewed as attractive. Discretion tends to be avoided when uncertainty seems to outweigh the organization's predictive capacity and when the consequences of error appear to be great. Organizations themselves foster avoidance of discretion by using inappropriate structures and assessment criteria, and by assessing performance on various incompatible criteria. Several of Thompson's propositions deal with multiple consequences of discretion:

1. Organizations seek to guard against deviant discretion by policing methods.
2. Where work loads exceed capacity and the individual has options, he is tempted to select tasks which promise to enhance his scores on assessment criteria.
3. Where work loads or resource supplies fluctuate, the individual is tempted to stockpile (empire build).

4. Where alternatives are present, the individual is tempted to report successes and suppress evidence of failure (Thompson 1967, pp. 122–24).

Individuals in highly discretionary positions such as top management characteristically seek to maintain power that exceeds their dependence on others in the organization. When this is not possible, the individual will seek a coalition that may include essential segments of the task environment. Certainly changes in environmental dependencies can serve to restructure coalitions.

The number of political positions or power bases in an organization increases with the number of sources of uncertainty and with the degree of decentralization. However, power bases and organizational goals can change rapidly under conditions of a dynamic task environment or technology. Generally such changes are functional for the organization, and for that reason commitments to entrenched power, as in the case of a founding entrepreneur, should be avoided.

Control. The propositions dealing with control draw heavily on the concept of coalition—primarily the dominant coalition—and on Thompson and Tuden's (1959) typology of decision making. The dominant coalition increases in size with increases in the number of areas in the organization where it is necessary to rely on a judgmental decision; thus a shift in one area from the predominance of computational to judgmental decisions can be expected to place a representative of that area in the dominant coalition. Similarly imperfections in the core technology and heterogeneity in the task environment foster coalition membership for task-environmental and technological specialists.

Conflict within the dominant coalition can be expected to increase (1) as interdependence increases, (2) as environmental forces require compromises on outcome preferences, and (3) as the variety of professions represented increases. When power is widely distributed within the dominant coalition, an inner circle emerges, without which the coalition would be immobilized. Under such circumstances the dominant coalition as a whole becomes a ratifying body. To the extent there is a central power figure, this individual is the one who can manage the dominant coalition.

At the conclusion of his book Thompson (1967) reemphasizes the importance of the open systems approach and of the dimension of certainty-uncertainty. Uncertainties come from inside and outside the organization. There are three major sources:

1. *Generalized uncertainty*, or lack of cause-effect understanding in the culture at large.

2. *Contingency,* in which the outcomes of organizational action are in part determined by the actions of environmental elements.

3. *Internal interdependence* of components.

As utilized by Thompson, the uncertainty concept is highly congruent with an open systems approach that emphasizes exchanges across organizational boundaries.

Later Papers

Thompson's writings after 1967 focus on two major themes. One involves extrapolating some of his ideas about organizations to other social units and in particular to society at large. The other involves speculations about social and organizational forms of the future. There is some minor reworking or reformulating of earlier views, but by and large the *Organizations in Action* propositions stand as *the* statements of the theory.

Thompson (1974a) extends his concept of technological determinism in organizations to society at large. In this view technology determines the type of interdependence, which in turn is a major factor in political orientations and societal identification. In considering interdependence, however, Thompson (1974a, 1974b) now utilizes a somewhat different set of categories. Pooled and sequential interdependence remain essentially unchanged, but the concept of *intensive* interdependence is drawn from the prior categorization of technologies and substituted for reciprocal interdependence. Intensive interdependence is concerned with knowledge generation and application, and a major characteristic is its lack of permanence. As with reciprocal interdependence, units need to adjust to feedback from others, and indeed mutual adjustment remains the essential method of coordination.

Thompson (1974b) believes the future will see much greater use of intensive interdependence and of temporary systems, often involving the actions of sets of organizations, not merely sets of individuals. In many respects his views parallel those of the theorists considered in Chapter 5. Of the organizational world of the year 2000, he says:

> Many of us, or our successors, will hold regular jobs in formal
> organizations with geographic identities and regularities, with
> recognized clienteles and functions. . . . But I believe such
> things will be routine, taken for granted, unproblematic. Our
> preoccupations as a society, I believe, will not be in this
> arena, but rather with what I have tried to designate as
> *complex organizations* of a much more fluid, ad hoc, flexible
> form. Perhaps these should not be designed organizations at

all, and the emphasis should instead be placed on the administration of temporarily organized activities . . . with the development of administration teams or cadres to specialize in a continuous process of synthesizing. Perhaps complex organizations of the future will be known not for their components but by their cadres, with each cadre devoted to mobilizing and deploying resources in shifting configurations, to employ changing technologies to meet changing demands (Thompson, 1973, in Rushing and Zald, 1976, p. 245).

Research Bearing on Sociological Open Systems Theory

Obviously, Thompson intended to state his propositions so that they might be tested. On the other hand, he is aware that he has not provided operational definitions of his variables, and he seems to have anticipated what has since turned out to be true—research tests have been few and far between:

The propositions . . . have been stated in the form which allows them to be negated if incorrect. . . . Testable form is not enough, however. We must have operations which will enable us to say the specific conditions do or do not exist. . . . Hopefully our propositions seem plausible and important, but it is unlikely that many will be treated as hypotheses for extensive testing, for in the process of the necessary conceptual refinement, more specific and subtle hypotheses will be generated (Thompson, 1967, p. 163).

Though there are some direct tests of one or more of Thompson's propositions, these are few. More commonly, certain theory concepts have been used in testing hypotheses that differ from, but are entirely consistent with, the hypotheses Thompson formulated. On occasion it seems that Thompson's propositions have been stretched to the breaking point to achieve consonance between them and the design or results of a particular study.

Co-optation and Coalition

The theory posits a hierarchy of procedures for dealing with environmental uncertainty running from the least costly, which is competition, through bargaining or contracting and co-optation, to the most costly, which is coalition or coalescing (Thompson and McEwen, 1958; Thompson, 1967). Though the preference hierarchy as such has not been studied, there is research evidence to support the hypothesis that co-optation and coalition are methods of dealing with uncertainty and interdependence.

Thus, Pfeffer (1972a) studied corporate board memberships, relating board composition to such factors as need for access to capital markets and the extent of governmental regulation. The expectation was that representatives of financial institutions, attorneys, and other outsiders would be co-opted onto boards to deal with these external dependencies. Data are presented that are consistent with this expectation. Furthermore, companies that deviated from an optimum board structure commensurate with the dependency requirements existing in their particular industries were less profitable.

In another study Pfeffer (1972b) looked at the use of merger as a method of coping with uncertainty and interdependence. He found that merger behavior was better explained as an attempt to deal with input and output dependencies than it was by any competing hypotheses. Evidence is also presented to show that mergers are often used to reduce the impact of competition within an industry, and to achieve diversification that will reduce the company's dependence on a limited set of other organizations.

A study by Nikolai and Bazley (1977) purports to deal with the coalition strategy also. These authors define the hiring of each other's graduates by university accounting departments as coalition and the hiring of one's own graduates (inbreeding) as vertical integration. Thompson (1967), however, associates vertical integration with a long-linked technology, not an intensive technology, which an accounting department is. The hiring of graduates of a competing program seems at least as likely to reflect co-optation as coalition formation. In any event the data indicate a tendency for high prestige departments to hire graduates of other high prestige departments, intermediate prestige departments to hire graduates of other intermediate prestige departments, and so on. Furthermore, inbreeding is positively correlated with prestige level. The data appear best interpreted as the use of prestige competition to cope with environmental contingencies, though the authors prefer to speak in terms of coalitions and vertical integration. These analyses dealing with co-optation, coalescing, and related concepts are probably best viewed as supporting the open systems approach generally, rather than Thompson's theory specifically. The findings fit well with Thompson's views, but they can be explained equally effectively by other theories of a similar nature.

Protecting the Technical Core

Research conducted by Williams (1977) attempts to study the use of buffering and forecasting mechanisms to protect the technical core. Specifically, Williams hypothesizes that there will be a greater investment in these mechanisms when they are particularly needed, because of a high degree of mechanization of the technical core. Hypotheses of this kind are more specific than the Thompson propositions, but are entirely consonant with them.

Consistent with the hypotheses, it was found that the use of buffering systems represented by disproportionately larger employment in the areas of facility maintenance, employee acquisition, and supervision was associated with various measures of throughput mechanization; the relationships are particularly strong for the extent of supervisory employment, with correlations in the .60s and .70s. Also employment of individuals to deal with output transactions and to survey and forecast the environment was associated with greater throughput mechanization, but only under conditions of high environmental competition. Where competition was minimal, heavy investment in boundary personnel of this kind apparently was not needed to protect the technical core.

There is also evidence that the degree of smoothing in input and output transactions such as sales, capital expenditures, and dividend payments is associated with uncertainty reduction, as reflected in the lower volatility of various common stock return measures (Lev, 1975). To the extent a company can achieve smooth flow across its boundaries from year to year, objective indexes of risk appear to be relatively low also. Data on this point for four industries in which twenty or more firms could be studied are given in Table 7–1.

Research of this kind dealing with methods of protecting the technical core tends to substantiate Thompson's hypotheses regarding specific mechanisms. However, nothing has been done to investigate the priorities of usage hypothesized by sociological open systems theory.

Varieties of Technology

Numerous studies have drawn on Thompson's typology of technologies to test various hypotheses about organizations and their members. These hypotheses often extend well beyond what Thompson actually said, and while they are typically confirmed by the research, the findings support his theoretical propositions only in a very general sense. Thus, Mahoney and Frost (1974) found differences in criteria of effectiveness associated with the dominant technology of a unit. Scheduling and coordination were important in achieving productivity in long-linked technology, and effectiveness was assessed without reference to interactions with other units. Interactions with other units became increasingly significant in assessing effectiveness as the technology changed to mediating and then to intensive; so, too, did quality of staff.

Table 7-1
Correlations Between Degree of Smoothness of Input and Output Transactions Over a Twenty-Year Period and Degree of Uncertainty Reduction as Reflected in a Lack of Stock Volatility by Industry Groups

| | Measure of Smoothness | | |
Measure of Uncertainty Reduction	Sales Volume	Capital Expenditures	Dividends Paid
Stability of overall stock returns			
Chemicals and drugs	(.38)	(.62)	(.48)
Metals producers	(.39)	(.66)	(.43)
Retail stores	(.71)	(.45)	(.41)
Food producers	.17	.18	(.52)
Stability of systematic stock returns			
Chemicals and drugs	(.45)	(.54)	(.66)
Metals producers	.27	(.49)	(.40)
Retail stores	(.41)	(.43)	(.43)
Food producers	.17	.21	(.50)

( ) Correlation statistically significant.

SOURCE: Adapted from Baruch Lev, "Environmental Uncertainty Reduction by Smoothing and Buffering: An Empirical Verification," *Academy of Management Journal,* 18 (1975), p. 870.

A series of studies by Rousseau has demonstrated numerous relationships between Thompson's technological forms and various individual variables. Though these relationships are not embodied in Thompson's propositions, they support the differential effects of varying technologies. Thus technology is related to variations in job attitudes, but only as mediated by job characteristics (Rousseau, 1978). Presumably the technology defines the various aspects of the job, which in turn influence the attitudes of incumbents.

Similarly, Vardi and Hammer (1977) have related Thompson's technological variable to various mobility patterns within an organization. Others have also demonstrated the significance of this kind of technological differentiation (Hitt and Middlemist, 1978; Morrissey and Gillespie, 1975). Clearly technology, as Thompson conceived it, can make a difference in organizations; whether it makes a difference in exactly the way Thompson proposed is another question. On that point the evidence is extremely sparse. The following quote reflects one major problem inhibiting research in this area.

Thompson's concepts are quite abstract, thus making them difficult to apply unambiguously even in a classification of organizations where one is provided with a great deal of information (Morrissey and Gillespie, 1975).

Interdependence and Coordination

There is considerable evidence to support Thompson's propositions relating coordination approach to type of interdependence. Thus, Reeves and Turner (1972) report that mutual adjustment appears to be the appropriate method of coordination under conditions of reciprocal interdependence. They base this conclusion on intensive case studies of batch production factories. However, they also report that high levels of uncertainty and complexity require the use of mutual adjustment as well, and that mutual adjustment may well be appropriate under uncertain conditions, irrespective of the nature of the interdependence. If anything, they believe that the uncertainty effects are greater than the interdependence effects.

Similarly, Baumler (1971) found in a simulation study that a coordination approach that approximated standardization yielded very positive results when interdependence was low, as in the pooled situation, but actually had a negative effect when interdependence was greater. On the other hand, a more informal approach approximating mutual adjustment worked well under conditions approaching reciprocal interdependence.

Van de Ven (1976) presents data bearing on the hypothesis that, as interdependence increases, there will be a shift from supervisory to group decision making. Though not specifically envisaged by Thompson, this result is certainly consistent with a shift from standardization to mutual adjustment as methods of coordination. In general the results support this expectation, but they also support an additional conclusion—the group decision making feeds back and actually increases the level of interdependence. Thus, though mutual adjustment would appear to be appropriate for dealing with high levels of interdependence, it also may further increase interdependence. One could thus hope for the development of an alternative approach.

Environmental Stability and Homogeneity

Research undertaken by Duncan (1972) offers considerable support for the homogeneity-heterogeneity and stability-variability dimensions of the environment formulated by Thompson. These dimensions appear to be important in managers' perceptions of environmental uncertainty. Thus in homogeneous-stable contexts little uncertainty is experienced, while in heterogeneous-variable situations it is considerable. Of the two dimensions, stability-variability seems to contribute more to uncertainty perceptions.

When one moves to the theory's more specific statements relating environmental characteristics to organizational structure, there is less support, however. For instance, a study conducted by Schmidt and Cummings (1976) failed to establish any relationship between environmental variability and structural differentiation. Initial analyses did suggest a relationship between environmental heterogeneity and differentiation. However, the size of the organization was found to mediate this relationship, and when these size effects were removed, heterogeneity and differentiation proved to be unrelated.

The general problem of how uncertainty about the environment affects organizational structure is a matter of concern for several theories considered in subsequent chapters. However, Thompson's propositions in this area are relatively specific. There is little research bearing on them, and what does exist is nonconfirming.

Assessment

Though research on Thompson's propositions dealing with the assessment of organizational effectiveness is minimal, some findings support the differentiation among efficiency, instrumental, and social tests and the relationship of the use of these tests to such matters as decision certainty, change, and technology (Mahoney and Weitzel, 1969).

A study by Schramm (1975) deals with the ways organizations such as universities seek to compete when they are forced to utilize social tests in comparisons with reference groups. From faculty salary information reported to the American Association of University Professors over a ten-year period it was apparent that reporting universities attempted to improve their relative positions along this dimension over time. Since salary levels have much to do with recruiting quality faculty (an area of much environmental dependence), competition on this variable is highly consistent with Thompson's hypotheses.

In addition, universities paying higher salaries and having other, higher-quality standards as well tended to join in the salary survey process at an earlier date, thus attempting to make their favorable assessment position visible. Universities that were not able to demonstrate a favorable rate of improvement in compensation tended to drop out of the survey process, presumably with a view to emphasizing other dimensions on which they could compete more effectively. Though not uniquely derivable from Thompson's propositions regarding assessment, Schramm's findings do support them in a number of respects.

Discretion and Control

Thompson posits that changes at the top levels of organizations should reflect a responsiveness to organizational demands. In this view one would expect organizations facing unstable and hostile

Table 7–2

Correlations Between the Length of a Hospital Chief Administrator's Tenure and Indexes of Instability and Hostility in the Environment

Index of Environmental Instability and Hostility	Correlation
Amount of competition for staff	(− .35)
Affiliation with a religious denomination	(− .29)
Poor relations with the local community	(− .29)
Poor relations with the business community	(− .24)
Amount of competition for funding	− .19
Lack of surplus in current budget	− .10
Amount of competition for patients	− .09

( ) Correlation statistically significant.

SOURCE: Adapted from Jeffrey Pfeffer and Gerald R. Salancik, "Organizational Context and the Characteristics and Tenure of Hospital Administrators," *Academy of Management Journal*, 20 (1977), p. 83.

environments to experience greater turnover at the top simply to adjust to new contingencies. Furthermore, these personnel changes should be consonant with the problems faced. Data on turnover for a group of hospital administrators are given in Table 7–2. Though the correlations are not high, they do reflect a consistent tendency for problem environments to be associated with low tenure; half of the correlations are statistically significant (Pfeffer and Salancik, 1977). Also, when the operating budget is obtained primarily from payments by private insurers, chief administrators with training in hospital administration tend to be brought in. There is a similar tendency to call in accountants. However, when private donations or government funds are critical to hospital operation, other personnel with more appropriate backgrounds are called in. Clearly organizational contingencies do relate to top-level staffing, as Thompson hypothesized.

There is other evidence that supports Thompson's propositions regarding discretion and control. Inner, elite circles are a reality in many organizations and serve as a major source of organizational innovation (Hage and Dewar, 1973). The case analyses of batch production firms yield results that are consistent with the hypothesis that less perfect technologies are likely to be represented in the dominant coalition (Reeves and Turner, 1972). However, the authors believe that the power of production management is as much a consequence of the critical role played in meeting market demand contingencies as it is a consequence of imperfections in the technology. All the evidence does not appear to be in on this proposition.

Conclusions

Sociological systems theory suffers from many of the same problems as its psychological sibling. Due to a high level of abstraction and the lack of operationalized constructs, the theory has inspired little research, and in those studies that have been done it is difficult to determine whether they are true tests of the theory or not. Furthermore, because the theory lacks logical interconnectedness, the verification of one theoretical proposition often does not increase confidence in the truth of other propositions not yet tested. And, then, there is the lack of any applications of the theory.

Goals of Application

Clearly, Thompson's theory is an applied theory of organizational structuring and operation; it deals with practical problems ranging from strategy formulation to unit staffing. To the extent one wishes to be rational (under norms of rationality), it is a normative theory that tells us what to do in a wide range of areas to make an organization more effective. But that is where it ends.

James Thompson was not a consultant to organizations (Perrow, 1976), and he did not implement his ideas to determine how they worked. Neither has anyone else. Except for a few laboratory studies, the research into Thompson's theory has not been experimental. It looks at what is, rather than what happens when experimental changes are introduced. Causation is therefore difficult to establish. It should be possible to develop a technology of organizational intervention that matches the theory, but Thompson did not do it, and as is typically the case under such circumstances, no one else has moved his theory across the application gap.

Scientific Goals

There can be no question that James Thompson's work is widely respected (Demerath, McEwen, Avery, Van Houten, and Rushing, 1974). Conceptually, Thompson's theory represented a major leap forward. Thompson used the deductive approach far more than any previous theorist to develop new constructs and new relationships. His work was, and remains, a tremendous creative accomplishment, and is cited extensively even now (Pondy and Mitroff, 1979).

Against this backdrop it is appropriate to consider not only the research evidence, but also the logical or conceptual criticisms that have been lodged against the theory. One such view is that Thompson is too uncritically accepting of current organizations and current organizational forms. He fails to deal with such problems as socially irresponsible behavior and illegal acts, the frustration of needs of lower-level employees by management, and the quality of work life (Perrow, 1976). Perrow contends that Thompson was wrong in being so uncritical and that his contribution would have been much richer had he been less detached (rational?). Perrow's criticism is in many ways more philosophical than scientific; in his writings Thompson was not the humanist others might have wished him to be. From a scientific viewpoint a theorist has a right to define his domain, and as long as the domain is not trivial (and Thompson's clearly was not), he cannot be faulted on that score. Thompson chose to ignore voluntary organizations and to emphasize management and top-level strategy formulation over individual employee concerns. Such domain limitations are often good theoretical strategy; some would even argue that Thompson attempted to cover too large a theoretical domain.

Argyris (1972) has lodged a similar set of criticisms. He maintains that one must deal with the irrational as well as the rational, the informal as well as the formal, the psychological as well as the sociological, if one is to understand organizations. Furthermore, Argyris (1972, p. 26) views sociological open systems theory as "an explication of scientific management and engineering economics." He continues:

> Although Thompson aspires to present a more realistic integration of the formal and natural system, the integration actually made favors the closed system, traditional management, economically oriented model which he rejects as incomplete. The "variable human" seems to be minimally variable and minimally human. . . . man turns out to be the closed system Thompson so cogently describes as ineffective for existing living systems. Group dynamics and interpersonal relations are not included (Argyris, 1972, pp. 33–34).

In line with his own theoretical formulations (Chapter 5) Argyris maintains that all organizations utilize reciprocal interdependence and coordinate by mutual adjustment and those that do not cannot cope with a dynamic environment. On this latter point Thompson would argue that "under norms of rationality" change should occur as environmental concerns and internal interdependencies require and that to use a more costly level of coordination than the current situation requires is not rational. Witness Van de Ven's (1976) finding that mutual adjustment can actually increase interdependence. The implication is that excessive use of mutual adjustment can escalate interdependence to a limit beyond which most organizations can cope with it, producing a state of near-anarchy.

Wanting sociological open systems theory to be and to do things that it cannot be and do is a pervasive problem. A recent paper by Pondy and Mitroff (1979) takes the theory to task for not being open enough. In fact the authors view the theory as essentially closed and controlled because it utilizes such concepts as standardization, buffering, and smoothing, which are attempts to introduce high degrees of certainty and stability into the organization. Pondy and Mitroff maintain that organizations need variety in their environments and without it they experience the equivalent of sensory deprivation; thus organizations should not strive for certainty, but rather should seek uncertainty and even evoke it in their environments. Under some circumstances this is probably correct, but the level of uncertainty can be so high that it threatens to overwhelm both organizations and individual human beings, and it was to such situations that Thompson addressed his theory.

At the level of what Thompson's theory is, rather than what it might be, there remain some definite problems. Perrow (1976) has raised questions about mediating technology and how it differs from long-linked technology. The two are actually much the same, with the major difference being that one deals with service industries and the other with production industries. With regard to Thompson's proposed differences, Perrow advances some very cogent arguments:

> Both have standardization and repetition as their basic characteristics. The only difference is that mediating technologies operate extensively with "multiple clients or customers distributed in time and space." But that is also true of firms with long-linked technologies, such as General Motors. And doesn't A. T. and T. or the post office (mediating technologies) use a highly standardized and repetitive technology, characteristic of the long-linked form? He says the organization with a mediating technology will handle uncertainty by increasing the populations served, while those with long-linked technologies integrate vertically. But Alcoa and G. M. certainly seek to increase the population served, and A. T. and T. has a significant degree of vertical integration (Perrow, 1976, p. 719).

Apparently those who have attempted to classify technologies according to Thompson's system also have had difficulties. The system is very abstract and should have been elaborated on with many more specific examples. Because the varieties of interdependence and of technology are so closely related, this matter of ambiguity and insufficient differentiation spills over into the interdependence formulations. Are intensive and reciprocal interdependence the same thing? What does pooled interdependence really mean? Users need a detailed guide for classifying organizations (or their units) by these typologies. Had Thompson applied his system he might have found that differences that appeared clear to him at a high level of abstraction were not nearly so clear at an operational level.

Many of Thompson's propositions have not as yet been adequately tested; we simply do not know if they are true or not. Yet other propositions have been supported, and even more seem to have been supported, though the hypotheses actually tested often are not the same as those proposed by Thompson. Only in the area of environmental effects on structure are there data that definitely question Thompson's propositions. The relationships with differentiation do not support his theory of environmental determinism. Many other studies raise serious questions about the validity of so-called structural-contingency models that utilize variables associated with uncertainty to moderate between dimensions of organizational structure and effectiveness (Pennings, 1975). Clearly numerous other factors, including the amount of internal control (Chapter 3), influence organizational effectiveness.

Without much more research into the propositions of sociological open systems theory extending across the whole span of its domain, one cannot be sure where its most pronounced weak spots lie. Such research has been distinctly on the wane in the last few years, to the point where our questions may never be answered. Thompson's creative genius deserves a better empirical response than it is receiving. At the same time, the abstract, unrelated hypotheses generated by systems theories appear to be self-defeating insofar as research confirmation is concerned. It may simply be that research into systems theories is not the best way to generate new knowledge within the field of organizational theory at the present time.

References

Argyris, Chris. *The Applicability of Organizational Sociology*. London: Cambridge University Press, 1972.

Baumler, John V. "Defined Criteria of Performance in Organizational Control," *Administrative Science Quarterly*, 16 (1971), 340–49.

Berelson, Bernard, and Gary A. Steiner. *Human Behavior: An Inventory of Scientific Findings*. New York: Harcourt, Brace, and World, 1964.

Demerath, Nicholas J., William J. McEwen, Robert W. Avery, Donald R. Van Houten, and William A. Rushing. "James D. Thompson: A Memorial," *Administrative Science Quarterly*, 19 (1974), 1–5.

Duncan, Robert B. "Characteristics of Organizational Environments and Perceived Environmental Uncertainty," *Administrative Science Quarterly*, 17 (1972), 313–27.

Hage, Jerald, and Robert Dewar. "Elite Values Versus Organizational Structure in Predicting Innovation," *Administrative Science Quarterly*, 18 (1973), 279–90.

Hitt, Michael A., and R. Dennis Middlemist. "The Measurement of Technology within Organizations," *Journal of Management*, 4 (1978), 47–67.

Lev, Baruch. "Environmental Uncertainty Reduction by Smoothing and Buffering: An Empirical Verification," *Academy of Management Journal*, 18 (1975), 864–71.

Mahoney, Thomas A., and Peter J. Frost. "The Role of Technology in Models of Organizational Effectiveness," *Organizational Behavior and Human Performance*, 11 (1974), 122–38.

Mahoney, Thomas A., and William Weitzel. "Managerial Models of Organizational Effectiveness," *Administrative Science Quarterly*, 14 (1969), 357–65.

March, James G., and Herbert A. Simon. *Organizations*. New York: Wiley, 1958.

McNeil, Kenneth, and James D. Thompson. "The Regeneration of Social Organizations," *American Sociological Review*, 36 (1971), 624–37.

Morrissey, Elizabeth, and David F. Gillespie. "Technology and the Conflict of Professionals in Bureaucratic Organizations," *Sociological Quarterly*, 16 (1975), 319–32.

Nikolai, Loren A., and John D. Bazley. "An Analysis of the Organizational Interaction of Accounting Departments," *Academy of Management Journal*, 20 (1977), 608–21.

Pennings, Johannes M. "The Relevance of the Structural-Contingency Model for Organizational Effectiveness," *Administrative Science Quarterly*, 20 (1975), 393–410.

Perrow, Charles. "Review of Organizations and Beyond: Selected Essays of James D. Thompson," *Administrative Science Quarterly*, 21 (1976), 718–21.

Pfeffer, Jeffrey. "Size and Composition of Corporate Boards of Directors: The Organization and Its Environment," *Administrative Science Quarterly*, 17 (1972a), 218–28.

―――. "Merger as a Response to Organizational Interdependence," *Administrative Science Quarterly*, 17 (1972b), 382–94.

Pfeffer, Jeffrey, and Gerald R. Salancik. "Organizational Context and the Characteristics and Tenure of Hospital Administrators," *Academy of Management Journal*, 20 (1977), 74–88.

Pondy, Louis R., and Ian I. Mitroff. "Beyond Open System Models of Organization," *Research in Organizational Behavior*, 1 (1979), 3–39.

Reeves, Tom K., and Barry A. Turner. "A Theory of Organization and Behavior in Batch Production Factories," *Administrative Science Quarterly*, 17 (1972), 81–98.

Rousseau, Denise M. "Measures of Technology as Predictors of Employee Attitude," *Journal of Applied Psychology*, 63 (1978), 213–18.

Rushing, William A., and Mayer N. Zald. *Organizations and Beyond: Selected Essays of James D. Thompson*. Lexington, Mass.: D. C. Heath, 1976.

Schmidt, Stuart M., and Larry L. Cummings. "Organizational Environment, Differentiation, and Perceived Environmental Uncertainty," *Decision Sciences*, 7 (1976), 447–67.

Schramm, Carl. J. "Thompson's Assessment of Organizations: Universities and the AAUP Salary Grades," *Administrative Science Quarterly*, 20 (1975), 87–96.

Thompson, James D. "Authority and Power in Identical Organizations," *American Journal of Sociology*, 62 (1956), 290–98.

―――. "Organizational Management of Conflict," *Administrative Science Quarterly*, 4 (1960), 389–409.

―――. "Organizations and Output Transactions," *American Journal of Sociology*, 67 (1962), 309–24.

―――. "Decision-Making, the Firm, and the Market." In William W. Cooper, Harold J. Leavitt, and Maynard W. Shelly (eds.), *New Perspectives in Organization Research*. New York: Wiley, 1964, pp. 334–48.

———. *Organizations in Action.* New York: McGraw-Hill, 1967.

———. "Society's Frontiers for Organizing Activities," *Public Administration Review*, 33 (1973), 327–35.

———. "Technology, Polity and Societal Development," *Administrative Science Quarterly*, 19 (1974a), 6–21.

———. "Social Interdependence, The Polity, and Public Administration," *Administration and Society*, 6 (1974b), 3–21.

Thompson, James D., and Frederick L. Bates. "Technology and Administration," *Administrative Science Quarterly*, 2 (1957), 325–43.

Thompson, James D., and Robert W. Hawkes. "Disaster, Community Organization, and Administrative Process." In George W. Baker and Dwight W. Chapman (eds.), *Man and Society in Disaster*. New York: Basic Books, 1962, pp. 268–300.

Thompson, James D., and William J. McEwen. "Organizational Goals and Environment: Goal-Setting as an Interaction Process," *American Sociological Review*, 23 (1958), 23–31.

Thompson, James D., and Arthur Tuden. "Strategies, Structures, and Processes of Organizational Decision." In James D. Thompson, P. B. Hammond, R. W. Hawkes, B. H. Junker, and A. Tuden (eds.), *Comparative Studies in Administration*. Pittsburgh, Pa.: University of Pittsburgh Press, 1959, pp. 195–216.

Thompson, James D., and Donald R. Van Houten. *The Behavioral Sciences: An Interpretation*. Reading, Mass.: Addison-Wesley, 1970.

Tosi, Henry L. *Theories of Organization*. Chicago, Ill.: St. Clair, 1975.

Van de Ven, Andrew H. "A Panel Study of Determinants of Authority Structures Within Organizational Units," *Academy of Management Proceedings*, 1976, pp. 256–62.

Vardi, Yoav, and Tove H. Hammer. "Intraorganizational Mobility and Career Perceptions Among Rank and File Employees in Different Technologies," *Academy of Management Journal*, 20 (1977), 622–34.

Williams, William W. "Organizational Size, Technology, and Employment Investments in Ancillary Specialisms," *Academy of Management Proceedings*, 1977, pp. 224–28.

8

The Technological Imperative

Technology plays an important role in sociological open systems theory, but it shares the spotlight with numerous other factors. For another group of theories, however, technology operates as a *major*, though never exclusive, determinant of organizational process and structure. This causal link between technology and organization has come to be known as "the technological imperative." The theorists who espouse it in one form or another have had a significant impact on the study of organizations.

The mother of this approach was Joan Woodward, who appears to have discovered technological determinism almost accidentally while searching for evidence to support classical management theory. Unfortunately, Woodward did not live to complete either the full statement of her theory or her research. Her first research was conducted from the University of Liverpool, but she began to develop her ideas on the role of technology while she was director of the Human Relations Research Unit at the South-East Essex College of Technology in the middle 1950s. She continued her work during the 1960s at the Imperial College of Science and Technology, University of London.

A second theory that concerns itself more with technological change than with the nature of technology itself comes from Tom Burns, also a sociologist, at the University of Edinburgh, who collaborated on his major work with G. M. Stalker, a psychologist. The Burns and Stalker theory in large part follows that of Woodward, though Woodward did use certain Burns and Stalker concepts in later analyses of her data.

A third theorist, Charles Perrow, who began to write about the technological imperative in the middle 1960s, has carried the approach the farthest. He trained in the Sociology Department at the University of California/Berkeley under Philip Selznick, one of the important figures in the early development of organizational study (Selznick, 1949). Perrow formulated his views while holding a series of faculty appointments at the universities of Michigan, Pittsburgh, and Wisconsin. Since the early 1970s, he has been in the Sociology Department of the State University of New York at Stony Brook.

The Theoretical Contributions of Woodward, Burns and Stalker, and Perrow

The theorists considered in this chapter have in common not only an interest in the role of technology in organizations, but also a commitment to the use of technological variations as a contingency variable. All agree that there is no one best way to structure organizations—that structure should and often does vary with particular technological conditions. Though they emphasize different aspects of technology and/or vary in their conceptualization of the varieties of technology to some degree, the three theories are much more alike than they are different.

Woodward's Technological Determinism

The Woodward theory is the outgrowth of an extensive research project utilizing data from 100 firms and, to a somewhat lesser degree, of a series of case studies. It is therefore inductive in nature. As with many organizational theories, the formulations represent post hoc interpretations of the research. Thus the research, though important in its own right, cannot be considered a validation of the technological theory. On the other hand, the research fails to support many hypotheses of classical management theory, which it was originally designed to test, and it was this outcome that sparked the search for an alternative interpretation.

Both the theory and the research are presented in three major publications—*Management and Technology* (Woodward, 1958), *Industrial Organization: Theory and Practice* (Woodward, 1965), and *Industrial Organization: Behavior and Control* (Woodward, 1970). The 1958 volume is a brief and preliminary version of the 1965 report. The 1970 book contains some theoretical extensions as well as additional case studies and certain reanalyses of the earlier data. In that book technology is defined as "the collection of plant, machines, tools, and recipes available at a given time for the execution of the production task and the rationale underlying their utilization" (Woodward, 1970, p. 4).

Technological Classification Systems. Woodward utilized three major classes of technologies—unit and small batch, large batch and mass production, and process. The scales to which these categorizations were applied varied slightly from the 1958 to the 1965 versions, as noted in Table 8–1. However, the scale utilized was one of increasing technical complexity in that the production process was more controllable and yielded more predictable results. No necessary relationship was assumed between this scale and either progressiveness or organizational size.

In essence the theory states that there is a causal impact of the system of production on organizational patterns:

> Different technologies imposed different kinds of demands on individuals and organizations, and these demands had to be met through an appropriate form of organization. There were still a number of differences between firms—related to such factors as history, background, and personalities—but these were not as significant as the differences between one

production group and another and their influence seemed to be limited by technical considerations (Woodward, 1958, p. 9).

Organizational Patterns. Certain effects that technology has on organization are a direct function of increasing complexity. Thus, as one moves up the scale from unit through large batch to process production, the number of levels of management would be expected to increase; so, too, would the span of control of the chief executive. Committees increasingly are needed toward the process end of the scale, thus reducing authoritarianism; there is more delegation and

Table 8–1

Original and Revised Systems for Classifying Technologies

Original System (Woodward, 1958)	Revised System (Woodward, 1965)
Unit and Small Batch Production	
1. Production of simple units to customers' orders	1. Production of units to customers' requirements
2. Production of technically complex units	2. Production of prototypes
3. Fabrication of large equipment in stages	3. Fabrication of large equipment in stages
4. Production of small batches	4. Production of small batches to customers' orders
Large Batch and Mass Production	
5. Production of large batches, assembly-line type	5. Production of large batches
	6. Production of large batches on assembly lines
6. Mass production	7. Mass production
Process Production	
7. Process production of chemicals in batches	8. Intermittent production of chemicals in multipurpose plant
8. Continuous flow production of liquids, gases, and solid shapes	9. Continuous flow production of liquids, gases, and crystalline substances
Combined Systems	
9. Production of components in large batches, subsequently assembled diversely	10. Production of standardized components in large batches, subsequently assembled diversely
10. Process production combined with the preparation of a product for sale by large batch or mass production methods	11. Process production of crystalline substances, subsequently prepared for sale by standardized production methods.

SOURCE: Adapted from Joan Woodward, *Management and Technology,* Problems of Progress in Industry, no. 3. London: Her Majesty's Stationery Office, 1958, p. 8. Joan Woodward, *Industrial Organization: Theory and Practice.* London: Oxford University Press, 1965, p. 39.

decentralization. Spans of control in middle management are expected to decrease with increasing technological complexity.

Labor costs should be relatively much lower and the proportion of managerial personnel higher in process firms. There are also likely to be more industrial relations specialists, and educational levels should be higher. Direct production work is the predominant source of employment in unit and small batch firms, with clerical and administrative employment increasing as one moves up the scale.

Additional factors are assumed to show a curvilinear relationship to technological complexity. One such factor is the span of control of production supervisors. This span should be greatest and the use of skilled workers least in large batch and mass production. In terms of the mechanistic-organic differentiation developed by Burns and Stalker (1961), mechanistic patterns with highly formalized structures should predominate in the middle of the technological complexity scale, while organic patterns with greater participativeness and flexibility in the production categories should predominate at the extremes. The traditional line-staff structure is also associated with firms in the middle range of technologies. At the extremes either line domination or a functional form with specialists making many key decisions should prevail. Written communication is expected to be more frequent in the large batch and mass production firms, while verbal communication is expected to predominate in firms at the ends of the scale. Quality and other pressures generally should be greater in the middle range, producing more negative attitudes and poorer labor relations.

Technology, Organization, and Success. The basic hypothesis of technological theory is that the firms most nearly approximating the typical structure for their technology should be the most successful. Firms that deviate in either direction from the ideal specified by their technology should be less successful. Thus success is a function of an appropriate technology-structure fit. Though this fit may be consciously planned, and should be in the large batch and mass production category, it arises spontaneously in many cases.

Success in the middle range of technology is thus associated with a mechanistic system:

In general, the administrative expedients associated with success in large-batch production firms were in line with the principles and ideas on which the teaching of management subjects is based. In all the successful large batch production firms there was not only a clear definition of duties and responsibilities ... but also an adherence to the principles of unity of command; a separation (at least on paper) of advisory from executive responsibilities, and a chief executive who controlled no more than the recommended five or six direct subordinates. The tendency to regard large batch production as the typical system of modern industry may be the explanation of this link between success and conformity with management theory (Woodward, 1965, p. 71).

In this view the application of classical management principles at the extremes of the technological complexity scale should be frequent but associated with ineffective organizational performance.

Technological change must be radical enough to influence the production system before structural change should be anticipated. Should the structure not be adapted to the new technology, however, technological innovations cannot be expected to bring success. Structural changes of an appropriate nature are made more difficult by the fact that development plays the dominant role in unit and small batch systems, while manufacturing dominates in large batch and mass production industry and marketing is most important in process systems. Thus, entrenched power positions may well have to change.

The Role of Control. The theory as set forth so far is logically consistent and in many respects logically compelling. However, like many such inductive theories, Woodward's is highly responsive to data, and here difficulties arise:

> Production organization did not appear to be as closely related to the scale of technology [Table 8–1] as other aspects of organization. In the categories at the extremes of the scale there were no problems. . . . But between these two extremes a relationship between production organization and technology was difficult to establish. The general impression obtained from the background survey—that there was greater variation in the way production operations were planned and controlled in firms in the middle ranges of the scale—was confirmed by the follow-up studies (Woodward, 1965, p. 155).

Attempts to deal with this conclusion within the theory have taken several forms, but the role of the control system as an intervening variable between technology and structure has been of continuing concern. The need for some additional theoretical construct was accentuated by the failure of the technology-structure fit to influence success consistently within the middle range of technology. At the same time it was within the middle range that social and technical objectives were at variance most frequently and complex control systems were most likely to appear. Accordingly, structure in the production component itself hypothetically reflected the control system as much as it did the technology, and the control system was often influenced by social and economic factors.

On logical grounds alone one might expect the technological imperative to operate with greatest strength close to the technology within the production component. Yet it is precisely at this point, at least in large batch and mass production systems, that an additional variable is introduced. Nevertheless an attempt is made to specify the relationships between different control systems and different organizational structures and processes (Woodward, 1970).

Control systems fall along two major dimensions: (1) the degree to which they are unitary as opposed to fragmented, and (2) the degree to which they are personal (hierarchical) as opposed to impersonal (mechanical). Controls in unit and small batch production would be expected to be unitary and personal, and in process production, unitary and impersonal (as a function of the technology itself). Within the more heterogeneous large batch and mass production category more diversity is expected, but fragmentation frequently should occur. Here the theory hypothesizes that firms with personal controls should be structured like unit and small batch organizations and those with impersonal controls like process firms.

Technological Determinism Revisited. With the introduction of control concepts Woodward's theory appears to be moving away from pure technological determinism. Control and technology together are said to determine uncertainty levels, and uncertainty influences structure. The technology scale (Table 8–1) covers a range of complexity or predictability, with uncertainty decreasing in the production process as one moves up the scale. Thus the creation of a common metric for technological and control variables seems feasible, but now one has an uncertainty imperative, not a technological imperative.

Woodward's theory was not entirely consistent on this matter at the time of Woodward's death. However, her commitment to technological determinism certainly was less strong than it had been at an earlier time:

> It is important to emphasize that the approach is not technological determinism. It is not suggested that technology is the only, or even the main, determinant of organizational behavior. All that is implied is that technological differences . . . provide a better basis for comparing organizational behavior from firm to firm than do the other comparative frameworks that currently are being used (Woodward, 1973, p. 60).

> Although . . . technology is regarded as a basis for comparison
> and not as the sole or even the major determinant of behavior,
> there is little doubt that an approach of this nature does
> suggest a degree of determinism (Woodward, 1973, p. 63).

Burns and Stalker's Mechanistic and Organic Systems

The theory of mechanistic and organic (or organismic) systems uses change rather than the nature of the technology itself as a contingency variable (Burns and Stalker, 1961; Burns, 1963). Though the major emphasis is on technological change, market change is also a consideration. Both exert certain pressures on the organization that make particular organizational forms desirable:

> As the rate of change increases in the technical field, so does
> the number of occasions which demand quick and effective
> interpretation between people working in different parts of
> the system. As the rate of change increases in the market field,
> so does the need to multiply the points of contact between the
> concern and the markets it wishes to explore and develop
> (Burns and Stalker, 1961, p. 231).

The theory grew out of a series of studies that ultimately encompassed twenty total firms or parts of firms, most of which had invested in electronic development. Several of these firms were also studied by Woodward. Burns and Stalker took an essentially anthropological approach and relied heavily on unstructured observation and interviews. They presented no quantitative data. As the authors themselves state, "All this is far removed from any investigation which could possibly be called scientific" (Burns and Stalker, 1961, p. 13). Thus the only value of the studies themselves is in the theory they generated; they *prove* nothing.

Ideal Types of Organization. Mechanistic systems, which are suited to stable conditions, and organic systems, which are appropriate to changing conditions that introduce new problems and unforeseen requirements for action, are posited as polarities, not as a dichotomy. Thus intermediate stages may occur between the extremes, as described in Table 8–2, and firms may operate within both systems at the same time.

Organic organizations are stratified primarily in terms of expertise, and leadership accrues to those who are the best informed and most capable. There is much more commitment to the organization, with the result that formal and informal systems become indistinguishable. A framework of values and beliefs, much like those characterizing a profession, develops that becomes an effective substitute for

Table 8–2

Characteristics of Mechanistic and Organic Systems

Mechanistic System (appropriate to stable conditions)	Organic System (appropriate to changing conditions)
1. The *specialized differentiation* of functional tasks into which the problems and tasks facing the concern as a whole are broken down.	1. The *contributive nature* of special knowledge and experience to the common task of the concern.
2. The *abstract nature* of each individual task, which is pursued with techniques and purposes distinct from those of the concern as a whole.	2. The *realistic nature* of the individual task, which is seen as set by the total situation of the concern.
3. The reconciliation, for each level in the hierarchy, of these distinct performances by the *immediate superiors*.	3. The adjustment and *continual redefinition* of individual tasks through interaction with others.
4. The *precise definition* of rights and obligations and technical methods attached to each functional role.	4. The *shedding of responsibility* as a limited field of rights, obligations, and methods. Thus problems may not be avoided as someone else's responsibility.
5. The *translation of rights* and obligations and methods into the responsibilities of a functional position.	5. The *spread of commitment* to the concern beyond any technical definition.
6. A *hierarchic structure* of control, authority and communication.	6. A *network structure* of control, authority and communication. Sanctions derive from presumed community of interest with the rest of the organization.
7. A reinforcement of the hierarchic structure by the location of *knowledge* of actualities exclusively *at the top* of the hierarchy.	7. *Knowledge* about the technical or commercial nature of the task may be located *anywhere*. This location becomes the ad hoc center of authority and communication.
8. A tendency for *interaction* between members of the concern to be *vertical.*	8. A *lateral* direction of *communication* through the organization, resembling consultation rather than command.
9. A tendency for operations and working behavior to be governed by the instructions and decisions issued by *superiors*.	9. A content of communication which consists of *information and advice* rather than instructions and decisions.
10. *Insistence on loyalty* to the concern and obedience to superiors as a condition of membership.	10. *Commitment* to the concern's tasks and to the technological ethos of material progress and expansion is more highly valued than loyalty and obedience.

Table 8–2 (Continued)

| 11. A greater importance and prestige attaching to *local* than to cosmopolitan knowledge, experience, and skill. | 11. Importance and prestige attach to *affiliations and expertise* valid in the industrial and technical and commercial milieu external to the firm. |

Note: Reprinted by permission of the publisher from Tom Burns and G. M. Stalker, *The Management of Innovation*. London: Tavistock Publications, 1961, pp. 120–22.

formal hierarchy. Yet the ambiguity and lack of structure can become a source of anxiety for many. Even when the organic system arises as a planned response to a rapidly changing technology that is little understood, managers often yearn for a greater degree of structure.

Pathological Forms of the Mechanistic System. The need for structure, combined with certain political and personal career factors, can block change from mechanistic to organic forms, when such a change would be appropriate; the result is often some pathological form of the mechanistic system and less effective organizational performance (Burns, 1963). Individuals in mechanistic systems may fail to adapt because they are committed to sectional groups or departments, and internal politics may serve to perpetuate existing forms. Similarly it may be in the interests of individuals and their long-term career plans to maintain the status quo.

Three possible pathological responses to change and the consequent uncertainty are noted. First is the *ambiguous figure* system wherein increasing numbers of exceptions to policy are referred to top-level managers, and lower-level managers start to bypass those above them to get decisions made. The result is an overloaded chief executive, considerable conflict, and a highly politicized organization. A second response is the *mechanistic jungle* in which more and more branches are added to the bureaucratic tree and increasing numbers of specialized positions are created to deal with new problems. Since the problems are often related to communication, the new positions tend to be of a liaison type, and the communication system becomes too complex to function. Finally, there is the *superpersonal* or committee system response to change and uncertainty that temporarily grafts committees on the mechanistic structure to deal with special problems, rather than making the needed change to an organic system.

The theory does not indicate when each of these responses might be anticipated, but all are considered nonfunctional under conditions of change.

Perrow's Comparative Framework

Perrow's concern with technology as a central factor in theorizing about organization appears to have been sparked by some of James Thompson's early work (see Chapter 7). It manifested itself first in an article dealing with the goal-setting process in organizations where technology was portrayed as influencing the operative goals—those goals reflected in the observed operating policies and day-to-day decisions of the organization (Perrow, 1961).

This way of thinking was developed further in an extensive review of the literature on hospitals (Perrow, 1965). In this paper he sets forth a view of organizations, emphasizing:

> . . . the work performed on the basic material which is to be altered, rather than focusing upon the interaction of organizational members or the function for society. From this perspective, organizations are viewed as systems which utilize energy (given up by humans and nonhuman devices) in a patterned, directed effort to alter the condition of basic materials in a predetermined manner. . . . Technology is a technique or complex of techniques employed to alter materials (human or nonhuman, mental or physical) in an anticipated manner (Perrow, 1965, pp. 913, 915).

Technology is a major factor determining structure, dominance relationships, and consequently operative goals. Thus, in hospitals, trustees would be expected to play the key role when the technology is simple, physicians when medical technology is central, and administrators when multiple technologies must be coordinated. Views of this kind clearly cast Perrow as a proponent of the technological imperative.

The Dimensions of Technology. Building on these beginnings, Perrow set forth his basic theory in somewhat different forms in several publications (1966, 1967, 1968, 1970a). Two aspects of technology are viewed as having major importance for organizational structure. One is the *number of exceptions* encountered in the work. Do the stimuli lack variability so that they can be handled in a highly programmed manner, or do they pose a constant variety so that every task seems to be a new one? Second, if there are exceptions, *search* must be instituted to determine the appropriate response. The search may be quite analyzable in that it involves routine, logical analysis—one can determine a response by looking it up in a book or by drawing on some other programmed solution. With unanalyzable search, ready-made solutions do not exist. Intuition, insight, experience, and the like are needed. Highly rationalized, programmed responses are not available.

Using this cognitive concept of technology, Perrow places organizations at various points in the two-dimensional space created by the two variables—the number of exceptions and the analyzability of search. Table 8–3 summarizes the results and indicates which of the four quadrants contains each type of organization. The two dimensions tend to be somewhat positively correlated. Thus one would not expect to find instances of tasks that have very few exceptions where search is distinctly unanalyzable, or cases of tasks with a great many exceptions where search is almost completely analyzable.

Paralleling the distinctions Perrow made with regard to technology is another set dealing with the characteristics of the raw material, which in certain cases may be human beings, as in educational institutions. This raw material may vary in the extent to which it is perceived as uniform and stable by members of the organization, paralleling the number of exceptions variable in technology. It may also vary in the degree to which it is well understood (analyzable). Organizations generally seek to standardize raw materials, making them as uniform and stable as possible to minimize the number of exceptions.

Table 8–3

Positions of Types of Firms on Perrow's Dimensions of Technology

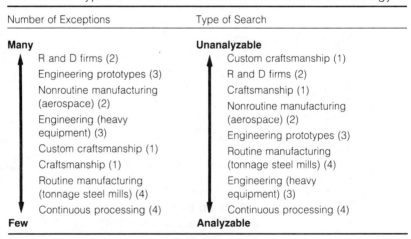

Number of Exceptions	Type of Search
Many	**Unanalyzable**
R and D firms (2)	Custom craftsmanship (1)
Engineering prototypes (3)	R and D firms (2)
Nonroutine manufacturing (aerospace) (2)	Craftsmanship (1)
Engineering (heavy equipment) (3)	Nonroutine manufacturing (aerospace) (2)
Custom craftsmanship (1)	Engineering prototypes (3)
Craftsmanship (1)	Routine manufacturing (tonnage steel mills) (4)
Routine manufacturing (tonnage steel mills) (4)	Engineering (heavy equipment) (3)
Continuous processing (4)	Continuous processing (4)
Few	**Analyzable**

NOTE: Figures in parentheses are the quadrant designations:
1 Craftsman (few exceptions–unanalyzable search)
2 Nonroutine (many exceptions–unanalyzable search)
3 Engineering (many exceptions–analyzable search)
4 Routine (few exceptions–analyzable search)

SOURCE: Adapted from Charles Perrow, "The Effect of Technological Change on the Structure of Business Firms." In B. C. Roberts (ed.), *Industrial Relations: Contemporary Issues.* New York: Macmillan, 1968, p. 211.

Technology and Structure. In relating technology to structure, Perrow makes a major distinction between quadrant 4 with its routine technology, which should foster bureaucratic organization, and quadrant 2 with its nonroutine technology, which requires nonbureaucratic forms. He also relates quadrant 4 to the mechanistic system posited by Burns and Stalker and quadrant 2 to the organic system. With regard to the Woodward classification of firms (see Table 8–1) he has this to say:

> Most of those in the general category "small batch and unit" are probably involved in nonroutine production; those in the "large batch and unit" are probably involved in routine production; those in the "large batch and mass production" category have a mixture of routine and nonroutine technologies, but are predominantly routine. If so, her findings would be consistent with our perspective. However, her analysis of continuous process firms unfortunately cannot easily be incorporated in the scheme advanced here (Perrow, 1967, p. 207).

In addition to these general statements about the routine to nonroutine continuum, Perrow extends his analysis to quadrants 1 and 3 and attempts to deal with task structure in more precise terms. The results of this process are presented in Table 8–4. The structural dimensions relate to control and coordination. The extent of *interdependence* of groups is also considered, though it is said to be high only in the flexible, polycentralized firms needed in quadrant 2, where a nonroutine technology predominates.

Control is defined in terms of the degree of *discretion* an individual or a group has in making decisions about how the work should be organized and carried out and in terms of the *power* to call upon resources and establish goals. Coordination is viewed as occurring either through *planning,* where the interaction of tasks is programmed in advance, either by rules or by the mechanical processes involved, or through *feedback,* where there are negotiated alterations in tasks involving two units (mutual adjustment).

These aspects of control and coordination are specified separately for middle management, which is understood to include technical staff control and support functions, and for direct, first-level supervision of production and marketing. In addition there is some consideration of the top management level where major strategies and policies are formulated, though specifics of structure are not stated in the same manner for this level and thus are not included in Table 8–4. All other things being equal, top management should have routine tasks and techniques in quadrants 4 and 1, nonroutine tasks

Table 8–4
Characteristics of Firms in Perrow's Four Quadrants (Technological Types)

	Quadrant 1 (Craftsman)	Quadrant 2 (Nonroutine)	Quadrant 3 (Engineering)	Quadrant 4 (Routine)
Technology	Few exceptions—unanalyzable search	Many exceptions—unanalyzable search	Many exceptions—analyzable search	Few exceptions—analyzable search
Raw material	Uniform and stable—not well understood	Nonuniform and unstable—not well understood	Nonuniform and unstable—not well understood	Uniform and stable—well understood
Appropriate task structure				
Interdependence of groups	Decentralized	Flexible—polycentralized	Flexible—centralized	Formal—centralized
	Low	High	Low	Low
Discretion				
Middle management	Low	High	High	Low
Direct supervision	High	High	Low	Low
Power				
Middle management	Low	High	High	High
Direct supervision	High	High	Low	Low
Coordination method within groups				
Middle management	Planning	Feedback	Feedback	Planning
Direct supervision	Feedback	Feedback	Planning	Planning
Appropriate social structure	Social identity (communal)	Goal identification (mission, distinctive competence)	Work or task identification (technical satisfactions)	Instrumental identification (job security, pay)
Appropriate goals				
System	Stability	High growth	Moderate growth	Stability
	Few risks	High risks	Some risks	Few risks
	Moderate to low profit emphasis	Low emphasis on profit	Moderate profit emphasis	High profit emphasis
Product	Quality	High quality	Reliability	Quantity
	No innovations	Innovation	Moderate innovations	No innovations
Derived	Conservative	Liberal	Liberal	Conservative

SOURCE: Adapted from Charles Perrow, "A Framework for the Comparative Analysis of Organizations," *American Sociological Review*, 32 (1967), pp. 196, 198–200, 203.

in quadrant 2, and somewhat nonroutine tasks in quadrant 3. However, the product environment (competitors, customers, suppliers, unions, and regulatory agencies) can have a major impact on top management structure. Thus nonroutine tasks may be introduced at this level by environmental forces, and major departures from technological determinism may result. The processes involved here are not spelled out in great detail; in some respects top management structure appears to be outside the domain of the theory.

Attention is also given to the social, as opposed to task, structure of the organization. Differences in organizationally relevant interactions are posited in relation to technology. In nonroutine firms (quadrant 2) these interactions deal with the long-range goals and direction of development of the organization. In craftsman firms (quadrant 1) the emphasis is on communal and personal satisfactions born of long and close associations. In quadrant 4 with its routine technology, the social structure has an instrumental identity, stressing job security, protection from arbitrary authority, pay, and other matters often of concern to unions. In engineering firms (quadrant 3) there is primarily work or task identification, with allied satisfactions.

Technology and Goals. As one moves from task structure to social structure to goals, correlations with technology may be expected to decrease appreciably. Thus technology sets only broad limits on possible goals. These goals are considered in three categories. System goals relate to the organization as a whole, but do not include its products, on which the second category of goals is based. Third, there are derived goals that define the uses to which power generated by the organization may be put in the larger society. Hypotheses with regard to these three types of goals as they operate in different technologies are given in Table 8–4.

Perrow (1967) is less certain about his statements on goals than he is about his statements on technology and structure. The influences of individual personalities and environmental forces on goals may be considerably greater than that of technology. The theory is indeed very tentative at this point.

Subsequent Developments. Shortly after the presentation of his theory, Perrow wrote a book dealing with organizations and their functioning. In it he devoted very little space to the technological imperative. A footnote is revealing: "For a not very successful attempt to spell out four models [of technology], rather than just two see Perrow, 'Framework for Comparative Organizational Analysis'" (Perrow, 1972, p. 170). Sometime in the early 1970s Perrow evidently became somewhat disillusioned with technological theory and the research on it. His only major work in the area in the mid-1970s was an article refuting the view that technological change has been widespread and rapid (and thus environments turbulent) in recent years (Perrow, 1974).

Recently, however, he has begun to give attention to a theme that he noted almost as an aside a number of years before—"For many purposes of organizational analysis technology might not be an independent variable but a dependent one" (Perrow, 1966, p. 163). More specifically on the basis of a historical analysis of the literature surrounding the industrial revolution, he concludes:

> The techniques of doing the work, the technology, the machines, the work flow, the layout, was designed to fit in with and to maximize the potential of this new social system. In contrast to present-day contingency theory, structure predicts to technology, not the other way around (I might add, as an aside, that it still does in its basic sense). . . . Machines were designed, in part, to be unobtrusive control devices, limiting discretion of the operative, pacing her or him faster, demanding continuous attendance, signalling a lapse of attention. The skilled worker was anathema to the factory system: her or his skills had to be dissolved in a machine, or, in Taylorism after the turn of the century, extracted from the worker and placed in the hands of management. . . . The organization came first, the technology second. (Perrow, 1978, pp. 6–8).

Though typically not fully committed to this position either, Perrow clearly does have doubts about technological determinism. He raises the question of whether "structural determinism" is not a more defensible position. His openness of mind is clearly intellectually admirable. But it is still important to establish the validity of the technological imperative.

Research by the Theorists

All of the theorists considered in the previous section conducted some research, though not necessarily as true tests of their theories. The Burns and Stalker (1961) study already noted was exploratory and not intended as scientific research. Accordingly, it is not considered further here. The other two theorists carried out significant research.

Woodward's Study of Manufacturing Firms

The Woodward (1958, 1965) study dealt with 100 manufacturing firms in the South Essex area of England. Roughly a third of these firms were branch factories of larger companies. Though firms with fewer than 100 employees were excluded, the sample still focused on smaller organizations, almost three-quarters of them having fewer than 500 employees. Data dealing with the background and objectives of the firm, manufacturing processes, organizational structure and processes, and financial success were obtained from records and interviews.

The initial analyses compared such factors as the number of levels of management, spans of control, managerial ratios, staff ratios, ratios of direct to indirect labor, and the use of organizational planning to financial success. The essential objective was to test certain principles of management derived from classical management theory. However, the Burns and Stalker organic-mechanistic classification was also utilized in the expectation that organicity would be associated with success because of pervasive, rapid, technological change in the area studied. Both successful and less successful firms differed widely on the variables studied, and none of the predicted relationships was identified. However, quantitative data on success relationships are not provided, nor are significance tests reported for them.

In exploring the data for some benefits to be salvaged from an extremely time-consuming data collection process, the researchers noted certain differences when the technological categories of Table 8–1 were utilized. In subsequent analyses by technological category combined systems were eliminated, and other cases had insufficient data. The reported findings, were consistent, of course, with the previously stated hypotheses, since the hypotheses derive from the findings. In general these findings are given in verbal terms only. The exceptions are shown in Table 8–5. Additional support for the theory is adduced from a limited number of case analyses (Woodward, 1965, 1970). A reanalysis of the data (Table 8–6) formed the basis for the control hypotheses.

Perrow's Measures and Research

Perrow (1970b, 1970c, 1973) conducted studies in fourteen firms or divisions of firms to investigate relationships between technology and structure. The data were obtained from questionnaire measures administered at the managerial level. This questionnaire contained a number of questions intended to get at dimensions of technology. However, in the final analysis Perrow rejected certain of these questions as inappropriate to the study of technology as he defined it. As a result, he ended with a measure focused on the single dimension running from routine (cell 4) to nonroutine (cell 2) of his theory, and did not operationalize the engineering and craftsman components. The questions in the final technology index asked for a rating of (1) the percent of time the respondents were not sure whether what they did would work or not, and (2) the probability that there

Table 8–5

Relationships Between Technology and Organizational Variables

	Technological Category					
	Unit and Small Batch		Large Batch and Mass		Process Production	
Organizational Variables	N	Median	N	Median	N	Median
Levels of management	24	3	31	4	25	6
Span of control of CEO	*	4	*	7	*	10
Percent of costs allocated to wages	23	36	28	33	20	15
Ratio of managers to nonmanagers	*	1:23	*	1:16	*	1:8
Number of direct workers to one indirect	24	9	28	6	23	1
Number of industrial workers to one staff	24	8	28	6	23	2
Span of control first-line supervisors	24	23	31	49	25	13

	Relative Successfulness of Firms by Category					
Percent with Each First-Line Span	More (N=5)	Less (N=5)	More (N=5)	Less (N=6)	More (N=6)	Less (N=4)
Less than 10	0	20	0	0	17	25
11 to 20	0	20	0	17	83	0
21 to 30	80	0	0	17	0	25
31 to 40	20	0	0	17	0	50
41 to 50	0	40	60	0	0	0
51 to 60	0	20	40	0	0	0
61 to 70	0	0	0	0	0	0
71 to 80	0	0	0	17	0	0
81 to 90	0	0	0	32	0	0

*Ns not reported

Source: Adapted from Joan Woodward, *Industrial Organization Theory and Practice*. London: Oxford University Press, 1965, pp. 52–55, 59–60, 69.

was someone else in the organization who could help them should they face a problem in their work that they could not handle.

Reports of the study do not systematically relate the findings to the theory, and the structural dimensions considered are neither consistently the same as those in Table 8–4 nor always differentiated by managerial level. The measures used deal with:

1. Clarity—clear lines of authority, written rules, precise duties and authority, and delegation.

Table 8–6
Woodward's Reanalysis of Management Study Data by
Technological Category and Type of Control

Controls	Technological Category		
	Unit	Large Batch	Process
Unitary and personal (N = 28)	75%	15%	0
Fragmented and personal (N = 21)	25	35	0
Fragmented and impersonal (N = 18)	0	40	5%
Unitary and impersonal (N = 33)	0	10	95

SOURCE: Adapted from Joan Woodward, *Industrial Organization: Behavior and Control.* London: Oxford University Press, 1970, p. 48.

2. Strictness—following orders, consistent use of procedures, and consistent reporting relationships.

3. Openness—use of group decisions, lower-level suggestions, interdepartmental teams, and individual initiative and judgment.

4. Influence—within the whole company and with supervisors.

5. Coordination—whether by planning and routine or by mutual adjustment and feedback.

6. Power—of management levels and functional areas.

Relationships were found that tied nonroutine technology with feedback coordination, low strictness, and possibly low clarity, but not with openness, individual influence, or power. These findings are summarized as follows:

> The relationship between technology and task-related aspects of structure was high, but the relationship between technology and subordinate power, influence, and discretion was attenuated. Apparently, considerations of organizational history and leadership variables, which were not measured, played an increasing role here (Perrow, 1970b, p. 82).

No findings related to social structure and goals are reported by Perrow, but Magnusen (1973) indicates there was some directional support for the goals formulations, but little for those regarding social structure.

The Aston Studies and Replications

A series of studies related to the technological imperative was initiated in the early 1960s at what was to become the University of Aston in Birmingham, England (Pugh and Hickson, 1976). This research has involved a rather large number of individuals, many of whom have continued their work at other universities. The unifying links in these studies are the use of relatively large samples of diverse organizations, often drawn to represent a given area, and the scoring of these organizations on standardized measures related to context and structure. Information for these latter scales was provided by top-level managers and existing records.

The Original Study

The original Aston study utilized a composite measure of technology dealing with the degree of automation, the rigidity of the workflow processes, the interdependence of workflow, and the extent to which operations were evaluated against precise specifications or plans. This primary measure of technology was considered to be an index of *workflow integration* (Hickson, Pugh, and Pheysey, 1969). An attempt also was made to develop a scale analogous to that originally devised by Woodward (1958), which applied to manufacturing organizations only. This latter measure, considered to be an index of *production continuity*, correlated .46 with the basic Aston measure.

Table 8–7 contains data for workflow integration, production continuity, and size as measured by number of employees, correlated with three composite measures of structure (structuring of activities, concentration of authority, control of workflow by line managers), their major component scales, and other indexes considered by Woodward. The findings do not provide strong support for the technological imperative. In manufacturing organizations, where one would expect the theory to apply, there are few significant correlations with any technology measure, and the significant correlations with technology that do emerge can be explained in terms of the larger and more frequently significant size correlations. Only a marginally significant curvilinear relationship to the first-line supervisor's span of control is as hypothesized.

Within the much more diverse total sample, technology does yield significant correlations, but those for size are usually larger. In general, technology tends to be the better predictor only when structural factors close to the workflow are considered. Given that most of their organizations were larger than Woodward's (none under 250 employees and 60 percent over 500), the authors hypothesize:

> Structural variables will be associated with operations technology only where they are centered on the workflow. The smaller the organization the more its structure will be pervaded by such technological effects: the larger the organization, the more these effects will be confined to variables such as job counts of employees on activities linked with the workflow itself, and will not be detectable in variables of the more remote administrative and hierarchical nature (Hickson, Pugh, and Pheysey, 1969, pp. 394–95).

Table 8–7

Statistically Significant Correlations of Technology Measures and Size with Structural Variables

Structural Variables	All Organizations (N=46)		Manufacturing Organizations (N=31)		
	Technology (Aston)	Size (Employees)	Technology (Aston)	Technology (Woodward)	Size (Employees)
Degree of structuring of activities	.34	.69	—	.41(.07)[a]	.78
Role specification	.38	.75	—	.52(.26)[a]	.83
Functional specialization	.44	.67	—	—	.75
Standardization of procedures	.46	.56	—	—	.65
Formalization of documentation	—	.55	—	—	.67
Degree of concentration of authority	−.30	—	—	—	—
Standardization of selection/promotion procedures	−.38	.31	—	.43(.29)[a]	.42
Centralization of decisions	—	−.39	—	—	−.47
Organizational autonomy	—	—	—	—	—
Degree of control of workflow by line managers	−.46	—	—	—	—
Formalization of role performance recording	.41	.42	—	—	.45
First-line span of control	.35	—	—	−(.36)[b]	—
Percent workflow managers	−.53	—	—	—	—
CEO span of control	—	.32	—	—	—
Levels of management	—	.67	—	.51(.26)[a]	.77
Percent direct workers	—	—	—	—	−.46
Percent nonworkflow personnel	.34	.36	—	—	.53
Size (number of employees)	—		—	.47	
Woodward technology measure			.46		

[a] Figures in parentheses are partial correlations with size removed—none significant.
[b] Curvilinear correlation in parentheses—significant and in accord with Woodward theory

SOURCE: Adapted from David J. Hickson, D. S. Pugh, and Diana C. Pheysey. "Operations Technology and Organization Structure: An Empirical Reappraisal," *Administrative Science Quarterly*, 14 (1969), pp. 386, 391.

Limited Scale Replications

There have been several replication studies conducted on a more limited scale that support the original Aston finding that size-structure correlations typically exceed those for technology and structure. Data from two such studies are given in Table 8–8. Again the correlations obtained with the Aston workflow integration measure of technology tend to shrink when the sample is limited to manufacturing firms only. Also, though size yields larger correlations, and more significant values as well, one cannot conclude that technology is unrelated to important structural dimensions.

The National Study

The most comprehensive attempt at replicating the original Aston results involved eighty-two firms distributed throughout England and Scotland, thus the designation "national study." All were in the business sector, and a predominant number were autonomous. The size scale was extended downward to 100 employees. The results relating to technology characteristically confirm the earlier Aston findings (Child, 1973a, 1973b, 1975; Child and Mansfield, 1972). Size continues to yield high correlations with structural variables, but those for technology are not negligible. Though significant correlations with technology occur close to the technology in various staffing ratios, they also emerge in relation to structuring activities generally.

In contrast to all preceding studies, the national research included measures of organizational performance bearing on Woodward's hypothesis that organizations in the middle range of structure for a technology group would be more successful. However, such data as have been reported are not very encouraging. Donaldson (1976, p. 267) indicates that, "Preliminary analysis of the relationships involving organizational structure shows little clear association with performance." On the other hand there are some positive findings, though not necessarily of the exact type Woodward anticipated:

> Correlations were computed separately for above and below average performance companies between a measure of rigidity in the main workflow and organizational variables. . . . although in both high and low performance companies maintenance roles become more specialized along with the use of more rigid technology (generally characterized by heavier and more specialized plant), it was only in faster growing and more profitable companies that the requirements of the more rigid technologies were met by allocating a larger

Table 8–8

Correlation of Technology and Size with Structural Variables in Two Studies

Structural Variables	Forty Organizations in the English Midlands		Twenty-five Midlands Manufacturing Firms		Twenty-one U.S. (Ohio) Manufacturing Firms	
	Technology (Aston measure)	Size (Employees)	Technology (Aston measure)	Size (Employees)	Technology (Aston measure)	Size (Employees)
Degree of structuring of activities	(.51)	(.61)	.30	(.71)	(.59)	(.72)
Functional specialization			.27	(.80)	(.64)	(.82)
Formalization of documentation			.26	(.51)	(.45)	(.48)
Degree of concentration of authority	(−.39)	.11	−.25	.00	.30	.35
Size	.23		.31		(.75)	

(   ) Correlations statistically significant.

Source: Adapted from J. H. K. Inkson, D. S. Pugh, and D. J. Hickson, "Organization Context and Structure: An Abbreviated Replication," *Administrative Science Quarterly*, 15 (1970), p. 321. J. H. K. Inkson, J. P. Schwitter, D. C. Pheysey, and D. J. Hickson, "A Comparison of Organization Structure and Managerial Roles: Ohio, U.S.A. and the Midlands, England," *Journal of Management Studies*, 7 (1970), p. 361.

percentage of total employment to maintenance services. A comparable distinction was apparent with dispatch and transport activities. In higher performance companies there was a significant positive relationship between rigidity of technology and a greater proportion of total employment being given over to these activities, in low performance companies there was no relationship. . . . Among the companies securing an above average level of income to sales, as rigidity of technology increased so did the proportion of employment devoted to market research activities and the level of specialization among employees in that function (Child, 1975, pp. 24–25).

The Aston researchers have consistently interpreted all of their findings as evidence against the technological imperative. Yet they report numerous relationships between technology and structure. Though the size correlations are often larger, they are rarely significantly larger. Furthermore, whether the technological effects are considered to be swamped by those of size is a consequence of one's assumptions about the causal processes involved (Aldrich, 1972; Pugh and Hickson, 1972). Longitudinal research that sorts out the causal sequencing among technology, size, and various aspects of structure is clearly needed. Aside from a small and inconclusive study by Inkson, Pugh, and Hickson (1970), the Aston researchers have focused on concurrent data. This appropriate first step has not answered all the questions.

Evaluations of the Theories

The Aston research was in large part a response to the Woodward hypotheses. To the extent it is generalizable to the technological imperative as a whole, it has implications for the Perrow and Burns and Stalker theories as well, but it is less directly relevant for them. On the other hand, there is a host of other studies that were designed to test one or the other theories independently.

Tests of the Woodward Theory

The research considered to this point has dealt with organizational, as opposed to subunit or work group, processes and structures. In addition it has focused on the manufacturing sector, though the Aston studies included other types of organizations as well. The total literature related to the technological imperative concerns itself with a more diverse range of organizations and includes subunit as well as total system levels of analysis (Reiman and Inzerilli, 1979). However, that portion of the literature that has utilized a measure of technology analogous to that employed by Woodward and accordingly purports to test the Woodward theory has continued the focus on manufacturing industry at the firm level.

The Zwerman Study. The most ambitious attempt to replicate the Woodward findings involved fifty-five firms in the Minneapolis area (Zwerman, 1970). This sample was restricted to organizations with more than 100 employees, but it contained disproportionately more large firms than did the Woodward study.

The data indicate that organic systems predominate at the extremes of the technology scale and mechanistic systems predominate in the intermediate, large-batch and mass production category. However, only when mechanistic systems are used with intermediate technologies is there any relationship to organizational success. Additional data on structural relationships are given in Table 8–9. With the exception of the span of control of first-line supervisors, the reported medians for technology groups follow a pattern consistent with the hypotheses. The differences are smaller than they were in the Woodward study, and significance levels are not reported. When success is considered, the expected pattern of more successful firms falling close to the median for the technology group

Table 8–9
Relationships among Technology, Success, and Structure in the Zwerman Sample

	Technology					
	Unit and Small Batch		Large Batch and Mass		Process	
Structural Variable	Successful (%)	Less Successful (%)	Successful (%)	Less Successful (%)	Successful (%)	Less Successful (%)
Span of control of CEO						
1–3	22	11	8	13	0	0
4–5	56	22	15	54	17	0
6–7	11	45	46	20	17	0
8–10	11	22	15	13	33	0
11 +	0	0	15	0	33	0
Medians		5		6		8.5
Ratio of nonmanagers to managers						
1–6	10	0	46	27	80	0
7–12	50	45	15	20	20	0
13–18	10	45	15	40	0	0
19 +	30	10	24	13	0	0
Medians		12		10.5		5
Levels of management						
2–3	45	45	0	6	0	0
4	22	11	20	40	0	0
5	33	22	33	27	17	0
6 +	0	22	47	27	83	0
Medians		4		5		6
Ratio of production to nonproduction workers						
1–	50	0	13	13	83	0
2–3	30	33	54	54	17	0
4–5	20	33	13	20	0	0
6 +	0	33	20	13	0	0
Medians		3		2		.6
Percent of costs allocated to wages						
12½%	11	20	0	22	0	0
12½–25%	11	0	10	0	60	0
26–50%	33	40	70	45	20	0
>50%	45	40	20	33	20	0
Medians		36		35		25
Span of control of first-line supervisors						
10–	22	0	15	7	25	0
11–20	45	50	38	53	50	0
21–30	0	0	8	13	0	0
31–40	33	50	23	13	25	0
41–50	0	0	8	7	0	0
51 +	0	0	8	7	0	0
Medians		20		20		17

SOURCE: Adapted from William L. Zwerman, *New Perspectives on Organization Theory*. Westport, Conn.: Greenwood, 1970, pp. 67, 71, 73, 100, 108, 184.

and the less successful falling at both extremes (see Table 8–5) is not obtained, though data on less successful process firms were not available. Overall, though the author interprets his findings as strongly supportive of the Woodward theory, this support is in fact rather weak (Donaldson, 1976).

Other Research. In general the limited research tests of Woodward's hypotheses on organizational effectiveness have not confirmed the theory. Some findings indicate an interplay between technology, structure, and effectiveness, however. Thus, Khandwalla (1974) found the hypothesized relationships between technology and structural dimensions such as decentralization among the more successful firms, but not among the less successful.

Tests dealing with the technological imperative itself yield extremely mixed results. There is some support for the Aston finding that certain personnel ratios and spans of control at the lowest level are related to technology (Blau, Falbe, McKinley, and Tracy, 1976). Yet these investigators did not find support for the views that structural variables directly linked to production are affected most or that technology exerts its most pervasive influence in small organizations. Characteristically, size relationships were greater than those involving technology.

A recent study by Reimann (1980) utilized an index of technology modeled on that of Woodward and found a limited number of relationships. Of eleven correlations with structural variables, three were significant—with formalization, centralization of operations, and size of the maintenance staff. Variables such as number of levels in the hierarchy and the various spans of control were unrelated to the technology measure. Surprisingly the presence or absence of an in-house computer yielded seven significant correlations, while size produced only five.

In reviewing the literature in this area, Reimann and Inzerilli (1979, pp. 181–82) conclude:

> ... findings with respect to the technology-structure relationship are difficult to compare, and, where they are comparable, often inconsistent. This, of course, was to be expected since many of the complex organizations studies may have been operating with several different workflow technologies (e.g., some unit, some mass, and some process production) and the aggregate measures used generally did not reflect this possible variety.

Tests of the Perrow Theory

In contrast to the research on the Woodward theory, that on the Perrow theory has focused on service rather than manufacturing organizations and frequently has utilized subunits rather than total systems as the basis for analysis. Within this primary context involving subunit-level analyses of service organizations, measures of Perrow's routine-nonroutine dimension have shown consistent relationships to structural factors (Reimann and Inzerilli, 1979). At this subunit level, sizable variations in technology within the unit are less likely to occur and thus one potential source of error in organizationwide studies such as those used to test the Woodward theory is eliminated.

Furthermore, there is some evidence here, for the first time, that technology can actually cause the structural effects (Van de Ven, 1977). Longitudinal analyses indicated that as the technology became more nonroutine supervisory decision making decreased and employee and group decision making increased—thus a certain type of decentralization occurred. These technological effects exceeded those for size. On the other hand, there are also data, though less powerful because they derive from concurrent analyses, suggesting that structural factors (in this case, division of labor) may influence the degree of routinization of work (Glisson, 1978). Actually there is no reason why the primary direction of causation could not vary from one structural variable to another.

Though the evidence bearing on the Perrow theory tends to be positive, a comparison with Table 8–4 indicates that only limited aspects of the basic theory have been tested. The focus has been entirely on a dimension running from quadrant 2 (nonroutine) to quadrant 4 (routine). Furthermore, the variables considered have rarely been identical with those Perrow proposed. Thus in a very real sense, in spite of extensive research, the Perrow theory remains untested.

Tests of the Burns and Stalker Theory

The Burns and Stalker theory deals with technological change, not technological type, and it incorporates market change as well. In this latter respect the theory moves beyond the technological imperative into the domain of contingency theory. Thus a full evaluation of the theory of mechanistic and organic systems must await the discussion in Chapter 9.

Ideally the hypothesis on technological change would be tested longitudinally. One such investigation compares increases in the scope of the technology in social service organizations with various structural changes (Dewar and Hage, 1978). The data are consistent with the view that technological change produces more diversified and specialized occupational structures, but the anticipated effects of technological change on levels of hierarchy and factors associated with spans of control were minimal at best.

In another series of studies, various indexes of technological change taking place over considerable periods of time prior to the study were related to measures of centralization, specialization, formalization, spans of control, levels of hierarchy, and various staff personnel indexes (Reimann, 1975; 1980). Though not specifically formulated in terms of the mechanistic-organic concept, many of the structural indexes clearly relate to it. Yet no significant relationships were found, nor were the variables of the study related to measures of organizational effectiveness. Keller, Slocum, and Susman (1974), utilizing a measure of the number of product changes in continuous process manufacturing organizations, also failed to find support for the Burns and Stalker theory, even though they made the mechanistic-organic differentiation explicit. Organic firms did prove to be more successful in process industries, but this was totally unrelated to the amount of technological change.

An earlier study by Harvey (1968) had utilized the product change measure and obtained more favorable results, though it did not include data on organizational effectiveness. The findings, given in Table 8–10, clearly indicate that greater technological change is associated with a more organic organizational form. These results cannot be attributed to size effects.

On balance, the evidence is not strongly supportive of the Burns and Stalker hypotheses regarding technology. The Harvey (1968) study provides the most positive evidence, but since it does not test the hypotheses regarding success, even this support is only partial.

Construct Validity and Measurement Problems

The studies of the technological imperative theories utilize a wide range of measures of both technology and structure. To some extent, especially in technology, divergence would be expected because the underlying theoretical constructs are different. However, this is not true in every case, and accordingly considerations such as construct validity, comparability of measures, and reliability become important for all the various measures employed.

Technology Variables. As noted in Table 8–7, the Aston researchers found a correlation of .46 between their own measure of technology and one developed to coincide with Woodward. Subsequent research suggests that values above this can be expected only rarely, even when essentially comparable technology constructs are involved (Lynch, 1974). Pierce and Dunham (1978) report that two questionnaire indexes of routinization-variability correlated .77, but findings of this kind are rare.

In general the rather low correlations do not appear to be attributable to unreliability of the measures (Dewar, Whetten, and Boje,

Table 8–10

Relationships Between Frequency of Product Changes and Aspects of Structure in Forty-Three Manufacturing Firms

Structural Variable	Frequency of Product Changes		
	Few (%)	Intermediate (%)	Many (%)
Number of subunits (Division of labor)			
Few	0	13	64
Intermediate	31	56	36
Many	69	31	0
Levels of hierarchy			
Few	0	19	64
Intermediate	38	44	36
Many	62	37	0
Number of managers per employee			
Few	0	6	79
Intermediate	31	63	21
Many	69	31	0
Extent of programming of roles, output, and communications			
Low (organic)	0	6	72
Intermediate	23	81	21
High (mechanistic)	77	13	7

SOURCE: Adapted from Edward Harvey, "Technology and the Structure of Organizations," *American Sociological Review*, 33 (1968), p. 255.

1980; Lynch, 1974; Pierce and Dunham, 1978). Some reported reliability coefficients drop into the .50s, but this is almost invariably a consequence of the use of very short instruments; usually the values are in the .70s or higher. Technology seems to be measured differently in many of the studies. If there were multiple technological imperatives, this would not be a problem. But the research findings are uneven. Some technology constructs and/or operationalizations of them seem to be more powerful than others.

One approach measures technology through the use of questionnaires on the perceptions of organization members, as in Perrow's (1970b, 1970c) own research. This approach is very similar to one used in studying jobs and job redesign at the micro level (see Miner, 1980), a similarity that led Pierce and Dunham (1978) to study the relationships empirically. They found very strong associations between technological routinization-variability and job-based feedback. This suggests that operationalizations of technology, if not the underlying constructs themselves, may well have moved a considerable distance away from what Woodward and the Aston researchers originally had in mind.

Structural Variables. Continuing the logic applied to technology, one might expect that questionnaire measures of structure administered across a broad base of organization members might also yield results different from those obtained through observation and through interviews with top-level executives. One early study compared various measures of centralization and formalization used in the Aston studies with questionnaire measures of comparable variables (Pennings, 1973). Though the various questionnaire measures tended to be related to each other, they were not related to the more objective measures with any consistency; this lack of association was particularly pronounced in the case of centralization. A subsequent study by Sathe (1978) that drew upon additional measures of the structural variables produced almost identical results. Other research using the same questionnaire and objective measures has had some very limited success in establishing construct validity for formalization, but overall, the lack of convergence between the two types of measures remains in evidence (Ford, 1979).

When questionnaire measures of structural variables such as centralization and formalization are related to micro-level variables drawn from job redesign research, problems similar to those with technology emerge. There are strong associations with job autonomy (Pierce and Dunham, 1978). The sparse research in this area suggests that at least some questionnaire measures that purport to measure aspects of *organizational* structure may not in fact have moved beyond the level of the individual position.

Though the reliabilities for structural measures, when reported, appear to be at least as good as those for technological measures (Dewar, Whetten, and Boje, 1980; Pierce and Dunham, 1978), it is questionable whether actual structural properties of organizations have been measured consistently. To the extent they have not, true tests of the technological imperative are lacking.

Conclusions

The literature related to the technological imperative is about as confused as any in the area of organizational theorizing. Major reviews of research come to almost diametrically opposed conclusions (Donaldson, 1976; Reimann and Inzerilli, 1979). Even the theorists themselves have basic disagreements. Thus, Woodward has the following to say:

> Although, however, Perrow develops his ideas as a basis for comparison, his attempts at measurement are of an elementary kind. . . . his attention seems to be focused on the perception by organization members of the constraints in the work

environment. . . . Indeed he does what the Imperial College team had tried to avoid from the outset; he classifies technology in terms that are themselves social (Woodward, 1970, p. 33).

And Perrow indicates:

It is impossible to determine how Woodward or Burns and Stalker arrived at their classifications of companies (Perrow, 1967, p. 208).

What conclusions (if any) can be reached, then, regarding this approach to theory construction?

Scientific Goals

The Individual Theories. Certain problems in the technological imperative literature relate to the individual theories; others relate to the general concept of a technological imperative itself. Two of the theorists, Woodward and Perrow, came very close to rejecting their own theories in the early 1970s, and Burns and Stalker appear to have largely abandoned theirs. Often the theorists have had difficulty making the theories work subsequently, either in individual case contexts or in more comprehensive organizational research.

The Woodward's theory is incomplete in the middle range of technology and the later resort to control systems as the explanatory variable (Woodward, 1970) introduces considerable theoretical confusion. It is not at all clear whether control procedures are part of technology, or structure, or some other category of variables such as organizational process. Research on the Woodward theory yields intermittent support at best. Early efforts to limit the domain of the theory to constructs close to the dominant technology have not proven particularly fruitful; the theory does not necessarily work better within the more limited domain.

The Burns and Stalker theory has the advantage of considerable parsimony. However, it fails to specify when the various pathological forms will emerge and to that extent is incomplete. The mechanistic-organic differentiation appears to be useful conceptually, but research evidence that this variable operates as hypothesized (at least in response to technological change) is sparse indeed; only the Harvey (1968) study can be said to provide results that consistently support the theory.

The Perrow theory is something of an enigma. It is presented as a theory of organizational level functioning analogous to the other two theories, and the examples Perrow cites are of this type (see Table 8–3). Yet the theoretical variables appear to deal more with individual or at best work group level concepts. This is manifest not only in the theoretical definitions, but also in Perrow's own operationalizations and in the level at which research designed to test the theory has been carried out. It is questionable whether the theory or the research generated by it should be extrapolated to the organizational level. Ultimately, Perrow (1972) appears to have recognized these problems also.

At the micro level Perrow's theory has received considerable support. In this research it emerges not so much as a broad theory of organization, but as a theory of job design focused on the routine-nonroutine dimension. Other aspects of the theory simply have not been tested sufficiently. Though these studies tend to aggregate data obtained from individuals, they do so within units where considerable task homogeneity exists. In addition they focus on only one aspect of the job—routineness—ignoring even the engineering-craftsman dimension that Perrow also proposed. Accordingly, it seems best to consider the Perrow theory as it has been operationalized and tested a limited-scale, micro-level theory of organizational behavior, rather than a theory of organizational process and structure. This conclusion is reinforced by Perrow's own tentativeness in hypothesizing about organizational social structure and goals and his recent indication (1978) that organizational technology operates more as a dependent than as an independent variable.

All the theories propose that when technology (by whatever definition) and structure fit in the appropriate manner the result will be greater organizational effectiveness. Tests extending to this effectiveness variable have been relatively few, compared to those merely relating technology and structure. What has been done provides little support for the normative aspect of the theories. The Woodward findings emerged only after an extensive post hoc search for relationships among many variables, and actual data are presented for only one structural factor—first-line span of control. Thus capitalization on chance remains a distinct possibility.

Technology Overall. Commentary on the technological imperative literature pinpoints a number of problem areas. One difficulty is that most organizations of any size have multiple technologies. To the degree this is true, striking an average or defining a dominant technology misrepresents the true state of affairs (Gerwin, 1979; Gillespie and Mileti, 1977). Segmenting the organization by subunits and testing the theory within units can well reduce this source of error, but fails to achieve a theory of *organization*. Furthermore, it appears that these subunit (or individual) level studies often do not deal with technology as Woodward originally used the term. Rather they measure task or job design factors at a micro level. The result is a considerable dilution of construct validity.

The dilution of construct validity is exaggerated by the fact that different definitions of technology and structure appear to overlap so that a given variable may be considered part of technology in one instance and of structure in another (Gerwin, 1979; Gillespie and Mileti, 1977; Stanfield, 1976). Classification problems are particularly pronounced when the technology is not of a manufacturing nature and with variables that reflect individual role prescriptions. As a result of inconsistencies in the applications of category boundaries, it is difficult to determine the comparability of different study results.

Another problem is the tendency to use limited sets of variables or even single variables to stand for the whole technology and/or structure construct. Generalization of this kind is risky in that different aspects of technology and of structure may in fact operate differently (Rousseau, 1979; Stanfield, 1976). The Woodward theory, for instance, hypothesizes different forms of relationships, even within the span of control concept, and in numerous instances aspects of formalization and centralization have acted differentially. Rousseau (1979) has shown that studies have dealt in various instances with input characteristics, input control, conversion processes, output control, and output characteristics while treating each of these as a proxy for technology as a whole. Similarly studies conducted at the individual, subunit, and organizational levels are used interchangeably to demonstrate relationships between organizational technology and organizational structure. Most of the research is much less generalizable than it has been made out to be. Thus failure to find a relationship may not sound the death knell of technological imperative theory as a whole, but finding one does not prove all versions to be true either.

Perhaps the most perplexing problem is causality. The theory includes a causal arrow. Yet we have little that even approximates a controlled study where a technology is introduced in one setting and not in another, and structural changes are measured. In no research has the technology-structure fit been manipulated and effectiveness then measured. Such studies are difficult to conduct, but tests of this kind have been applied to other theories. They are badly needed in the case of the technological imperative.

Some longitudinal research has been done and path analysis has been used to extract causal generalizations from concurrent data. Path analysis appears to be less useful than longitudinal studies, depending as it does on certain very limiting assumptions. In fact, two different applications have produced what appear to be directly antithetical conclusions—that technology causes structure (Aldrich, 1972) and that structure causes technology (Glisson, 1978). One is left with a feeling that something other than concurrent data are needed.

Longitudinal data indicate that technology does not have much causal impact. Thus a shift in a large hospital kitchen from batch to mass production technology was found to produce certain changes in job characteristics for those close to the change, but no other structural alterations (Billings, Klimoski, and Breaugh, 1977). Other research indicates that technological changes can be accompanied by the introduction of new specialists and thus a more differentiated work force. To the extent these specialists are able to exercise expert power of the kind typically invoked by professionals, it appears that some decentralization close to the technology may occur. There is no reason why, in the case of a major upgrading of technology, these structural effects might not reverberate out to more distant parts of the organization, but the findings to date indicate this is not a very common occurrence.

If the causal impact of technology is as limited as the data appear to imply, how can one account for those findings that emerge from certain concurrent studies indicating that relationships between technological and structural variables do exist? Argyris (1972) and others have suggested that psychological variables should be introduced into what have been essentially sociological equations. Actually, Perrow raised this possibility at an early point, but did not pursue it, and Child (1972) emphasized the role of choice in organizational structuring.

The point is, as Pfeffer (1978) notes, that both the technologies and the structures of an organization are chosen at a point in time by an individual or individuals who have sufficient control over resources to implement these technologies and structures. Once chosen, both sets of variables may exert controls on organization members and operate as constraints on further change. As noted, the choices involving technology may carry with them certain implications for structure, as when professionals are needed. Also choices regarding structure, for instance the introduction of small autonomous work groups, may carry implications for technology. However, at a higher level both technology and structure are chosen and thus caused by the same third factor. Until changes in either technology or structure are introduced, the original choices are continually reaffirmed, and when changes do occur, they also come about as a result of choice.

In this view the primary causal variable is a decision or choice, not technology or structure. To the extent certain correlations between technological and structural variables exist in the minds of the choosers, these will be perpetuated in organizations and found in research. Though some such correlations in the minds of decision makers may yield patterns that make for more effective organizations, research focused on technological considerations has produced little to confirm this hypothesis.

Giving the primary emphasis to the causal effects of choice, which operates conjointly on technology and structure, severely limits the role of the technological imperative. To the extent the choosers in organizations are influenced by common philosophies or achieve a degree of consensus as a result of interoganizational communications, patterns of relationships may emerge with some consistency, as they did in the Aston studies. Such a theory suggests a change in research strategy to focus on organizational decision makers and the procedures they use to make choices about technology and structure. Pursuing the technological imperative alone seems no more likely to be fruitful in the future than it has been in the past.

Goals of Application

This chapter has given scant attention to applications of technological imperative theories. This is not an oversight; rather, it reflects the realities in this area of theory construction. The Woodward research was originally undertaken to influence the content of management courses and thereby management practice. In reporting on that research the author notes:

> It was hoped that this research would produce findings on which the management course offered in the South East Essex Technical College could be appraised. At first sight this report may suggest that these courses have limited usefulness and can in some circumstances be misleading to students. The danger lies in the tendency to teach the principles of administration as though they were scientific laws (Woodward, 1958, p. 34).

Though the research generated caution in teaching the principles of classical management theory, it did not generate a new course based on the technological imperative or a design to help organizations fit their structures to their technologies more appropriately. Clear-cut guides to action are almost totally lacking. In this sense the technological imperative theory has not generated the technology for its own application.

Actually, Perrow envisaged the development of such a technology at an early point:

Students must not only learn discrete techniques or even analytical skills, but also acquire the ability to see when a technique is or is not applicable because of the technological and structural situation in which it might be applied. . . . More generally, the perspective has implications for management practices: Why do you have so much trouble when you try to combine routine and nonroutine production techniques in the same plant? Not just because metallurgists and old time production men won't mix. When should you isolate production lines or even phases of production? Classical management theory will not help here. When should you buy the latest book by MacGregor, Bennis, or Argyris and order participative management to come into effect, by next Thursday? Not if you have a routine operation, and only in some units if it is a craft or engineering operation (Perrow, 1966, pp. 161–62).

Perrow's ideas could have been extended in practice, and research could have been designed to test their utility. But one could seriously question whether the scientific foundation is strong enough to support a sound technological superstructure.

References

Aldrich, Howard E. "Technology and Organizational Structure: A Reexamination of the Findings of the Aston Group," *Administrative Science Quarterly*, 17 (1972), 26–43.

Argyris, Chris. *The Applicability of Organizational Sociology.* Cambridge, England: Cambridge University Press, 1972.

Billings, Robert S., Richard J. Klimoski, and James A. Breaugh. "The Impact of a Change in Technology on Job Characteristics: A Quasi-Experiment," *Administrative Science Quarterly*, 22 (1977), 318–39.

Blau, Peter M., Cecilia M. Falbe, William McKinley, and Phelps K. Tracy. "Technology and Organization in Manufacturing," *Administrative Science Quarterly*, 21 (1976), 20–40.

Burns, Tom. "Industry in a New Age," *New Society*, 31 (January 1963), 17–20.

Burns, Tom, and G.M. Stalker. *The Management of Innovation.* London: Tavistock Publications, 1961.

Child, John. "Organizational Structure and Strategies of Control: A Replication of the Aston Study," *Administrative Science Quarterly*, 17 (1972), 163–77.

———. "Predicting and Understanding Organization Structure," *Administrative Science Quarterly*, 18 (1973a), 168–85.

———. "Parkinson's Progress: Accounting for the Number of Specialists in Organizations," *Administrative Science Quarterly*, 18 (1973b), 328–48.

―――. "Managerial and Organizational Factors Associated with Company Performance—Part II. A Contingency Analysis," *Journal of Management Studies*, 12 (1975), 12–27.

Child, John, and Roger Mansfield. "Technology, Size and Organizational Structure," *Sociology*, 6 (1972), 369–93.

Dewar, Robert D., and Jerald Hage. "Size, Technology, Complexity, and Structural Differentiation: Toward a Theoretical Synthesis," *Administrative Science Quarterly*, 23 (1978), 111–36.

Dewar, Robert D., David A. Whetten, and David Boje. "An Examination of the Reliability and Validity of the Aiken and Hage Scales of Centralization, Formalization, and Task Routineness," *Administrative Science Quarterly*, 25 (1980), 120–28.

Donaldson, Lex. "Woodward, Technology, Organizational Structure and Performance—A Critique of the Universal Generalization," *Journal of Management Studies*, 13 (1976), 255–73.

Ford, Jeffrey D. "Institutional Versus Questionnaire Measures of Organizational Structure: A Reexamination," *Academy of Management Journal*, 22 (1979), 601–10.

Gerwin, Donald. "Comparative Analysis of Structure and Technology: A Critical Appraisal," *Academy of Management Review*, 4 (1979), 41–51.

Gillespie, David F., and Dennis S. Mileti. "Technology and the Study of Organizations: An Overview and Appraisal," *Academy of Management Review*, 2 (1977), 7–16.

Glisson, Charles A. "Dependence of Technological Routinization on Structural Variables in Human Service Organizations," *Administrative Science Quarterly*, 23 (1978), 383–95.

Harvey, Edward. "Technology and the Structure of Organizations," *American Sociological Review*, 33 (1968), 247–59.

Hickson, David J., D. S. Pugh, and Diana C. Pheysey. "Operations Technology and Organization Structure: An Empirical Reappraisal," *Administrative Science Quarterly*, 14 (1969), 378–97.

Inkson, J. H. K., D. S. Pugh, and D. J. Hickson. "Organization Context and Structure: An Abbreviated Replication," *Administrative Science Quarterly*, 15 (1970), 318–29.

Inkson, J. H. K., J. P. Schwitter, D. C. Pheysey, and D. J. Hickson. "A Comparison of Organization Structure and Managerial Roles: Ohio, U.S.A. and the Midlands, England," *Journal of Management Studies*, 7 (1970), 347–63.

Keller, Robert T., John W. Slocum, and Gerald I. Susman. "Uncertainty and Type of Management System in Continuous Process Organizations," *Academy of Management Journal*, 17 (1974), 56–68.

Khandwalla, Pradip N. "Mass Output Orientation of Operations Technology and Organizational Structure," *Administrative Science Quarterly*, 19 (1974), 74–97.

Lynch, Beverly P. "An Empirical Assessment of Perrow's Technology Construct," *Administrative Science Quarterly*, 19 (1974), 338–56.

Magnusen, Karl O. "Perspectives on Organizational Design and Development," Unpublished Research Paper No. 21, Graduate School of Business, Columbia University, 1973.

Miner, John B. *Theories of Organizational Behavior*. Hinsdale, Ill.: Dryden, 1980.

Pennings, Johannes. "Measures of Organizational Structure: A Methodological Note," *American Journal of Sociology*, 79 (1973), 686–704.

Perrow, Charles. "The Analysis of Goals in Complex Organizations," *American Sociological Review*, 26 (1961), 854–66.

―――. "Hospitals: Technology, Structure, and Goals." In James G. March (ed.), *Handbook of Organizations*. Chicago: Rand, McNally, 1965, pp. 910–71.

―――. "Technology and Organizational Structure," *Industrial Relations Research Association Proceedings, 1966*, pp. 156–63.

———. "A Framework for the Comparative Analysis of Organizations," *American Sociological Review*, 32 (1967), 194–208.

———. "The Effect of Technological Change on the Structure of Business Firms." In B. C. Roberts (ed.), *Industrial Relations: Contemporary Issues*. New York: Macmillan, 1968, pp. 205–19.

———. *Organizational Analysis: A Sociological View*. Belmont, Calif.: Wadsworth, 1970a.

———. "Departmental Power and Perspectives in Industrial Firms." In Mayer Zald (ed.), *Power in Organizations*. Nashville, Tenn.: Vanderbilt University Press, 1970b, pp. 59–89.

———. "Working Paper on Technology and Structure." Unpublished paper, University of Wisconsin, 1970c.

———. *Complex Organizations: A Critical Essay*. Glenview, Ill.: Scott, Foresman, 1972.

———. "Some Reflections on Technology and Organizational Analysis." In Anant R. Negandhi (ed.), *Modern Organizational Theory: Contextual, Environmental, and Socio-Cultural Variables*. Kent, Ohio: Kent State University Press, 1973, pp. 47–57.

———. "Is Business Really Changing?" *Organizational Dynamics*, 3, no. 1 (1974), 31–44.

———. "The Emergence of a Society of Organizations." Unpublished paper, State University of New York at Stony Brook, 1978.

Pfeffer, Jeffrey. *Organizational Design*. Arlington Heights, Ill.: AHM Publishing, 1978.

Pierce, Jon L., and Randall B. Dunham. "An Empirical Demonstration of the Convergence of Common Macro- and Micro-organization Measures," *Academy of Management Journal*, 21 (1978), 410–18.

Pugh, D. S., and David J. Hickson. "Causal Inference and the Aston Studies," *Administrative Science Quarterly*, 17 (1972), 273–76.

———. *Organizational Structure in Its Context: The Aston Programme I*. Lexington, Mass.: D. C. Heath, 1976.

Reimann, Bernard C. "Organizational Effectiveness and Management's Public Values: A Canonical Analysis," *Academy of Management Journal*, 18 (1975), 224–41.

———. "Organization Structure and Technology in Manufacturing: System Versus Work Flow Level Perspectives," *Academy of Management Journal*, 23 (1980), 61–77.

Reimann, Bernard C., and Giorgio Inzerilli. "A Comparative Analysis of Empirical Research on Technology and Structure," *Journal of Management*, 5 (1979), 167–92.

Rousseau, Denise M. "Assessment of Technology in Organizations: Closed Versus Open Systems Approaches," *Academy of Management Review*, 4 (1979), 531–42.

Sathe, Vijay. "Institutional Versus Questionnaire Measures of Organizational Structure," *Academy of Management Journal*, 21 (1978), 227–38.

Selznick, Philip. *TVA and the Grass Roots*. Berkeley: University of California Press, 1949.

Stanfield, Gary G. "Technology and Organization Structure as Theoretical Categories," *Administrative Science Quarterly*, 21 (1976), 489–93.

Van de Ven, Andrew H. "A Panel Study on the Effects of Task Uncertainty, Interdependence, and Size on Unit Decision Making," *Organization and Administrative Sciences*, 8 (1977), 237–53.

Woodward, Joan. *Management and Technology*. Problems of Progress in Industry, no. 3. London: Her Majesty's Stationery Office, 1958.

———. *Industrial Organization: Theory and Practice*. London: Oxford University Press, 1965.

———. *Industrial Organization: Behavior and Control*. London: Oxford University Press, 1970.

————. "Technology, Material Control, and Organizational Behavior." In Anant R. Negandhi (ed.), *Modern Organizational Theory: Contextual, Environmental, and Socio-Cultural Variables.* Kent, Ohio: Kent State University Press, 1973, pp. 58–68.

Zwerman, William L. *New Perspectives on Organization Theory.* Westport, Conn.: Greenwood, 1970.

Contingency Theory of Organization: Differentiation and Integration

Certainly theories related to the technological imperative are contingency theories, as are systems theories in many respects. All these theories say there is no one best way to structure organizations. But the term *contingency theory* as it is used in the field of macro organization study has become associated primarily with the views of Paul Lawrence and Jay Lorsch at Harvard University. Both Lawrence and Lorsch have been at Harvard for many years, and publications related to the theory, among them a number of doctoral dissertations, have been emerging from that institution since the mid-1960s.

The basic statements of the theory appear in an article (Lawrence and Lorsch, 1967a) and in a book (Lawrence and Lorsch, 1967b), though reports on pilot studies and preliminary hypotheses that exerted considerable influence on these formulations were published earlier (Lorsch, 1965; Lorsch and Lawrence, 1965). Since the 1960s, several extensions to the theory have been published, some of them growing out of the participation of individuals working on their dissertations at Harvard under the major theorists.

The Lawrence and Lorsch Theory

Though the contingency theorists acknowledge a number of debts in presenting their views, their most influential sources appear to be the technological imperative theorists discussed in Chapter 8, particularly Woodward, and Burns and Stalker. In its emphasis on the importance of environmental change and uncertainty, and in other respects as well, contingency theory has much in common with the mechanistic-organic formulations; contingency theory is, however, much more complex.

The Initial Hypotheses

The first formal statement of the contingency theory defined an organization as follows:

A system of interrelated behaviors of people who are performing a task that has been differentiated into several distinct subsystems, each subsystem performing a portion of the task, and the efforts of each being integrated to achieve effective performance of the system (Lawrence and Lorsch, 1967a, p. 3).

The task was to account for a whole input-transformation-output cycle, and the early formulations were focused on research, production, and sales subsystems. Unique to the definition, however, is the inclusion of differentiation and integration, which are defined as follows:

Differentiation . . . the state of segmentation of the organizational system into subsystems, each of which tends to develop particular attributes in relation to the requirements posed by its relevant external environment.
Integration . . . the process of achieving unity of effort among the various subsystems in the accomplishment of the organization's task (Lawrence and Lorsch, 1967a, pp. 3–4).

Differentiation of subsystems was viewed in terms of four factors. In addition to the frequently cited *formalization of structure*, these were *orientation of members toward others, time orientation* of members, and *goal orientation* of the subsystem members. The three orientation factors are behavioral attributes. Hypotheses stating the relationships of these factors to the environment are as follows:

1. The greater the certainty of the relevant subenvironment, the more formalized the structure of the subsystem.
2. Subsystems dealing with environments of moderate certainty will have members with more social interpersonal orientations, whereas subsystems coping with either very certain environments or very uncertain environments will have members with more task-oriented interpersonal orientations.
3. The time orientations of subsystem members will vary directly with the modal time required to get definitive feedback from the relevant subenvironment.
4. The members of a subsystem will develop a primary concern with the goals of coping with their particular subenvironment (Lawrence and Lorsch, 1967a, pp. 6–8).

Three additional hypotheses include the concept of integration and relate it to the environment and to differentiation:

5. Within any organizational system, given a similar degree of requisite integration, the greater the degree of

differentiation in subsystem attributes between pairs of subsystems, the less effective will be the integration achieved between them.

6. Overall performance in coping with the external environment will be related to there being a degree of differentiation among subsystems consistent with the requirements of their relevant subenvironments and a degree of integration consistent with requirements of the total environment.

7. When the environment requires both a high degree of system differentiation and a high degree of integration, integrative devices will tend to emerge (Lawrence and Lorsch, 1967a, pp. 10–12).

In these formulations no distinction was made between the actual environment and the environment as perceived by management.

Early Elaboration

The more extensive publication of the theory in book form (Lawrence and Lorsch, 1967b) does not formally restate the seven hypotheses, though it does not clearly depart from them. However, differentiation and integration are defined somewhat differently:

> *Differentiation* . . . the difference in cognitive and emotional orientation among managers in different functional departments.*
> *Integration* . . . the quality of the state of collaboration that exists among departments that are required to achieve unity of effort by the demands of the environment (Lawrence and Lorsch, 1967b, p. 11).

Differentiation among functional specialists almost invariably creates a potential for conflict. Integration is the means by which conflicts are resolved. At the very simplest level, integration is achieved through adjudication within the management hierarchy. However, sizable demands created by the environment, which are typically mediated through the degree of differentiation, require the use of more extensive integration devices at lower levels. Among these integrative positions are product manager, program coordinator, project leader, planning director, and systems designer that cut across and link major subsystems (Lawrence and Lorsch, 1967c).

The environment includes not only forces external to the organization, but also "the physical machinery, the nonhuman aspect of

*This was later amended to include "and the differences in formal structure among these departments" (Dalton, Lawrence, and Lorsch, 1970, p. 5).

production.'' The authors maintain that uncertainty may reside in equipment performance, as well as factors outside the firm's boundaries. Uncertainty is a product of unclear information, uncertain causal relationships, and long feedback spans from the environment. Accordingly, uncertainty would be greater for the research component of an organization than for the production subsystem. Highly uncertain environments require high degrees of differentiation and integration for effective performance (a state of unstable equilibrium). More certain environments typically require neither.

Integration is most appropriately achieved through confrontation or negotiated problem solving, rather than through the smoothing over of differences or the forcing of resolutions through the use of power or authority. Thus in uncertain environments, where the demand for integration is high, effective organizations will use confrontation. In addition, influence should be based on competence and expertise, and insofar as special integrator positions have emerged, incumbents in those positions should maintain a balanced orientation toward the separate subsystems and convey a feeling that conflict resolution will be rewarded.

The Lorsch and Allen Extensions

Though the original theory dealt with differentiation among departmental subsystems organized on a functional basis, Lorsch and Allen (1973) subsequently extended it to cover corporate-divisional and interdivisional relationships in firms organized into multiple product divisions. This extension provided hypotheses for the authors' own research. After carrying out this research, they formulated a set of hypotheses based on their findings and on the earlier hypotheses of Lawrence and Lorsch (1967b).

In all, Lorsch and Allen stated thirty-nine hypotheses. Many of these represent extensions of the earlier concepts to the more complex relationships of product division organization. Thus the environment for a division comes to include the corporate headquarters, and the complexity of the interdependence between headquarters and the division becomes a consideration in integration.

Lorsch and Allen add some new concepts to the theory. A factor influencing the extent of differentiation is the *cognitive limitation* imposed by individual information processing capabilities. *Economic risk* becomes a factor influencing integration:

> Within a firm the greater the differentiation between any division and the corporate headquarters and the greater the economic risk posed by that division, the greater the difficulties of achieving integration between these two units (Lorsch and Allen, 1973, p. 179).

The concept of *integrative effort* is introduced in the following hypothesis:

> Either an excess or a deficit of integrative effort relative to the degree of interdependence and of differentiation required at the corporate-divisional interface will tend to lead to less effective relationships among these units (Lorsch and Allen, 1973, p. 182).

Certain hypotheses are stated in such general terms it would be difficult to test them. For example:

> Corporations will tend to develop divisional performance evaluation systems which are broadly consistent with the overall uncertainty and the patterns of diversity and interdependence which characterize their total environments (Lorsch and Allen, 1973, p. 187).

In this volume, as in more recent writings (1976), Lorsch gives somewhat less emphasis to environmental uncertainty as a contingency variable, while extending the contingency concept to other aspects of the environment. In particular he emphasizes the homogeneity versus heterogeneity or diversity aspect of the environment. Heterogeneity may be correlated with uncertainty, but it is not the same thing.

The Lorsch and Morse Extensions

The formulations and extensions of contingency theory considered to this point deal with organization and environment and with the fit between the two. The work of Lorsch and Morse (1974) extends the theory to individual members of organizations and thus enters the domain of organizational behavior theories. Lorsch and Morse view organizational (and unit) effectiveness as dependent on a total fit between environment, organization, and the individual. The original pattern is depicted as shown in Figure 9–1.

Figure 9–1

Lorsch-Morse Statement of Original Environment-Organization Fit

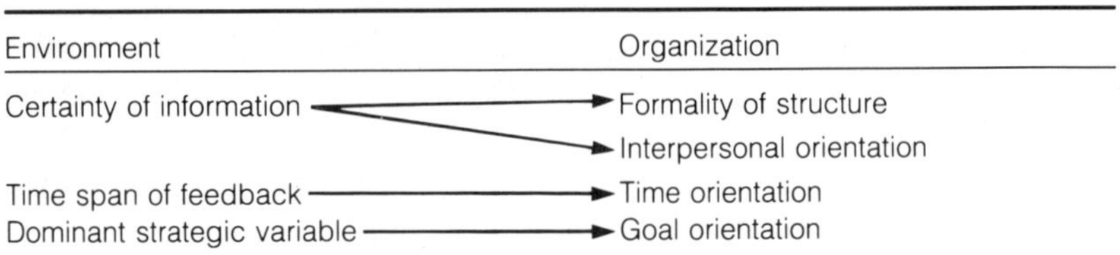

Environment	Organization
Certainty of information	Formality of structure
	Interpersonal orientation
Time span of feedback	Time orientation
Dominant strategic variable	Goal orientation

Table 9–1

Examples of High Environment-Organization-Individual Fit in Production and in Research and Development Units

	Manufacturing Plant	Research Laboratory
Nature of environment	Certain	Uncertain
Organizational structures and processes	Short time orientation	Long time orientation
	Strong technoeconomic goals	Strong scientific goals
	High formality of structure	Low formality of structure
	Influence concentrated at the top—directive	Influence diffused through many levels—participative
	High coordination	Low coordination
	Confrontation to resolve conflicts	Confrontation to resolve conflicts
Individual characteristics	Low cognitive complexity	High cognitive complexity
	Low tolerance for ambiguity	High tolerance for ambiguity
	Dependency in authority relationships	Independence in authority relationships
	Preference for group interaction	Preference for working alone
	High feeling of competence	High feeling of competence
Performance outcome	Effective	Effective

SOURCE: Adapted from Jay W. Lorsch and John J. Morse, *Organizations and Their Members: A Contingency Approach*. New York: Harper & Row, 1974, pp. 52, 112.

To this framework, Lorsch and Morse add as organizational factors the amount of *control* or *influence* members are expected to have over their own and others' activities and the degree to which members are expected to *coordinate* their activities. Table 9–1 gives the essence of the resulting theory. Manufacturing plants operating in environments with high certainty should exhibit the pattern shown on the left in the table. To the extent they depart from that pattern, they should be less effective. Similarly the pattern on the right fits uncertain environments of the kind research units often face. If the organization and its members do not operate as indicated, effectiveness should be low.

When organizational subsystems are structured and staffed in a manner appropriate to their environments, differentiation will result, given that the environments differ insofar as the hypothesized contingency variables are concerned. Thus, if the manufacturing plant and the research laboratory of Table 9–1 were in the same company, the differentiation would be appropriate because the company environment contains uncertainty as well as diversity (certainty and uncertainty) (Lorsch, 1977). On the other hand, in a highly uncertain environment the uncertainty might be diffused through all subsystems (at least in this sense, diversity would be minimal). Under these circumstances all subsystems would tend to approximate the right side of Table 9–1 and differentiation would be low. Yet the theory argues for differentiation in the face of uncertainty. There appears to be a logical problem here. Under conditions of high uncertainty in all subsystems of the organization, should one differentiate the subsystems in terms other than goals, and if so how?

The Harvard-Based Research

The unfolding of contingency theory has in each instance coincided with a major research study conducted by the theorists. The usual pattern has been to undertake an exploratory study on a very limited sample, firm up the hypotheses on the basis of that work, and then extend the research to a larger sample as a full test of the theory. To the extent that the hypotheses tested in the final study are influenced by the pilot study findings and the organizations involved in the pilot study also are used in the final study, there is potential contamination in this strategy. This appears to have been the case in the Harvard studies, and so they cannot be considered full tests of the theory. Yet the studies constitute an important and widely cited body of research.

Studies in the Plastics, Foods, and Containers Industries

The pilot work for the research done in the plastics, foods, and containers industries made use of two firms in the plastics industry (Lorsch, 1965; Lorsch and Lawrence, 1965). The final study involved six firms in the plastics industry (Lawrence and Lorsch, 1967a; 1967b) and two firms each in the foods and containers industries (Lawrence and Lorsch, 1967b). Data were gathered on theoretically relevant variables using questionnaires and interviews with thirty to fifty managers in each company.

Within the plastics industry uncertainty was found to be at medium levels for the technoeconomic (manufacturing) and market environments, but very high for the scientific environment. For the foods companies technoeconomic uncertainty was also medium, but market and scientific uncertainty were both considerably higher. As a result, the total environmental uncertainty for the foods companies was only slightly below that for plastics. On the other hand, the containers firms were found to operate in a more homogeneous environment of medium to low uncertainty throughout.

Table 9–2

Relationships of Environmental Uncertainty to Differentiation,
Integration, and Effectiveness

Environment	Financial Effectiveness Rank of Firms	Extent of Differentiation		Effectiveness of Integration	
		Rank	Score	Rank	Score
Plastics industry	1	4	8.7	2	5.6
(Relatively uncertain;	2	1	9.4	1	5.7
considerable diversity of	3	5	7.5	3	5.3
uncertainty)	4	2.5	9.0	4	5.1
	5	6	6.3	6	4.7
	6	2.5	9.0	5	4.9
Foods industry	1	1	8.0	1	5.3
(Relatively uncertain;	2	2	6.5	2	5.0
considerable diversity of					
uncertainty)					
Containers industry	1	1.5	5.7	1	5.7
(Low to medium	2	1.5	5.7	2	4.8
uncertainty; less diversity					
of uncertainty)					

Source: Adapted from Paul R. Lawrence and Jay W. Lorsch. *Organization and Environment: Managing Differentiation and Integration.* Boston, Mass.: Graduate School of Business Administration, Harvard University, 1967, pp. 50, 103.

Differentiation and Integration. Table 9–2 contains the results of the research insofar as differentiation and integration are concerned. In the plastics industry, differentiation should be highly correlated with financial effectiveness; it is not. However, the relationship between differentiation and effectiveness in the foods industry is as hypothesized, though a somewhat higher differentiation score might have been expected in the more successful firm. In the containers industry differentiation is low, but the anticipated difference in financial effectiveness does not emerge; the more successful company does not fit its environment any better than the less successful. These data do not strongly support the differentiation hypotheses, though the authors cite more impressionistic findings that do.

The results involving integration are different. The findings are in accord with the theory for the plastics industry, and to a somewhat lesser degree for the foods industry. But in the more certain containers industry the original theory would have predicted that success would be associated with low integration. This is clearly not the case. The data from all three industries are consistent with the view that integration helps performance, and this appears to be true irrespective of any possible contingencies introduced by environmental uncertainty.

Integration and Conflict Resolution. The major role of integrating units and individuals is hypothesized to be resolving conflicts among functional departments. These conflicts were expected to be greatest in more effective firms in highly uncertain environments; thus the influence of integrators should be greater there. The data indicate, however, that integrator influence was high in all six plastics firms, irrespective of performance level. This appears consistent with the similarity of differentiation scores among these firms.

The findings do suggest that integrators in the more successful plastics firms tend to be intermediate with regard to goal, time, and interpersonal orientations, as well as formality of structure between the functional departments they integrate. They are also more likely to feel rewarded for resolving conflicts. There was a highly significant tendency for more effective plastics companies to use confrontation to resolve conflicts. On the other hand, the smoothing over of differences was used less in these more effective firms. However, in the foods industry, confrontation was most pronounced in the low-performance company and differences in smoothing scores were nonexistent. In the containers industry the successful firm used both confrontation and smoothing more, and forcing less.

Studies in Conglomerates and the Paper Industry

The pilot study for research done among six multidivision firms made use of two conglomerates (Lorsch, 1968). The research was then extended to include two more conglomerates and two paper companies. The divisions in all six firms handled different product lines (Lorsch and Allen, 1973). Data were collected by interviews and questionnaires.

Findings on the major theoretical variables are given in Table 9–3. The first two firms listed are conglomerates, the second two are paper companies, and the third two are conglomerates. The data on integrative effort indicate that this variable cannot be substituted for integration in the theory; in fact it is difficult to interpret the data in any manner. In a division-by-division analysis, integrative effort was correlated $-.70$ with differentiation, the reverse of what might have been expected.

Among the three effective firms the first appears to fit the theory, the second is generally satisfactory though it lacks integration, and the third is too integrated and probably too differentiated to be as effective as it is in its homogeneous and clearly very certain environment. The fourth firm also requires low differentiation and integration, but its moderate success level would lead one to expect somewhat higher differentiation scores. The fifth firm has a performance pattern consistent with its uncertainty scores, but totally inconsistent with the degree of environmental diversity. The final firm

Table 9–3

Data on Environments, Effectiveness, Differentiation, and Integration Based on Rankings for Six Firms

| Environments | | Financial Effectiveness | Differentiation | | Integration | | |
| | | | | | Corporate-Divisional | | Interdivisional Effort |
Diversity	Uncertainty		Corporate-Divisional	Total Firm	Actual	Effort	
1	1	1 (High)	3	1	1	6	5
3	3	2 (High)	1	2	4	5	6
4	5	3 (High)	2	4	2	2	1
5	6	4 (Moderate)	4	5	3	3	4
6	2	5 (Low)	6	6	6	1	3
2	4	6 (Low)	5	3	5	4	2

SOURCE: Adapted from Jay W. Lorsch and Stephen A. Allen. *Managing Diversity and Interdependence: An Organizational Study of Multidivisional Firms.* Boston, Mass.: Graduate School of Business Administration, Harvard University, 1973, pp. 143, 153.

exhibits the reverse pattern—the performance results fit well for diversity, but one would expect a higher level of performance, given the uncertainty level.

Overall, the data do not provide any greater support for environmental diversity as a contingency variable than for uncertainty. Any way one computes it, the theory fails in two instances, succeeds in two, and yields somewhat equivocal results in the other two. Generally the straight, noncontingent relationships between differentiation and integration scores and effectiveness appear considerably more promising than the contingency hypotheses. However, division-by-division analyses within the conglomerates yield a significant relationship for integration only (.62), not for differentiation. Across the two industrial environments it is clearly integration and not differentiation that is associated with success (Miner, 1979).

One problem with the Lorsch and Allen (1973) report is that a great volume of data is presented, but not necessarily in a manner that makes it easy to relate the findings to the theoretical hypotheses. However, confrontation of conflict is associated with effective integration as expected, and confrontation also is related positively to firm effectiveness. Smoothing had no relationship to effectiveness, and forcing predominated in the less effective firms. In general this indicates the value of rationality in decision making. High performance in both the conglomerates and paper firms was reported to be associated with:

1. Intermediate orientation toward time, goals, and interpersonal relations, and high influence of linking functions.

2. Corporate-divisional influence balance.

3. Modes of resolving conflicts—the degree to which confrontation or problem solving was used.

4. Overall quality of upward and downward information flows.

These findings support the idea that integration is a source of effectiveness, but since the variables involved are not related to environmental characteristics, it is impossible to consider them in the context of contingency theory itself.

Studies in Manufacturing and Research and Development

The pilot research for the Harvard study of manufacturing and R and D divisions in five companies was conducted in two containers plants of a single company and in two communications research laboratories of another company (Morse and Lorsch, 1970). Subsequently the sample was extended to include a pair of plants manufacturing household appliances, two research laboratories working with proprietary drugs, and two medical technology laboratories (Lorsch and Morse, 1974). In each company pair, one installation was considered to be effective and the other less so. Certain early analyses dealing with the relationship between uncertainty and personality considered only the four manufacturing plants and four of the research laboratories (Morse and Young, 1973). In addition to interviews and questionnaires, psychological tests were administered to a cross section of managers in the plants, and managers and professionals in the laboratories.

The manufacturing plants were originally selected to represent an environment of some certainty, and their mean score of 6.3 on the uncertainty measure supports this conclusion. In contrast, the research laboratories had a mean uncertainty score of 15.4. The two groups were sharply distinguished on this index.

Individual Characteristics. If one contrasts the data of Table 9–4 with the hypotheses embodied in Table 9–1, some striking disparities appear. Effective plants do not have lower scores than the ineffective plants on the personality variables, and the effective laboratories do not have higher scores. The only differences associated with organizational effectiveness are the scores on the feeling of competence measures, and these are as hypothesized. Since those who work in the more effective systems presumably are more competent, a finding that they feel so is not unexpected.

On the other hand, what emerges from the data is a clear indication that those individuals who work in research laboratories are more cognitively complex, more tolerant of ambiguity, more independent of authority, and more individualistic. Presumably that is a function of some combination of self-selection, professional selection, and acculturation.

Table 9–4
Individual Characteristics in Effective and Ineffective Organizations in Certain and Uncertain Environments

Individual Characteristic	Certain (Plants)		Uncertain (Laboratories)		Certain Total	Uncertain Total
	Effective	Ineffective	Effective	Ineffective		
Cognitive complexity	4.2	4.2	5.2	5.2	(4.2	5.2)
Tolerance for ambiguity	2.6	2.5	2.9	2.9	(2.6	2.9)
Independence in authority relationships	2.2	2.1	2.8	2.9	(2.2	2.8)
Preference for working alone	2.4	2.4	3.0	3.0	(2.4	3.0)
Feeling of competence						
Measure 1	(1.2	.5)	(1.2	.2)	.8	.7
Measure 2	(2.4	1.2)	(2.3	1.0)	1.8	1.7

( ) Difference statistically significant.
Source: Adapted from Jay W. Lorsch and John J. Morse. *Organizations and Their Members: A Contingency Approach*. Boston, Mass.: Graduate School of Business Administration, Harvard University, 1974, pp. 40–41, 43–44, 53–55.

Organizational Characteristics. In the manufacturing plants, time orientation did not differentiate the effective and ineffective organizations—in both, the time orientation was short. But all other structure and process variables in Table 9–1 did differentiate effective and ineffective organizations and in the predicted direction. The more effective plants had stronger technoeconomic goals, more formality of structure, greater influence at the top exercised in a more directive manner, a higher degree of coordination, and a greater use of confrontation to resolve conflicts.

In the research laboratories the pattern is almost completely reversed, as suggested by the hypotheses of Table 9–1. The more effective laboratories exhibit a longer time orientation, a greater commitment to scientific goals, less formality of structure, more influence at lower organizational levels, a more participative style, less coordination, and a greater use of confrontation. Clearly success is associated with very different organizational characteristics in the research and manufacturing contexts.

These results say nothing about the original *organizational* theory of differentiation and integration. The data are for single subsystems only. Furthermore, being concurrent, they are subject to multiple explanations. Though the authors emphasize the role of the fit between environment and organization, the findings may be explained without recourse to the environmental level and thus to the dimension of certainty-uncertainty:

1. The effective research units appear to have relied strongly on professional norms to induce and control individual efforts toward goal achievement. The less effective research units appear to have confounded the already existing professional system of norms by adding in a sizable amount of hierarchic pressures as well. That this should create role conflict and lower performance levels is entirely consistent with research findings.

2. The effective manufacturing plants clearly place strong reliance on hierarchic authority to induce goal contributions. . . . the low performing manufacturing plants are often characterized by a basically laissez-faire approach, where strong inducements of any kind are lacking. Extrapolation from research on leadership would indicate that just such performance problems should occur in a laissez-faire context.

3. On occasion low performance in the manufacturing context was associated with a confounding of a hierarchic authority system with an inducement system which made use of group norms and pressures (participative decision making of a kind) to induce contributions. Again, the potential for role conflict was sizable, and the likelihood that this contributed to the performance deficiencies considerable (Miner, 1979, pp. 290–91).

Case Studies

In addition to the full-scale studies noted previously, Lorsch and Lawrence (1970) edited a volume of studies, primarily doctoral dissertations, dealing with contingency theory. Included are the pilot studies for the Lorsch and Allen (1973) and Lorsch and Morse (1974) investigations.

The remaining papers, to the extent they report research at all, are case studies dealing with one or, at most, two organizations. Quantitative data are rarely included. Though this volume provides considerable insight into the intellectual climate contingency theory created at Harvard during the 1960s, it does not contain any generalizable findings that bear directly on the contingency theory hypotheses. For this reason the specific case studies are not considered individually here.

An exception is Neilsen's (1974) study of two relatively small firms that utilized the Lawrence and Lorsch measures and reported quantitative results. Both firms were highly effective, but one faced an environment that was both more uncertain and contained a greater diversity of uncertainty levels. This greater uncertainty and diversity would have been expected to elicit more differentiation and integration to achieve such high effectiveness, but it did not. Overall, the two firms were equally differentiated. On the integration measures the firm facing the somewhat more certain and less diverse environment scored the highest. Since actual effectiveness data are not given, one cannot say whether this greater integration was related to better financial results. In any event the pattern of the findings does not fit theoretical expectations.

Independent Evaluations of the Theory

The Harvard research suffers from a potential source of contamination in moving from pilot study to theory to a research test that included the pilot data. The research considered in the following section does not suffer from this problem.

Measurement and Construct Validity Problems

One line of investigation has focused on the effectiveness of the Lawrence and Lorsch uncertainty measure in categorizing environments. Because this measure was used in the initial work with the plastics industry and in subsequent Harvard research, it is important to establish its value.

The Tosi, Aldag, and Storey Study. The initial methodological analyses of the uncertainty scale were carried out on a sample of more than 100 managers at the middle and top levels (Tosi, Aldag, and Storey, 1973). The overall reliability of the scale was found to be .51, and the subscale values were .11 for research, .38 for manufacturing, and .52 for marketing. These values are low but not surprising, considering the shortness of the instrument.

To get at construct validity, measures of volatility in the external environment were established from the range of fluctuations over a ten-year period. Technological, income, and sales volatility measures were calculated for the industry as a whole and for the firm in which each manager-respondent worked. The correlations between the uncertainty scale and these measures of actual environmental variation were uniformly low and, to the extent they were statistically significant, negative. A reanalysis of specific functions and their relevant environments did little to improve the degree or direction of the correlations.

In reply, Lawrence and Lorsch (1973) argue that the volatility measures do not tap what they meant by uncertainty and that the Tosi, Aldag, and Storey (1973) findings do not adequately reflect construct validity. Furthermore, the theorists note that they confirmed the results from the uncertainty scale in other ways in their research and that the Tosi, Aldag, and Storey subjects were not the best qualified to complete the scale. Overall, the result of this first methodological investigation appears to be a standoff, but it raises serious questions about scale reliability and the degree of match between uncertainty as perceived by managers and as reflected in the actual environment.

Perceived Uncertainty, the Environment, and the Individual. Lawrence and Lorsch (1967b) clearly utilize a measure of uncertainty as perceived by organizational decision makers, but they view it as roughly equivalent to external circumstances. Others have tended to emphasize the perceptual aspects more and the realities of the environment somewhat less, while noting that individual characteristics may also play a role in uncertainty perception (Downey and Slocum, 1975).

Downey, Hellriegel, and Slocum (1975) report low reliabilities for the uncertainty scale as utilized by Lawrence and Lorsch among the division managers of a conglomerate. They also utilized industry volatility data and the managers' perceptions of a number of variables such as competition that are related to uncertainty. Overall, the data provide no evidence of construct validity. Even an alternative measure of the Lawrence and Lorsch uncertainty construct proved to be unrelated to the original scale. On the other hand, in an extension of this study the authors found that a characteristic of the individual manager, degree of cognitive complexity, was positively associated with the perception of environmental uncertainty (Downey, Hellriegel, and Slocum, 1977).

Other data indicate a more positive relationship between perceived uncertainty and environmental aspects—change rate, in particular, but also complexity and routineness (Tung, 1979). However, all these variables were measured by one questionnaire administered at one time to one individual per organizational unit. The possibility that common method variance may have confounded the results cannot be excluded. Thus these results require further external substantiation before they can be accepted, especially in view of conflicting findings from other studies.

It is becoming increasingly clear that individual differences can influence perceptions of uncertainty. One laboratory study developed evidence that preexisting tolerance for ambiguity can be an important determinant of these perceptions (McCaskey, 1976). The following quotes raise important new questions regarding contingency theory relationships:

> A person high in tolerance for ambiguity may take the same situation and make it into something more complex and uncertain than a person low in tolerance for ambiguity does.

. . . Organization members seem to adjust the level of environmental uncertainty they perceive to fit their own needs for stimulation and closure. People more tolerant of ambiguity seem to want the challenge of working with greater uncertainty, even to the point of creating it themselves. . . . For some jobs, for some organizations, greater tolerance for ambiguity is desirable. In other cases, if high tolerance for ambiguity people see and maybe create uncertainty even in relatively well-defined situations, high tolerance for ambiguity can be dysfunctional (McCaskey, 1976, p. 75).

Processes such as these, if they operate among top-level executives, could create havoc for the hypotheses of the Lawrence and Lorsch theory simply because environmental uncertainty (as perceived) now becomes a function of what the individual desires.

Research Bearing on Theoretical Hypotheses

There is little research that might be considered a true replication of the Harvard studies. One exception is a study conducted in three banks that follows the original Lawrence and Lorsch (1967b) design closely (Herbert and Matthews, 1977). In general, data at the subunit level for operations, customer service, and marketing are compatible with expectations. As a group, the banks operate in a moderately uncertain environment, below the plastics industry but by no means as certain as containers, the marketing environment appears particularly uncertain. In this context one would expect a moderate degree of differentiation *and* integration to yield financial success.

In actuality the most successful bank was the least differentiated but the most integrated. The differentiation level of this high performer might well be theoretically appropriate, and the low performing bank's high differentiation excessive, as the authors suggest. Yet the uncertainty score for the low performer was right up with the plastics firms, suggesting a possible need for its high differentiation. Differentiation and integration ranks were perfectly negatively correlated across the three banks, and in this instance, as in prior studies, it was integration that was correlated positively with success. The parsimonious explanation is that effective integration contributes to success, that differentiation matters little, and that environmental uncertainty as measured is not relevant.

Duncan's Research. In a series of studies Duncan attempts to add a greater degree of precision to the uncertainty construct and to investigate various methods of adaptation. In the process Duncan (1972) developed a new measure of uncertainty that differentiated simple-complex and static-dynamic dimensions of the environment.

He found, as hypothesized, that perceived uncertainty was greatest where the environment was experienced as dynamic and complex. Of the two environmental components the static-dynamic contributed more to the perception of uncertainty. However, the uncertainty measure used, though conceptually similar to the measure used by Lawrence and Lorsch, does not appear to be closely related empirically (Downey, Hellriegel, and Slocum, 1975). Furthermore, Downey, Hellriegel, and Slocum were unable to replicate Duncan's findings regarding the role of the simple-complex dimension in perceived environmental uncertainty.

Duncan (1973) also studied structural differences at the subunit level (not the total organization) as related to environmental uncertainty. He found that when uncertainty was high the more effective units were more likely to utilize different structures to deal with routine and nonroutine decisions. Thus there was differentiation within the same department. Though consistent with the perspective of Lawrence and Lorsch, this finding clearly goes beyond their actual theoretical statements. As anticipated, uncertainty was associated with a less structured hierarchy of authority, more participation, fewer rules and procedures, and less division of labor for nonroutine decisions (Duncan, 1974).

The Negandhi and Reimann Studies. In their initial study Negandhi and Reimann (1973) considered thirty diverse manufacturing firms operating under pervasive growth market conditions in India. Construing the environment as stable and relatively certain overall, and extrapolating from contingency theory of organization, the authors hypothesized that centralization of decision making would be associated with organizational effectiveness. However, the results showed just the reverse; there was a marked tendency for the decentralized firms to be more effective. In the more effective firms the decentralization was particularly likely to be accompanied by formalized systems dealing with manpower planning, employee selection, compensation, appraisal, and training (Reimann and Negandhi, 1975).

Though the above results provide little support for contingency theory, an analysis in terms of market competition yields somewhat more favorable results (Negandhi and Reimann, 1972). Under competitive circumstances decentralization was strongly associated with effectiveness. However, a significant though smaller relationship of the same kind was found under conditions of little competition. The authors interpret this as a reflection of the cultural context in India, thus adding another contingency variable to the theory.

Research conducted in Mexico and Italy yields support for the original theory without the need for cultural modification (Simonetti and Boseman, 1975). In Italy decentralization was related positively to economic effectiveness in competitive markets and negatively under conditions of minimal competition. No significant differences were found in Mexico under limited competition; only the positive relationship between decentralization and effectiveness with high competition was significant.

Khandwalla's Research. Working from an initial finding that companies operating under conditions of high environmental uncertainty tended to use uncertainty reduction mechanisms such as staff services and vertical integration extensively, Khandwalla (1972, 1973) correlated these uncertainty-related variables with various indexes of differentiation and integration for high- and low-profit firms. Though the measures of variables are different from those of Lawrence and Lorsch, in part because they were obtained from a mail survey, there is enough conceptual similarity to view the research as relevant for contingency theory. Under that theory one would expect higher levels of uncertainty to be compensated with greater differentiation and integration in the more effective firms, but not in the less effective.

The data of Table 9–5 yield mixed support for that expectation. As in other studies, uncertainty relates to decentralization, but the additional relationship to profitability is minimal. Only in the case of the vertical integration index can structural differentiation be said to be functional in the face of uncertainty. With regard to integration, the use of team decision making at the top level, and not the use of sophisticated controls, follows the theory. In this sense uncertainty,

Table 9–5

Relationships Between Uncertainty and Differentiation and Integration Indexes in Profitable and Less Profitable Firms

| | Uncertainty Index | | | |
| | Utilization of Staff Services | | Vertical Integration | |
Organizational Variables	Profit High	Profit Low	Profit High	Profit Low
Differentiation Indexes				
Decentralization	(.56)	(.51)	(.55)	(.31)
Functional departmentalization	.07	−.07	(.36)	−.09
Divisionalization	(.57)	(.32)	(.28)	−.01
Integration Indexes				
Use of sophisticated controls	(.34)	(.30)	.22	(.33)
Participative management at the top level	(.43)	.00	(.38)	.00

( ) Values statistically significant.

Source: Adapted from Pradip N. Khandwalla, "Viable and Effective Organizational Designs of Firms," *Academy of Management Journal,* 16 (1973), p. 490.

coupled with integration, is associated with profitability; a lack of association is not. The total theory, that uncertainty requires differentiation and then, in turn, integration to produce effectiveness, appears to be supported in two of twelve variable sets. Neither differentiation nor integration appears to be related consistently in a noncontingent manner to effectiveness. However, such noncontingent relationships do appear to exist for the decentralization measure of differentiation and the controls measure of integration—two of the five indexes.

Nonsupportive Findings. Though the results considered to this point do not consistently support contingency theory, there are some positive findings. Another group of studies present a considerably less favorable picture, however. Pennings (1975) studied forty brokerage offices of a single firm and found no evidence of a tie between various uncertainty-related environmental variables, indexes of structure, and effectiveness. The various environmental measures exhibited no consistent relationship with structure, and with uncertainty no relationship at all, nor did these variables relate to effectiveness. On the other hand, structure alone was closely tied to effectiveness:

> If the employees of the organization were left on their own,
> did not share ideas, were not informationally integrated, did
> not participate in decisions, and did not receive support, the
> effectiveness on any criterion will be below average. This is
> probably the best single statement that could summarize the
> relationship between structural variables and effectiveness.
> . . . From the results obtained, one questions the usefulness of
> the structural-contingency model (Pennings, 1975, p. 405).

Osborn (1976) studied antipoverty agencies, which were described as highly mechanistic in structure, and correlated the perceived uncertainty of their environments with their effectiveness. One would expect from contingency theory that the mechanistic structure would be functional in more certain environments; thus a negative relationship should emerge. This did not occur, and in fact there was no evidence of any relationship at all.

Child (1975) tested contingency theory in England using an objective measure of industry variability as the environmental moderator. Variability was found to be associated with the employment of more people in specialized roles (differentiation), but this was true irrespective of the organization's effectiveness. Various indexes of formalization such as standardization of procedures, documentation, and written performance records also were correlated with environmental variability to test the hypothesis that low formalization is a prerequisite for success in uncertain environments. Profitability as an index of effectiveness produced no support for the hypothesis, but growth rate as an index did. Though the Lawrence and Lorsch theory is concerned primarily with the profit criterion, the results can be interpreted as tangential support for their theory.

Schmidt and Cummings (1976) related various indexes of environmental change and perceived uncertainty to differentiation, but without considering the effectiveness levels of their organizational units (employment service offices). Though the design is hardly a test of the Lawrence and Lorsch theory, its few significant findings reflect a tendency for greater differentiation to be associated with *less* uncertainty. This apparent departure from contingency theory is attributed to the fact that differentiation permits more effective coping with environmental uncertainty and thus reduces the extent to which it is perceived to exist.

A similar phenomenon emerges in three laboratory studies conducted by Bourgeois, McAllister, and Mitchell (1978) with students and with practicing managers. They note:

> The hypothesis that managers would respond mechanistically in a turbulent environment and organically in a stable one was supported by the data. . . . they did shift to a more mechanistic mode when turbulence followed stability; but they did not shift to a more organic mode when the environment became more stable. . . . there is a compelling argument for reciprocal causation between environmental uncertainty and organization structure (Bourgeois, McAllister, and Mitchell, 1978, pp. 512–13).

Here, too, effectiveness was not considered; the observed responses were assumed to be dysfunctional, but there is no basis for concluding this with confidence. Overall, these studies raise a number of new questions for contingency theory, while doing little to answer the old ones.

Applications: Organization Development and Matrix Organization

From its beginnings contingency theory of organization has been closely tied to application. The original studies were part of organizational change programs that were first described in a paper written in 1965, though not published until later (Lorsch and Lawrence, 1969). The theory rapidly became associated with the organization development movement (Lawrence and Lorsch, 1969). In general, Lorsch has remained involved in the development of such applications (Lorsch, 1977). Meanwhile, Lawrence has increasingly focused on the development of matrix organization structures, which, though they are in no sense a derivative of contingency theory, fit well with the differentiation and integration concepts (Davis and Lawrence, 1977).

The Contingency Approach to Organization Development

The approach taken in the initial change programs is described as follows:

> Our general approach, then, has been to spend considerable time and effort through the use of questionnaires and a systematic interviewing program in gathering data to be analyzed in terms of a conceptual framework developed in our research efforts [contingency theory]. Having collected and analyzed these data we have then educated management to our conceptual scheme and have fed the data back to them, working through with them the meanings and the limitations of the data. The managers themselves have worked out whatever structural changes seemed required and have collaborated with us in the formulation of specific development programs to alleviate specific reorganizational problems (Lorsch and Lawrence, 1969, p. 471).

One type of specific development program frequently mentioned was a training effort in which members of differentiated departments were brought together for the purpose of gaining a better understanding of each other's roles. The objective was to confront sources of conflict and attempt to resolve them through mutual understanding (Lawrence and Lorsch, 1967b; Lorsch and Lawrence, 1969). In general these descriptions deal with the high differentiation and integration situation associated with high uncertainty. Though it is recognized that an environmental fit may require little differentiation or integration and that a change toward such a situation may also be facilitated through training, little attention is given to this type of contingency. It clearly is not what the authors are interested in.

Dealing with Interfaces. For purposes of organization development there are three important interfaces—organization-environment, group-group, and individual-organization (Lawrence and Lorsch, 1969). First, sources of uncertainty in the environment and the needs of organization members are diagnosed and a picture of what the organization should be is drawn up. Then data are obtained on existing differentiation levels, integration methods, conflict resolution processes, and sources of dissatisfaction. By comparing what is with what should be, one can obtain a blueprint for change that is tailored to the specific organization.

In initiating change at the organization-environment interface many different approaches may be employed, ranging from training, to internal realignments of departments, to major structural reorganizations. Realignments and reorganizations are intended to overcome pressures for consistency across departments, to adjust unit differentiation to changes in the environment, to create new departments to cope with new environmental elements, and to adapt to growth. At this interface the major goal is the appropriate type and degree of differentiation. As a result, a major structural intervention may be introduced at an early stage of the organization development program, rather than after extensive process interventions, as in most other organization development approaches.

However, once appropriate differentiation is achieved, there arises a need to effect integration and collaboration among the diverse elements. The basic sequence of activities is diagnosis, design, action planning, implementation, and evaluation. Diagnostic data are fed back to organization members in much the same manner as they are with other organization development approaches. This typically eventuates in a *differentiation laboratory* designed to provide understanding of the varying outlooks of different units. It is focused on the group-group interface and constitutes both action planning and implementation. Business games may also be used for this purpose. The intended outcome is the development of new behavior patterns that will facilitate collaboration and integration.

The authors contrast their contingent approach at this interface to the more universalistic approach of other practitioners:

> They argue that all organizations need . . . the development of trust and understanding between groups and the confrontation of conflict. . . . our model also leads us to see confrontation of conflict as necessary. Where we differ from these other practitioners is in placing emphasis on the requirement for other conflict-management variables which are contingent on environmental demands; on the required state of differentiation; and also on the design of appropriate structural devices for achieving integration. . . . They focus on educational interventions which emphasize face-to-face group process and interpersonal skill. We recognize these as important, but again would go further. . . . we have also used diagnostic data and have encouraged managers to use other means to alter expectations and behavior (i.e., formal organizational changes, redefinition of tasks, and other educational techniques) (Lawrence and Lorsch, 1969, pp. 58–59).

As application moves to the individual-organization interface, it abandons contingency theory as its conceptual base and begins to draw heavily on the views of another Harvard-based theorist, David McClelland (1961), especially his views on the roles of achievement, affiliation, and power motives in performance. This theory has been considered at length elsewhere (Miner, 1980), and because it is essentially a theory of organizational behavior at the micro level, it will not be developed here.

Recent Extensions. In his writing during the 1970s Lorsch has tended to emphasize the implications of theory and research for applications, rather than additional approaches to organization development. The Lorsch and Allen (1973) volume deals with differentiation within the hierarchy (decentralization) as well as with differentiation among functional departments. In the Lorsch and Morse (1974) book, concepts from achievement motivation theory are replaced with other individual constructs such as cognitive complexity, tolerance for ambiguity, and independence in authority relationships in matters involving the individual-organization interface. These books contain some interesting chapters on applications in the areas of organizational structure and process, but little is said about specific procedures and techniques. Almost every statement follows directly from the theory.

Lorsch (1977) now seems less inclined to use precise measurement instruments and more favorably disposed toward diagnosis based on clinical insights derived from top-level interviews. He also emphasizes that organizational design changes must be congruent with the preferences of top management to be effectively implemented. Finally, changes must be consistent with each other so that they all move toward the same objective. All too often, changes prove to be offsetting, and nothing actually happens.

Though the change sequence proposed includes an evaluation phase, little has been done to determine the effectiveness of the contingency approach to organization development. The authors cite case studies in support of their procedures, but offer no solid evaluation research of a longitudinal nature.

Matrix Organization

In a sense contingency theory of organization has adopted matrix organization. The matrix structure was noted in the early theoretical publications as congruent with the needs created by a highly uncertain environment, but more recently Lawrence has focused major attention on the matrix form (Davis and Lawrence, 1977, 1978; Lawrence, Kolodny, and Davis, 1977). In these writings matrix is defined as "any organization that employs a *multiple command system* that includes not only a multiple command structure but also related support mechanisms and an associated organizational culture and behavior patterns."

Conditions for Use. The value of matrix form is inherent in its potential for greater flexibility in responding to environmental pressures. Since environments vary in the pressures they produce, there are conditions under which matrix organization may not be needed, or may even be dysfunctional. Accordingly, one would not expect to find this type of structure emerging in all organizations.

There are three conditions (all of which must be present) under which the matrix is the preferred mode. First, two or more critical sectors such as functions, products, services, markets, or geographic areas must be highly salient for goal accomplishment at the same time. Second, the need to perform uncertain, complex, and interdependent tasks must exist so that a sizable information-processing capacity is required. Third, there must be a need to realize economies of scale by utilizing scarce human resources effectively.

Though these conditions are not specified in terms of contingency theory, they clearly assume a complex, uncertain, and perhaps highly competitive environment. The theory would posit a need for differentiation to process various types of information and for integration to coordinate the differentiation. The matrix organization contains both. Such an organization is specified, as one would expect from contingency theory, in terms of not only its structure, but also its systems, culture, and behaviors—just as differentiation is.

Phases of Development. The matrix emerges from the classical pyramidal form in which all members have one boss. In the next phase a temporary overlay is added to the functional structure in the form of project management. Typically these projects do not contain their own resources and draw on a variety of outside sources for this purpose. The key aspects of organization are a project manager, decentralized resource support, and centralized planning and control. Clearly the project aspect is not yet the coequal of the functional.

In phase three the overlay becomes permanent, with a product or brand manager whose task is to maintain product viability in the marketplace and stable membership. Yet the overlay is still complementary to functional organization. Finally, in the mature matrix, a dual authority relationship emerges in which the power is balanced. There are two bosses representing two bases of organization. Typically these are function and product, but other bases may be used, even to the point of extending the matrix beyond two dimensions. The key roles are top leadership, which actually is outside the matrix, matrix managers who share subordinates with other matrix managers, and subordinate managers, who have two bosses.

Methods of Introduction. Matrix forms involve increased interdependencies and thus increased communication and opportunity for conflict. As in contingency theory, confrontation is proposed as the best method of dealing with this conflict. The matrix structure requires collaboration to function, and the key ingredient for collaboration is said to be trust.

All this means that new patterns of behavior must be learned if people are to function effectively in the new structure. This is facilitated through a *team-banding* process that may utilize a staff professional or process consultant in the role of catalyst. Team-building meetings are held that appear to have much in common with the differentiation laboratories previously discussed. These are aimed at identifying expectations and dealing with such matters as objectives, frequency of meetings, leadership, roles and responsibilities, decision modes, communication and conflict resolution patterns, and interpersonal problems.

In addition to such group procedures there is a need for individual development to provide knowledge and skills relevant to the matrix form. A training program for matrix managers involving skill training, experiential learning, and team-building is recommended. The elements are as follows:

1. Knowledge input about matrix organizations and information about why their organization is adopting matrix. This would include top management's philosophy.

2. Lecture, discussion, and exercises about effective communication and group process.

3. Lecture and exercises on concepts and techniques relevant to the kind of business problem solving expected.

4. A simulation in which individuals are randomly placed in groups and given a business task. Each member is given a role to play and each experiences directly the problem of making and implementing decisions. Each examines the experience with the help of a trainer and learns from it.

5. The actual teams are brought together to work on a number of exercises to create a low-risk setting for self-examination and learning.

6. A team-building meeting is conducted, with a professional, as a process consultant, to go over the important startup questions (Davis and Lawrence, 1977, p. 113).

At this point implementation of the matrix takes on many qualities of "traditional" organization development (see Chapter 5).

Potential Problems. Many things can go wrong in organizations moving to the matrix structure (Davis and Lawrence, 1978). A state of confusion may develop where no clear lines of authority are recognized (anarchy). An excessive amount of conflict related to a state of free-floating power (power struggles) may emerge. Matrix management may become equated with group decision making to an inappropriate degree (severe groupitis). Under conditions of business decline the matrix may be blamed for what is in fact poor management and be eliminated (collapse during economic crunch). Failure to realize possible economies of scale may occur, with the result that costs become excessive (excessive overhead). The matrix structure may gravitate from the higher levels of the organization downward, so that it exists only at the group and division levels (sinking to lower levels). Matrices within matrices within matrices often develop out of power fights rather than the logic of design (uncontrolled layering). Internal preoccupations may become so compelling that contact with the realities of the market is lost (navel gazing). There may be so much democracy that action is not taken when needed (decision strangulation).

These problems can be overcome if the organization is aware of them, but to some extent they are inherent in the form itself. To these must be added the very real possibility of major role conflicts (see Chapter 6).

Medical Center Research. With the exception of their own work in several medical centers, the authors cite practically no research dealing with the matrix form. Thus, evaluation is very difficult. Even the medical center research does not actually test the matrix form (Charns, Lawrence, and Weisbord, 1977; Weisbord, Lawrence, and Charns, 1978).

Interviews and questionnaires explicitly based on contingency theory were administered in nine medical centers. Differentiation and integration were found to be inadequate to environmental demands. Differences associated with technical specialties (departments) and functions (M.D. education, Ph.D. education, internship and residency training, research, and patient care) were in evidence, but there was considerable blurring in perceptions of them. Confrontation was not widely used to resolve conflicts.

The three conditions for the use of matrix organization appeared to be present. Greater differentiation and integration were needed, and the matrix form seemed to be an ideal method of accomplishing this. However, the research did not relate differentiation and integration measures to the effectiveness of the centers. Nor is there a report on the consequences of introducing a matrix structure. In essence the research stops at the diagnostic stage, and the implications drawn must be accepted on the basis of faith in the underlying contingency theory and in the matrix application of it.

Conclusions

Contingency theory of organization introduces several major advances over its sister theory, the technological imperative. For one thing it deals with organizational subunits and their environments separately, thus avoiding the pitfalls of organizational averaging and abstractions; differentiated subunits are in fact a major component of the theory. Second, it addresses the problem of achieving organized effort toward goals through the introduction of the integration concept. This concept in one form or another has shown much promise in organization theory. Its inclusion in contingency theory appears to advance understanding considerably. Finally, contingency theory has spawned and lent support to applications, which though inadequately tested have the merit of bridging the gap between theory and practice.

Scientific Goals

In one respect contingency theory exhibits much the same vulnerability as technological theory, and that is in the area of its contingency variable. Environmental uncertainty suffers from most of the difficulties that technology does, plus a few of its own. The overwhelming problem is that of construct validity. What is uncertainty? It is not environmental change, as the mechanistic-organic formulations might suggest, because with improvements in forecasting techniques, many changes have become highly predictable and thus no longer a source of uncertainty (Miner, 1978). Uncertainty is not environmental diversity either, as the extensions to contingency theory might suggest. On logical as well as empirical grounds this equation breaks down. Under conditions of high uncertainty across all organizational subunits, uncertainty is at a maximum, but diversity (at least on the uncertainty variable) is low.

Contingency theory has been criticized for confusing internal technological uncertainty with its external environmental counterpart and for inappropriately equating subjective and objective uncertainty. Though the scope of the uncertainty variable Lawrence and Lorsch envisaged may well have been so great as to make it unmanageable, the greatest difficulties seem to revolve around the perceived uncertainty concept. Empirically it has proved almost impossible to demonstrate construct validity, and unreliable measures have emerged often enough to suggest an underlying ambiguity in the basic construct.

Perceived uncertainty is not just a function of the objective environment. It is strongly influenced by characteristics of the perceiver. Some people desire uncertainty and create it by stirring up the environment, or by penetrating more deeply into it so that there is more of it to cope with, or by distorting their world. Others become extremely anxious in the face of uncertainty and eliminate it wherever possible, not only by controlling the environment, but also by limiting it drastically, or by ignoring and even denying aspects of it. Clearly organizations can fail because key decision makers distort uncertainty levels both upward and downward to an excessive degree and adjust organization structures and functioning inappropriately to something that is not really there. Numerous cases in the business policy/strategy area demonstrate this again and again. It is particularly common to keep perceived uncertainty low by totally ignoring major threats in the environment until it is too late. Here subjective and objective uncertainty are far from being the same thing.

To the extent the same individuals in a firm report on certainty levels in the environment and actually determine internal structures, there is a good probability that environmental uncertainty will be matched with internal structural uncertainty (organic forms) and environmental certainty with structural certainty (mechanistic forms). This is simply because those who prefer one or the other are likely to prefer it everywhere and to create a world to match. There is no reason why all this should have much to do with organizational effectiveness, and it typically does not.

At present it would appear that environmental uncertainty, at least as Lawrence and Lorsch conceived it, is a construct that is no longer theoretically useful. There may very well be something here that can contribute to a greater understanding of organizational functioning, but to get at that something is going to require breaking the current global construct down into constituent parts that can be defined, measured, and validated with sufficient precision.

The other components of contingency theory fare somewhat better in the research, though as one might suspect, once the contingency variable's imperfections are understood, not in a contingent manner. Confrontation as a means of conflict resolution and integration is not contingent on other variables. It is hypothesized to have universally positive consequences, and the research overall supports this. One might only question the nature of the construct itself. The items actually used to measure confrontation suggest that a high score is associated more with rational decision making than with anything else. Perhaps what we have in this instance is an index of the rationality that Weber associates with the ideal bureaucracy (see Chapter 13).

If one follows the logic of the confrontation variable, one would expect other integration indexes to have a general rather than a contingent relationship to success. In Tables 9–2 and 9–3 and elsewhere in the research this is the case. One of the few consistent findings is that more integrated firms are more effective, irrespective of their environments. The definition of integration used in contingency theory is not identical with that of either Argyris (Chapter 5) or Stogdill (Chapter 6), but there is enough conceptual similarity so that previously reported findings can provide a degree of confidence in those reported in this chapter. Integration in some form keeps emerging from the research with something positive to say. Even in the case of control theory (Chapter 3), McMahon and Ivancevich (1976) found that concordance among views from different parts of the organization (integration) was associated with success.

The data reported for differentiation do not present nearly as consistent a picture as those for integration. They do not match the hypotheses of contingency theory with anything approaching the necessary regularity, but neither do they fit a general, noncontingent formulation. When one sticks strictly to the numerical data, even the Harvard studies do not give reason to consider differentiation an important organizational variable. The authors might well argue that their clinical findings from interviews provide greater support for their theory, but until we know the processes through which those findings can be independently replicated, the clinical data cannot be considered part of the body of scientific knowledge.

One additional problem clouds the understanding of differentiation-integration-uncertainty relationships as set forth by the theory. Several writers have noted that in a mature context concurrent studies should yield high levels of differentiation and integration in an environment of *low* perceived uncertainty, because the organizational variables should have acted over time to tame the environment. Such effects, coupled with a sampling of organizations at different stages of adaptive change, could completely confound concurrent research results. The theory does not deal with such matters as time lags and reciprocal effects between organization and environment. Child (1977) has noted there is a need for longitudinal research that would deal with these issues, but there is also a need for theoretical extensions that indicate what to expect if such research were conducted.

Numerous environmental factors within a rather wide band of variation currently may have little relevance for many organizations (Child, 1977). Certainly this is true for the company that has established a monopoly, or carved out a solid market niche, or operates in a pervasive growth market. Furthermore, a variety of structures may be adequate to the demands of any given environmental context (Aldrich and Pfeffer, 1976). To the extent these conclusions are valid, contingency theory needs considerable revision to match the realities of the organizational world.

Extensions of the theory to date have not been in the directions noted above. When the theory for single-product firms was extended to conglomerates, the results tended to parallel those obtained in the original studies (Lorsch and Allen, 1973). In retrospect this theoretical expansion does not appear to have been very great. In the case of the theory of environment-organization-individual fit, a sizable theoretical leap did occur, but empirical support did not cover the same ground (Lorsch and Morse, 1974). The data did not consistently support the hypotheses, and even more important, the controls used were insufficient to permit confidence in the researchers' interpretation of their results (Johnston, 1975; Miner, 1979).

It is now possible to complete the evaluation of the Burns and Stalker theory initiated in Chapter 8. There it was concluded that even the limited amount of research dealing explicitly with the technological change variable did not consistently support the theory. There has been even less research done explicitly on market change as a contingency variable, probably because of the need to conduct analyses over time. However, if one accepts surrogate variables such as competition and uncertainty, these data do not consistently support the mechanistic-organic theory. The study by Pennings (1975) employed a particularly wide range of environmental variables and did not obtain support. Overall, though definitive tests of the theory at the technological and environmental levels are lacking, results from related research suggest that theory-specific tests of the Burns and Stalker hypotheses would probably be unproductive.

Goals of Application

In prior chapters the subject of organization development has been considered in relation to system 4 theory (Chapter 2), sociotechnical systems theory (Chapter 4), and goal congruence theory (Chapter 5). In these instances the changes introduced have affected process more than structure, except for the lower-level changes with autonomous work groups, and a considerable amount of research has been conducted to evaluate the changes. In type of change and in evaluation the applications derived from or associated with contingency theory present a different picture. Structural changes throughout the organization to produce a more theoretically appropriate fit often are required, and they may well be implemented through the existing hierarchy of authority at an early stage (Lorsch, 1977). For all practical purposes the consequences for an organization of these changes based on contingency theory have never been studied.

Given that this is a different approach to organization development and that the matrix form represents a sizable departure from existing line-staff structures, the lack of research is troublesome. Evaluation must be extrapolated from conceptually distant sources. One source is a small body of research dealing with the use of project overlays of various kinds (Miner, 1978). These studies indicate that the two-boss concept, which is basic to matrix organization, can yield considerable role conflict and ambiguity, as might be expected, and that negative consequences such as increased anxiety levels can be anticipated. Whether other advantages such as increased flexibility outweigh these negative considerations and whether the role conflict can be neutralized under certain circumstances simply is not known. Nevertheless, the matrix structure continues to have many distinguished and highly persuasive advocates (Galbraith, 1977; Knight, 1977).

Evaluating applications by extrapolating from research on the basic theory raises some serious questions. We do not know that organizations should differentiate and integrate in the face of uncertainty, though greater integration will probably yield positive consequences in any event. We do not even know what uncertainty is, and identifying its presence more clinically, as Lorsch (1977) proposes, is not likely to help solve the problem. Furthermore, the applications deal only with more differentiation and integration in a system. What if the diagnosis calls for a reduction in differentiation and integration? What should be done then? On the evidence a shift to less integration would appear to be foolhardy.

Existing evidence does not support organization development based on contingency theory, though subsequent research into applications may well modify this conclusion in certain respects. About matrix structures we really know relatively little. Arguments from role theory and its related research appear much stronger than those from either contingency theory of organization or system 4 theory (the cross-functional team route to the matrix). And role theory would clearly indicate a great deal of caution in adopting the matrix structure, unless conflict can be reduced by building effective methods of coordinating or stratifying role senders into the system.

References

Aldrich, Howard E., and Jeffrey Pfeffer. "Environments of Organizations," *Annual Review of Sociology*, 2 (1976), 79–105.

Bourgeois, L. J., Daniel W. McAllister, and Terence R. Mitchell. "The Effects of Different Organizational Environments upon Decisions about Organizational Structure," *Academy of Management Journal*, 21 (1978), 503–14.

Charns, Martin P., Paul R. Lawrence, and Marvin R. Weisbord. "Organizing Multiple-function Professionals in Academic Medical Centers." In Paul C. Nystrom and William H. Starbuck (eds.), *Prescriptive Models of Organizations*. New York: North-Holland, 1977, pp. 71–88.

Child, John. "Managerial and Organizational Factors Associated with Company Performance—Part II. A Contingency Analysis," *Journal of Management Studies*, 12 (1975), 12–27.

———. "Organizational Design and Performance: Contingency Theory and Beyond." In Elmer H. Burack and Anant R. Negandhi (eds.), *Organizational Design: Theoretical Perspectives and Empirical Findings*. Kent, Ohio: Kent State University Press, 1977, pp. 169–83.

Dalton, Gene W., Paul R. Lawrence, and Jay W. Lorsch. *Organizational Structure and Design*. Homewood, Ill.: Irwin-Dorsey, 1970.

Davis, Stanley M., and Paul R. Lawrence. *Matrix*. Reading, Mass.: Addison-Wesley, 1977.

———. "Problems of Matrix Organizations," *Harvard Business Review*, 56, no. 3 (1978), 131–42.

Downey, H. Kirk, Don Hellriegel, and John W. Slocum. "Environmental Uncertainty: The Construct and Its Application," *Administrative Science Quarterly*, 20 (1975), 613–29.

———. "Individual Characteristics as Sources of Perceived Uncertainty Variability," *Human Relations*, 30 (1977), 161–74.

Downey, H. Kirk, and John W. Slocum. "Uncertainty: Measures, Research, and Sources of Variation," *Academy of Management Journal*, 18 (1975), 562–78.

Duncan, Robert B. "Characteristics of Organizational Environments and Perceived Environmental Uncertainty," *Administrative Science Quarterly*, 17 (1972), 313–27.

———. "Multiple Decision-making Structures in Adapting to Environmental Uncertainty: The Impact on Organizational Effectiveness," *Human Relations*, 26 (1973), 273–91.

———. "Modifications in Decision Structure in Adapting to the Environment: Some Implications for Organizational Learning," *Decision Sciences*, 5, no. 4 (1974), 122–42.

Galbraith, Jay R. *Organization Design*. Reading, Mass.: Addison-Wesley, 1977.

Herbert, Theodore T., and Ronald D. Mathews. "Is the Contingency Theory of Organization a Technology-Bound Conceptualization?" *Journal of Management*, 3 (1977), 1–10.

Johnston, Russ. Review of *Organizations and Their Members: A Contingency Approach*," *Administrative Science Quarterly*, 20 (1975), 133–36, 631.

Khandwalla, Pradip N. "Environment and Its Impact on the Organization," *International Studies of Management and Organization*, 2 (1972), 297–313.

———. "Viable and Effective Organizational Designs of Firms," *Academy of Management Journal*, 16 (1973), 481–95.

Knight, Kenneth. *Matrix Management*. Westmead, England: Gower Press, 1977.

Lawrence, Paul R., Harvey F. Kolodny, and Stanley M. Davis. "The Human Side of the Matrix," *Organizational Dynamics*, 6, no. 1 (1977), 43–61.

Lawrence, Paul R., and Jay W. Lorsch. "Differentiation and Integration in Complex Organizations," *Administrative Science Quarterly*, 12 (1967a), 1–47.

———. *Organization and Environment: Managing Differentiation and Integration*. Boston, Mass.: Graduate School of Business Administration, Harvard University, 1967b.

———. "New Management Job: The Integrator," *Harvard Business Review*, 45, no. 6 (1967c), 142–51.

———. *Developing Organizations: Diagnosis and Action*. Reading, Mass.: Addison-Wesley, 1969.

————. "A Reply to Tosi, Aldag, and Storey," *Administrative Science Quarterly*, 18 (1973), 397–98.

Lorsch, Jay W. *Product Innovation and Organization*. New York: Macmillan, 1965.

————. "Organizing for Diversification," *Academy of Management Proceedings*, 1968, pp. 87–100.

————. "Contingency Theory and Organization Design: A Personal Odyssey." In Ralph H. Kilman, Louis R. Pondy, and Dennis P. Slevin (eds.), *The Management of Organization Design: Strategies and Implementation*. New York: North-Holland, 1976, pp. 141–65.

————. "Organizational Design: A Situational Perspective," *Organizational Dynamics*, 6, no. 2 (1977), 2–14.

Lorsch, Jay W., and Stephen A. Allen. *Managing Diversity and Interdependence: An Organizational Study of Multidivisional Firms*. Boston, Mass.: Graduate School of Business Administration, Harvard University, 1973.

Lorsch, Jay W., and Paul R. Lawrence. "Organizing for Product Innovation," *Harvard Business Review*, 43, no. 1 (1965).

————. "The Diagnosis of Organizational Problems." In Warren G. Bennis, Kenneth D. Benne, and Robert Chin (eds.), *The Planning of Change*. New York: Holt, Rinehart, and Winston, 1969, pp. 468–76.

————. *Studies in Organization Design*. Homewood, Ill.: Irwin-Dorsey, 1970.

Lorsch, Jay W., and John J. Morse. *Organizations and Their Members: A Contingency Approach*. New York: Harper & Row, 1974.

McCaskey, Michael B. "Tolerance for Ambiguity and the Perception of Uncertainty in Organization Design." In Ralph H. Kilman, Louis R. Pondy, and Dennis P. Slevin (eds.), *The Management of Organization Design: Research and Methodology*. New York: North-Holland, 1976, pp. 59–85.

McClelland, David C. *The Achieving Society*. Princeton, N. J.: Van Nostrand, 1961.

McMahon, J. Timothy, and John M. Ivancevich. "A Study of Control in a Manufacturing Organization: Managers and Nonmanagers," *Administrative Science Quarterly*, 21 (1976), 66–83.

Miner, John B. *The Management Process: Theory, Research, and Practice*. New York: Macmillan, 1978.

————. "The Role of Organizational Structure and Process in Strategy Implementation: Commentary." In Don E. Schendel and Charles W. Hofer (eds.), *Strategic Management: A New View of Business Policy and Planning*. Boston, Mass.: Little, Brown, 1979, pp. 289–302.

————. *Theories of Organizational Behavior*. Hinsdale, Ill.: Dryden, 1980.

Morse, John J., and Jay W. Lorsch. "Beyond Theory Y," *Harvard Business Review*, 48 no. 3 (1970), 61–68.

Morse, John J., and Darroch F. Young. "Personality Development and Task Choices: A Systems View," *Human Relations*, 26 (1973), 307–24.

Negandhi, Anant R., and Bernard C. Reimann. "A Contingency Theory of Organization Re-Examined in the Context of a Developing Country," *Academy of Management Journal*, 15 (1972), 137–46.

————. "Task Environment, Decentralization, and Organizational Effectiveness," *Human Relations*, 26 (1973), 203–14.

Neilsen, Eric H. "Contingency Theory Applied to Small Business Organizations," *Human Relations*, 27 (1974), 357–79.

Osborn, Richard N. "The Search for Environmental Complexity," *Human Relations*, 29 (1976), 179–91.

Pennings, Johannes M. "The Relevance of the Structural-Contingency Model for Organizational Effectiveness," *Administrative Science Quarterly*, 20 (1975), 393–410.

Reimann, Bernard C., and Anant R. Negandhi. "Strategies of Administrative Control and Organizational Effectiveness," *Human Relations*, 28 (1975), 475–86.

Schmidt, Stuart M., and Larry L. Cummings. "Organizational Environment, Differentiation, and Perceived Environmental Uncertainty," *Decision Sciences, 7* (1976), 447–67.

Simonetti, Jack L., and F. Glenn Boseman. "The Impact of Market Competition on Organization Structure and Effectiveness: A Cross-Cultural Study," *Academy of Management Journal*, 18 (1975), 631–38.

Tosi, Henry, Ramon Aldag, and Ronald Storey. "On the Measurement of the Environment: An Assessment of the Lawrence and Lorsch Environmental Uncertainty Questionnaire," *Administrative Science Quarterly*, 18 (1973), 27–36.

Tung, Rosalie L. "Dimensions of Organizational Environments: An Exploratory Study of Their Impact on Organization Structure," *Academy of Management Journal*, 22 (1979), 672–93.

Weisbord, Marvin R., Paul R. Lawrence, and Martin P. Charns. "Three Dilemmas of Academic Medical Centers," *Journal of Applied Behavioral Science*, 14 (1978), 284–304.

10

Strategy and Structure

The theoretical work of Alfred du Pont Chandler differs in a number of respects from the theories considered up to now. The previous theorists were social scientists with strong ties to disciplines such as psychology, sociology, and cultural anthropology. Chandler served on the history faculty at Massachusetts Institute of Technology for a number of years before moving to the Harvard Business School. He approaches theory construction through analysis of historical data. The technique is inductive, but draws on existing organizational records and public documents rather than on social science research.

Chandler's theory of strategy and structure is more a part of the literature of the business policy field than of organizational study. The borderlines between policy/strategy and organizational study become blurred here. Certainly the writings of the sociological open systems and contingency theorists have considerable relevance for the policy discipline also. Yet, among the theorists considered in this book, only Chandler has won acceptance as a major contributor to the business policy/strategy field.

Chandler's Historical Theory

The theory of strategy and structure emerged gradually through a series of articles published in the late 1950s and early 1960s, but was not formally stated until the publication of the book *Strategy and Structure: Chapters in the History of the American Industrial Enterprise* (Chandler, 1962). The starting point was a study of patterns of decentralization over periods of growth in fifty large corporations (Chandler, 1956). This was the structure part of the theory. The strategy part came somewhat later. Strategy was defined in terms of decisions made by the top team holding ultimate authority with regard to such matters as goal determination, planning, and budgeting (Chandler and Redlich, 1961).

The Formal Statement

Within Chandler's writings it is practically impossible to disentangle historical analysis and theory formulation; the two go hand in hand. Much of the historical analysis associated with strategy/structure theory utilizes case history data, particularly from those firms that adopted the decentralized structure at an early point such as du Pont, General Motors, Standard Oil of New Jersey, and Sears, Roebuck. Ultimately, Chandler (1962) drew on the administrative histories of almost 100 companies. But he did not carry out statistical or even quantitative studies relating measures of strategy, structure, and success to each other. Basically the data remained in case form. Because of this and the impossibility of separating theory and data, it is not possible to consider Chandler's rich historical descriptions as providing tests of the theory (Miner, 1979). That task remained to others.

Definitions. The theory holds only for the limited domain of the *industrial enterprise,* defined as:

A large private, profit-oriented business firm involved in the handling of goods in some or all of the successive industrial processes from the procurement of the raw material to the sale to the ultimate customer (Chandler, 1962, p. 8).

Administration refers to executive actions, orders, and decisions that coordinate, appraise, and plan the work of the industrial enterprise, as well as allocate resources. A decentralized company is administered from four successively higher positions or offices:

1. *Field unit.* Runs a plant or works, a branch or district sales office, a purchasing office, an engineering or research laboratory, an accounting or other financial office, and the like.
2. *Departmental headquarters.* Coordinates, appraises and plans for a number of field units.
3. *Division central office.* Administers a number of departments . . . responsible for the administration of a major function—manufacturing, selling, purchasing or producing of raw materials, engineering, research, finance, and the like.
4. *General office.* Executives and staff specialists coordinate, appraise, and plan goals and policies and allocate resources for a number of quasi-autonomous, fairly self-contained divisions. Each division handles a major product line or carries on the firm's activities in one large geographical area (Chandler, 1962, p. 9).

In an earlier formulation Chandler and Redlich (1961) identified only three levels within decentralized systems. However, all levels need not be present in a given firm. Figure 10–1 depicts the structure involved. Overall, *structure* is defined as:

The design of organization through which the enterprise is administered. . . . It includes, first, the lines of authority and communication between the different administrative offices and officers and, second, the information and data that flow through these lines of communication and authority (Chandler, 1962, p. 14).

While tactical decisions are concerned primarily with day-to-day operating matters, strategic decisions relate to the longer term. Strategy is defined as:

Figure 10–1

Structure of the Decentralized Firm

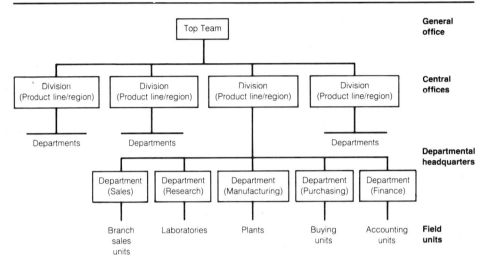

The determination of the basic long-term goals and objectives of an enterprise, and the adoption of courses of action and the allocation of resources necessary for carrying out these goals. Decisions to expand the volume of activities, to set up distant plants and offices, to move into new economic functions, or become diversified along many lines of business involve the defining of new basic goals (Chandler, 1962, p. 13).

From Chandler's historical perspective, which was the period of major industrial expansion in the United States, Chandler clearly meant growth strategy when he used the term *strategy*. Growth was his major concern, and his theory realistically must be considered to be bounded by this more limited concept of strategy.

Propositions. The initial propositions of strategy/structure theory deal with administration:

1. Administration is an identifiable activity that . . . differs from the actual buying, selling, processing, or transporting of the goods. . . . In the large industrial enterprise the concern of the executives is more with administration than with the performance of functional work.

2. The administrator must handle two types of administrative tasks when he is coordinating, appraising, and planning the activities of the enterprise. . . . The first type of activity calls for concentration on long-term planning and appraisal, the second for meeting immediate problems and

needs and for handling unexpected contingencies or crises (Chandler, 1962, pp. 8–9).

Long-term activities are predominantly a general office concern, as is the allocation of resources to divisions. If the general office fails to perform such roles and concentrates on immediate problems, the firm will be less effective.

This decentralized structure is the result of several basic strategies, i.e., "structure follows strategy." A growth strategy resulting in expanded volume creates the need for an administrative office to handle one function in one area. A growth strategy resulting in geographic dispersion creates the need for departmental headquarters to administer several such field units. A growth strategy resulting in expansion into new types of functions via vertical integration creates the need for divisional central offices and a multidepartment structure. A growth strategy resulting in the development of new lines of products via diversification or major geographic expansion creates the need for a general office to coordinate the divisions.

For a number of reasons there may be a delay between the acceptance of a strategy and the emergence of the needed structure. The result is increasing inefficiency. This lag is discussed as follows:

> Necessary reorganization came only after the retirement and occasionally not until the death of a powerful executive or dominant group of managers. . . . the timing of these changes has been greatly influenced by the turnover of top management personnel. . . . except for crisis, age was the primary reason for changes in the top management (Chandler, 1956, pp. 172–73).

The theory clearly states that delays or failure to adopt the decentralized structure required by growth strategies leads to inefficiency; in this sense the theory is normative in nature. Yet there is also the implication of a strategy imperative—that ultimately the structure will follow from the strategy; in this sense the theory is descriptive as well. As formulated by Chandler, strategy/structure theory applies only to growth strategies and to the decentralized multidivisional structure. The theory may have wider applications, but these are not discussed.

The source of the growth strategies themselves is multifaceted. The development of new products, changing and expanding markets both within the United States and abroad, and economic prosperity all appear to be important. However, a major factor historically was the existence of excess capacity. Growth strategies were often adopted to utilize existing personnel and facilities more fully. There appears to have been a cyclical but gradually escalating effect, with growth strategies being formulated to handle excess capacity, only to create some new excess capacity that required further growth, which was typically achieved through either vertical integration or diversification.

If the structure that emerged from these strategies contained a general office and at least two major multidepartmental divisions that were relatively autonomous, the conditions for the decentralized form were met. Within the general office the preferred form of decision making was by a team or group. However, below this level, operating decisions typically were made in a more individualized manner. Thus the term *decentralization* applied primarily to the relationship between the general office and the central office. Decentralization of decisions down through the structure to departmental and field unit levels was not implied.

Though the most complete formal statement of the theory appears in Chandler (1962), there have been numerous articles elaborating the historical underpinnings and restating parts of the theory since. Some of these, like the major statement, have focused on the United States experience (Chandler, 1969; 1977a). Others have compared this experience with developments in other countries (Chandler, 1975; 1976). None of these articles appears to have extended the theory to any meaningful degree.

Broader Concepts

In a book entitled *The Visible Hand: The Managerial Revolution in American Business,* Chandler (1977b) develops certain concepts that extend or, perhaps more appropriately, fill in blanks in the strategy/structure theory. A paper by Chandler and Daems (1979) further elaborates this thrust. Here the view that organizational structures and processes are a consequence of decisions by managers becomes increasingly manifest. Here also Chandler (1977b) makes it very clear that any generalizations presented are derived from the historical analyses. "The data have not been selected to test and validate hypotheses or general theories" (p. 6).

Propositions. Eight propositions dealing with the emergence and continued growth of divisionalized firms are set forth:

1. Modern multiunit business enterprise replaced small traditional enterprise when administrative coordination permitted greater productivity, lower costs, and higher profits than coordination by market mechanisms.

2. The advantages of internalizing the activities of many business units within a single enterprise could not be realized until a managerial hierarchy had been created.

3. Modern business enterprise appeared for the first time in history when the volume of economic activities reached a level that made administrative coordination more efficient and more profitable than market coordination.

4. Once a managerial hierarchy had been formed and had successfully carried out its function of administrative coordination, the hierarchy itself became a source of permanence, power, and continued growth.

5. The careers of the salaried managers who directed these hierarchies became increasingly technical and professional.

6. As the multiunit business enterprise grew in size and diversity and as its managers became more professional, the management of the enterprise became separated from its ownership.

7. In making administrative decisions, career managers preferred policies that favored the long-term stability and growth of their enterprises to those that maximized current profits.

8. As the large enterprises grew and dominated major sectors of the economy, they altered the basic structure of these sectors and of the economy as a whole (Chandler, 1977b, pp. 6–10).

This process of moving from small, family enterprises to large, divisionalized structures staffed by salaried managers appeared first in the railroads. Its spread to other industries was facilitated by economies of speed in transportation, communications, production, distribution, and merchandising. Growth occurred both internally and through mergers, but in both cases vertical integration was a necessary condition for continued profitability.

Allocation, Monitoring, and Coordination. Ultimately the decentralized firm with a general office emerged as a method of carrying out necessary allocation, monitoring, and coordination activities (Chandler and Daems, 1979). Allocation is providing human, material, and financial resources to organizational components. Monitoring is checking on and rewarding accordingly the performance of these components. Coordination is structuring and facilitating transactions between interdependent components.

Coordination appears to have emerged first, followed shortly by monitoring. Instruments for allocating resources came much later. Coordination was a means to achieve economies of speed, and indeed without these economies the decentralized structure had little value. Opportunities for improved coordination were thus a consequence of technological changes in transportation, communication, and later production, as well as changes in the volume and composition of demand. Given these opportunities, growth strategies could be activated and economies of speed achieved. Monitoring systems were then needed to determine whether the potential economies of speed were in fact realized. Resource allocation procedures came only as increased cash flow resulted in sizable internally generated funds and organizational components began to compete for these funds as sources of expansion capital. An essential element in the administration of coordination, monitoring, and allocation was the creation of accounting procedures and controls. Thus developments in corporate accounting closely paralleled the rise of the new structures.

Chandler and Daems (1979) note that the lag in moving to new structures and processes was much greater in Europe than in the United States. This lag is attributed to the predominant role of the family in European enterprise, the unequal distribution of income that hampered the development of mass markets, and the existence of interfirm agreements that limited competition. Here, as elsewhere (Chandler, 1956), there is the implication that strategy/structure theory holds only under conditions of competition.

Elaborations by Others

Chandler's thinking and historical analyses have had a considerable impact on the theoretical contributions of others. One of the best known examples is the work of Oliver Williamson (1970, 1975) in the field of institutional economics. Williamson develops the view that firms, especially those using the multidivisional form, may serve as effective substitutes for markets in the conduct of economic transactions. Though it draws extensively on organizational constructs, the theory falls more clearly in the area of microeconomics than in organizational theory, and accordingly will not be considered at length here. Nevertheless, its existence is a highly visible indication of Chandler's influence.

Two other thrusts in theory development are more closely related to the organizational field and deserve consideration. One involves the extension of Chandler's ideas about a fit between strategy and structure to other fits within the firm itself. The other involves the specification of organizational growth or life cycles based on the historical sequences Chandler depicted.

Organizational Fit Theory. Organizational fit theory is the creation of Galbraith and Nathanson (1978). It is an amalgam of Chandler's concept of strategy/structure fit and those extensions of contingency theory that go beyond environment and structure to other aspects of the organization, including the selection of people to staff organizations (see Chapter 9). Such a theory covers a much wider domain than Chandler envisaged, extending from business policy at one end to personality theory at the other. At present it lacks specific statements of what the various fits and nonfits actually are. However, the component variables among which fits should occur have been indicated and are noted in Figure 10–2.

Figure 10–2
Flow of Relationships in Organizational Fit Theory

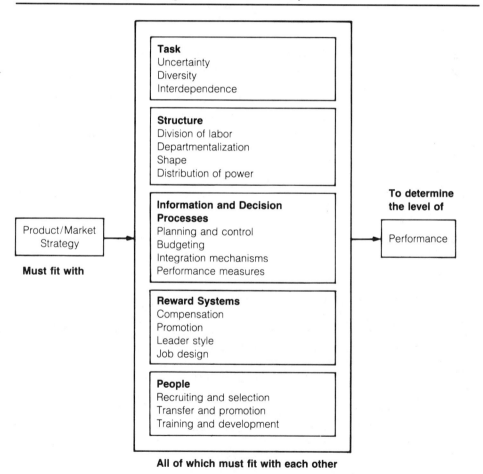

All of which must fit with each other

Source: Adapted from Jay R. Galbraith and Daniel A. Nathanson, *Strategy Implementation: The Role of Structure and Process*. St. Paul, Minn.: West, 1978, p. 96.

The most specific statement of the theory is as follows:

The product-market strategy chosen by the firm determines to a large extent the task diversity and uncertainty with which the organization must cope. The organization must then match the people with task through selection, recruitment, and training and development practices. The people must also match the structure. The structure, also chosen to fit the task, is specified by choices of the division of labor (amount of role differentiation), the departmental structure, the shape (number of levels, spans of control), and the distribution of power (both horizontal and vertical). Across the structure, processes are overlaid to allocate resources and coordinate activities not handled by the departmental structure. These information and decision processes are planning and control systems, budgeting processes, integration mechanisms, and performance measurements. And finally, the reward system must be matched with the task and structure through choices of compensation practices, career paths, leader behavior, and the design of work. In total, all of these choices must create an internally consistent design. If one of the practices is changed, the other dimensions must be altered to maintain fit. Similarly, if the strategy is changed, then all the dimensions may need to be altered (Galbraith and Nathanson, 1978, p. 95).

The debt to Chandler is evident at many points in this statement. The theory, like Chandler's, is normative. Furthermore, the concept of competition is again introduced as a domain-limiting variable; the extended fit theory is a theory for competitive circumstances.

Organizational Growth Models. The literature on organizational growth or life cycle models that have their origins in Chandler's formulations has been extensively reviewed (Galbraith and Nathanson, 1978; Steiner and Miner, 1982). Chandler (1962) saw as the historical sequence (1) initial expansion and accumulation of resources, (2) rationalization of the use of resources within complex functional and vertically integrated forms, (3) further expansion into new markets and lines to assure continued use of resources, and (4) rationalization of the use of these expanded resources within the multidivision, decentralized form.

Many elaborations on this sequence have emerged. Most of them are somewhat more detailed than Chandler's, while emphasizing a necessary sequence, thus introducing a normative element; firms should pass through the successive stages as they grow if they are to be effective, though they need not move all the way up the scale under all circumstances. The number of stages introduced varies, depending on whether decline, international expansion, or the like are considered. The following three-stage development model closely resembles Chandler's:

I. Single product or single line; distribution via one channel or set of channels; little or no formal structure (one man show); R & D organization not institutionalized (guided by owner-manager); performance measurement by personal contact and subjective criteria; rewards unsystematic and often paternalistic; personal control of both strategic and operating decisions; strategic choices relate to needs of owner versus needs of company.

II. Single product line; one set of distribution channels; specialization based on function; integrated pattern of product-service transactions; increasingly institutionalized search for product or process improvements; performance measurement increasingly impersonal using technical and/or cost criteria; rewards increasingly systematic, with emphasis on stability and service; personal control of strategic decisions, with increasing delegation of operating decisions through policy; strategic choices relate to degree of integration; market share objective, breadth of product-line.

III. Multiple product lines; multiple distribution channels; specialization based on product-market relationships, nonintegrated pattern of product-service transactions; institutionalized search for *new* products as well as for improvements; performance measurement increasingly impersonal using *market* criteria (return on investment and market share); rewards increasingly systematic, with variability related to performance; delegation of product-market decisions within existing businesses, with indirect control based on analyses of results; strategic choices relate to entry and exit from industries, allocation of resources by industry, rate of growth (Scott, 1973, p. 137).

Here there is a shift from entrepreneurial to functional to multi-divisional forms. A single product firm could stay at stage II and grow very large, in some cases larger and more profitable than certain stage III diversified firms. But if the growth strategy changes, the structure had best change to fit also.

Research on Strategy and Structure

A sizable amount of literature follows Chandler in the business history tradition and analyzes developmental sequences of firms in various countries and societies (Hannah, 1976; H. Williamson, 1975). This is a rich literature from a theoretical perspective, but it is not part of science because the results cannot be replicated and tested for generalizability. Fortunately there are other studies of strategy and structure in a more scientific tradition.

The Harvard Studies

In the late 1960s and early 1970s a number of studies were conducted at Harvard utilizing companies in both the United States and Europe. These studies were a direct outgrowth of Chandler's theory. Most were submitted as dissertations at the Harvard Business School. Though the extent to which this research actually tests the Chandler hypotheses varies considerably, all the studies are relevant in one way or another.

Stopford. This program of research includes the Stopford (1968) dissertation and certain related studies (Fouraker and Stopford, 1968; Stopford and Wells, 1972). There is consistent evidence that product diversification is associated with the multidivisional forms and that this is true whether the data are analyzed on a company-by-company basis or across industries.

Much of the research focuses on companies that have expanded into international markets. Initially this tends to involve the establishment of a single, overarching international division, which is analogous to the functional structure and inappropriate to the diversification strategy. The ideal fit for an international diversification strategy is hypothesized to be the worldwide product division structure, though in some instances this might be applied only to a few major products, and the area division structure, broken down by country or groups of countries, might be applied to the rest. As anticipated, worldwide product divisions predominated under conditions of high foreign product diversity, and international divisions predominated where there was no such diversity. Under conditions of some but low diversity, international divisions also predominated, but worldwide product divisions and mixed product-area forms were also frequent. The pure area division form was most likely to be associated with no foreign product diversity.

Though reorganizations tended to occur when foreign product sales reached numbers that would require the shift, there were many instances in which sales growth was slow and the lag in years between strategy and structure quite sizable. Thus at any given time the actual extent of strategy/structure fit was far from perfect.

Perhaps the most theoretically important results obtained from this research relate to the effectiveness of the firms. Comparisons were made for firms whose strategies fit their structures—international or area divisions under conditions of no diversification, and worldwide product divisions under conditions of considerable diversification—and for firms whose strategies and structures did not fit. The results are contained in Table 10–1. Though statistical significance levels are not reported, growth in sales is greatest when a diversified growth strategy is coupled with the appropriate structure. In general on this growth variable, success appears to be associated with both fit and the adoption of a diversified growth strategy. On profitability, as measured by return on investment (in the last of the six years), diversification does not show a similar advantage, and strategy/structure fit appears to be really advantageous only under conditions of a high diversification strategy. Differences in firm size, however measured, cannot account for these results. These and other findings often tend to support the theory, but not as consistently or as strongly as one might anticipate.

Wrigley. The Wrigley research dealt with Fortune 500 firms and relationships between their growth strategies and structures (Scott, 1973; Wrigley, 1970). Strategies were differentiated as single business (with no diversification), dominant business (with 70–95 percent of sales coming from one business or a vertically integrated chain), related business (with diversification in related areas, no one of which accounts for more than 70 percent of sales), and unrelated business (with diversification into unrelated areas and no business having more than 70 percent of sales). Of these, the related business strategy was by far the most frequent, and such firms almost always had a multidivisional structure. The unrelated business strategy was always associated with the multidivisional form, and the single business strategy was always carried out within a functional structure.

Table 10–1

Effectiveness of Multinational Firms Whose Structure Does and Does Not Match Their Strategy (N = 162)

Strategy as Reflected in Foreign Product Diversity	Growth in Foreign Sales over Six Years		Foreign Return on Investment	
	Structure/ Strategy Fit	Structure/ Strategy Misfit	Structure/ Strategy Fit	Structure/ Strategy Misfit
All products in one industry	12.0%	*	11.9%	*
Products in more than one industry, but one product line dominates	14.9	13.8	11.3	10.1%
Products in many industries and no dominant product line	19.3	13.5	10.0	7.5

*No such cases reported.

Source: Adapted from John M. Stopford and Louis T. Wells, *Managing the Multinational Enterprise: Organization of the Firm and Ownership of the Subsidiaries.* New York: Basic Books, 1972, p. 82.

The dominant business strategy was associated with no single structure consistently. These results are generally in agreement with expectations from strategy/structure theory.

Channon. In a study covering the period from 1950 to 1970 Channon (1973) collected data on 100 of the largest manufacturing firms in Great Britain. During this period single business firms decreased from 34 to 6 percent of the total, dominant business firms remained roughly stable in frequency, and related businesses increased from 23 to 54 percent. Unrelated businesses were not a major factor in British enterprise over this period. In general the single business firms did not use a multidivisional structure, though there were instances where this occurred. The dominant business firms shifted increasingly to this structure over time; 11 percent were multidivisional in 1950, and 70 percent by 1970. The same pattern appears among the related businesses, which rose from 29 percent to 78 percent. Among the limited number of unrelated business firms, the multidivisional structure increased, but in all periods there were companies that departed from theoretical expectations.

Analyses of changes over time indicated a frequent tendency for the diversified growth strategy to precede the shift to a multidivisional form. However, the lags involved often extended over many years. These lags were particularly characteristic of companies controlled by families. In 1970 there were still a number of companies pursuing diversification strategies without multidivisional structures. Yet three companies had modified their structures for the purpose of pursuing a diversification strategy subsequently. Here one might argue that strategy followed structure. In one sense this is true, but it is perhaps more correct to say that strategy implementation followed structure. The formulated strategy appears to have existed at the top-management level prior to both the structural change and the subsequent strategy implementation.

Channon (1973) notes at several points that declining profits preceded structural change, but no actual data are provided on this point. Furthermore, increasing competition appears to have fostered diversification through acquisition and later the adoption of a multidivisional structure. A major factor in both the strategic and the structural shifts was often a management consulting firm. Almost without exception these firms recommended the adoption of a multidivisional form.

Dyas. Studies utilizing the same procedure as that employed by Channon in Great Britain were carried out in France, Germany, and Italy. The French research was conducted by Dyas (Dyas and Thanheiser, 1976). Over the period from 1950 to 1970 single business firms decreased sharply, while increases occurred in all the other categories. By 1970, 60 percent of the dominant businesses, 64 percent of the related businesses, and only 50 percent of the unrelated businesses had adopted the multidivisional structure. Though functional forms predominated in the single business category, 19 percent of these companies were utilizing a multidivisional structure. These figures reflect sharp increases in the amount of multidivisional organization over the twenty years. Though unrelated business strategies were rare in 1950, dominant and particularly related businesses were reasonably common. Yet there were very few multidivisional structures to match these strategies. These and other data indicate that, while strategy tended to precede structure, the structures were very slow to change.

In general the move to multidivisional organization occurred much later in France than in the United States:

> Moves to a more diversified category, though frequently
> involving some shift in organizational form, had not led
> directly to the adoption of the divisional organization. While
> diversification was a necessary condition for divisionalization,
> the advent of the latter occurred late, but rapidly, in France,
> and had seemingly little connection with the pattern of moves
> to greater diversity (Dyas and Thanheiser, 1976, p. 262).

A major factor associated with this pattern noted by the authors is the lack of competitive pressure in the French environment over the period of study. When competition increased during the 1960s, multidivisional structures were adopted at an accelerated pace, and the overall amount of strategy/structure fit expanded. Such a hypothesis is consistent with Chandler's theoretical statements regarding the role of competition, but because the Dyas study lacks actual measures of competitive pressures or of organizational effectiveness, it offers no test of Chandler's views in this regard.

Thanheiser. The German pattern differed in several respects from that in France (Dyas and Thanheiser, 1976). Single businesses declined some, but many remained in 1970. There were increases in the related and unrelated business categories, but they were not accompanied by any meaningful shift in the dominant businesses. Overall, strategies changed much less than structures—the multidivisional form increased dramatically, especially during the late 1960s. The result was a substantial upward shift in the number of diversified firms with multidivisional structures, from 7 percent in 1950 to 67 percent in 1970. Again there were often sizable lags. Overall, the data are consistent with theoretical expectations. Though structural changes followed strategy changes in thirty-three cases over the twenty-year period, there were only two instances in which the structural shift occurred first.

Here, as in France, competitive pressures increased during the late 1960s; so, too, did the influence of major U.S.-based consulting firms. Both of these factors appear to have offset the resistance to a decentralized form, which the multidivisional structure is, that is inherent in traditional German attitudes toward authority. As in prior studies, the failure to obtain measures of these contingency or domain-defining variables and of organizational success limits the value of the research.

Pavan. In Italy between 1950 and 1970 single business firms decreased, while dominant and related businesses increased and unrelated businesses were of little significance (Pavan, 1976). At the same time, the functional form decreased, but even so it was at 36 percent in 1970, and the multidivisional form increased from less than 10 percent in 1950 to 48 percent in 1970. These patterns are not unlike those in other countries, but the degree of acceptance of the diversified, multidivisional concept is much less. Among strictly Italian-owned firms only 35 percent of those with related or unrelated business strategies had a multidivisional structure in 1970.

Furthermore, when Italian businesses found the multidivisional form, they tended to decentralize less, and the resource allocation, monitoring, and coordination processes often operated in a manner not totally consistent with the Chandler concept. Family firms were particularly likely to have adopted a diversified strategy without following up with divisionalization of structure. The extent to which these departures from theoretical expectations are associated with restricted competition (protective tariffs, cartels, and the like) and substandard profit performance cannot be determined from the data.

Franko. Another investigation focused on large firms in a number of countries in Europe, and particularly multinational companies. The data indicate a marked acceleration in the adoption of the multidivisional structure during the late 1960s and early 1970s (Franko, 1974). By 1972, 70 percent of the major manufacturers in Great Britain, France, Germany, and Italy, as well as Switzerland, Holland, Belgium, Luxembourg, and Sweden, had shifted to the structure.

It is evident that the decentralized, multidivisional form that Chandler had in mind is a latecomer on the European scene and that European multinationals have characteristically utilized a very different structure until recently, even when their strategy was diversified; many companies continued to maintain a particular type of structure other than the multidivisional (Franko, 1976). This structure involved an informal, personal relationship between the parent company president and presidents of subsidiaries operated in each foreign country. This geographic differentiation was not coupled with the types of decentralization, personal responsibility, and controls inherent in the multidivisional form. Often there were strong family and friendship ties between parent and subsidiary, hence the title "mother-daughter" form. Characteristically the predominant organization structure in the home country was functional, perhaps with some domestic subsidiaries as well.

Table 10–2 shows the relationships between strategy and structure among the large continental European multinationals in 1971. British companies, which already had adopted the multidivisional form quite extensively, are not included. It is clear that greater product diversity is associated with a move away from international divisions, area structures, and world-functional structures, and to worldwide product divisions, as theory would predict. But the mother-daughter form is practically impervious to strategy.

There is evidence now that many companies have been abandoning the mother-daughter organization. This occurred before 1968 almost entirely among those with large U.S. operations. This type of change has been particularly characteristic of companies operating in industries invaded by competition. The change to a multidivisional structure was continuing until at least 1974, with a decrease of over 40 percent in mother-daughter organizations in a three-year period. These shifts are shown to be highly correlated with tariff reductions in the European Economic Community, changes in laws relating to antitrust and cartels, and other forces making for a more competitive business environment. In short, exposure to competition is said to have caused structure to move to a better fit with strategy:

> In Continental Europe, structure did not follow strategy until there was a change in the competitive environment. The average Continental European enterprise was actually more likely to be diversified both at home and abroad than was the average American multinational. Whereas 16% of American multinationals had all their domestic operations in one industry, only 11% of Continental multinationals were similarly undiversified at home. While 35% of the American multinationals had their foreign operations in one industry, only 16% of the Continental multinationals were undiversified abroad. Had structure followed strategy in the Continental European environment, one would have expected nearly universal use of the product-division structure (Franko, 1976, p. 204).

Franko views international consulting firms as a major source, but not a cause, of the exportation of the multidivisional structure to Europe. He also recognizes the need for data on company success to test strategy/structure theory fully, while indicating how difficult

Table 10–2

Extent of Use of Various Structures by European Multinationals in 1971 and Relationship to Degree of Foreign Product Diversity*

Structure	Percent Using Structure	Percent of Firms with Various Amounts of Diversity		
		None (N = 8)	Low (N = 21)	High (N = 31)
Mother-daughter	37	38	29	39
International division	16	38	24	6
Worldwide product divisions	34	12	29	42
Area and world-functional	4	12	9	0
Mixed	9	0	9	13

*Does not include Great Britain.

SOURCE: Adapted from Lawrence G. Franko, *The European Multinationals*. Stamford, Conn.: Greylock, 1976, pp. 188, 193.

it is to develop such data in standardized form for companies based in a number of countries.

Rumelt. The major United States study of Chandler's strategy/structure theory utilized randomly selected samples of 100 each from the top 500 industrials for the years 1947, 1959, and 1969 (Rumelt, 1974). Because of duplications, the total number of firms was 246. The 1969 sample overlaps the sample used by Wrigley (1970) to a considerable extent, and thus comparisons can be made between the two studies with regard to the strategic classifications. The two studies disagree in categorization of the same firms 28 percent of the time. In part this is attributable to Rumelt's efforts to develop more precise criteria for establishing a firm's strategic posture, but it is somewhat disconcerting nevertheless. The degree of comparability across studies may not be as great as it appears on the surface. None of the Harvard researchers has carried out a reliability check using additional judges to determine if high levels of agreement on classifications can be obtained.

Over the twenty years of the study there was a sharp decline in single businesses, with the greatest growth occurring in the related businesses and the next greatest in the unrelated businesses. This rush to diversification was matched by a drastic drop in functionally organized firms and a comparable rise in the use of the product division form. Though part of the shift to the divisionalized form can be attributed to diversification, an almost equal amount appears to be due to an overall tendency to opt for the divisional structure, irrespective of strategy, and thus to follow the fashion of the times.

Diversification and change to the multidivisional form are clearly linked only for companies originally using the single business strategy. Here there does tend to be a causal arrow from strategy to structure. There is also evidence during the 1950s (but not the 1960s) that already divisionalized firms were more likely to adopt a more aggressive diversification strategy. Again it is not clear whether it is strategy, or merely strategy implementation, that follows structure in these cases.

As noted in Table 10–3, the strategy/structure tie clearly did exist at all three points in time. Nevertheless there were numerous departures from the theoretically favored fit. Were those departures less successful? Unfortunately a full-scale test of the Chandler hypothesis was not carried out. The analysis was restricted to the related business category in the expectation that those divisionalized firms would be more successful than functionally organized companies. The evidence does not support this hypothesis. The multidivisional companies showed a significantly greater growth in sales, but not in profits, even though several different profitability indexes were employed. The major predictor of success in this study was

Table 10–3

Relationships Among Strategy and Structure in Fortune 500 U.S. Firms

Strategy by Year	Percent in Each Structural Category		
	Functional	Product Division	Other
Single business			
1949	94.7	2.7	2.6
1959	96.4	0	3.6
1969	76.5	14.2	9.3
Dominant business			
1949	80.0	17.1	2.9
1959	58.8	34.5	6.7
1969	38.2	60.3	1.5
Related business			
1949	56.4	40.3	3.3
1959	28.4	71.6	0
1969	9.5	89.5	1.0
Unrelated business			
1949	0	61.2	38.8
1959	0	93.3	6.7
1969	2.3	85.3	12.4

SOURCE: Adapted from Richard P. Rumelt, *Strategy, Structure, and Economic Performance.* Boston, Mass.: Graduate School of Business Administration, Harvard University, 1974, p. 71.

not strategy/structure fit, but the adoption of a particular type of either dominant business or related business strategy labeled "constrained." In these instances there was diversification, but it tended to be close to home, building on some particular skill or resource originally possessed by the company.

Recent Research

Certainly the best known and most widely cited studies related to strategy and structure theory are those done at Harvard. For a number of years they were the only studies. Recently some additional research has been conducted, and certain studies originally carried out for other purposes have some bearing on the theory.

Armour and Teece. The objective of the Armour and Teece (1978) study was to test Oliver Williamson's (1970, 1975) propositions regarding the economic consequences of adopting the multidivisional structure. As conducted, the research deals only with structure, and not with strategy/structure fit. However, because the data derive from twenty-eight firms in the Fortune 500 who obtain the majority of their revenues from petroleum, it is possible to construct a reasonably good picture of prevailing strategies. In the period covered, from 1955 to 1973, the industry was characterized by the use of a vertically integrated dominant business strategy (Rumelt, 1974). In most cases this represented a move from a single business approach during the 1960s, though some firms were in the dominant category throughout the period. In any event product diversification was not pronounced in the industry. Accordingly, one would expect the best structural fit to come from some combination of functional, geographic division, and small product division forms, but not from a full-fledged, decentralized, multiproduct divisional structure (Chandler, 1962).

Armour and Teece (1978) report that during the 1955–68 period a multidivisional structure was associated with a significantly higher return on stockholder's equity, roughly 2 percentage points above the 7.5 percent attained by companies with a predominantly functional form. In the 1969–73 period this superiority no longer existed, but all but a handful of relatively small firms were described as multidivisional. As a whole, these data do not support strategy/structure theory; rather, they suggest a generalized tendency for the multidivisional structure to yield at least an initial advantage.

This conclusion must be questioned in view of the lack of congruence between the structural classifications employed by Armour and Teece (1978) and Rumelt (1974). Not only is there considerable disagreement between them in describing the same firms at the same times, but Rumelt consistently indicates less divisionalization.

Changes that Armour and Teece say yield a product-based multidivisional structure are considered by Rumelt to yield a basically functional form with subsidiaries. The latter would appear to represent a better fit with the prevailing dominant business strategy. Thus, if one accepts the extrapolations from the Rumelt research, the initial findings for the 1955–68 period do appear to substantiate strategy/structure theory. On the other hand, the continuing problems in classifying firms represent a major source of concern; in this instance agreement was less than 50 percent.

Grinyer, Yasai-Ardekani, and Al-Bazzaz. A second study was conducted in Great Britain with forty-eight large firms (Grinyer, Yasai-Ardekani, and Al-Bazzaz, 1980). When these firms were classified in accordance with the Wrigley (1970) procedure, single business firms tended to be functionally organized, dominant businesses were split, related businesses most frequently utilized some product division structure (though 30 percent were functional), and unrelated businesses used product divisions. There was a correlation of .36 between the extent of diversification in the firm's strategy and the degree of divisionalization of structure. This value, though not large, remained essentially the same when a number of other factors were controlled; it does not appear to be attributable to the influence of any third variable. On the other hand, a wide range of variables other than strategy are also correlated with the structure measure.

The extent of strategy/structure fit was analyzed in relation to indexes of turbulence, change, hostility, and competitiveness in the environment. As perceptual measures, these indexes may not reflect the actual situation (see Chapter 9). These pressures were perceived as consistently less when the strategy/structure fit was good, which implies that an appropriate fit, such as a single business with functional structure or a related business with multidivisional structure, helps those in the firm cope with environmental forces. However, fit may merely produce a *feeling* of coping effectively.

Analyses of financial data bear on this issue. In general the hypothesis that strategy/structure fit yields greater success is not supported. Various financial measures were employed, and a number of correlations were computed. Of the forty-nine coefficients shown, seven were significant and in the direction expected, while four were significant, but in the opposite direction. Almost all the findings tending to support the theory involved growth in size (sales and number of employees), rather than growth in profitability. In this respect the findings closely parallel those obtained by Rumelt (1974). On the evidence from this study it appears that the theoretically specified fit may create some confidence in coping with the environment, which though perhaps justified by the firm's growth, has no necessary basis in improved financial performance.

Other Data. With the exception of the Armour and Teece (1978) study, published research on strategy/structure theory has not controlled for differences associated with the specific industries. This now appears to be an important consideration (Beard and Dess, 1979). A sizable proportion of the profits achieved by a diversified firm depend on the particular industries into which the firm diversifies. Thus, to identify the effects of strategy/structure fit alone, one may have to control for these industry effects. Certainly the Armour and Teece (1978) findings suggest that such a research strategy should be seriously considered in future studies.

The findings from studies of strategy/structure fit related to financial performance are uncertain, and one could hope for more data on this point. Studies of this kind are the crucial tests of theory. Galbraith and Nathanson (1978) note several additional unpublished investigations that bear mention. In one instance a small superiority for profit center firms (apparently diversified and multidivisional) over functionally organized companies was noted. Another case produced a similar finding when decentralized multidivisionals and functionally structured single businesses were categorized together as an "optimal form" and compared with all other combinations. Several other findings relate to strategy and structure separately, but not in the specific manner Chandler hypothesized. Galbraith and Nathanson (1978) note certain problems in the design of all these studies, in particular the inability to establish the direction of causation from concurrent analyses. The studies do provide certain limited support for strategy/structure theory, and certainly they are not inconsistent with it.

Galbraith and Nathanson (1978) also cite several studies considered in Chapter 9 as evidence that, under conditions of competition, structure will and should move to a position of closer alignment with strategy. In these studies a competitive environment tends to be associated with a decentralized structure and with more formalized procedures. This picture fits the multidivisional form described by Chandler. In this sense the research can be considered support for the theory, but on the other hand the organizations studied tend to be so small that a diversification strategy is not likely. Once again the findings are congruent with the theory, but do not approximate a crucial test.

Conclusions

Goals of Application

The theory of strategy and structure presents certain conceptual problems insofar as applications are concerned. As a theory derived from practice, applications may be said to have preceded the theory. Yet, once the theory was developed and stated, it probably served to accelerate the spread of the multidivisional form both within the United States and throughout the world.

Chandler was based at the Harvard Business School, and his ideas appear to have influenced faculty and students at that school from an early date. Many of these students subsequently joined major international consulting firms, advising clients on the conduct of diversification strategies and the introduction of multidivisional structures. In this sense strategy/structure theory, though it did not actually spawn any new applications, appears to have exerted a sizable influence on business practice, especially during the period of rapid conversion to multidivisional structures on the part of firms based in Europe. Whether this influence has been desirable for the organizations involved rests on an assessment of the scientific validity of the theory.

Scientific Goals

The theory of strategy and structure covers a rather narrow domain. Strategy is limited to a particular type of growth strategy; structure is limited to a handful of alternatives, all focused on the top levels of bureaucratically organized business firms. Historically these variables have been of considerable importance. Whether they will remain so is an open question. Numerous new organizational structures and processes have appeared on the horizon, and most of these receive no attention from strategy/structure theory. Nevertheless, the domain occupied by the theory has been, and still is, one of major significance for society. It is important to determine how effectively this stewardship has been carried out.

There appears to be little question that strategy influences structure at the top levels of business firms. The evidence on this point is overwhelming. While many companies in recent years have adopted the multidivisional form because it was the thing to do, many others have or have not adopted it because of the particular strategies they were pursuing. Structure may influence strategy as well; certainly it is a logical possibility, as when a multidivisional structure is installed because everyone else is doing it and then an acquisition strategy is developed to make the structure viable. It is more likely that in cases where strategy is said to follow structure, a strategy was formulated before any changes occurred and then was implemented after the new structure was in place.

When cross-sectional data are used and structure does not match strategy, the disparity often is attributed to lag. This concept applies only to diversified companies *without* a multidivisional structure, however. It will not handle single businesses *with* a multidivisional structure, and such businesses do exist. Furthermore, the lag concept is not well developed. Lag is said to be reduced by retirements, crises, reduced family involvement, and competition, but the theory does not actually provide a fully developed set of testable hypotheses. Thus the lag concept becomes a theoretical escape hatch. If the data do not come out right, wait a while and the lag will end. But how long must one wait? In many instances these lags have extended over such long periods that it makes little sense to couple a new structure with a strategy that has existed for many years. Too many other things have happened in the interim that might better account for the change.

Competition is one factor that seems to lead to structural change. The evidence here is rather compelling. Many studies invoke the concept without providing data to support its use, but Franko (1976) provides the data, and the research relating market competition to decentralization gives added support. On the other hand, such change may be as well explained by the more general concept that if one is faced with competition and does not wish to lose, one should "get one's house in order." Strategy/structure fit may be just one of many changes that occur with the advent of competition.

In view of the strong support for the descriptive theory, it is surprising that the normative strategy/structure theory fares so poorly. It appears that growth is facilitated by the use of a multidivisional structure among those with a diversification strategy. However, when profit indexes are used as criteria, the picture becomes much less clear. There are some positive findings, but there are more negative findings, and the few studies that report a relationship between fit and financial performance do so only under certain conditions— a limited time period or a specific type of fit. Furthermore, the qualifications on the relationship provided by one study do not match up with those from another. A company considering a major reorganization certainly should have good reason to believe that the time, effort, and expense of change will prove financially worthwhile. At present there is no evidence that reorganization will be profitable.

The difficulty in demonstrating the profitability of a strategy/structure fit may lie in the research itself. Growth effects may be stronger and more pervasive than profit effects. When this difference is combined with research procedures that introduce or permit wide error variance, the profit effects may be eclipsed. Two sources of possible error have been noted previously. One is the frequent failure to separate industry and company effects. Firms make domain decisions that determine what industry or industries they will operate in; they also make decisions about whether they wish to grow, and if so, how. The Chandler theory deals only with growth as an overall company strategy. Ideally the domain decision factor should be eliminated from tests of the theory, but it rarely has been. The Armour and Teece (1978) results suggest that eliminating industry effects might improve predictions of profit performance.

The variability of strategy and structure classifications in the research raises serious questions. Though few studies yield data on this point, disagreements in classifications tend to be pronounced. In part the problem arises out of disagreements over category definitions—this should yield constant errors that reflect construct validity problems and seriously limit the comparability of studies. But there are also cases in which category definitions are sufficiently loose to permit two companies with the same strategies (or structures) to be classified differently—this should yield unreliability of measurement and a sizable error variance. The answer to both problems would appear to be the development of highly specific category descriptions with examples and perhaps the setting of quantitative bounds on various dimensional measures. A finer breakdown of categories often facilitates the classification process, because fewer broad abstractions are required. Rumelt (1974) moved in this direction, but perhaps not far enough. Recent research attempts by Allen (1978) to develop a taxonomy of divisionalized structures are the kind needed to deal with this issue.

Strategy/structure theory has not been the source of a large number of studies. Furthermore, the research that has been done has given little direct attention to the role of resource allocation, monitoring, and coordination processes as they relate to economies of speed and to the development of accounting procedures. The only findings noted to this point that bear on these factors are those that relate competitiveness in the environment to decentralization and formalization as well as to the use of sophisticated controls (see Chapter 9). However, additional research in this area is considered in Chapter 13 in the context of bureaucratic theory.

When a company moves to a multidivisional structure, the changes typically introduced cover a broad range. Though Chandler views them all as logically interlocking parts of an inherent whole, it is possible that only certain changes affect growth (and profits, if they are affected at all) and that other changes are extraneous. Perhaps the theory can be further simplified to focus on key change variables that maximize results. Conceivably actual structural change may not matter at all, and observed effects may arise from clearer role prescriptions and the monitoring of role behavior.

Strategy/structure theory itself operates within a limited domain, but the variables with which it deals encourage its expansion to a broader arena. Strategy, for instance, is much more than a limited set of growth strategies. The theory has already been elaborated along the growth dimension. The growth models, though probably not yet fully developed, are good examples of how Chandler's ideas may be expanded. The following statement sums up the existing knowledge in this regard:

> As organizations come from different sized countries, face domestic markets varying in competitiveness, and grow by acquisition rather than internally, they choose different but predictable paths to a similar final stage. However, the more detailed the specification of the stage, the less predictable the sequential movement. As long as we conceive of only three stages, with global forms considered to be a Stage III type, the stages of growth model holds. As soon as we consider other types of global structure or consider substages such as the international division phase, more alternative paths appear, more outcomes are possible, and more detailed specifications of strategy such as Rumelt's nine categories, are required in order to match strategy with structure and process (Galbraith and Nathanson, 1978, p. 113).

The Galbraith and Nathanson (1978) organizational fit theory itself appears to be too loosely stated to constitute a true theory. It relies heavily on a single study, that of Lorsch and Morse (1974), which as noted in Chapter 9 is subject to multiple interpretations. The authors appear to be striving for a grand theory covering a very broad domain. Such theories have not characteristically had much success in the field of organization study (Miner, 1980). Yet, if we view the ideas expressed in Figure 10–2 as a conceptual framework for a number of middle-range theories (Pinder and Moore, 1980), then the approach taken by Galbraith and Nathanson appears to make considerable sense.

Within such a framework various structures may turn out to be effective in implementing a given strategy. The key may not be so much which structure is chosen, as how that structure is staffed and operated once it is chosen. This would imply that the fit, or set of possible fits, between strategy and structure, may be loose indeed at the decision-making stage but much more precise within the organization once a structural decision has been reached.

The theory of strategy and structure has brought the concept of organizational decision making and choice clearly into focus as a major variable in organizational theory. Decision makers are not viewed as pawns moved about by various imperatives, but rather as key sources of variance in their own right. Both the theory and the research on strategy and structure support this conclusion, and in so doing fill a major theoretical void.

References

Allen, Stephen A. "Organizational Choices and General Management Influence Networks in Divisionalized Companies," *Academy of Management Journal*, 21 (1978), 341–65.

Armour, Henry O., and David J. Teece. "Organizational Structure and Economic Performance: A Test of the Multidivisional Hypothesis," *Bell Journal of Economics*, 9 (1978), 106–22.

Beard, Donald W., and George G. Dess. "Industry Profitability and Firm Performance: A Preliminary Analysis of the Firm Portfolio Question," *Academy of Management Proceedings*, 1979, pp. 123–27.

Chandler, Alfred D. "Management Decentralization: An Historical Analysis," *Business History Review*, 30 (1956), 111–74.

———. *Strategy and Structure: Chapters in the History of the American Industrial Enterprise.* Cambridge, Mass.: MIT Press, 1962.

———. "The Structure of American Industry in the Twentieth Century: A Historical Overview," *Business History Review*, 43 (1969), 255–97.

———. "The Multi-Unit Enterprise: A Historical and International Comparative Analysis and Summary." In Harold F. Williamson (ed.), *Evolution of International Management Structures.* Newark, Del.: University of Delaware Press, 1975, pp. 225–54.

———. "Institutional Integration: An Approach to Comparative Studies of the History of Large-Scale Business Enterprise." In Keiichiro Nakagawa (ed.), *Strategy and Structure of Big Business.* Tokyo: University of Tokyo Press, 1976, pp. 121–47.

———. "The United States: The Evolution of Enterprise," *Cambridge Economic History of Europe*, 7, pt. 2 (1977a), 70–133.

———. *The Visible Hand: The Managerial Revolution in American Business.* Cambridge, Mass.: Harvard University Press, 1977b.

Chandler, Alfred D., and Herman Daems. "Administrative Coordination, Allocation, and Monitoring: Concepts and Comparisons." In Norbert Horn and Jürgen Kocka (eds.), *Law and the Formation of the Big Enterprises in the 19th and Early 20th Centuries.* Göttingen, West Germany: Vandenhoeck and Ruprecht, 1979, pp. 28–54.

Chandler, Alfred D., and Fritz Redlich. "Recent Developments in American Business Administration and Their Conceptualization," *Business History Review*, 35 (1961), 1–27.

Channon, Derek F. *The Strategy and Structure of British Enterprise.* Boston, Mass.: Graduate School of Business Administration, Harvard University, 1973.

Dyas, Gareth P., and Heinz T. Thanheiser. *The Emerging European Enterprise: Strategy and Structure in French and German Industry.* Boulder, Col.: Westview Press, 1976.

Fouraker, Lawrence E., and John M. Stopford. "Organizational Structure and the Multinational Strategy," *Administrative Science Quarterly*, 13 (1968), 47–64.

Franko, Lawrence G. "The Move Toward a Multidivisional Structure in European Organizations," *Administrative Science Quarterly*, 19 (1974), 493–506.

———. *The European Multinationals: A Renewed Challenge to American and British Big Business.* Stamford, Conn.: Greylock, 1976. ·

Galbraith, Jay R., and Daniel A. Nathanson. *Strategy Implementation: The Role of Structure and Process.* St. Paul, Minn.: West, 1978.

Grinyer, Peter H., Masoud Yasai-Ardekani, and Shawki Al-Bazzaz. "Strategy, Structure, the Environment, and Financial Performance in 48 United Kingdom Companies," *Academy of Management Journal*, 23 (1980), 193–226.

Hannah, Leslie. *The Rise of the Corporate Economy: The British Experience.* Baltimore, Md.: Johns Hopkins University Press, 1976.

Lorsch, Jay W., and John J. Morse. *Organizations and Their Members: A Contingency Approach.* New York: Harper & Row, 1974.

Miner, John B. "The Role of Organizational Structure and Process in Strategy Implementation: Commentary." In Dan E. Schendel and Charles W. Hofer (eds.), *Strategic Management: A New View of Business Policy and Planning.* Boston: Little, Brown, 1979, pp. 289–302.

———. *Theories of Organizational Behavior.* Hinsdale, Ill.: Dryden, 1980.

Pavan, Robert J. "Strategy and Structure: The Italian Experience," *Journal of Economics and Business,* 28 (1976), 254–60.

Pinder, Craig C., and Larry F. Moore. *Middle Range Theory and the Study of Organizations.* Boston: Martinus Nijhoff, 1980.

Rumelt, Richard P. *Strategy, Structure, and Economic Performance.* Boston, Mass.: Graduate School of Business Administration, Harvard University, 1974.

Scott, Bruce R. "The Industrial State: Old Myths and New Realities," *Harvard Business Review,* 51, no. 2 (1973), 133–48.

Steiner, George A., and John B. Miner. *Management Policy and Strategy.* New York: Macmillan, 1982.

Stopford, John M. "Growth and Organizational Change in the Multinational Firm." D.B.A. dissertation, Harvard Business School, 1968.

Stopford, John M., and Louis T. Wells. *Managing the Multinational Enterprise: Organization of the Firm and Ownership of the Subsidiaries.* New York: Basic Books, 1972.

Williamson, Harold F. *Evolution of International Management Structures.* Newark, Del.: University of Delaware, 1975.

Williamson, Oliver E. *Corporate Control and Business Behavior: An Inquiry into the Effects of Organization Form on Enterprise Behavior.* Englewood Cliffs, N.J.: Prentice-Hall, 1970.

———. *Markets and Hierarchies: Analysis and Antitrust Implications: A Study in the Economics of Internal Organization.* New York: Free Press, 1975.

Wrigley, Leonard. "Divisional Autonomy and Diversification." D.B.A. dissertation, Harvard Business School, 1970.

11

Administrative Behavior, Organizations, and the Behavioral Theory of the Firm

The title of this chapter echoes the titles of three books whose authors are the major contributors to a theoretical perspective based on organizational decision making. Organizational functioning under their decision-making approach is in some ways conceptually akin to that of strategy/structure theory. However, the similarities lie primarily in the emphasis given to choices and decisions rather than in specific theoretical content, and there is little reason to believe the two theories influenced each other at all. On the other hand, early statements of the views considered in this chapter did influence sociological open systems theory (Chapter 7).

The three books that contain among them the foundations of the theory discussed here are *Administrative Behavior* by Herbert Simon (1947); *Organizations* by James March and Simon (1958); and *A Behavioral Theory of the Firm* by Richard Cyert and March (1963). All three authors have made significant theoretical contributions before and since publication of these books, but the essential elements of their thinking are contained in these volumes. All three authors were together at Carnegie Institute of Technology (now Carnegie-Mellon) for a number of years.

Herbert Simon obtained his degree in political science from the University of Chicago and held a brief appointment in the Bureau of Public Administration at the University of California (Berkeley). He subsequently served on the political science faculty at Illinois Institute of Technology, before moving to the Graduate School of Industrial Administration at Carnegie Institute in 1949. At present he holds appointments in psychology and computer science at that university, though his contributions have spanned the whole range of social science. He has been awarded a Nobel prize in economics.

James March, serving at Stanford University since 1970, has an equally diverse array of disciplinary associations, including appointments in political science, education, sociology, and business administration. He, too, started in the field of political science with a degree from Yale. From 1953 to 1964 he was with Simon at Carnegie before taking an administrative position at the University of California (Irvine). In contrast to Simon and March, Richard Cyert has remained much more closely associated with Carnegie and with the discipline of economics. Since obtaining his doctorate from Columbia, Cyert has served both as dean of the graduate school of industrial administration and as president of Carnegie-Mellon University—the latter a position he currently holds.

The Theoretical Formulations of Simon, March, and Cyert

Though the theories considered in this chapter tend to focus on decision making, and in recent years to focus on that subject more and more, they cover a number of the conventional components of organizational functioning that they characteristically relate to the decision process. Furthermore, we are not dealing with a single, cohesive theory. As conceptual development has continued, there has been some splintering among the authors at various points. Though the central theme has remained stable, the authors have tended to develop that theme in different ways. Thus it is more appropriate to speak of the authors' theoretical formulations than of their theory.

The Debt to Chester Barnard

Emphasizing the views of Simon, March, and Cyert should not be seen as an attempt to minimize the contributions of Chester Barnard, who developed his personal observations as a corporate officer into an influential set of concepts at an early date (Barnard, 1938). Simon was strongly influenced by Barnard and acknowledges his influence repeatedly in *Administrative Behavior* (1947). In fact Barnard critically reviewed the original manuscript and wrote a foreword to the first edition of that book. Simon's views on the decision to participate in an organization and on organizational authority were derived from Barnard. Barnard himself appears to have believed that Simon's stress on the importance of decision making also came from him. However, this seems unlikely, even though Barnard certainly influenced Simon in certain specific formulations about decision making (Wolf, 1974).

Barnard's theory is not considered in this volume because many of his views have been superseded by those of Simon, March, and Cyert. Barnard (1938) was as much a philosopher as a theorist, and his highly abstract statements have spawned little research. The Simon, March, and Cyert formulations fall more clearly in the realm of science and are more appropriate to present purposes.

Administrative Behavior

Simon's *Administrative Behavior* (1947) is unusual in several respects. Like so many others, Simon first attempts to demolish classical management theory, but instead of arguing on grounds of humanitarianism or adaptive inflexibility, he attacks it for logical inconsistency and failure to measure up to the demands of science (see Chapter 1). These considerations are treated at some length in Chapter 12 where classical theory is discussed. While rejecting the normative principles of classical theory, Simon does not then advocate a new normative theory to replace them. Instead, he takes only a first step toward reconstruction—the setting forth of a vocabulary and conceptual framework.

Limits to Rationality. A central thesis in Simon's thinking is that rational decision making is limited or bounded by (1) a person's skills, habits, and reflexes, (2) the values and concepts of purpose that influence the decision, and (3) the person's knowledge, particularly of the consequences of alternatives. Inherent in this view is the idea that decisions involve not only factual judgments, but also ethical or value judgments that relate to the goals and purposes to be served. In a very rough sense *administration* relates to factual judgments and *policy* to value judgments. In the same sense, facts more often tend to be related to means and values to ends.

Simon's views in this area must be set against the prevailing concept of a highly rational, maximizing decision maker, as epitomized by *economic man:*

> It is impossible for the behavior of a single, isolated individual to reach any high degree of rationality. The number of alternatives he must explore is so great, the information he would need to evaluate them so vast that even an approximation to objective rationality is hard to conceive. Individual choice takes place in an environment of "givens"—premises that are accepted by the subject as bases for his choice; and behavior is adaptive only within the limits set by these "givens" (Simon, 1947, p. 79).

Behavior thus fails of objective rationality in several respects:

> 1. Rationality requires a complete knowledge and anticipation of the consequences that will follow on each choice. In fact, knowledge of consequences is always fragmentary.
> 2. Since these consequences lie in the future, imagination must supply the lack of experienced feeling in attaching value to them. But values can be only imperfectly anticipated.
> 3. Rationality requires a choice among all possible alternative behaviors. In actual behavior, only a very few of all these possible alternatives ever come to mind (Simon, 1947, p. 81).

Within an organization the decision process begins with *substantive planning*—the broad decisions affecting values, methods of attaining those values, and needed knowledge, skills, and information. Second, there is *procedural planning*, involving decisions about mechanisms to direct attention and channel information in accordance with the substantive plan. Finally, there is *execution* based on day-to-day decisions. The hierarchy of steps increasingly restricts alternatives and limits the decision process. Consistent with this objective, work is divided among members, standard practices are introduced, decisions are transmitted through the organization, and members are trained in matters related to their decisions. Thus much of organizational structure and process is explained in relation to making decisions manageable.

Simon (1947) devotes considerable attention to the criterion of efficiency, which requires that the alternative selected be the one that will yield greatest net return. If costs are fixed, the decision should maximize income, and if income is fixed, it should minimize costs. When efficiency is the accepted criterion, rationality governs decision making, much as it does in economic theory when an attempt is made to maximize utility. Given the limits to rationality, Simon does not assert that managerial decisions are characteristically dominated by the criterion of efficiency. Yet, Simon seems to favor that end highly and to argue for maximization of efficiency and rational decisions to the extent that available data permit. On occasion he even seems to imply that rationality often is attainable. In subsequent treatments, however, he is less optimistic (Simon, 1957a; Simon, Smithburg, and Thompson, 1950).

Inducements-Contributions Equilibrium. Business organizations have at least three kinds of participants—entrepreneurs, employees, and customers. Entrepreneurs enter into contracts with employees to obtain their time and effort and with customers to obtain their money to pay wages and thus maintain the employment contract. Though in businesses the inducement—money—is indirect, in some organizations such as churches the inducement for members may be some direct personal value. In any event a necessary condition for gaining and continuing to belong to an organization is some form of inducements-contributions agreement.

When the contributions are adequate to attract what is needed to provide the appropriate kinds and amounts of inducements, the organization prospers. One kind of contribution in such situations is a willingness to accept authority. This willingness extends over a zone of acceptance whose width is determined by the nature and extent of inducements. If the employment contract terms, implicit or explicit, are favorable, an employee can be expected to contribute willingly over a broad range of activities. But if the inducements provide little satisfaction of personal goals, contributions and the zone of acceptance shrink.

In these relationships authority is defined as "the power to make decisions which guide the actions of another" (Simon, 1947, p. 125). Authority is only one form of influence, which also includes persuasion and suggestion. Authority exists only as long as it is accepted, and thus only as long as what is required falls within the zone of acceptance.

Models of Man and Other Extensions. In the period following the first publication of *Administrative Behavior*, Simon developed his concepts more fully in a number of articles. These articles, as well as others unrelated to organizational structure and process, were brought together in a single volume entitled *Models of Man* (Simon, 1957b). In the same year *Administrative Behavior* (1957a) was republished with a lengthy introduction qualifying and extending Simon's earlier views. In both publications the term *satisficing* is now used to refer to the behavior of those who "have not the wits to maximize."

In elaborating on the idea that administrative theory is, in fact, synonymous with the theory of intended and bounded rationality, Simon amended his prior views to include the satisficing concept:

1. While economic man maximizes—selects the best alternative from among all those available to him, his cousin, whom we shall call administrative man—satisfices—looks for a course of action that is satisfactory or "good enough."

2. Economic man deals with the "real world" in all its complexity. Administrative man recognizes that the world he perceives is a drastically simplified model of the buzzing, blooming confusion that constitutes the real world. He is content with this gross simplification because he believes that the real world is mostly empty—that most of the facts of the real world have no great relevance to any particular situation he is facing. . . . He makes his choices using a simple picture of the situation that takes into account just a few of the factors that he regards as most relevant and crucial. . . . Administrative man is able to make his decisions with relatively simple rules of thumb that do not make impossible demands upon his capacity for thought (Simon, 1957a, pp. xxv-xxvi).

In publication after publication Simon attacks the economic theory that assumes perfect knowledge and ignores the reality of bounded rationality. Under bounded rationality the decision maker, instead of maximizing, searches only until he finds an alternative where the payoff is good enough. There is no need to look beyond this point for an alternative that will yield an even higher payoff. In formulating the satisficing concept, Simon assumes a sequential pattern of choice:

The aspiration level, which defines a satisfactory alternative, may change from point to point in this sequence of trials. A vague principle would be that as the individual, in his exploration of alternatives, finds it easy to discover satisfactory alternatives, his aspiration level rises; as he finds it difficult to discover satisfactory alternatives, his aspiration level falls. . . . Such changes in aspiration level would tend to bring about a "near-uniqueness" of the satisfactory solutions, and would also tend to guarantee the existence of satisfactory solutions. For the failure to discover a solution would depress the aspiration level and bring satisfactory solutions into existence (Simon, 1957b, p. 253).

Elaborating further on the inducements-contributions equilibrium, Simon notes that employment contracts and sales contracts differ in that the former specify only a zone of acceptance of authority (and perhaps areas of nonacceptance), rather than specific terms and actions for each party. Yet, as Simon himself recognizes, his theory tends somewhat inconsistently to assume rational, utility-maximizing behavior in the employment relationship:

> Each participant will remain in the organization if the satisfaction (or utility) he derives from the net balance of inducements over contributions (measured in terms of their utility to him) is greater than the satisfaction he could obtain if he withdrew. The zero point in such a "satisfaction function" is defined, therefore, in terms of the opportunity cost of participation (Simon, 1957b, p. 173).

Organizations

The book *Organizations* (March and Simon, 1958) has much in common with Thompson's *Organizations in Action* (1967). However, March and Simon's inventory of propositions is largely induced from empirical research, while Thompson's derives from conceptual premises. Many March and Simon hypotheses deal with variables such as motivation, group behavior, and leadership that fall entirely within the confines of organizational behavior at the micro level (Miner, 1980). At the micro level March and Simon's theory is now primarily of historical interest, having been superseded by other, more sophisticated formulations. The following discussion will focus on the theory's more comprehensive concepts and propositions relating to the organization as a whole, including its processes of decision making.

Satisficing and Bounded Rationality. The March and Simon (1958) discussion of decision making follows already familiar lines. However, some new concepts are added and old ones are developed more fully. The concept of performance program, which appears to be roughly analogous to role prescription, is invoked in the discussion of control and coordination systems. Performance programs, though intended to make behavior within an organization more predictable, are themselves selected on a satisficing basis, thus making it difficult to predict which performance programs will be chosen. Programs differ in their degree of stress on means and ends, and thus in the amount of discretion they permit.

Division of work is viewed as a means of simplifying the decision process. Units are established on the basis of purpose, and subgoals are introduced so that decision makers may face problems with which they can cope. Once units are created, the problem of interdependence arises. In stable, predictable environments there is considerable tolerance for interdependence, and process specialization can be carried quite far. In more rapidly changing environments specialization carries much higher risks. Thus organizations attempt to stabilize their environments by homogenizing materials, using interchangeable parts, holding buffer inventories, and the like to maintain specialization. Yet coordination problems remain:

> We may label coordination based on pre-established schedules *coordination by plan,* and coordination that involves transmission of new information *coordination by feedback.* The more stable and predictable the situation, the greater the reliance on coordination by plan; the more variable and unpredictable the situation, the greater the reliance on coordination by feedback (March and Simon, 1958, p. 160).

The influence of March and Simon on Thompson (1967) becomes very apparent in such formulations.

In general, highly programmed tasks drive out unprogrammed tasks. Organizations that do not give special consideration to this fact will fail to plan and innovate. To obtain unprogrammed action, organizations must establish specially budgeted planning units with their own specific goals or introduce hard-and-fast deadlines for the completion of unprogrammed tasks. Whether innovation occurs at the top levels of an organization depends on the type of coordination used. Feedback coordination facilitates, and coordination by plan limits, innovative decision making at the top.

The concept of bounded rationality provides a rationale not only for the division of work, but also for the decentralization of decision making. Given existing limits on human capacity, decentralized systems in which decisions are moved down and out to larger numbers of individuals are preferred over centralized systems.

The Decision to Participate. A stable inducements-contributions equilibrium is posited as a necessary condition for organizational survival. Increases in inducements decrease the tendency for an individual to leave the organization. The inducements-contributions balance is influenced by both perceived desirability and perceived ease of leaving. Propositions relating various factors to both per-

Figure 11–1

Major Factors Influencing Perceived Desirability and Ease of Movement from the Organization

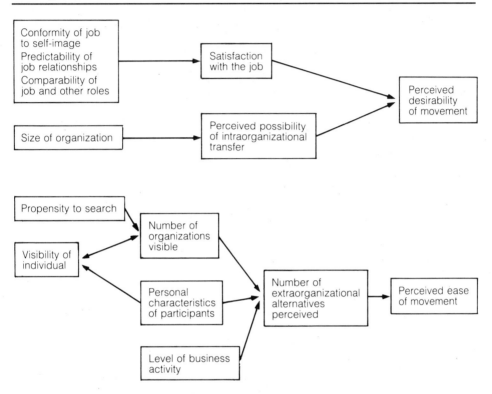

SOURCE: Adapted from James G. March and Herbert A. Simon, *Organizations*. New York: Wiley, 1958, pp. 99, 106.

ceived desirability of movement and perceived ease of movement are shown in Figure 11–1.

Conflict. Conflict in organizations may be within the individual, in that known, acceptable, decision alternatives are not available, or between individuals (or groups), in that different individuals make different choices. Conflict of the latter type is of prime concern here. Conflict within the individual is important too, in that it retards choice, and choice is a necessary condition for intergroup conflict.

Figure 11–2 outlines the major propositions involving intergroup conflict. The formulations relating to joint decision making are of particular interest. Sharing a common service unit and being adjacent to another unit in a flow-chart sense are given as examples of situations calling for joint decision making. Conflict is expected to

Figure 11–2
Major Factors Influencing Intergroup Conflict

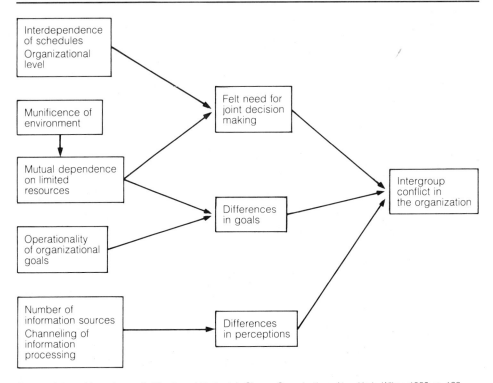

SOURCE: Adapted from James G. March and Herbert A. Simon, *Organizations*. New York: Wiley, 1958, p. 128.

be high in these instances. Conflict is most likely to be related to budgeting and monetary allocations and will tend to increase when overall resources are reduced.

Reactions to conflict include (1) problem solving, often with a search for new alternatives; (2) persuasion, often with a search for previously unconsidered superordinate objectives; (3) bargaining, where goal disagreements are taken as inevitable; and (4) politics, where the conflict arena is expanded to include other groups and constituencies. Typically, managerial hierarchies prefer problem solving and persuasion to bargaining and politics and will prefer to use them in conflict resolution. Problem solving and persuasion put less strain on the status and power systems.

Behavioral Theory of the Firm

Building on a collaboration begun a number of years before, Cyert and March (1955, 1956) extended their early ideas in various papers and ultimately published the most fully developed version of their theory in *A Behavioral Theory of the Firm* (1963). The theory takes the firm as its basic unit, attempts to predict firm behavior with regard to pricing, output, resource allocation, and the like, and focuses on the actual processes of organizational decision making.

Goal Formation. The firm is viewed as a coalition of managers, workers, stockholders, customers, and others, each with their own goals. The objectives that emerge out of this coalition are determined by bargaining, stabilized by various internal control processes, and adjusted over time in response to environmental change. Within the coalition some members exert greater influence and make greater demands for policy commitments than others. Such commitments, once made, become stabilized in the form of budget allocations, particular divisions of labor, and the like. At the same time clear, logical conflicts between the demands of different coalition members often remain unresolved in the goal structure. Conflicts may remain unresolved because attention tends to focus sequentially on first one goal and then another, thus skirting the need to deal with incompatibilities.

A coalition is viable, and thus an organization exists, if the payments (inducements), including influence over goals, are adequate to keep coalition members in the organization. These demands of members tend to be roughly correlated with the resources available to the organization, but the correlation is indeed rough:

> Because of these frictions in the mutual adjustment of payments and demands, there is ordinarily a disparity between the resources available to the organization and the payments required to maintain the coalition. This difference between total resources and total necessary payments is what we have called *organizational slack*. Slack consists in payments to members of the coalition in excess of what is required to maintain the organization (Cyert and March, 1963, p. 36).

Examples cited are excessively high dividends or wages, unnecessary public services, overstaffing, and the like. Such slack tends to absorb variability in the firm's environment; it increases when the environment is munificent and decreases as the cycle shifts toward the barren.

Though the goals that emerge out of bargaining within the coalition may vary widely, a limited set is considered sufficient to account for most of the variance. These are classifiable as production goals (with regard to both the smoothing and the level of production), inventory goals, sales goals, market share goals, and profit goals. Goal conflict in these areas is rarely fully resolved. Rather it tends to be suffered through mechanisms such as decentralization of goal attention, sequential attention to various goals, and adjustments in slack.

Expectations and Choice. The concepts of organizational expectations and choice set forth by Cyert and March (1963) closely follow those considered previously. However, the authors provide certain more specific formulations. They develop an executive decision-tree model as follows:

1. *Forecast competitors' behavior*
2. *Forecast demand*
3. *Estimate costs*
4. *Specify objectives*

These four steps are taken in no particular order. When all four are completed, the organization moves to:

5. *Evaluate plan* by examining the results of steps 1–3 to see if at least one alternative meets the objectives of step 4. If one does, the organization immediately moves to step 9.

6. *Reexamine costs* if step 5 does not yield a satisfactory alternative. After reexamination, return to step 5.

7. *Reexamine demand* if step 5 still fails to yield a satisfactory alternative. Again, return to step 5 after the reexamination.

8. *Reexamine objectives,* following the same pattern as that followed in steps 6 and 7. There is a tendency to revise objectives downward as necessary.

9. *Select alternative.*

Such a decision system is viewed as adaptive in the following sense:

1. There exist a number of states of the system. At any point in time the system in some sense "prefers" some of these states to others.

2. There exists an external source of disturbance or shock to the system. These shocks cannot be controlled.

3. There exist a number of decision variables internal to the system. These variables are manipulated according to some decision rules.

4. Each combination of external shocks and decision variables in the system changes the state of the system. Thus, given an existing state, an external shock, and a decision, the next state is determined.

5. Any decision rule that leads to a preferred state at one point in time is more likely to be used in the future than it was in the past (Cyert and March, 1963, p. 99).

The decision rules or standard operating procedures are both general and specific. Three basic principles appear to govern at the general level—avoid uncertainty, maintain the rules, and use simple rules. At the specific level there are four major types of procedures—task performance rules, continuing records and reports, information-handling rules, and plans. Plans are defined at one and the same time as goals, schedules, theories, and precedents.

These standard operating procedures exert a major impact on decision-making behavior within the firm as follows:

1. *Effects on individual goals within the organization.* The specification of a plan or other rule has a direct effect on the desires and expectations of organizational members.

2. *Effects on individual perceptions of the state of the environment.* Different parts of the organization see different environments, and the environments they see depend on the rules for recording and processing information.

3. *Effects on the range of alternatives considered* by organization members in arriving at operating decisions. The way in which the organization searches for alternatives is substantially a function of the operating rule it has.

4. *Effects on the managerial decision rules used* in the organization. In fact, these rules frequently are specified explicitly (Cyert and March, 1963, p. 112).

What these theorists have done is develop more fully the idea that various "rules of thumb" are used in reaching decisions when satisficing occurs.

Relational Concepts. Underlying the formulations on organizational goals, expectations, and choice are four major relational concepts: (1) *quasi resolution of conflict,* which involves goals that operate as aspiration-level constraints imposed by the demands of coalition members; (2) *uncertainty avoidance,* which is accomplished by focusing on more predictable short-term environments and short-run feedback or by arranging a negotiated environment; (3) *problemistic search,* which is concerned with engineering a solution to a specific problem—a solution that is motivated, simple-minded to the degree possible, and biased by the prior training, hopes, and conflicting goals of those involved; (4) *organizational learning,* which results in changes and adaptations in goals, in attention rules, and in search rules. The way these concepts enter into the organizational decision process is outlined in the decision tree of Figure 11–3.

As developed, the theory is essentially descriptive in nature. It attempts to understand and predict what executives do and will do, rather than to state what they should do. To the extent there are normative implications, these appear to have emerged as an afterthought; they have clearly not been the central focus of the theorists' efforts.

Figure 11–3

Organizational Decision Process at Abstract Level
(Start *is at the point of receiving feedback from past decisions*)

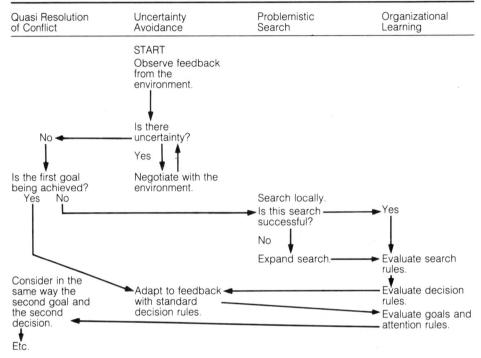

SOURCE: Adapted from Richard M. Cyert and James G. March, *A Behavioral Theory of the Firm*. Englewood Cliffs, N.J.: Prentice-Hall, 1963, p. 126.

Extensions Beyond the Basic Statements—Simon

The three books considered and certain elaborations on them represent the basic building blocks of the theory. Since the publication of his book with March, Cyert has worked on relating the basic formulations to ecomomic theory per se (Cyert and Hedrick, 1972), to using those formulations as a framework for looking at organization theory (Cyert and MacCrimmon, 1968), and to commenting on the field of university administration (Cyert, 1975). The result has not been so much a further extension of the theory as a placing of its major concepts in perspective.

Simon has continued to build on the theory. For the past twenty years or so he has devoted himself to extending the concepts of bounded rationality in the areas of human problem solving and computer science—areas that have only tangential relevance for the study of organizations (Simon, 1969; Newell and Simon, 1972). Yet some of Simon's extensions lie within the confines of the original theoretical structure.

Organizational Goals. In 1964 Simon published an article dealing with goals that he subsequently included in the third edition of *Administrative Behavior*. His discussion is described as "generally compatible with, but not identical to, that of my colleagues, R. M. Cyert and J. G. March" (Simon, 1976, p. 257). In fact it appears to be the beginning of a separation in viewpoints that has taken Simon and March in different directions since their collaboration on *Organizations* in 1958.

For Simon, goals are value premises for decisions and must be clearly distinguished from individual motives. In his view goals become synonymous with constraints:

> A course of action, to be acceptable, must satisfy a whole set of requirements, or constraints. Sometimes one of these requirements is singled out and referred to as the goal of the action. But the choice of one of the constraints, from many, is to a large extent arbitrary. For many purposes it is more meaningful to refer to the whole set of requirements as the (complex) goal of the action. This conclusion applies both to individual and organizational decision-making (Simon, 1976, p. 262).

These goals/constraints can serve to generate alternatives or, in the more traditional role of goals, to test alternatives. Used in the former sense there appears to be little goal congruence among the subunits of an organization, and goal conflict seems rampant. Used in the latter sense the sharing of constraint sets becomes much more widespread.

Simon (1976) gives less emphasis to bargaining and loosely bound coalitions than Cyert and March (1963) do. The goals/constraints emerge out of the inducements-contributions equilibrium, but they are also strongly influenced by the system of organizational roles in which decisions made in one unit serve as constraints for other parts of the organization. The coupling here is loose, but the decisions that produce the role structure can be measured against various organizational goals (other constraints) and corrected accordingly. Personal motives become much less important in organizational decisions than programmed organizational roles. Furthermore, given a hierarchical system, it is logical to use the term *organizational goal* to refer to "the constraint sets and criteria of search that define roles at the upper levels" (Simon, 1976, p. 277) and "to describe most business firms as directed toward profit making—subject to a number of side constraints" (p. 278).

Computers, Decisions, and Structures. From an early period Simon has been concerned with the influence of computers on organizational decision making and, because decisions are the raison d'être for structure, on organizational design as well. His current views appear in what is essentially the third edition of a book first published in 1960 entitled *The New Science of Management Decision* (Simon, 1977). In this book Simon describes progammed and nonprogrammed decisions and the techniques applicable to each. Simon's views in this regard are contained in Table 11–1.

Basically, Simon (1977) views hierarchy as an essential feature of large, complex systems of any kind. Applying this concept to organizations, nonprogrammed decision making is characteristic at the top levels, programmed decision making at the middle level, and the basic work processes, the actual doing, at the bottom level. The same hierarchical structure and subdivision into units is ascribed to computer systems, a natural outgrowth of the decision-making focus involved. "Hierarchy is the adaptive form for finite intelligence to assume in the face of complexity" (Simon, 1977, p. 114). Thus adding computers to the decision process should not change the essentially hierarchical nature of organizations.

Earlier, Simon (March and Simon, 1958) espoused decentralization to facilitate coping with complex decisions. Now he says about a historical period covered in the previous chapter:

> In the first twenty years after the Second World War there was a movement toward decentralization in large American business firms. This movement was probably a sound development, but it did not signify that more decentralization at all times and under all circumstances is a good thing. It signified that at a particular time in history, many American firms, which had experienced almost continuous long-term growth and diversification, discovered that they could operate more effectively if they brought together all the activities relating to individual products or groups of similar products and decentralized a great deal of decision making to the departments handling these products or product groups. . . . In the past ten years we have heard less about decentralization. . . . Some of this reversal of trend was produced by second thoughts after the earlier enthusiasm for product-group divisionalization. . . . A second force working toward recentralization of decisions has been the introduction of computers and automation (Simon, 1977, p. 116).

In short, computers now make it unnecessary to decentralize to handle complex decisions, and combined with operations research techniques, computers tend to foster coordination and planning at

Table 11–1

Techniques of Decision Making Utilized in Programmed and Nonprogrammed Approaches

Types of Decisions	Techniques Applicable
1. Programmed Repetitive and routine A definite procedure has been worked out so that decisions do not have to be handled de novo each time they occur	**Traditional** 1. Habit 2. Standard operating procedures 3. Organizational structure **Modern** 1. Operations research 2. Electronic data processing
2. Nonprogrammed Novel, unstructured, and unusually consequential No cut-and-dried method for handling the problem because it has not arisen before, or because its precise nature and structure are elusive and complex, or because it is so important that it deserves a custom-tailored treatment	**Traditional** 1. Judgment, intuition, and creativity 2. Selection and training of executives **Modern** 1. Heuristic problem solving applied to training humans 2. Constructing heuristic computer programs

SOURCE: Adapted from Herbert A. Simon, *The New Science of Management Decision.* Englewood Cliffs, N.J.: Prentice-Hall, 1977, pp. 46, 48.

superordinate levels—thus centralization. The result is a greater rationalization of the system, perhaps with fewer levels of hierarchy, but with a greater broadening through the addition of staff positions. "For some managers, important satisfactions derived in the past from certain kinds of interpersonal relations with others will be lost. For other managers, important satisfactions from a feeling of the adequacy of their professional skills will be gained" (Simon, 1977, p. 133). It is clear, though he does not say so explicitly, that Simon views strategy/structure theory as deficient in its failure to include the computer variable.

The Garbage Can Model

Throughout Simon's writings one finds an implicit, normative underpinning that says some type of rationality, to the extent it is possible, is always to be desired. In contrast March has increasingly moved away from such a position. The following statement appears to epitomize his views:

Interesting people and interesting organizations construct complicated theories of themselves. In order to do this, they need to supplement the technology of reason with a technology of foolishness. Individuals and organizations need ways of doing things for which they have no good reason. Not always. Not usually. But sometimes. They need to act before they think (March, 1972, p. 423).

From this orientation the so-called garbage can model of organizational choice emerged (Cohen, March, and Olsen, 1972; Cohen and March, 1974; March and Olsen, 1976).

Organized Anarchies. The garbage can model applies in situations where organized anarchies exist, and the university setting is cited as a prime example of such a context. The characteristics of an organized anarchy are:

1. *Problematic goals*—preferences are ill-defined and inconsistent, and are discovered most frequently through action rather than serving as a basis for action.

2. *Unclear technology*—the organization does not understand its own processes and thus operates from trial and error, learning from accidents of the past, imitation, and the power of necessity.

3. *Fluid participation*—participants change frequently and the amount of attention given to the organization by any one participant can vary significantly.

In such an organization issues tend to have low salience for most participants, being important primarily for symbolic reasons; there is a great deal of inertia; the occasion of a decision provides a garbage can into which all types of problems of current concern may be thrown; choice processes are easily overloaded; and the information base available for search and learning tends to be very limited. Ambiguity permeates not only the goal structure and the understanding of technologies and environments, but also the interpretation of past events, the organization's history, and even the concept of organizational membership.

Organizational Choice. The concept of organizational choice is described as follows:

> Although organizations can often be viewed as vehicles for solving well-defined problems and as structures within which conflict is resolved through bargaining, there are also sets of procedures through which organizational participants arrive at an interpretation of what they are doing and what they have done while doing it. From this point of view, an organization is a collection of choices looking for problems, issues and feelings looking for decision situations in which they might be aired, solutions looking for issues to which they might be the answer, and decision makers looking for work. . . . A key to understanding the processes within organizations is to view a choice opportunity as a garbage can into which various

problems and solutions are dumped by participants (Cohen and March, 1974, p. 81).

Among the hypotheses proposed are:

1. As the load on the decision system increases, so too does the number of decisions made by flight (problems leaving choices thus making a choice which solves nothing possible) and oversight (choices being activated without being attached to problems, with the result that there is speedy acceptance).

2. Which problems and solutions are attended to in the context of which choices depends on the timing of appearance and who is available at the time to participate.

3. Problems, solutions, and attitudes that are persistently present are attended to more consistently than those that are sporadic.

4. Rules limiting the flow of problems to choices and the flow of participants to choice (controlling who may participate in the decision) change the process and the outcomes.

5. Given the widespread use of flight and oversight, the movement of certain problems to certain choices affects not only the choices to which the problems move, but the choices left alone as well.

6. Problems and solutions are debated to a degree because of the positive rewards associated with participation in the process of debate, rather than with decision outcomes (March and Olsen, 1976).

The elements of the theory are best understood in the context of a computer simulation (Cohen, March, and Olsen, 1972). In this simulation certain factors are fixed—the number of time periods considered, the number of choice opportunities, the number of decision makers involved, the number of problems, and the solution coefficient for each time period. Entry times for choices and problems were varied across time periods using randomly generated sequences. Net energy load on the organization, which was defined as the difference between the participant energy required to solve all problems and the total amount of such energy available to the organization, varied from light to moderate to heavy. The relation between problems and choices (access structure) was established in three ways—(1) any active problem has access to any active choice; (2) important problems have access to many choices, and important choices are accessible to important problems only; (3) access between problems and choices is highly constrained and specialized. A similar structuring process was used to establish the relation between decision makers and choices (the decision structure), and the categories were again unsegmented, hierarchical, and specialized. The distribution of energy among decision makers, reflecting the amount of time spent by each on organizational problems, varied from important people with low energy, through equal energy for all decision makers, to important people with high energy.

When such a simulation is run, certain consistencies appear that might best be considered specific hypotheses for subsequent empirical investigation:

1. Resolution of problems as a style for making decisions is not the most common style, except under conditions where flight is severely restricted (for instance, specialized access) or a few conditions under light load. Decision making by flight and oversight is a major feature of the process in general.

2. The process is quite thoroughly and quite generally sensitive to variations in load. . . . an increase in the net energy load on the system generally increases problem activity, decision maker activity, decision difficulty, and the uses of flight and oversight.

3. A typical feature of the model is the tendency of decision makers and problems to track each other through choices. . . . both decision makers and problems tend to move together from choice to choice.

4. There are some important interconnections among three key aspects of the efficiency of the decision processes specified. The first is problem activity . . . a rough measure of the potential for decision conflict. . . . The second aspect is problem latency, the amount of time problems spend activated but not linked to choices. The third aspect is decision time, the persistence of choices. Presumably a good organizational structure would keep both problem activity and problem latency low through rapid problem solution in its choices. In the garbage can process such a result was never observed.

5. The process is frequently sharply interactive. . . . phenomena are . . . dependent on the particular combination of structures involved. . . . High segmentation of access structure generally produces slow decision time. . . . a specialized access structure, in combination with an unsegmented decision structure, produces quick decisions.

6. Important problems are more likely to be solved than unimportant ones. Problems which appear early are more likely to be resolved than later ones.

7. Important choices are less likely to resolve problems than unimportant choices. Important choices are made by

oversight and flight. Unimportant choices are made by resolution.

8. Although a large proportion of the choices are made, the choice failures that do occur are concentrated among the most important and least important choices. Choices of intermediate importance are virtually always made (Cohen, March, and Olsen, 1972, pp. 9–11).

Organizational Attention. Such concepts as net energy load refer to the matter of participant attention. What happens in a decision situation is strongly dependent on who pays attention to what, and when (March and Olsen, 1976). Organizational structures, rules, and role expectations have a lot to do with this process; they serve as constraints on attention, while normally specifying only upper and lower limits for involvement. As with access and decision structures, attention may be organized so that all are affected equally by constraints, on a specialized basis, or on a hierarchical basis. Which attention structure will predominate is a function of the interdependencies of individual and group actions and the distribution of competencies, values, and resources.

Attention is often a consequence of competing demands on an individual's time, and as a result those who end up making a decision tend to be those who have nothing better to do. This is particularly true in unsegmented, permissive attention structures. Since status tends to attach more to the right to attend to a particular decision than to actual participation in it, individuals often compete for the right and then fail to attend. Nevertheless, more than any other factor, attention is predictable from a knowledge of standard operating procedures and administrative role.

Learning under Ambiguity. The preceding theory of organizational attention contains a number of concepts and variables, but the theoretical relationships are not fully developed. The same may be said of formulations relating to organizational learning (March and Olsen, 1976). The major focus of organizational learning is on the individual, and thus all but a few of the formulations are of more relevance for the study of organizational behavior than of organizational structure and process.

A primary point is that organizational learning is not necessarily adaptive or a source of wisdom and improved performance under conditions of ambiguity. Learning may well yield myths, fictions, folklore, and illusions rather than improvement. This is because it is not always obvious what happened, or why it happened, or whether what happened is a good thing. Given this ambiguity, learning can get far removed from what rationality would indicate.

Under such circumstances a theory of organizational learning would need to include:

1. Ideas about the ways in which information exposure, organizational memory, and the retrieval of history vary across individuals and subunits.

2. Ideas about how incentives and motivation for various forms of learning operate.

3. Ideas about how preexisting understandings, beliefs, and attitudes may condition learning.

4. Ideas about how the timing, order, and context of information influence the development of beliefs.

Specific hypotheses at the organizational level regarding such variables are not presented.

Research and Applications by the Theorists

The three theorists all have carried out studies related to their formulations, some in collaboration with each other. There has been little explicit emphasis on applications—a not entirely unexpected outcome, given the basically descriptive rather than normative nature of the theory. However, the Simon, Smithburg, and Thompson (1950) text in public administration was strongly influenced by Simon's views regarding decision making.

In recent years only March has been actively involved in research on organizations. Cyert's writing has been largely nonempirical, and Simon's research has been conducted within the field of cognitive psychology (Simon, 1979).

Simon's Early Studies

Initially, Simon conducted studies in the field of governmental administration that, though applied in nature, had little relationship to his theories. There were, for instance, analyses of optimal case loads for welfare workers (Simon and Devine, 1941) and of the fiscal factors associated with consolidating local governments (Simon, 1943). A later study dealt with the organization of the accounting function in seven companies (Simon, Guetzkow, Kozmetsky, and Tyndall, 1954). Though the research provides some qualified support for segmentation and decentralization, it does not relate these factors to the need to simplify decision making. In fact the research appears to have been conducted without reference to theoretical concepts of any kind.

Subsequent studies were more closely related to the theory. A laboratory investigation of behavior in varied communication nets demonstrated the impact of programming differences on problem solving (Guetzkow and Simon, 1955). A detailed analysis of the decision processes employed by a company investigating the feasibility of utilizing electronic data processing equipment demonstrated both a tendency to break down the decision into more manageable units and the use of extensive search procedures, which were terminated in accordance with the theory of satisficing (Cyert, Simon, and Trow, 1956). A study of executives working in different functional areas of a business indicated, as expected, that the executives' departmental identifications exerted considerable influence on the ways they perceived problems (Dearborn and Simon, 1958). Though limited by small sample sizes and other considerations, and thus far from conclusive in and of themselves, these studies begin to build a structure of support for the theory.

Research in the Context of the Behavioral Theory of the Firm

A second group of studies appears to have contributed in large part to the development of the behavioral theory of the firm, rather than tested the theory. Throughout the middle and late 1950s March conducted a number of studies related to group processes and the dynamics of influence (for example, see March, 1956), but it was only toward the very end of the decade that he and Cyert began to collaborate on the research that provided an underpinning for their theory.

In one instance a series of decisions dealing with renovating old equipment, finding new working quarters, selecting a consulting firm, and choosing a data processing system were studied in much the same manner as Cyert, Simon, and Trow (1956) had done. It was found that marginal advantages of alternatives were considered only in the grossest sense, search was carried out in a bargaining context, computations were simple and focused on feasibility considerations, and individual and unit biases permeated the decisions (Cyert, Dill, and March, 1958). A subsequent laboratory study substantiated the existence of bias in sales and cost estimates, but found in addition that those obtaining the false information tended to apply a suitable bias discount (Cyert, March, and Starbuck, 1961). This finding, that bias may not be a significant factor in overall organizational decisions, as opposed to individual decisions, is not fully congruent with the theory, and the authors note the need for further study on this point.

Cyert and March (1963) report on several studies in which their formulations regarding expectation and choice processes were used to develop computer models. The results obtained were then compared with actual empirical data. A duopoly model was used to generate profit figures, which were then compared with longitudinal results reported for American Can Company and Continental Can Company. The fit, though by no means perfect, is reasonably good. This was also true of a model constructed to predict price and output decisions in a department store. Actual decisions were predicted accurately in 88 to 96 percent of the cases, depending on the particular output or price index used. Though the behavioral theory of the firm was not compared with alternative theories in these studies, its predictive power appears to be considerable.

Research in the Garbage Can

March views educational institutions as the prime examples of organized anarchies, and he has conducted considerable research on educational organizations. Much of this research is tangential to the garbage can model, however, and some is totally unrelated. The original presentation of the model discussed extensively the expected consequences of reduced slack for universities that were rich and poor, small and large (Cohen, March, and Olsen, 1972). Specific predictions were made in a computer model for universities in the various categories. The results are interesting and provocative, but they say little about the validity of the theory. In the words of the authors:

> The application of the model to this particular situation among American colleges and universities clearly depends upon a large number of assumptions. Other assumptions would lead to other interpretations of the impact of adversity within a garbage can decision process. Nevertheless, the derivations from the model have some face validity as a description of some aspects of recent life in American higher education (Cohen, March, and Olsen, 1972, p. 15).

Unfortunately, hard data were not available to the authors.

Similarly, March's basic studies of college administrators, though intended to illustrate the garbage can model, fail to prove its validity (Cohen and March, 1974; March and Olsen, 1976). They simply were not designed for this purpose. On the other hand, certain case studies described by March and Romelaer in the March and Olsen volume deal with decisions such as eliminating a program in speech, transferring a program in architecture, changing a grading system, and introducing a new doctoral field in economics that are clearly understandable within the garbage can framework.

Several investigations by March also touch on the garbage can model without really testing it. Thus a study extending over more than thirty years of the positions held by school superintendents indicates an almost random pattern, with the performance of individuals having practically no significance. This finding is at least consistent with the concept of the nonheroic, somewhat powerless top administrator in organized anarchies (March and March, 1977), but it does not deal with why the results occur. In another study it was found university departments attempt to change their curriculums to make them more attractive to students when the university is experiencing financial difficulty, but that this effect is less pronounced in departments with greater research reputations (Manns and March, 1978). These results say something about coalitions, bargaining power, and the like, but they do not provide direct support for the garbage can model.

Thus research evidence in support of the theory remains inadequate, awaiting studies by individuals other than March. The following prescription for action in university settings also must be held in abeyance for lack of evidence:

> One of the complications in accomplishing something in a garbage can decision-making process is the tendency for any particular project to become entwined with a variety of other issues simply because those issues exist at the time the project is before the organization. A proposal for curricular reform becomes an arena for a concern for social justice. . . . A proposal for bicycle paths becomes an arena for discussion of sexual inequality. It is pointless to try to react to such problems by attempting to enforce rules of relevance. . . . The appropriate tactical response is to provide garbage cans into which wide varieties of problems can be dumped. The more conspicuous the can, the more garbage it will attract away from other projects. . . . On a grand scale, discussions of overall organizational objectives or overall organizational long-term plans are classic first-quality cans. . . . On a smaller scale, the first item on a meeting agenda is an obvious garbage can (Cohen and March, 1974, p. 211).

The Wider Research Arena

Research on the theories of Simon, March, and Cyert tended originally to concentrate at Carnegie-Mellon, and even now many researchers in the area have had some connection with one or more of the theorists. In terms of overall impact on research the effects of the theories have been sizable. The amount and quality of work being done in cognitive psychology, behavioral decision theory, and related areas is impressive, and much of it was sparked initially by the writings we have considered. Yet a relatively small proportion of this research represents a direct test of theoretical hypotheses about organizations.

Bounded Rationality and Satisficing

Writing in the introduction to the third edition of *Administrative Behavior*, Simon (1976) notes:

> In view of the substantial body of evidence now available in support of the concept of bounded rationality, of satisficing, and of the limited rationality of administrative man, I do not regard the description of human rationality . . . as hypothetical but as now having been verified in its main features (p. xxxi).

In this connection he mentions a study by Clarkson described in Cyert and March (1963) and another by Soelberg (1966), as well as research conducted by the theorists themselves. The Clarkson study compared predictions made from a model developed from the Cyert and March (1963) theory with actual portfolio decisions made by a bank trust officer. Insofar as quasi resolution of conflict and uncertainty avoidance are concerned, the model agrees almost perfectly with the theory. Problemistic search and organizational learning are less clearly represented. Yet the decision-making process modeled is, in a sense, simple-minded, constrained in its computations, and adaptively rational. As Table 11–2 indicates, such a theory-based model comes close to depicting reality.

The Soelberg (1966) study confirms the theory only in part. What emerges from this and other studies is a frequent tendency to search beyond the point of choice, but not with a view to maximizing; rather the objective is to validate or confirm the choice (Steiner and Miner, 1982). Furthermore, there are sizable differences between individuals in the degree to which their decisions approach the maximizing, validating or confirming, and satisficing modes. To the extent evidence is available, goals other than profit appear to influence top-level decisions, and firms in which the rationality is less bounded are more likely to be profitable, in spite of the frequent use of satisficing. Managers are more likely to approximate rationality in their decision making than unskilled and semiskilled workers (Arroba, 1978). Overall, it seems apparent that bounded rationality and satisficing in one form or another are indeed important aspects of the decison-making process, but that more complex, specific, and probably more normative formulations are needed to improve understanding, prediction, and practice (Park, 1978; Taylor, 1975).

Table 11–2

Comparison of Results Obtained with a Computer Model Based on the Theory of Cyert and March and Actual Decision Outcomes

		Portfolio (Number of Shares) Selected by	
		Computer Program	Trust Officer
Account #1 (Growth)	General American Transportation	60	0
	Corning Glass	0	30
	Dow Chemical	50	50
	IBM	10	10
	Merck and Company	60	50
	Owens Corning Fiberglass	45	50
Account #2 (Income and growth)	American Can	100	100
	Continental Insurance	100	100
	Equitable Gas	100	100
	Duquesne Light	100	0
	General Public Utilities	0	100
	Libby Owens Ford	100	100
	International Harvester	100	0
	National Lead	0	50
	Philadelphia Electric	100	100
	Phillips Petroleum	100	100
	Socony Mobil	100	100
Account #3 (Income and growth)	American Can	100	100
	Continental Insurance	100	100
	Duquesne Light	100	100
	Equitable Gas	100	100
	Pennsylvania Power and Light	100	0
	General Public Utilities	0	100
	International Harvester	100	100
	Libby Owens Ford	100	100
	Socony Mobil	100	100
Account #4 (Income)	American Can	100	100
	Continental Insurance	100	100
	Duquesne Light	100	100
	Equitable Gas	100	100
	Pennsylvania Power and Light	100	0
	General Public Utilities	0	100
	International Harvester	100	100
	Phillips Petroleum	100	100

Source: Adapted from G. P. E. Clarkson, "A Model of Trust Investment Behavior," Chapter 10 in Richard M. Cyert and James G. March, *A Behavioral Theory of the Firm*. Englewood Cliffs, N.J.: Prentice-Hall, 1963, pp. 265–66.

Decisions in Coalitions

The concept of the organization as a coalition in which goals and decision outcomes are determined by bargaining has been studied primarily through analysis of actual decisions in organizations. One area of study has been budget decisions in universities. In one study it was found that budget allocations to departments are closely related to power position within the coalition, irrespective of actual departmental needs as reflected in work load, number of faculty, and the like (Pfeffer and Salancik, 1974). Very similar conclusions in support of a coalition model of university budget allocations were reported by Hills and Mahoney (1978). The power of certain departments was particularly manifest during periods of scarcity.

Other research indicates that repetitive, programmable decisions in business firms tend to coincide closely with expectations from the Cyert and March (1963) theory. Factors such as multiple goals, constraints, satisficing, uncertainty avoidance, bargaining, standard operating procedures, and rules of thumb were all in evidence in the weekly advertising decisions of a supermarket chain, and these factors tended to operate as the theory would predict (Rados, 1972).

On the other hand, to predict top-level strategy decisions that are one of a kind, the Cyert and March (1963) theory, though still applicable, needs considerable elaboration. In a field study of decisions related to investments and acquisitions by a rapidly growing computer firm it was found that sequential bargaining across hierarchical levels played an important role, that uncertainty of outcome tends to elicit a greater number of criteria or goals, and that search may be elicited by factors other than problems, and by opportunities in particular (Carter, 1971). The original theory seems to need a greater degree of specification if it is to be applied to strategic decisions, though there is not enough research to indicate exactly what form or forms this specification should take.

Inducements and Contributions

The inducements-contributions component of the theory can be derived from a number of theories of organizational behavior, at least as it relates to individual satisfaction, turnover, and performance. There are no comparative studies available that would indicate that the theory, as stated here, is superior. Nevertheless, there are studies that establish some validity for the inducements-contributions formulations (Portwood and Miller, 1976; Staw, 1974). Changes, and particularly reductions, in inducements tend to increase turnover and reduce overall contributions.

Research relating this factor to organizational survival is lacking. Furthermore, there have been few attempts to identify the limits of the zone of acceptance under specific circumstances. How do variations in inducements actually influence contributions? For whom? When? What kinds of inducements and contributions? The theory as stated is difficult to test because of its broad nature. There is a need for specific hypotheses that go beyond the general framework.

Organized Anarchies

In the preceding discussion of evidence bearing on the theories of Simon, March, and Cyert there has been frequent mention of case studies of decisions in which observation, interviews, and occasionally records were used to obtain data. In these instances the data collection is characteristically unstandardized, and replication of the research would be impossible, even if exactly the same decision situation could be identified. Such analyses of small numbers of cases are very useful for constructing descriptive theories, but much less useful for testing them. Unfortunately the research on organized anarchies and the garbage can model tends to be almost entirely observational (March and Olsen, 1976; McCaskey, 1979).

The March and Olsen (1976) volume contains descriptions of a university dean selection decision (by Olsen), a medical school location decision (by Kare Rommetveit), decision making in an experimental free school (by Kristian Kreiner and Soren Christensen), a racial desegregation decision in a school district (by Stephen Weiner), and a university reorganization decision (by Olsen). These decisions are said to be consistent with the garbage can model, and they appear to have much in common with that model, as does the R and D department decision making described by McCaskey (1979). The model unquestionably "rings a bell" when held up against the realities of these decision situations. On the other hand, none of these studies explicitly tests hypotheses derived from the theory.

One study in the March and Olsen volume tests hypotheses based on the theory in a context that could possibly qualify as organized anarchy. This research (by Per Stava) deals with certain college location decisions in Norway that were inherently political in nature. Various demographic indexes were used to predict where the colleges would be located, and these predictions were then compared with the actual decisions made by the Norwegian parliament. The results are rather surprising:

> Our analysis supports legal-bureaucratic theories of political choice. . . . Not power, not interest groups, not voters, but some simple, even sensible, rules come to dominate—without explicit computation. . . . the system pursues a political solution within highly restrictive normative rules of equity. Although, as far as we know, no one in the system calculated

anything approximating our weighted distance criterion, the process constrained itself to solutions consistent with such a conception of fairness and need. . . . our analysis indicates a case for treating decisions as explainable in terms of stable, structural elements in the situation (Stava in March and Olsen, 1976, p. 217).

If the context was that of organized anarchy, then the findings do not fit the hypothesized garbage can model.

One additional study deserves mention, not because it provides evidence on the garbage can model, but because it might erroneously be interpreted as doing so. This is a longitudinal investigation of innovation in thirteen high school districts (Daft and Becker, 1978). As originally formulated, the research hypotheses did not derive from the garbage can model, nor was the study designed with that model in mind. However, after the fact, the authors found garbage can concepts useful in explaining their findings, many of which were unexpected. On an ad hoc basis the data appear amenable to interpretation in garbage can terms, but they do not provide a test of the theory.

Conclusions

Though the theories we have been considering exhibit many common threads, both historically and conceptually, they have arrived at rather disparate points on the current theoretical landscape. March's emphasis on the value of foolishness in organizational decision making is distinctly at variance with Simon's stress on the intendedly rational. In fact foolishness appears to be strongly aligned with Barnard's (1938) appeal to intuition which Simon rejected. Similarly the organized anarchy view of universities that March propounds does not fit well with the much more rational view that Cyert (1975) has come to espouse as a university president. Cyert himself explains the difference in viewpoint as largely temporal, with the organized anarchy concepts applying in times of high slack and his own current views being more descriptive of what happens under low-slack conditions. However, March himself does not propose that slack be used as a contingency variable, and the research on university budgeting only partially supports Cyert's suggestion.

Scientific Goals

Argyris (1973, 1976) has been a continuing critic of the theoretical positions taken by Simon, March, and Cyert. His initial concern, consistent with his own theoretical views as elucidated in Chapter

5, was that all three of the theorists' basic books espoused a traditional, pyramidal organization that did not adequately consider man's self-actualizing and often nonrational nature. Theory of this type, though said to be descriptive, inevitably becomes normative and incorrectly perpetuates the status quo.

In reply to this attack Simon (1973) cites a number of instances in which Argyris (1973) misrepresents or misinterprets his views. More important, however, Simon seriously questions Argyris's essential assumption:

> The charge is not that the theories are wrong, but that, right or wrong, they are anti-revolutionary and reactionary. We are not to describe social phenomena as they are, because describing them legitimizes them, and makes them harder to change. . . . Argyris' argument that we must not describe the world as it is lest we prevent its reform is of a piece with the general anti-rationalism of the contemporary counter culture. . . . knowledge about the world and about ourselves is better than ignorance. Nothing in human history refutes that belief, or suggests that we can save mankind by halting descriptive research on the rational aspects of human behavior (Simon, 1973, p. 351).

Argyris (1976) takes a different tack with the Cohen and March theory. He accuses the theorists of Machiavellian tactics, such as the suggestion that garbage cans be created to attract problems away from other projects, and of sanctioning deceit. Again, the charge is that the theory fosters the status quo, though now the status quo is organized anarchy. But to this is added a charge of thwarting openness and trust. To know how the organizational world is and to develop tactics for coping with reality hardly seem to be undesirable scientific goals. In fact we often must understand reality before we can decide whether it should be and can be changed. One must question whether Argyris's criticisms are consistent with the goals of science as considered in Chapter 1.

A more balanced view of the work of Simon, March, and Cyert would be to recognize the fact that there is considerable research support for a number of their theoretical propositions, but also certain shortcomings in their formulations. In a rough sense research confirms the formulations on bounded rationality and satisficing, as Simon contends. Yet it is also true that organizations may extend a search for the purpose of confirming a satisficing decision and that sizable individual differences exist among decision makers that are not explained at all by the theory. Overall, programmable decisions are handled much more effectively than strategic, top-level choices that pratically never recur in the same form, at least within a given organization. However, the theory could possibly be extended to such unprogrammable decisions if norms, laws, and interorganizational conventions were taken as constraints and standard operating procedures. The findings obtained by Stava (in March and Olsen, 1976) appear promising in this regard. Perhaps all decisions are potentially programmable within some larger framework.

Other aspects of the theories, such as the inducements-contributions equilibrium, have research support, so at least the broad outline of the theory seems to be valid. However, many blanks remain to be filled in. In fact, given the long history of much of the theory, the small amount of research on certain aspects is surprising. There is little evidence bearing on the conflict-related formulations, for instance, and on the degree to which computers may operate as a contingency variable in moderating the relationship between centralization-decentralization and effectiveness.

The research that has been done on the Simon, March, and Cyert formulations often raises more questions than it resolves. The tentative finding that organizations may characteristically correct for biased inputs suggests a major difference between individual and organizational decision making and cries for further investigation. Yet that finding has been largely ignored.

Lack of operational definitions and measures of variables has limited systematic research on the theories and led to heavy reliance on observation. The theorists have focused more on computer representations of variables than on actual measures. Researchers developed some measures of decision making at a relatively early point, though little is known about the psychometric adequacy of the measures. Practically no other measures have been developed. The key concept of slack, for instance, has remained virtually unmeasured until recently (Kmetz, 1980). The concept of loose coupling has been extracted from the theory and stressed by a number of writers (for example, see Weick, 1976). But no one knows how much or how little coupling is required to say that the coupling is loose, because no measures of this variable exist. Research on a theory requires measures of the theory's key variables, and in this instance such measures have emerged very slowly.

Simon first set out to establish a descriptive framework and a vocabulary for dealing with organizations. He, and March and Cyert, too, were highly successful in this endeavor. But the framework is still only a framework; few details between the supporting timbers have been filled in, either by research or by further theorizing. Descriptive theory can give rise to normative theory, but except for a certain implicit, normative flavor that Argyris detected and some recent formulations by March and his coauthors, this has not happened. The framework appears solid and awaits further construction. Of all the theoretical orientations considered in this volume, the one arising originally from collaborations at Carnegie Institute of Technology is one of the most promising, but it has not been fully developed or used.

Goals of Application

As guides for organizational action, one would expect little from these essentially descriptive rather than normative theories. In large part this expectation is fulfilled. The theories begin to move into the gap opened by strategy/structure theory, but they do not move far. They say little about the content of strategy or the details of structure, except that there are good reasons for things being as they are. At best, the theories give organization members a way to look at and talk about their organizational world and to understand it better.

Cohen and March (1974) provide a set of rules for operating in a garbage can context. Briefly these rules are: spend time, persist, exchange status for substance, facilitate opposition participation, overload the system, provide garbage cans, manage unobtrusively, and interpret history—guidelines that Argyris considered Machiavellian. These guidelines appear to make sense, given a controlled anarchy. But such face validity, rather than true empirical evidence, argues for caution in accepting the theory of organized anarchy in the first place. We do not know the limits or domain of that theory. It may be valid within a small domain, or not at all. Accordingly, without further research, it cannot be accepted as a basis for action, however tempting it may be to do so.

References

Argyris, Chris. "Some Limits of Rational Man Organizational Theory," *Public Administration Review*, 33 (1973), 253–67.

———. "Single-Loop and Double-Loop Models in Research on Decision Making," *Administrative Science Quarterly*, 21 (1976), 363–75.

Arroba, Tanya Y. "Decision-Making Style as a Function of Occupational Group, Decision Content and Perceived Importance," *Journal of Occupational Psychology*, 51 (1978), 219–26.

Barnard, Chester I. *The Functions of the Executive*. Cambridge, Mass.: Harvard University Press, 1938.

Carter, E. Eugene. "The Behavioral Theory of the Firm and Top-Level Corporate Decisions," *Administrative Science Quarterly*, 16 (1971), 413–28.

Cohen, Michael D., and James G. March. *Leadership and Ambiguity: The American College President*. New York: McGraw-Hill, 1974.

Cohen, Michael D., James G. March, and Johan P. Olsen. "A Garbage Can Model of Organizational Choice," *Administrative Science Quarterly*, 17 (1972), 1–25.

Cyert, Richard M. *The Management of Nonprofit Organizations.* Lexington, Mass.: D. C. Heath, 1975.

Cyert, Richard M., William R. Dill, and James G. March. "The Role of Expectations in Business Decision Making," *Administrative Science Quarterly*, 3 (1958), 307–40.

Cyert, Richard M., and Charles L. Hedrick. "Theory of the Firm: Past, Present, and Future; An Interpretation," *Journal of Economic Literature*, 10 (1972), 398–412.

Cyert, Richard M., and Kenneth R. MacCrimmon. "Organizations." In Gardner Lindsey and Elliot Aronsen (eds.), *Handbook of Social Psychology.* Reading, Mass.: Addison Wesley, 1968, pp. 568–611.

Cyert, Richard M., and James G. March. "Organizational Structure and Pricing Behavior in an Oligopolistic Market," *American Economic Review*, 45 (1955), 129–39.

———. "Organizational Factors in the Theory of Oligopoly," *Quarterly Journal of Economics*, 70 (1956), 44–64.

———. *A Behavioral Theory of the Firm.* Englewood Cliffs, N.J.: Prentice-Hall, 1963.

Cyert, Richard M., James G. March, and William H. Starbuck. "Two Experiments on Bias and Conflict in Organizational Estimation," *Management Science*, 7 (1961), 254–64.

Cyert, Richard M., Herbert A. Simon, and Donald B. Trow. "Observations of a Business Decision," *Journal of Business*, 29 (1956), 237–48.

Daft, Richard L., and Selwyn W. Becker. *Innovation in Organizations.* New York: Elsevier, 1978.

Dearborn, DeWitt C., and Herbert A. Simon. "Selective Perception: A Note on the Departmental Identifications of Executives," *Sociometry*, 21 (1958), 140–44.

Guetzkow, Harold, and Herbert A. Simon. "The Impact of Certain Communication Nets Upon Organization and Performance in Task-oriented Groups," *Management Science*, 1 (1955), 233–50.

Hills, Frederick S., and Thomas A. Mahoney. "University Budgets and Organizational Decision Making," *Administrative Science Quarterly*, 23 (1978), 454–65.

Kmetz, John L. "A Preliminary Test of Relationships Between Organizational Slack and Theoretically Related Variables," *Academy of Management Proceedings*, 1980, pp. 246–50.

Manns, Curtis L., and James G. March. "Financial Adversity, Internal Competition, and Curriculum Change in a University," *Administrative Science Quarterly*, 23 (1978). 541–52.

March, James C., and James G. March. "Almost Random Careers: The Wisconsin School Superintendency, 1940–72," *Administrative Science Quarterly*, 22 (1977), 377–409.

March, James G. "Influence Measurement in Experimental and Semi-Experimental Groups," *Sociometry*, 19 (1956), 260–71.

———. "Model Bias in Social Action," *Review of Educational Research*, 42 (1972), 413–29.

March, James G., and Johan P. Olsen. *Ambiguity and Choice in Organizations.* Bergen, Norway: Universitetsforlaget, 1976.

March, James G., and Herbert A. Simon. *Organizations.* New York: Wiley, 1958.

McCaskey, Michael B. "The Management of Ambiguity," *Organizational Dynamics*, 7, no. 4 (1979), 31–48.

Miner, John B. *Theories of Organizational Behavior.* Hinsdale, Ill.: Dryden, 1980.

Newell, Allen, and Herbert A. Simon. *Human Problem Solving.* Englewood Cliffs, N.J.: Prentice-Hall, 1972.

Park, C. Whan. "A Seven-Point Scale and a Decision-Maker's Simplifying Choice Strategy: An Operationalized Satisficing-Plus Model," *Organizational Behavior and Human Performance*, 21 (1978), 252–71.

Pfeffer, Jeffrey, and Gerald R. Salancik. "Organizational Decision Making as a Political Process: The Case of a University Budget," *Administrative Science Quarterly*, 19 (1974), 135–51.

Portwood, James D., and Edwin L. Miller. "Evaluating the Psychological Contract: Its Implications for Employee Job Satisfaction and Work Behavior," *Academy of Management Proceedings*, 1976, pp. 109–93.

Rados, David L. "Selection and Evaluation of Alternatives in Repetitive Decision Making," *Administrative Science Quarterly*, 17 (1972), 196–206.

Simon, Herbert A. *Fiscal Aspects of Metropolitan Consolidation*. Berkeley, Calif.: Bureau of Public Administration, University of California, 1943.

———. *Administrative Behavior: A Study of Decision-Making Processes in Administrative Organization*. New York: Free Press, 1947; second edition, 1957a; third edition, 1976.

———. *Models of Man: Social and Rational*. New York: Wiley, 1957b.

———. *The Sciences of the Artificial*. Cambridge, Mass.: MIT Press, 1969.

———. "Organization Man: Rational or Self-Actualizing?" *Public Administration Review*, 33 (1973), 346–53.

———. *The New Science of Management Decision*. Englewood Cliffs, N.J.: Prentice-Hall, 1977.

———. "Information Processing Models of Cognition," *Annual Review of Psychology*, 30 (1979), 363–96.

Simon, Herbert A., and William R. Devine. "Controlling Human Factors in an Administrative Experiment," *Public Administration Review*, 1 (1941), 485–92.

Simon, Herbert A., Harold Guetzkow, George Kozmetsky, and Gordon Tyndall. *Centralization vs. Decentralization in Organizing the Controller's Department*. New York: Controllership Foundation, 1954.

Simon, Herbert A., Donald W. Smithburg, and Victor A. Thompson. *Public Administration*. New York: Knopf, 1950.

Soelberg, Peer. "Unprogrammed Decision Making," *Academy of Management Proceedings*, 1966, pp. 3–16.

Staw, Barry M. "Attitudinal and Behavioral Consequences of Changing a Major Organizational Reward: A Natural Field Experiment," *Journal of Personality and Social Psychology*, 29 (1974), 742–51.

Steiner, George A., and John B. Miner. *Management Policy and Strategy*. New York: Macmillan, 1982.

Taylor, Ronald N. "Psychological Determinants of Bounded Rationality: Implications for Decision-Making Strategies," *Decision Sciences*, 6 (1975), 409–29.

Thompson, James. *Organizations in Action*. New York: McGraw-Hill, 1967.

Weick, Karl E. "Educational Organizations as Loosely Coupled Systems," *Administrative Science Quarterly*, 21 (1976), 1–19.

Wolf, William B. *The Basic Barnard: An Introduction to Chester I. Barnard and His Theories of Organization and Management*. Ithaca, N.Y.: New York State School of Industrial and Labor Relations, Cornell University, 1974.

12

Classical Management Theory

A number of the theorists considered in preceding chapters have used classical management theory (and on occasion bureaucratic theory) as a foil for their own positions. Viewed in this way, the theory is seen as inhumane, outdated, and just plain not very good. Yet what has been depicted may be a straw man, a caricature of the theory as it really is. Whether this is so can only be determined in the light of balanced study. Classical management theory is important for two reasons — because so many other theories have been set in opposition to it *and* because, as a major theory in its own right, it has had a significant impact on various practices.

In many treatments of the subject the term *classical management theory* (or its equivalent) refers to a set of formulations extending from Taylor (1911) to Fayol (1949) and on to a long list of individuals who elaborated on the ideas of both. Taylor and his followers focused largely on the individual worker and thus made their primary contribution to organizational behavior theory; their work is not considered here in any detail.

Fayol's work spawned a number of elaborations and extensions, especially in the years immediately following its major translation into English; among the best known are those of Urwick (1952), Ralph C. Davis (1951), and Koontz and O'Donnell (1955). Subsequent statements in the classical tradition have appeared largely in management textbooks, again with considerable variation around the central themes (Miner, 1971). Earlier formulations in a similar vein are presented in books by Mooney and Reiley (1931) and Gulick and Urwick (1937), for example.

To cover all of these theories in a single chapter would be impossible. So Henri Fayol, described by Koontz and O'Donnell (1976) as the "father of modern operational-management theory," has been chosen as the central focus for the discussion; other formulations in the classical tradition are given relatively little attention, except as they overlap with the ideas of Fayol, which they often do.

Fayol was a French mining engineer who became the chief executive officer of the Commentary-Fourchambault-Décazeville coal and iron combine in 1888. His writings on management came late in his career. The major theoretical publication appeared in 1916 when Fayol was seventy-five and still active as an executive. He continued to write on the subject of management until his death in 1925 (Bedeian, 1979).

Fayol's Original Statement of Management Theory

Fayol's (1949) major theoretical work in the field of management was entitled *Administration Industrielle et Générale*. It consisted of two parts—"Necessity and Possibility of Teaching Management" and "Principles and Elements of Management." Two additional parts, "Personal Observations and Experience" and "Lessons of the War," were projected but never published. These latter parts were to deal with applications, some of which were discussed in Fayol's later writings and speeches (see Brodie, 1967).

At the time Fayol wrote, theory was distinctly lacking in the management field. Fayol felt that there was a great need for management education to supplement technical education such as the training he himself had received in engineering, and he believed that the existence of a body of theory was a necessary precondition for such education. This was the underlying rationale for his theorizing.

Definition of Management and Related Abilities

Fayol specified essential activities or functions of industrial organizations as follows:

1. Technical—production, manufacture, adaptation.
2. Commercial—buying, selling, exchange.
3. Financial—search for and optimum use of capital.
4. Security—protection of property and persons.
5. Accounting—stocktaking, balance sheets, costs, statistics.
6. Managerial—planning, organization, command, co-ordination, control (Fayol, 1949, p. 3).

Management is "spread like all other activities, between head and members of the body corporate," but it is concentrated particularly within top management. The distinct increase in hypothesized need for managerial ability, as compared with the decrease or stability of other abilities, that comes with an increase in occupational level is given in Table 12–1. At the lower levels it is technical ability that matters most; at higher levels it is managerial ability. The definition of technical ability varies, of course, within commercial, financial, and other functions. The head of a very small firm will need considerable technical ability, but this need, like that for commercial ability, will decrease with increasing size; in contrast, managerial ability requirements will increase with size.

Principles of Management

> For preference I shall adopt the term principles whilst dissociating it from any suggestion of rigidity, for there is nothing rigid or absolute in management affairs, it is all a question of proportion. . . . principles are flexible and capable of adaptation to every need; it is a matter of knowing how to make use of them, which is a difficult art requiring intelligence, experience, decision, and proportion (Fayol, 1949, p. 19).

Table 12–1

Hypothesized Ability Requirements at Various Occupational Levels

Occupational Level	Distribution of Required Abilities (Percent)					
	Technical	Commercial	Financial	Security	Accounting	Managerial
Production worker	85	—	—	5	5	5
Foreman	60	5	—	10	10	15
Superintendent	45	5	—	10	15	25
Section head	30	5	5	10	20	30
Department head	30	10	5	10	10	35
Plant manager	15	15	10	10	10	40
General manager	10	10	10	10	10	50

SOURCE: Adapted from Henri Fayol, *General and Industrial Management.* London: Pitman, 1949, p. 8.

The following are fourteen of the principles of management. Behavior in accord with them will contribute to a more effective organization. The list is not exhaustive, but widespread generality of application is hypothesized.

This code is indispensable. Be it a case of commerce, industry, politics, religion, war, or philanthropy, in every concern there is a management function to be performed, and for its performance there must be principles, that is to say acknowledged truths regarded as proven on which to rely (Fayol, 1949, pp. 41–42).

Division of Work. Division of labor or specialization at the worker and managerial levels reduces the number of objects to which attention must be given and therefore yields increased quality and quantity of output for the same amount of overall effort. There are limits beyond which division of work should not be carried, however. How these limits may be determined is not clearly specified.

Authority and Responsibility. Managers should exercise authority, both as it derives from the office held and as it derives from the intelligence, experience, and other personal qualities of the manager. At the same time responsiblity must be commensurate with authority in that rewards and penalties accrue, depending on how effectively authority is used. Determining and measuring the authority of a given manager as it relates to a particular outcome and establishing appropriate sanctions are viewed as major difficulties. Fayol recognizes the underlying measurement problems here; he also recognizes a natural tendency to seek authority and avoid responsibility. In neither case does he present a solution, other than to call for integrity and moral character.

Discipline. Discipline is a necessary condition for the effective operation of a business. It consists of obedience, application, energy, behavior, and outward marks of respect, all given on the basis of some formal or informal employment contract between the individual and the firm. To function as it should, discipline requires good managers, clear and equitable agreements, and the judicious application of sanctions such as warnings, fines, suspensions, and other, similar disciplinary actions.

Unity of Command. An individual should receive orders with regard to a particular action from one source only. Dual command is to be avoided. Examples of situations where dual command may arise are superiors bypassing subordinate managers to direct that manager's subordinates, two friends or family members both heading up a firm, unclear boundaries between two departments at the same level, and conditions of role ambiguity in general.

Unity of Direction. Unity of direction applies to coordination of effort and is a principle of organizations. A group of activities having the same objective should be placed under a single head and a single plan. Fayol does not discuss the bases for differentiating objectives that might be applied here.

Subordination of Individual Interest to General Interest. For effective functioning the interests of the organization as a whole must take precedence over those of individuals or groups. Subordination of interests is one basis for reconciling conflicting interests. In some instances interests of a different order appear to have equal claims. Such conflicts must be reconciled rather than being permitted to continue. Possible means to this end are the firmness and good example of managers, fair agreements, and constant supervision.

Remuneration of Personnel. Insofar as possible, payments should be fair and equitable, should reward well-directed effort, and should not exceed reasonable limits. Various methods of achieving these goals are discussed, but without any clear resolution. One index of effective remuneration is that the pay agreement afford satisfaction to employee and employer alike, but it is recognized that this may not be possible. There is a need for precise definitions and operationalizations of concepts such as fairness, reasonable limits, and the like.

Centralization. The amount of centralization, as opposed to decentralization, should be optimal for the particular concern. Contingency variables are firm size, personal character of the manager, manager's moral worth, reliability of subordinates, and condition of the business. The degree of centralization may vary considerably, depending on the relative potential effectiveness of the manager or subordinate. Fayol's formulations in this area are not specific, but he does recognize a number of relevant contingency factors.

Scalar Chain. In the simplest case communication should occur up and down the scalar chain of authority—in Figure 12–1 from E_1 up to A, and if necessary, back down to E_2. But vertical communication through this many steps may consume too much time. Where speed is essential, firms should resort to what has been called Fayol's gang-plank—horizontal communication authorized by managers at the next higher level. This, too, is indicated in Figure 12–1. In general, Fayol seems to think that horizontal communication should be used more widely than it is:

> It is an error to depart needlessly from the line of authority, but it is an even greater one to keep to it when detriment to the business ensues. . . . When a employee is obliged to choose between the two practices and it is impossible to take advice from his superior, he should be courageous enough and feel free enough to adopt the line dictated by the general interest (Fayol, 1949, p. 36).

Surprisingly, Fayol did not include the scalar chain principle in all versions of his theory (Brodie, 1967).

Order. To avoid loss of material, there should be a place for everything and everything in its place. In addition, the prescribed place should be one that facilitates the carrying out of necessary activities. However, the principle of order applies not only to material things,

Figure 12–1
The Scalar Chain and the Gangplank

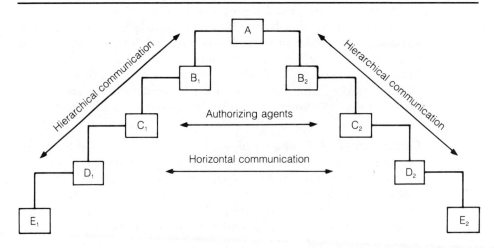

but also to people. Thus there should be an appointed place for each employee, and each employee should be in that place. Again, the appointed place should be appropriate to the task to be performed. This principle means good organization and selection, and it implies the existence of an organization chart.

Equity. Employees should be treated with kindness and justice, which together equal equity. The object is to elicit devotion and loyalty in return. Ideally a sense of equity will permeate the whole scalar chain.

Stability of Tenure of Personnel. Employees and managers alike need time to settle into their jobs before they can achieve maximum performance. They should be given this opportunity, and thus considerable stability of personnel should prevail. A lack of stability is both a cause and effect of poor management. At the same time there can be too much stability. "In common with all the other principles, therefore, stability of tenure of personnel is also a question of proportion" (Fayol, 1949, p. 39). No specific guidelines for establishing when the correct proportion exists are given, however.

Initiative. Initiative is thinking out a plan and executing it, as well as having the freedom to do these things. Initiative of this kind should be encouraged; it is particularly valuable to an organization in difficult times. The manager who facilitates the initiative of subordinates is far superior to the manager who does not, because initiative can serve as a source of both satisfaction and motivation.

Esprit de Corps. Essentially this is a principle of unity. Harmony should be fostered and conflict minimized. Unity of command is one means to this end. Fayol comes out strongly against the application of such ideas as "divide and conquer" in the organization. Creating dissension among one's subordinates thwarts coordination and teamwork. Verbal communication should be used whenever possible because, being two-way, it permits rapid resolution of conflicts. Written communication often fosters conflict.

Elements of Management

Fayol (1949) specified five elements of managerial work—planning, organizing, command, coordination, and control—though certain functions he considers could be split into other elements.

Planning. Planning involves foresight—assessing the future and making provision for it. It requires the development of a plan of action based on contributions from throughout the business. Fayol comes out strongly in favor of planning that is characterized by unity, continuity, flexibility, and precision.

The plan of action facilitates the utilization of the firm's resources and the choice of best methods to use for attaining the objective. It suppresses or reduces hesitancy, false steps, unwarranted changes of course, and helps to improve personnel. It is a precious managerial instrument (Fayol, 1949, p. 50).

One would expect more effective organizations to be characterized by a greater use of planning and forecasting.

Organizing. Though a distinction is made between the material organization and the human, only the latter is considered. The human organization is established to carry out managerial functions and implement the principles of management. The basic structure is pyramidal in that "each fresh group of ten, twenty, thirty workers brings in a fresh foreman; two, three or four foremen make necessary a superintendent, two or three superintendents give rise to a department manager, and the number of links of the scalar chain continues to increase in this way up to the ultimate superior, each new superior having usually no more than four or five immediate subordinates" (Fayol, 1949, p. 55). What Fayol is describing is a line organization.

Fayol considers staffing the structure part of the organizing function. In addition to the line positions extending from operatives to the board of directors, it is necessary to fill certain staff positions attached to the general manager's office that serve to complement the general manager's capabilities. This is the general staff concept, and there are no levels of authority within this component. Such staff members may be consultants, and they may devote only part of their time to the staff position. To the extent it violates unity of command, Fayol rejects direct supervision of one person by several functional specialists, as in Taylor's functional foremanship.

Evaluation, especially of managerial personnel, is also part of the organizing function. Among the factors to be considered are health and physical fitness, intelligence, moral qualities, general education, management knowledge, knowledge of the other functions (technical, commercial, etc.), and specialized ability characteristic of the concern. Only the latter requirement varies from one business to another; thus managerial capabilities are highly transferable.

Command. Command energizes the organization structure. It involves knowing the personnel thoroughly, eliminating incompetents, being knowledgeable about employer-employee agreements, setting a good example, conducting periodic organization audits, setting up conferences among one's chief assistants to establish unity of direction, avoiding an excess of detail, and generally fostering unity, energy, initiative, and loyalty. Being knowledgeable about subordinates, and command in general, is facilitated by a limited span of control:

> Whatever his level of authority, one head only has direct command over a small number of subordinates, less than six normally. Only the superior S^1 (foreman or his equivalent) is in direct command of twenty or thirty men, when the work is simple (Fayol, 1949, p. 98).

Effective performance of the command function is in part a matter of personal skill and in part a result of having a good grasp of management principles.

Coordination. The separate activities of an organization must be harmonized into a single whole, and that is the function of coordination. Basically it is a matter of establishing "rightful proportions" for the parts, ensuring that these proportions are maintained and adapting means to ends. Under such conditions:

1. The various departments work in harmony with each other, communicating as needed, rather than operating in isolation as ends in themselves.

2. Component units know their role in the total effort and what interdependencies exist with other units; they do not become watertight compartments, hiding themselves behind paperwork to avoid responsibility.

3. Departmental scheduling is constantly fine-tuned to external circumstances, rather than carried out without reference to organizational goals, loyalties, and needs for initiative.

The prime method of achieving coordination is a periodic conference of department heads. Where this is physically not possible, an alternative is the use of liaison officers attached to the staff to coordinate departments. In either case the need to facilitate horizontal communication clearly is evident.

Control. Control is the process of checking the realities of operations against plans and taking steps to correct deviations. It assumes the existence of up-to-date plans and the use of sanctions to achieve compatibility with them in a timely manner. Fayol notes that control systems may create duality of management if not devised correctly and monitored effectively. To the extent inspection is inherent in the control system, it should be impartial and objective.

Additional Formulations

Fayol continued to write on the subject of management during the nine years between the publication of *General and Industrial Management* in 1916 and his death. Much of this material is not generally available. There have been a few translations into English

(Fayol, 1937; 1970) and several summarizations of other works (Bedeian, 1979; Brodie, 1967).

Little modification occurred after publication of the primary theory. Many of the later papers deal with applications, and there are numerous restatements of parts of the theory. Fayol did come to view his own formulations and the scientific management ideas of Frederick Taylor (1911) as more complementary than conflicting.

There has been some controversy over the various translations of Fayol's work (Breeze and Miner, 1980; Wren, 1972). Typically this involves terms such as *administration* and *management, planning* and *foresight,* and the like; the impact of these matters on understanding the theory appears slight. Fayol modified some of his views on the role of management vis à vis other essential activities of organizations (technical, commercial, etc.) toward the end of his life (Breeze and Miner, 1980). Originally there were six such activities, including management; Fayol also referred rather vaguely to the overarching role of government within the organization. Later formulations dealt with only five essential activities and gave management (planning, organizing, directing, coordinating, and controlling) the overarching role previously assigned to organizational government. The theory was thus somewhat tightened conceptually.

Evaluations Stemming from Values, Logic, and Research

Certain difficulties in evaluating classical management theory should be noted. Though Fayol's training as a mining engineer was scientific in nature and resulted in his carrying out significant research in that field, he did not apply his research skills to the field of management. His contributions to management were entirely theoretical, and this was true of his immediate followers and interpreters as well. As so frequently happens, his theory was accepted uncritically without that acceptance being solidly grounded in research. As a result, it became vulnerable to widespread criticism, based largely on Fayol's failure to operationalize the major variables.

More recently, measures of key variables have been developed and a certain amount of research has been conducted. In addition, alternative formulations have been tested that bear on the hypotheses of classical management theory. Finally, there is a body of research dealing with other theoretical statements that appear to have some conceptual similarity to classical management theory. This latter research raises certain questions. How close is the conceptual similarity? Was Fayol really saying much the same thing as some later theorist? What should be included and what left out? The answers given here admittedly reflect only one person's judgment.

Attacks from the Human Relations Vantage Point

Historically the most significant criticisms of classical management theory have emerged from the human relations tradition, beginning with the now famous Hawthorne studies (Roethlisberger and Dickson, 1939; Cass and Zimmer, 1975). Whatever the scientific value of the Hawthorne research itself, and that is open to serious question (Filley, House, and Kerr, 1976; Franke and Kaul, 1978), it raises the point that classical theory ignores the human element in organization—the informal group, intrinsic motivation, and the like—a point that has been made often enough and cogently enough now to demand considerable attention.

Of the theories considered in this book, those of Likert (Chapter 2), Trist (Chapter 4), Argyris (Chapter 5), Bennis (Chapter 5), Woodward (Chapter 8), Burns and Stalker (Chapter 8), and Lawrence and Lorsch (Chapter 9) are the most explicit in their attacks on classical management theory from a human relations perspective. Several theories of organizational behavior, including those of Maslow, Herzberg, and McGregor, can be added to this list (see Miner, 1980, for discussions of these theories).

These theorists argue that the classical theory is inadequate as a comprehensive general theory of management because it fails to predict and explain a large number of phenomena. Under a variety of conditions of organizational membership, technology, environmental context, and the like, the theory does not work. The human relations theorists have a point. Fayol envisaged what amounts to a grand theory of management for all organizations. It seems safe to conclude on the basis of the human relations arguments and research that the effective domain of the theory (if there is one) is at least much smaller than that originally envisaged.

The human relations argument also includes criticisms of classical theory on the philosophical grounds that it is inherently inhumane. This criticism is beyond the purview of a book concerned with scientific theory, and thus is not considered further here.

Attacks by Simon and the Carnegie Theorists

As noted in Chapter 11, theorists associated with the Carnegie Institute of Technology, beginning with Simon, also viewed classical management theory as distinctly lacking (Simon, 1947; March and Simon, 1958; Simon, 1964). Their concern was its failure to meet the requirements for good theory, as reflected in a pervasive ambiguity of statement and lack of logical consistency.

This line of criticism draws on the writings of a number of classical theorists, and part of the ambiguity noted stems from certain disagreements among these theorists. Furthermore, Simon (1947) initially appears to have been unaware of Fayol's writings. These factors make certain criticisms less applicable to the present discussion than they might otherwise be. Nevertheless, extensive reference is made to the various writings of Lyndall Urwick, who was the major interpreter of Fayol's views. It would seem that at least some criticism of Urwick is applicable to Fayol.

The theory is criticized for not specifying for such concepts as specialization, unity of command, and span of control in what way, how much, and under what circumstances to apply them. How does one know when the optimum degree of centralization-decentralization has been achieved, for instance? Making the theory usable would require a great deal of research. Yet even its critics admit some share in the blame:

> Perhaps the most critical failure of classical administrative science is that it does not confront theory with evidence. In part, this is a consequence of the difficulties of operationalism. . . . The theories tend to dissolve when put into testable form. This, however, does not account completely for the neglect of empirical work. . . . we must share the onus of blame for the paucity of empirical evidence (March and Simon, 1958, p. 32).

Against this background, Simon (1964) views the theories of Fayol and others as more codifications of folk wisdom than contributions to mature science. He is particularly concerned about the unrelated nature of the "principles," whereby a test of one contributes nothing to verification of the others. In short, he views such theory as prescientific and rejects the arguments of those such as Koontz (1964) who believe it can be a way out of "the management theory jungle."

Research on Management Ability

The problems associated with defining and operationalizing variables are amply demonstrated in the area of management ability. Ghiselli (1971) has developed an adjective checklist of what he terms "supervisory ability." He makes no reference to Fayol, and Fayol gives no indication of how managerial ability might best be measured. Yet the Ghiselli index yields results that are consistent with the hypothesized ability requirements given in Table 12–1 for occupational levels. Does this mean the Ghiselli results support classical management theory? How would this research have been interpreted had the Ghiselli data indicated no relationship between supervisory ability and managerial level? Clearly there is a problem in using this type of research as evidence for Fayol's theory.

Yet, if a number of studies using various instruments produce converging evidence, one can have more confidence in the validity of some underlying construct—quite possibly the one Fayol had in mind. There is some evidence to support this conclusion, if—and this is an important qualification—one is willing to accept an essentially motivational definition of managerial ability (Miner, 1977; 1978a). A sentence completion measure of managerial motivation that differentiates managerial levels in much the same manner as indicated in Table 12–1 has been found to yield low but consistently significant correlations with other measures of similar variables, including Ghiselli's supervisory ability.

Overall, Fayol seems to have made an important beginning in this area, exactly how his views or any other version of the classical theory might have influenced the thinking of those who were doing the research many years later is not clear. Probably numerous other influences were at least as important.

Research on the Principles

Problems of construct definition and validity also plague research into Fayol's principles of management, though a number of measures have been developed (Price, 1972), We cannot be sure that today's operationalizations represent what Fayol had in mind; furthermore, measures are rarely tied directly to classical theory. However, conceptual similarities do exist.

The variables Fayol had in mind appear to have persisted in research. Many of them have persisted in theory also, and they remain a major factor in the vocabularies of practicing managers around the world (Negandhi, 1975). The problem is not that Fayol picked the wrong variables. Rather, his descriptions and hypotheses (principles) relating these variables to organizational effectiveness are very broad, all-encompassing, and vague.

A major difficulty is predicting the circumstances under which a particular organization will be successful. There is ample evidence that the range on the independent variables is wide in practice (Holden, Pederson, and Germane, 1968; Stogdill, 1965). It should be possible to associate scores at certain levels with success and scores at other levels with failure. Given the ambiguity of the principles as they are stated and the frequent iteration of the need for flexible application in the appropriate proportion and for adaptation to the requirements of the situation (whatever these may be), one is left with little basis for making specific predictions. Flexibility is admirable, if specific contingent hypotheses are stated to deal with it. Otherwise it is simply an escape valve that makes the rejection or verification of hypotheses impossible. Unfortunately, Fayol, while appearing to exercise a certain theoretical virtuosity, was guilty of a major theoretical sin; specific predictions from the theory cannot be made within an extremely wide range of variation on the key independent variables.

The Principles and Effectiveness. In Chapter 8 it was noted that the Woodward (1965) research was originally conducted to test certain classical management principles and that it came up empty in this regard. A later study by Zwerman (1970) produced a similar result, this time in the United States rather than Great Britain. In both instances, if the classical concepts proved valid in relation to success at all, it was in large batch, mass production firms—within the limited domain of assembly line technology.

A recent review considered a wide range of studies in which certain variables utilized by Fayol were related to organizational effectiveness (Dalton, Todor, Spendolini, Fielding, and Porter, 1980). The following quotes give a picture of the authors' conclusions:

> The association between specialization and performance has not been clearly demonstrated (p. 58).
> An association between levels of formalization and performance has not been convincingly demonstrated (p. 58).
> The evidence supports a conclusion that centralization is negatively associated with performance. We, however, are disinclined to firmly state this conclusion (p. 59).
> The literature on structure-performance relationships is among the most vexing and ambiguous in the field of management and organizational behavior (p. 60).

Research to date on classical management theory has not produced consistent results. Within a particular domain (such as an assembly line production system) a pattern may well emerge and approximate what Fayol predicted. On the other hand, within a very broad range these variables may not have any discernible influence on effectiveness, and the research may not have sampled effects with any consistency outside this broad range. Unfortunately neither Fayol nor his successors developed specific contingency hypotheses or specific statements about operative ranges for key variables.

Unity of Command and Role Conflict. In Chapter 6 the concepts of role conflict and role ambiguity were discussed and the negative consequences associated with each were considered. Though the role concepts are more comprehensive than Fayol's concept of unity of command, they are generally considered closely related (House, 1970). Accordingly, sizable support for the classical theory appears to exist in this area. One might argue that matrix organization, with its utilization of a multiple command structure, presents contrary evidence. Yet research on the effectiveness of matrix structures is lacking. That multiple command structures exist provides no evidence at all about the relative performance levels involved.

One investigation conducted within a governmental bureaucracy compared outcomes associated with reporting to two or more superiors (Gannon and Paine, 1974). Those working in a multiple command system more frequently felt that:

1. Promotions and other rewards were *not* based on ability, talent, competence, and good job performance.

2. Job assignments were frequently conflicting, there was considerable question as to who one's superior really was, and pressure was often needed to get a job done right.

3. Training was inadequate, work was often left incomplete, and there was a general lack of agreement on what had to be done.

4. Those at higher levels were doing too much lower level work and were involved in decisions that could better have been delegated to lower levels.

Violation of unity of command clearly appears to be associated with a host of negative outcomes.

Span of Control. Fayol (1949) considered the span of control in the context of elements rather than principles of management, first in connection with organizing and later when discussing command. Yet his statements in this area fit best with the principles, and it has become increasingly common practice to speak of the span of control *principle* (Urwick, 1974).

Fayol first says that above the first level, managers should have "no more than four or five immediate subordinates" and that foremen should have between ten and thirty. Later he uses the words "less than six" for the first group and "twenty or thirty" for the latter. The emphasis is on the upper limit, not the lower.

Writing and research on the span of control has been voluminous (Van Fleet and Bedeian, 1977). Yet much of the research has been descriptive and offers no test of the normative span of control principle (Dalton et al., 1980). When spans have been related to effectiveness indexes, the results have been conflicting. Also there has been some confusion over whether one should test the principle on raw data or on data corrected for the proportion of time devoted to supervision. The measures are not the same (Ouchi and Dowling, 1974). Once again, research on classical management theory has been plagued by vague definition of variables.

When one looks at the research broadly, it becomes evident that a wide range of phenomena may influence the span of control (House and Miner, 1969; Van Fleet and Bedeian, 1977). Under some circumstances spans can be too small as well as too large. If there is an optimal span, it is in the range of five to ten immediate subordinates, with spans of eight to ten being most appropriate at upper managerial levels, rather than the four to five that Fayol noted. Furthermore, narrow spans produce longer hierarchical chains and higher administrative overhead. Fayol was obviously taking such factors into account in prescribing for the lowest levels, but he chose to ignore them above that point. A more fully developed theory would build these factors into explicit hypotheses. In any event it seems likely now that most organizations are relatively insensitive to variations in the span of control over a broad band of values. If this is so, the span of control concept would appear not to be very important in practice, as Suojanen (1955) indicated a number of years ago.

Research on the Elements

Fayol notes five managerial elements or functions of the management process. Others have produced both shorter and much longer lists, and yet others have presented a completely different way of looking at managerial work. What is the evidence from job observation and analysis in this area? Does the effective performance of various managerial functions relate to organizational success?

The Classical Functions. Though the number of studies of managerial work has been sizable, the number bearing specifically on Fayol's hypotheses is much more limited (Mintzberg, 1973). Furthermore, a variety of techniques have been employed, including questionnaires, interviews, diaries, and observation. Each approach has its particular advantages and disadvantages, yet the multimethod study that looks for convergence among techniques is a distinct rarity.

Two questionnaire studies—one of thirteen different companies and one of a single, large bank—considered some of Fayol's functions. The results are given in Table 12–2. The data do not bear directly on organizing, and they deal with controlling only as it may be reflected in investigating and in aspects of evaluating. The functions of negotiating and representing are not explicitly mentioned by Fayol. Overall, it would appear that to the extent they were studied, Fayol's elements of management are supported, but then so, too, is negotiating among the bank managers, and sizable differences exist between the percentages obtained in the two studies. Not shown in Table 12–2 are additional differences related to managerial level, department, and job type (Mahoney, Jerdee, and Carroll, 1965; Haas, Porat, and Vaughan, 1969). Planning takes up 39 percent of the time of managers who are predominantly planners, but only

Table 12–2

Proportion of Time Devoted to Various Managerial Functions in Two Groups of Managers

	Managers Studied	
Function	452 Managers at All Levels in Thirteen Companies (Percent)	355 Officers of a Large Bank (Percent)
Planning	20	13
Command (Supervising)	30	21
Coordination	16	14
Investigating	13	13
Evaluating	13	14
Negotiating and Representing	8	25

SOURCE: Adapted from Thomas A. Mahoney, Thomas H. Jerdee, and Stephen J. Carroll, "The Job(s) of Management," *Industrial Relations*, 4 (1965), p. 103. John A. Haas, Avner M. Porat, and James A. Vaughan, "Actual vs. Ideal Time Allocations Reported by Managers: A Study of Managerial Behavior," *Personnel Psychology*, 22 (1969), p. 66.

12 percent of the time of those who are essentially coordinators. Similarly, the coordinators spend 39 percent of their time in that activity and the planners only 13 percent. Those who are essentially supervisors (mostly at lower management levels) devote 50 percent of their time to command; no other group devotes more than 21 percent.

This and other research makes it clear that managerial jobs differ significantly, so much so that it may not be meaningful to speak of essential activities, even within hierarchical organizations. There clearly are major differences between managers in what they do (Stewart, 1976), and it appears likely that the commonalities occur at the level of motivation and abilities, rather than in behavior and knowledge.

Taking the research as a whole, planning, command, coordination, and control often appear to be significant managerial activities, though one or more of these may be a negligible factor in any specific job. Organizing in a structural sense has been studied very little, but would appear to be unimportant at the lower managerial levels. Fayol included staffing and evaluating within organizing, however, and both of these activities have emerged as important for some groups of managers (and not for others). In addition some studies have found negotiating, investigating, communicating, representing, and decision making to be significant managerial activities (Miner, 1971; 1978b).

To what extent Fayol might have considered the additional elements noted above as falling within the boundaries of his basic five is unknown.This dilemma points up again the pervasive ambiguity in Fayol's definitions. If he had given us operational measures of planning, organizing, and the like, it would have been possible to know what was and was not included; without them, we can only guess.

Managerial Roles. Like his principles of management, Fayol's elements of management have been the subject of frequent attack, some of it stemming from behavior modification or social learning theory (Davis and Luthans, 1980) and some from work roles theory (Mintzberg, 1975). The latter represents a major alternative to management process formulations of any kind and has spawned a growing body of research. The initial research produced the ten roles described in Table 12–3 (Mintzberg, 1973).

Subsequent research suggests that, of the ten roles listed by Mintzberg, the leader, liaison, monitor, spokesman, entrepreneur, and resource allocator roles are generally distinct within managerial work. The remaining four roles are less clearly established (McCall and Segrist, 1980). As with management process, there appear to be differences in roles associated with both managerial level and functional area (Alexander, 1979). The entrepreneur and liaison roles are uniquely important in top management, but the figurehead, monitor, disseminator, spokesman, and negotiator roles are all more characteristic of managers at higher levels. The various decisional roles are more characteristic in production, the interpersonal in sales, and the informational in accounting. There also is some evidence that the ten roles may be telescoped into two rather than three categories— informational and decisional (Shapira and Dunbar, 1980). Furthermore, clear differences in role requirements for managers in different organizations have been noted (Morse and Wagner, 1978).

Given these findings, the managerial roles approach may not be as different as its proponents suggest. The data from research, and on occasion the nomenclature too, suggest many parallels with management functions. There are no comparative studies that would establish the superiority of one approach over the other. Thus without evidence, managerial roles formulations and related research cannot be used to discredit positions such as that taken by Fayol.

Planning vs. Not Planning. Fayol's views on the elements of management are descriptive as well as normative. Planning, organizing, command, coordination, and control not only describe what managers do, but what they should do. Accordingly, doing these things would be expected to be associated with success. Ideally research in this area would cover all five functions, but this has not happened. Only with regard to the scope of planning activities is there a significant body of evidence relating it to indexes of effectiveness.

Table 12–3
Mintzberg's Ten Work Roles

Role	Description	Typical Activities
Interpersonal roles		
Figurehead	Symbolic head; performs routine duties of a legal or social nature	Ceremony, status request
Leader	Responsible for motivation of subordinates and for staffing and training	Almost all managerial activities involving subordinates
Liaison	Maintains network of outside contacts to obtain favors and information	Handling mail, external board work, telephone calls
Informational roles		
Monitor	Seeks and receives information to obtain thorough understanding of organization and environment	Reading periodicals, observational tours
Disseminator	Transmits information received from outsiders or insiders to other organization members	Forwarding mail, review sessions with subordinates
Spokesman	Transmits information to outsiders on organization plans, policies, actions	Board meetings, handling mail
Decisional roles		
Entrepreneur	Initiates and supervises design of organizational improvement projects as opportunities arise	Strategy and review sessions regarding change efforts
Disturbance handler	Responsible for corrective action when organization faces unexpected crises	Strategy and review sessions regarding disturbances
Resource allocator	Responsible for allocation of human, monetary, and material resources	Scheduling, requests for authorization, budgeting
Negotiator	Responsible for representing the organization in bargaining negotiations	Collective bargaining, purchasing

SOURCE: Adapted from Henry Mintzberg, *The Nature of Managerial Work*. New York: Harper & Row, 1973, pp. 92–93.

This evidence indicates, as Fayol hypothesized, that formal, long-range planning at the corporate level can yield a sizable payoff (Miner, 1978b; Steiner and Miner, 1982). Some studies do not support this conclusion, but these studies are few. The greatest competitive advantages from planning appear to accrue when there are other companies in the industry that do little or no planning, and when the planning leads to a more effective set of strategies than had existed previously.

Certainly planning can go wrong. In one study of corporate failures a consistent tendency toward overly optimistic forecasting and planning was found (Richards, 1973). Contrary evidence was ignored and high-risk strategies were endorsed without adequate information. Findings such as these do not negate Fayol's statements, however. Clearly he was endorsing *effective* planning. On the other hand, he does not define effective planning, and in this respect his theory appears deficient.

At levels below the top, planning also appears to be desirable. Whether this planning should be carried all the way down to the worker level is subject to a number of qualifications and contingencies, but Fayol was talking about managerial planning, and there the evidence tends to be positive (Miner, 1978b).

Applications of Classical Management Theory

There is little question that classical management theory has had a strong influence on practice. Managers use the terminology of the theory widely, and consultants still call on its precepts to substantiate their recommendations, and perhaps to develop them, too. Textbooks have characteristically been modeled around the elements of management for a number of years. Yet studies designed to measure the effects of applications directly are practically nonexistent. There are cross-sectional studies such as Woodward's (1965) and endless anecdotal testimonials. What is lacking are instances in which classical precepts are implemented, potential consequences are measured before and after, and the results are compared with similar results obtained under controlled conditions.

Fayol's Applications

Fayol himself was involved in three applications, or potential applications, of his ideas. One was a study within the company he headed, Commentary-Fourchambault-Décazeville (Fayol, 1970); the second was a consulting engagement with the French government in the Department of Posts, Telegraphs, and Telephones (Fayol, 1937; Brodie, 1967); and the third was a similar engagement with the tobacco monopoly in France (Brodie, 1967).

Of the three, only the company application can make any claim to success. The firm:

> . . . was declining and on the road to bankruptcy, when a
> change occurred in 1888, in the way in which the
> administrative function was carried out; and, without
> modification of anything else, without improvement in any of

the adverse factors, the business began to prosper and has not stopped growing since. With the same mines and factories, with the same financial resources, the same markets, the same board of directors and the same personnel, solely because of a new method of administration the company experienced a rise comparable to its earlier fall (Fayol, 1970, p. 148).

Success is attributed specifically to a strategic action program based on annual and ten-year forecasts, the existence of an organization chart, observation of the necessary principles with regard to command, meetings of department and division heads, and universal control based on accounting data.

In the case of the Department of Posts, Telegraphs, and Telephones, Fayol (1937) points out many departures from his theoretical prescriptions and recommends appropriate corrections; span of control is a major concern. He recommended plans of action, regular meetings, organization charts, horizontal communication, and time study, among other changes. Yet the results were disappointing:

> . . . not even those recommendations which were of immediate applicability had been taken up. . . . In subsequent years some changes, mainly on the financial side, were introduced, but by and large Fayol's ideas and proposals never became translated into the administrative practice of the P.T.T. (Brodie, 1967, pp. 28–29).

The recommendations and results in the case of the tobacco monopoly were much the same. However, Fayol clearly recognized in this governmental application the differences between a state undertaking and private firms, particularly as they relate to goals.

Consulting Applications

Many individuals followed in Fayol's footsteps, using his concepts as a basis for consulting. Perhaps the best-known early example is Lyndall Urwick of Urwick, Orr, and Partners in Great Britain. Modern-day consulting seems to have begun with the scientific management movement and Frederick Taylor (Hunt, 1977). However, as consulting increasingly became an adjunct to top management, Fayol's concepts became more and more relevant. In one form or another they influence many of the top consulting firms today. This may well be due more to the lack of alternative, practical theories than to the enduring value of Fayol's concepts. Consultants have had an impact in spreading classical management theory that is at least as great as their impact in spreading the theory of strategy and structure.

The Structuring of Textbooks

For many years the introductory course in the field of management has been modeled on classical management theory. The course is still typically called "Principles of Management" and is organized around some version of the management elements or functions. This is one of the few instances in which the introductory course in a discipline has been so completely dominated by a single theoretical orientation.

Whether the field has been served well by this continuing domination is a question. Woodward (1965) concludes on the basis of her research that management has not benefited. Recent texts often have bent and distorted the classical framework to accommodate modern research findings. An analysis of nine textbooks (Miner, 1971) once revealed anywhere from four to eight management functions, with only planning included in all the lists. At least twenty different functions may be identified in one textbook or another. Of Fayol's five functions, planning, organizing, command (supervising, directing, or leading), and control appear frequently; coordination is rarely considered. But in many cases additional functions are introduced. The impact of classical theory on management texts is both a testimonial to the enduring quality of the theory itself and evidence of the limitations of the theory's constructs.

Conclusions

Many others have followed Fayol in classical management theory. Their principles have differed in number, in form, and in content, as have their elements of management. However, none of the research findings or analyses of theoretical logic favors one version of the theory over any other. Thus it seems justified to view the following discussion as applying to the theoretical variants as well as to Fayol's version.

Scientific Goals

One reviewer of Fayol's theory concludes:

> Inevitably the debt we owe to Fayol diminishes as time and greater complexity make his day and age seem more and more remote. At the time his attempt, the only one of its kind, to build a basic theory of management was invaluable. It was incomplete . . . too narrow . . . , but there was a great deal of value in it. . . . there are, for those who can separate the wheat from the chaff, principles and guidelines in Fayol's work which we would do well to remember today (Pollard, 1974, p. 99).

This statement contains two important points—one intended, the other probably not. First, it distinguishes between the historical significance of Fayol's ideas and the current viability of his theory. In its time the theory was at the leading edge of knowledge and served to stimulate both thinking and practice in the field. At the present time the theory contributes little, either as a stimulant to research or as a source of conceptual innovation.

Pollard also notes the need to separate the theoretical wheat from the chaff in utilizing Fayol's ideas. Here, perhaps unintentionally, he gets at the root of the problem. Fayol does not tell us how to do this, his followers have not told us, and research that would accomplish this has not been forthcoming. In areas such as managerial ability and formal planning, Fayol's views have been substantiated somewhat. But in many other areas research bearing directly on his hypotheses is either nonexistent or nonsupportive.

Not all of the criticisms leveled at classical management theory are justified, even now. Koontz and O'Donnell (1976), in responding to some of the attacks on the theory, contend that Fayol and the others did not view man as an inert instrument or present a closed system of management. Fayol proposed principles of initiative and equity that appear to assume considerable dynamism among organization members. Furthermore, in limiting his domain of concern, as any theorist must, Fayol appropriately gave less attention to employee dynamics than human relations theorists such as Argyris (Chapter 5) might consider desirable.

On the matter of closed versus open systems, Katz and Kahn (Chapter 6), among others, have argued convincingly for an open systems approach and criticized classical theory in this regard. Again, Fayol did not make organization-environment interaction the central focus of his theory, but he did not ignore it either. His discussions of planning and forecasting and of the commercial function reflect considerable concern for environmental factors. Here, as previously, the theory simply focused on a particular, limited domain— one that other theorists may consider trivial or unproductive, but important nevertheless for practice.

The question of domain is tantalizing. Classical theory aspires to both breadth and limitation, but the research suggests a domain that differs from either. In one sense the theory is grand in nature, covering a diverse array of organizations and managers. However, we have noted its limitations in the fields of organizational behavior and organization-environment interaction. These self-established limitations appear valid, but in addition there are limitations on the extent to which various organizational contexts are relevant. Certain findings indicate that the appropriate domain is production operations of the kind currently epitomized by the assembly line. This domain may be too narrow, but certainly the theory does not apply in professional contexts such as research and development, and even Fayol came to have questions regarding its applicability in highly politicized governmental contexts.

In the early stages of its development, classical management theory aspired to a domain beyond its capabilities. Once this fact is established, the theory is thrown back on research to chart its actual domain. The work of Lawrence and Lorsch (Chapter 9) suggests that a highly certain environment is the determining factor. Woodward and others (Chapter 8) suggest particular technological constraints. Overall, we really do not know the domain of the theory except that it is considerably narrower than had been originally proposed.

Whatever the domain, one is still faced with the problems of ambiguous definition and uncertain construct validity. Examples have been noted throughout the preceding discussion. The problem is not one of historical contribution, but viability as a modern theory. Fayol produced a terminology for the management field—a vocabulary. But he did not move beyond this to effective operationalization. Those who have taken this additional step have typically done so in the context of some newer theory; they have not attempted to test the classical theory itself. One can only conclude that classical management theory has served its purpose. The future calls for more precise formulations, subject to the kind of empirical test that will permit definitive statements regarding validity. Classical theory itself is simply not adequate in this regard.

Classical management theory, like other theories, lacks integration. Its hypotheses are such that a test of one says nothing about the validity of any other. On occasion, deficiencies of this kind are remedied as a theory matures, and new concepts are added. In this instance, however, the principles and elements remain just as separate and distinct today as they were in 1916.

Fayol was constrained by the limited information available to him. Well before Fayol wrote, a line-staff structure had emerged among the railroads of the United States and spread into manufacturing (Chandler and Daems, 1979). Such a structure facilitates horizontal communication by introducing hierarchy into the staff component and thus moves well beyond Fayol's general staff and gangplank formulations. How Fayol would have reacted to such a structure is unknown. He might well have been concerned about unity of command. In any event he did not react because he did not know about it. Many new ideas have come into being since that time—matrix structure, autonomous work groups, organization development in its many forms, and the like. Classical theory has not kept up with such changes, even in the domain to which it aspires. New theorists have not emerged to elaborate on and update the ideas of Fayol. Perhaps this reflects the shortcomings of the theory itself.

Goals of Application

The following comment summarizes much of what has been said in this chapter regarding applications of the classical theory:

> Management thought has contributed to a working vocabulary and has supplied a historical perspective on the evolution of management. However, management thought has contributed little to establishing a transferable set of concepts, methods of translating principles to specific practical applications, or guides for designing management systems. . . . Managers and consultants may have adapted certain concepts as starting points for diagnosing problems, constructing management processes, and formulating individual styles and values that influence how they do their work (Brandenburg, 1974, p. 112).

Current practice has generally moved beyond classical management theory. The major area where practice has continued to utilize the theory is in the structuring of management textbooks. Given the status of the research evidence and current theory it would appear time to introduce change in this area. Justifying the use of what is now an essentially outmoded theory to introduce students to the management field is becoming increasingly difficult. On this score the author has been equally culpable with other writers in the past (Miner, 1978b).

References

Alexander, Larry D. "The Effect Level in the Hierarchy and Functional Area Have on the Extent Mintzberg's Roles Are Required by Managerial Jobs," *Academy of Management Proceedings*, 1979, pp. 186–89.

Bedeian, Arthur G. *The Administrative Writings of Henri Fayol: A Bibliographic Investigation*. Monticello, Ill.: Vance Bibliographies, 1979.

Brandenburg, Richard G. "The Usefulness of Management Thought for Management." In Joseph W. McGuire (ed.), *Contemporary Management: Issues and Viewpoints*. Englewood Cliffs, N.J.: Prentice-Hall, 1974, pp. 99–113.

Breeze, John D., and Frederick C. Miner. "Henri Fayol: A New Definition of Administration." *Academy of Management Proceedings*, 1980, pp. 110–13.

Brodie, M. B. *Fayol on Administration*. London: Lyon, Grant and Green, 1967.

Cass, Eugene L., and Frederick G. Zimmer. *Man and Work in Society*. New York: Van Nostrand Reinhold, 1975.

Chandler, Alfred D., and Herman Daems. "Administrative Coordination, Allocation, and Monitoring: Concepts and Comparisons." In Norbert Horn and Jürgen Kocka (eds.), *Law and the Formation of the Big Enterprises in the 19th and Early 20th Centuries*. Göttingen, Germany: Vandenhoeck and Ruprecht, 1979, pp. 28–54.

Dalton, Dan R., William D. Todor, Michael J. Spendolini, Gordon J. Fielding, and Lyman W. Porter. "Organization Structure and Performance: A Critical Review," *Academy of Management Review*, 5 (1980), 49–64.

Davis, Ralph C. *The Fundamentals of Top Management*. New York: Harper & Row, 1951.

Davis, Tim R. V., and Fred Luthans. "Managers in Action: A New Look at Their Behavior and Operating Modes," *Organizational Dynamics*, 9, no. 1 (1980), 64–80.

Fayol, Henri. "The Administrative Theory in the State." In Luther Gulick and Lyndall F. Urwick (eds.), *Papers on the Science of Administration*. New York: Institute of Public Administration, 1937, pp. 99–114.

———. *General and Industrial Management*. Translated by Constance Storrs. London: Pitman, 1949.

———. "The Importance of the Administrative Factor." In Ernest Dale (ed.), *Readings in Management: Landmarks and New Frontiers*. New York: McGraw-Hill, 1970, pp. 148–49.

Filley, Alan C., Robert J. House, and Steven Kerr. *Managerial Process and Organizational Behavior*. Glenview, Ill.: Scott, Foresman, 1976.

Franke, Richard H., and James D. Kaul. "The Hawthorne Experiments: First Statistical Interpretation," *American Sociological Review*, 43 (1978), 623–43.

Gannon, Martin J., and Frank T. Paine. "Unity of Command and Job Attitudes of Managers in a Bureaucratic Organization," *Journal of Applied Psychology*, 59 (1974), 392–94.

Ghiselli, Edwin E. *Explorations in Managerial Talent*. Pacific Palisades, Calif.: Goodyear, 1971.

Gulick, Luther, and Lyndall F. Urwick. *Papers on the Science of Administration*. New York: Institute of Public Administration, 1937.

Haas, John A., Avner M. Porat, and James A. Vaughan. "Actual vs. Ideal Time Allocations Reported by Managers: A Study of Managerial Behavior," *Personnel Psychology*, 22 (1969), 61–75.

Holden, Paul E., Carlton A. Pederson, and Gayton E. Germane. *Top Management*. New York: McGraw-Hill, 1968.

House, Robert J. "Role Conflict and Multiple Authority in Complex Organizations," *California Management Review*, 12, no. 4 (1970), 53–60.

House, Robert, J., and John B. Miner. "Merging Management and Behavioral Theory: The Interaction between Span of Control and Group Size," *Administrative Science Quarterly*, 14 (1969), 451–64.

Hunt, Alfred. *The Management Consultant*. New York: Ronald, 1977.

Koontz, Harold. *Toward a Unified Theory of Management*. New York: McGraw-Hill, 1964.

Koontz, Harold, and Cyril O'Donnell. *Principles of Management: An Analysis of Managerial Functions*. New York: McGraw-Hill, 1955.

———. *Management: A Systems and Contingency Analysis of Managerial Functions*. New York: McGraw-Hill, 1976.

McCall, Morgan W., and Cheryl A. Segrist. *In Pursuit of the Manager's Job: Building on Mintzberg*. Greensboro, N.C.: Center for Creative Leadership, 1980.

Mahoney, Thomas A., Thomas H. Jerdee, and Stephen J. Carroll. "The Job(s) of Management," *Industrial Relations*, 4 (1965), 97–110.

March, James G., and Herbert A. Simon. *Organizations*. New York: Wiley, 1958.

Miner, John B. *Management Theory*. New York: Macmillan, 1971.

———. *Motivation to Manage: A Ten Year Update on the Studies in Management Education Research*. Atlanta, Ga.: Organizational Measurement Systems Press, 1977.

———. "Twenty Years of Research on Role-Motivation Theory of Managerial Effectiveness," *Personnel Psychology*, 31 (1978a), 739–60.

―――. *The Management Process: Theory, Research, and Practice.* New York: Macmillan, 1978b.

―――. *Theories of Organizational Behavior.* Hinsdale, Ill.: Dryden, 1980.

Mintzberg, Henry. *The Nature of Managerial Work.* New York: Harper & Row, 1973.

―――. "The Manager's Job: Folklore and Fact," *Harvard Business Review*, 53, no. 4 (1975), 49–61.

Mooney, James D., and Alan C. Reiley. *Onward Industry! The Principles of Organization and Their Significance to Modern Industry.* New York: Harper & Row, 1931.

Morse, John J., and Francis R. Wagner. "Measuring the Process of Managerial Effectiveness," *Academy of Management Journal*, 21 (1978), 23–35.

Negandhi, Anant R. *Organization Theory in an Open System.* New York: Dunellen, 1975.

Ouchi, William G., and John B. Dowling. "Defining the Span of Control," *Administrative Science Quarterly*, 19 (1974), 357–65.

Pollard, Harold R. *Developments in Management Thought.* New York: Crane, Russak, 1974.

Price, James L. *Handbook of Organizational Measurement.* Lexington, Mass.: D. C. Heath, 1972.

Richards, Max D. "An Exploratory Study of Strategic Failure," *Academy of Management Proceedings*, 1973, pp. 40–46.

Roethlisberger, F. J., and William J. Dickson. *Management and the Worker.* Cambridge, Mass.: Harvard University Press, 1939.

Shapira, Zur, and Roger L. M. Dunbar. "Testing Mintzberg's Managerial Roles Classification Using an In-Basket Simulation," *Journal of Applied Psychology*, 65 (1980), 87–95.

Simon, Herbert A. *Administrative Behavior: A Study of Decision-Making Processes in Administrative Organization.* New York: Free Press, 1947.

―――. "Approaching the Theory of Management." In Harold Koontz (ed.), *Toward a Unified Theory of Management.* New York: McGraw-Hill, 1964.

Steiner, George A., and John B. Miner. *Management Policy and Strategy.* New York: Macmillan, 1982.

Stewart, Rosemary. "To Understand the Manager's Job: Consider Demands, Constraints, Choices," *Organizational Dynamics*, 4, no. 4 (1976), 22–32.

Stogdill, Ralph M. *Managers, Employees, Organizations.* Columbus, Ohio: Bureau of Business Research, Ohio State University, 1965.

Suojanen, Waino W. "The Span of Control—Fact or Fable?" *Advanced Management*, 20 (1955), 5–13.

Taylor, Frederick W. *The Principles of Scientific Management.* New York: Harper & Row, 1911.

Urwick, Lyndall F. *Notes on the Theory of Organization.* New York: American Management Association, 1952.

―――. "V. A. Graicunas and the Span of Control," *Academy of Management Journal*, 17 (1974), 349–54.

Van Fleet, David D., and Arthur G. Bedeian. "A History of the Span of Management," *Academy of Management Review*, 2 (1977), 356–72.

Woodward, Joan. *Industrial Organization: Theory and Practice.* London: Oxford University Press, 1965.

Wren, Daniel A. *The Evolution of Management Thought.* New York: Ronald, 1972.

Zwerman, William L. *New Perspectives on Organization Theory.* Westport, Conn.: Greenwood, 1970.

13

Theory of Bureaucracy

The Theory as Formulated by Weber
The nature of organization
The pure types of authority
  Rational-legal authority
  Traditional authority
  Charismatic authority
Combined authority in organizations
The bureaucratic organization
  Aspects of bureaucracy
  Normative statements
  Contrasts with other forms

Theoretical Elaborations with Special Emphasis on Blau and Victor Thompson
The theoretical elaborations of Peter Blau
  Basic critiques of the Weber theory
  Professionalism, expert knowledge, and bureaucracy
  Differentiation in organizations
  Decentralization in bureaucracies
The theoretical elaborations of Victor Thompson
  Modern organization
  Bureaucracy and innovation
  Without sympathy or enthusiasm

Bureaucracy and the modern world
Specifications in terms of types

Research on Bureaucratic Structure and Process
Blau's comparative studies
  Differentiation
  Decentralization
The Aston research and subsequent extensions
  The British research
  Less comprehensive studies
The knowledge factor
Personality considerations
Normative research
  Research reviews
  Selected studies
Innovation and bureaucracy
  Dual hierarchies
  Venture teams
Problems of measurement

Conclusions
Scientific goals
  Weber's theory
  Blau's theory
  Victor Thompson's theory
  Bureaucratic and nonbureaucratic systems
Goals of application

Unlike classical management theory, bureaucratic theory has undergone considerable, varied revision since its original development by Max Weber during the first two decades of this century. Consequently, research designed to test one version of the theory often does not provide evidence for other versions. So, one must consider not only Weber's views, but also the views of those who have elaborated on them, often for the purpose of integrating the theory with human relations concepts and findings.

Weber was originally educated in Germany as a lawyer. Much of his early writing dealt with legal history. In addition to law and history Weber produced major contributions in the fields of economics, religion, and political science. However, he became best known in sociology, the field in which his theory of bureaucracy had the greatest impact. Though associated with several German and Austrian universities, Weber stayed longest at the University of Heidelberg. Due to a substantial inheritance and intermittent periods of debilitating depression, he did not teach regularly and in fact spent a number of years as a private scholar (Marianne Weber, 1975). He died in 1920 at the age of 56.

Weber's writings have been introduced in the United States through a variety of translations and compilations. The most comprehensive, though still incomplete, early statements of his theory of bureaucracy appeared in the translations by Gerth and Mills (Weber, 1946) and by Parsons and Henderson (Weber, 1947). The period of Weber's major impact in this country thus coincides with that of Fayol. The following discussion draws primarily on the comprehensive, three-volume *Economy and Society* translated by Roth and Wittich (Weber, 1968), and especially on the first and third volumes. This work contains no reference to the writings of Henri Fayol, just as Fayol did not consider Weber.

The Theory as Formulated by Weber

Weber's approach to theory construction is scholarly, and his statements often are documented from a historical perspective. Though some people, particularly those of a human relations bent, typically view classical management theory and bureaucratic theory as comparable, even to the point of not differentiating between them, a reading of the two indicates major differences. Weber is primarily interested in the role of bureaucracy in the historical development of society and its organizational forms; Fayol focuses on problems of managerial practice. Both fail to operationalize variables and conduct relevant research, but Weber is much more concerned with clarity of definition.

The Nature of Organization

Weber sees an organization as a particular type of social relationship that is either closed to outsiders or limits their admission and has its regulations enforced by a chief, usually with the assistance of an administrative staff. The key factor is some hierarchy of authority that serves to ensure that members will carry out the order governing the organization. This order may be self-enacted or imposed by an outside agency. Organizational structure refers to the specific manner in which the authority is distributed.

The concept of rules plays an important role in Weber's theory, especially rationally established rules. A *formal organization* is one with a "continuously and rationally operating staff." Such a staff possesses power—a probability that it will be able to carry out its own desires even in the face of resistance. It exercises domination or authority—a probability that its commands will be obeyed. It utilizes discipline—a probability that as a result of habit, commands will result in immediate and automatic obedience.

This staff, which is comparable to the managerial component of today's organizations, is a special group that can be trusted to execute existing policy and carry out commands. It may be tied to the chief in a number of ways, including custom, emotion, and material interest. A key factor in the continued domination of the organization by those at the top is the "law of the small number":

> The ruling minority can quickly reach understanding among its members; it is thus able at any time quickly to initiate that rationally organized action which is necessary to preserve its position of power. Consequently it can easily squelch any action of the masses threatening its power. . . . Another benefit of the small number is the ease of secrecy as to the intentions and resolutions of the rulers and the state of their information (Weber, 1968, p. 952).

The Pure Types of Authority

Weber's theory gives considerable attention to concepts such as authority, domination, command, power, and discipline; this focus appears to have alienated theorists of a human relations orientation. Yet these are important concepts for organizational theory.

Authority is said to be legitimized or validated by appeal to one or more of three possible grounds—rational-legal rules, personal authority invested with the force of tradition, and charisma. These are pure types that rarely occur alone in nature. In practice, systems of authority typically are mixtures or modifications of the three.

Rational-Legal Authority. Rational-legal authority provides a basis for the organizational structure termed bureaucracy. It involves:

> ... a system of consciously made *rational* rules (which may be agreed upon or imposed from above), which meet with obedience as generally binding norms whenever such obedience is claimed by him whom the rule designates. In that case every single bearer of powers of command is legitimated by the system of rational norms, and his power is legitimate insofar as it corresponds with the norm. Obedience is thus given to the norms rather than to the person (Weber, 1968, p. 954).

Norms are established because of expediency and/or value-rationality; they apply to the members of the organization, but may extend beyond that to the sphere of power of the organization. There is a consistent system of rules—stated in the abstract, but applied to particular cases. Even those in authority are thus subject to an impersonal order. An individual obeys only as an organization member and in response to the law or an impersonal order, not to an individual. Thus obedience is required only within a legitimate, rationally established jurisdiction.

The categories of rational-legal authority are described as follows:

1. A continuous rule-bound conduct of official business.
2. A specified sphere of competence (jurisdiction). This involves:
   a. A sphere of obligations to perform functions which have been marked off as part of a systematic division of labor.
   b. The provision of the incumbent with the necessary powers.
   c. That the necessary means of compulsion are clearly defined and their use is subject to definite conditions. . . .
3. The organization of offices follows the principle of hierarchy; that is, each lower office is under the control and supervision of a higher one. . . .
4. The rules which regulate the conduct of an office may be technical rules or norms.
5. . . . it is a matter of principle that the members of the administrative staff should be completely separated from ownership of the means of production. . . . There exists, furthermore, in principle complete separation of the organization's property (respectively capital), and the personal property (household) of the official.

6. . . . there is also a complete absence of appropriation of his official position by the incumbent. . . .

7. Administrative acts, decisions, and rules are formulated and recorded in writing.

8. Legal authority can be exercised in a wide variety of different forms (Weber, 1968, pp. 218–19).

Traditional Authority. Traditional authority derives from the personal loyalty associated with a common upbringing. It is based on the sanctity of long-standing rules and powers, on tradition, and custom. To some extent these traditions specify the exact content of command, but they may also provide a wide range for individual discretion. Thus traditional authority attaches to the person, not to an impersonal position. It tends to be present where positions of power are filled on the basis of family membership, as in kingdoms and family-owned firms. Here, as in the traditional family, obedience is to the person.

Charismatic Authority. Like traditional authority, charismatic authority is also personal. The leader's personality interacts with followers so that they attribute supernatural, superhuman, or at least exceptional powers to the leader. Charismatic authority rests on recognition by others and results in complete devotion to the leader. The hierarchical powers on which charisma is based must be frequently demonstrated and serve to benefit the followers, or authority will disappear. Typically, a charismatic community emerges over which the leader often exercises arbitrary control. Irrationality and emotional ties are characteristic. Economic considerations are downplayed. Free of ties to rules, whether rationally or traditionally derived, this kind of authority can be a major force for change and revolution.

Combined Authority in Organizations

Authority and willingness to obey are based on beliefs. These beliefs, which bestow prestige, are typically complex, and accordingly few organizations operate from a single authority base. Rational-legal authority tends to become infused with tradition over time. Bureaucratic organizations tend to be headed at the very top by charismatic leaders, not bureaucratic officials, and they function more effectively if this is so.

Historically, many organizations develop from charismatic, to rational-legal, to traditional, and then as traditional authority fails, organizations return to the revolutionary charismatic form. Charismatic authority alone is highly unstable. The charismatic community that maintains itself over time must become rationalized or traditionalized to some degree. This routinization of charisma is particularly important to succession.

Weber views the emergence of an administrative staff as essential to stable organization. Continued obedience requires an effort to enforce the existing order, and this in turn is a consequence of a solidarity of interests, a consistent value system extending between the chief and the staff. At some points Weber appears to equate the very existence of an organization with some degree of rationalized bureaucracy, but he is not consistent in this regard.

Though a generally authoritarian orientation is often attributed to bureaucratic theory, Weber is clearly positively disposed toward certain democratic and collegial forms. In establishing patterns of succession and routinizing charismatic systems, elections and other democratic procedures may emerge. Such procedures can be a major antiauthoritarian force and a force for rationality. As organizations become large, full collegiality is no longer possible, but other forms of democracy involving representation are still viable. In fact Weber tends to associate the democratization of society with the growth of bureaucratic organizations. Under such conditions bureaucracy contributes to the leveling of social and economic differences. At the same time democracy may come into conflict with bureaucratic tendencies under certain conditions; for instance, a bureaucratic emphasis on career service may conflict with democratic endorsements of election for short terms and the possibility of recall from office.

The Bureaucratic Organization

Many aspects of bureaucracy have been considered as a natural outgrowth of the discussion of different types of legitimate authority—especially the rational-legal type—but other factors are involved. Furthermore, Weber viewed bureaucracy as a modern organizational form, superior to other forms in a number of respects. He tended to associate it not only with societal, if not organizational, democracy, but also with the growth of a capitalistic economic system and with a certain disesteem for "irrational" religion.

Aspects of Bureaucracy. Bureaucracy involves sets of jurisdictional areas ordered by rules. Needed activities are assigned to jurisdictions as duties, authority to elicit behavior to carry out these duties is strictly defined and delimited, and the filling of positions is based on preestablished qualifications. There is a clearly established hierarchy of subordination and appeal. Management of the organization is based on written documents (the files). Management positions presuppose thorough training in a specialized area. In addition a comprehensive knowledge of the organization's rules is required. In a fully developed bureaucracy the needs for the various kinds of knowledge and expertise and for their application are sufficient to produce a full-time position.

Entry into bureaucratic management is based on a set course of training and usually on performance on prescribed examinations. Appointment tends to be by superior authority (election represents a departure from true bureaucracy). After appointment, the individual enters on a career in the organization and can expect to progress up the hierarchy. Compensation is a salary plus a pension in old age. Certain rights go with appointment to the office and protect an encumbent against arbitrary, personal action.

Bureaucratic systems dominate through knowledge, and this fact gives them their rationality. The result is a climate of formal impersonality "without hatred or passion and hence without affection or enthusiasm." Movement toward such an organizational form is fostered by sheer growth of an organization, and consequently of the administrative task. Bureaucracy is also fostered by the qualitative expansion of administrative tasks—the knowledge explosion and the taking on of added activities by the organization.

Normative Statements. Weber (1968) described bureaucracy at considerable length and placed it in historical perspective, but he also hypothesized that the kind of organization he described would be more effective than alternative forms on a number of counts:

> The purely bureaucratic type of administrative organization—that is, the monocratic variety of bureaucracy—is, from a purely technical point of view, capable of attaining the highest degree of efficiency and is in this sense formally the most rational known means of exercising authority over human beings. It is superior to any other form in precision, in stability, in the stringency of its discipline, and in its reliability. It thus makes possible a particularly high degree of calculability of results for the heads of the organization and for those acting in relation to it. It is finally superior both in intensive efficiency and in the scope of its operations, and is formally capable of application to all kinds of administrative tasks (p. 223).

And again:

> The fully developed bureaucratic apparatus compares with other organizations exactly as does the machine with the non-mechanical modes of production. Precision, speed, unambiguity, knowledge of the files, continuity, discretion, unity, strict subordination, reduction of friction and of material and personal costs—these are raised to the optimum point in the strictly bureaucratic administration. . . . As far as

complicated tasks are concerned, paid bureaucratic work is not only more precise but, in the last analysis, it is often cheaper than even formally unremunerated honorific service (pp. 973–74).

Nowhere does Weber contend that the members of such organizations will be happier or more satisfied, but he does contend that bureaucracy works, and to some degree it works for individual members also by freeing them from the inequities of arbitrary authority. Ultimately, bureaucracy works so well that it is practically indestructible. Once such a system is set in motion it is almost impossible to stop, except from the very top; the sum of the parts is an effective organization, but no one part, no single official, is powerful enough to disrupt the whole.

Contrasts with Other Forms. Weber contrasts bureaucracy with other types of organizations that rely more heavily on traditional and charismatic authority, what he calls prebureaucratic forms. Traditional authority is particularly manifest in patrimonial organizations, which lack the bureaucratic separation of private and official spheres. Under traditional conditions, decisions tend to be *ad hoc* rather than predetermined by rules, and loyalty is not to the duties of an impersonal office, but to a ruler as a person. Ineffectiveness becomes a matter of arousing the ruler's disfavor rather than failing to perform the duties of the position. Feudalism involves much that is patrimonial, but relationships are more fixed than in many other such forms. Elements of routinized charisma are in evidence as well.

In a sense charismatic authority is antithetical to the idea of organization. Yet a personal staff of disciples characteristically arises to form a charismatic aristocracy. The basic system tends to be communal, with the leader issuing dispensations according to his personal desires. Under such conditions the leader can introduce changes rapidly—there are no rules or traditions to block them. Bureaucracy can produce change as well, but it does so by first changing the material and social order along rational lines, and then the individuals.

Discipline in a modern factory is much the same as in the military or on a plantation, but it is more rational:

With the help of suitable methods of measurement, the optimum profitability of the individual worker is calculated like that of any material means of production. On this basis the American system of scientific management triumphantly proceeds with its rational conditioning and training of work performances, thus drawing the ultimate conclusions from the mechanization and discipline of the plant. . . . This whole process of rationalization, in the factory as elsewhere, and especially in the bureaucratic state machine, parallels the centralization of the material implements of organization in the hands of the master. Thus, discipline inexorably takes over ever larger areas as the satisfaction of political and economic needs is increasingly rationalized. This universal phenomenon more and more restricts the importance of charisma and of individually differentiated conduct (Weber, 1968, p. 1156).

Weber does not say he likes all this; his writing is in fact quite objective and neutral. But he certainly respects it, and he appears to be to some degree afraid of it as well.

Theoretical Elaborations with Special Emphasis on Blau and Victor Thompson

Elaborations of Weber's theory have taken a variety of forms. A major theoretical thrust has been toward the specification of dysfunctional side effects of bureaucracy. Another has formulated more precise theoretical hypotheses and developed operational definitions of variables. And yet another has differentiated various types of bureaucracies within the broad framework established by Weber.

Preceding chapters have considered a number of the hypotheses about unintended consequences of bureaucracy. The positions taken by Argyris and Bennis (Chapter 5) represent two more fully developed statements along these lines. Though these and other theorists have viewed the dysfunctions of the bureaucratic form as so overriding as to argue against its use altogether, others have remained content to point up the difficulties in bureaucratic systems without abandoning the underlying theory. Early examples of this latter approach that emerged from intensive case studies were Selznick's (1949) analysis of the Tennessee Valley Authority and Gouldner's (1954) study of a gypsum plant. These two formulations and a similar model developed by Merton (1940) are analyzed by March and Simon (1958) as major examples of the dysfunctions type of theory.

Discussion of the many elaborations on bureaucratic theory here will focus on the work of Peter Blau and Victor Thompson and give some additional attention to the differentiation of bureaucratic types by the Aston researchers (Chapter 8). Blau, a sociologist now at the State University of New York at Albany, spent a number of years at the University of Chicago and Columbia University. He has been an active researcher and theoretician in the field of bureaucracy. Victor Thompson, a political scientist, worked and published with Herbert Simon at IIT (Simon, Smithbury, and Thompson, 1950).

Subsequently he has held appointments at Syracuse University, the University of Illinois, and the University of Florida. Though limiting the treatment of theoretical elaborations in the manner proposed may do some disservice to specific theorists in the field, the major theoretical thrusts that have emerged since Weber are considered.

The Theoretical Elaborations of Peter Blau

Blau's writings on bureaucracy originally appeared as articles in the sociological literature. These have been compiled in a volume entitled *On the Nature of Organizations* (Blau, 1974), and it is to this volume that primary reference will be made.

Basic Critiques of the Weber Theory. Blau accepts a number of the criticisms of Weber developed by others. He agrees that Weber failed to recognize certain dysfunctions created by bureaucracy such as the encouragement of less personally responsible behavior. Basically, Weber focused on the functions of bureaucratic institutions within the larger society and failed to deal effectively with many problems of their internal workings. In discussing promotion he emphasized the use of objective, rational procedures, but failed to deal with the relative worth of seniority and merit. In the same vein, while noting numerous departures from the bureaucratic ideal, Weber does not recognize the existence and role of informal organization as a social entity.

Blau (1974) notes certain difficulties inherent in Weber's concept of authority, in his utilization of the ideal type or pure case, and in his handling of the interface between bureaucracy and democracy. These difficulties are exacerbated by the fact that Weber is not entirely consistent in his treatment of these matters.

The theory recognizes both a voluntary element and imperative control in rational-legal authority, but it does not attempt to reconcile the two. Blau proposes that the key factor is the development of norms of compliance within the subordinate group. The individual complies in part because the power to orchestrate sanctions resides in the superior and creates subordinate dependence, but in the context of group norms subordinates may obey even when they would not otherwise voluntarily comply.

One difficulty with the use of ideal types such as bureaucracy is that they freeze relationships so that factors must covary together, when in fact these factors may vary independently under certain conditions. As an approach to theory construction, the ideal type is at one and the same time a conceptual scheme and a set of hypotheses. It specifies aspects of a bureaucracy that are highly salient, and criteria for identifying bureaucracy in terms of these aspects.

But it also states hypotheses about relationships among the aspects and their relation to efficiency that are empirically testable. If the empirical facts do not confirm the hypotheses in all respects, the ideal type becomes meaningless. Blau argues for abandoning ideal-type constructs in bureaucratic theory in favor of a set of hypotheses relating key variables under specified circumstances.

Weber discusses democracy and collegiality on numerous occasions, but he never distinguishes between them and bureaucracy in any systematic manner. It is almost as if Weber does not know quite what to do with democracy within his historical framework. He borders on, but does not actually deal with, the distinction posed by sociotechnical theory (Chapter 4). Blau suggests that bureaucratic and democratic (group) systems are different and should be treated as such.

Blau departs from Weber in a number of respects, yet his overall debt is clear:

> Perhaps the most difficult task for a scholar is to develop a new approach to the study of reality. . . . It is no exaggeration to say that Weber was one of the rare men who has done just this (Blau, 1974, p. 57).

In addition Blau has given particular attention to operationalizing the constructs of bureaucratic theory—size, complexity, specialization, expertness, administrative staff, hierarchy, rules, impersonality, and career stability.

Professionalism, Expert Knowledge, and Bureaucracy. For Weber the major source of rational-legal authority was expert knowledge that accrued to those at higher levels in the bureaucratic system in increasing proportions. In many respects Weber was right. Communication comes down through a bureaucracy, and thus each higher level can know more. Knowledge that is idiosyncratic to the particular organization—knowledge of rules and information related to strategic decision making—is clearly a function of hierarchical position. But Weber failed to reckon with the organizational value of professional knowledge (legal, scientific, medical, and the like), which enters the organization through professional components and often at relatively low levels. Under such circumstances a hierarchical superior may be expert on strictly organizational issues, but not on professional knowledge relevant to the concern.

The relationship between expertise and hierarchy may not be quite as Weber viewed it, and thus rational-legal authority may flow in somewhat different directions. Blau recognized this problem and viewed professional authority as a separate entity that need not co-vary with bureaucratic variables such as the specialized division of labor. In this he follows a number of sociologists dating back to Parsons in his translation of Weber (1947).

Certainly, there are marked similarities between bureaucratic and professional systems—impersonality, rational decision making, and an emphasis on technical expertness. But there are many differences also. In stressing the differences and noting the potential sources of conflict between the two types of authority Blau departs significantly from Weber's theory.

Differentiation in Organizations. Building on the results of a study of governmental employment security units, Blau (1974) developed a theory of differentiation in organizations that primarily extends Weber's position rather than opposes it. Differentiation occurs when the number of geographical branches, occupational positions, hierarchical levels, and divisions, or units within branches or divisions, increases. The hypotheses are:

1. Increasing size generates structural differentiation in organizations along various dimensions at decelerating rates.
    1A. Large size promotes structural differentiation.
    1B. Large size promotes differentiation along several different lines.
    1C. The rate of differentiation declines with expanding size.
    1.1. As the size of organizations increases, its marginal influence on differentiation decreases.
    1.2. The larger an organization is, the larger is the average size of its structural components of all kinds.
    1.3. The proportionate size of the average structural component, as distinguished from the absolute size, decreases with increases in organizational size.
    1.4. The larger the organization is, the wider the supervisory span of control.
    1.5. Organizations exhibit an economy of scale in management.
    1.6. The economy of scale in administrative overhead itself declines with increasing organizational size.
2. Structural differentiation in organizations enlarges the administrative component.
    2.1. The large size of an organization indirectly raises the ratio of administrative personnel through the structural differentiation it generates.
    2.2. The direct effects of large organizational size lowering the administrative ratio exceed its indirect effects raising it owing to the structural differentiation it generates.

2.3. The differentiation of large organizations into subunits stems the decline in the economy of scale in management with increasing size (Blau, 1974, pp. 302–17).

Decentralization in Bureaucracies. Blau (1974) makes a distinction between managing through direct and indirect controls. Direct control involves close observation and corrective orders. Indirect control relies more on impersonal procedures that automatically limit behavior. Examples of indirect controls are automation and merit personnel standards. Clearly, indirect control has been expedited with the aid of computers. Direct control reflects centralization, while indirect control indicates standardization or formalization.

Weber leads one to expect that centralization and formalization both increase with greater bureaucratization; the two go together. Blau (1970) proposes, however, that formalization through indirect controls actually restricts the manager and serves as a means of decentralization. In this view direct and indirect control are alternatives, and define two different types of bureaucracies. Modern bureaucracies stress the formalization of indirect control and are more decentralized. These variables do not covary in the manner Weber appears to have envisaged.

Whether this is a true departure from Weber depends on whether one interprets the use of indirect controls as formalization or simply as another type of authority. Comments by discussants following the presentation of Blau's (1970) paper reflect uncertainty on this point and raise questions of construct validity for the Weber theory. In any event Blau's theory of alternative control procedures can stand on its own merits; it parallels Chandler's formulations rather closely (Chapter 10).

The Theoretical Elaborations of Victor Thompson

While Blau has moved back and forth between theory and research, Thompson has devoted himself primarily to theory. He has largely emphasized the dysfunctions and inadequacies of bureaucratic theory. Yet, like Blau, Thompson remains generally committed to the genius of Max Weber. Victor Thompson has presented his ideas in a series of books over a fifteen-year period.

Modern Organization. The major problem for modern bureaucracies according to Thompson (1961) is the imbalance between ability and authority. Increasingly the knowledge needed to operate the organization is to be found among specialists and professionals who do not have significant positions of authority. At the same time bureaucracy by its very nature places the right to exercise authority and the responsibility for outcomes in the hands of hierarchical superiors. The result is continuing confusion and conflict.

The characteristics of bureaucracy listed by Thompson are similar to Weber's:

1. A spirit of rationalism, with science and technology as major contributors.

2. Highly trained specialists appointed by merit to a system of assured careers.

3. Routinization of organizational activities.

4. Factoring of the general goal of the organization into subgoals for units along the lines of differentiation.

5. Apparent inversion of ends and means such that the total organizational goal becomes lost to view and the subgoals of units become ends in themselves.

6. A formalistic impersonality.

7. Categorization of data in accordance with the needs of specialists.

8. Classification of clients to minimize discrimination.

9. Seeming slowness to act or change as a result of resistance to change and preoccupation with hierarchy.

Those who come into contact with bureaucracies must adjust to these characteristics. Certain people (Thompson calls them *bureautics*) are too immature to adjust and react with an overwhelming suspicion. Bureausis is considered a disease that normally prevents people from rising in the hierarchy.

In addition to bureausis and adaptive bureaucratic behavior, Thompson describes bureaupathic behavior created by anxiety and insecurity. This phenomenon results in large part from the gap between the rights and duties of the hierarchical superior and the specialized ability to solve problems, a gap which in turn makes the superior dependent upon specialist subordinates. Often superiors react to this situation with an excessive need for control, an overemphasis on compliance with rules, exaggerated aloofness, resistance to change, and insistence on the rights of office. Such bureaupathology is a function of the insecurity of authority produced in large part by increasing specialization.

Minimal attention is given to solving these problems, but several approaches are noted:

1. Give most persons in supervisory positions some specific instrumental functions in addition to the exercise of authority, such as the factory foreman and the college-department chairman have.

2. Establish two equal salary scales, one for specialists and one for the hierarchy.

3. The division of labor in each organization should be re-examined to bring it into line with the needs of specialization. Wherever machine technology allows, the microdivision of labor should be ended.

4. All organizational processes and arrangements should have as a manifest purpose the furthering of cooperation (Thompson, 1961, pp. 195–97).

Bureaucracy and Innovation. It is Thompson's (1969) thesis that bureaucracies are under-innovative and that they need to perform a more entrepreneurial function for society than they do. He treats creativity and innovation as essentially the same and the rigidity of bureaucracy as a bar to either.

Thompson considered professionalism an alternative to bureaucracy, much the same as Blau did. Furthermore, he calls professional systems more innovative than bureaucratic systems. This is because they are "pluralistic and collegiate rather than monocratic and hierarchical." Professionalizing an organization decreases administration, top-down command, unquestioning obedience, constriction of communication, and interunit conflict. The associated shift to professional peer control should yield increased flexibility, variety, and receptivity to change, and thus innovation. Structurally there would be greater use of certain project forms.

Innovative, professional organizations would dispense with performance ratings by superiors and with most job descriptions. Thompson (1965) views the small technical organization headed by a creative entrepreneur and staffed with a small group of "able and personally loyal" peers as the prototype for innovation. To the extent this structure can be incorporated in or grafted onto them, large organizations might be expected to become more innovative.

Without Sympathy or Enthusiasm. In a small book aptly entitled by paraphrasing Weber's wording, Thompson (1975) takes up another potential dysfunction of bureaucracy—its lack of compassion for the individual. As Weber stated, bureaucracy by its very nature is impersonal—it lacks sympathy (affection) and enthusiasm, but also hatred and passion. It is not disposed to bend its rules positively in favor of individually perceived equity, but neither is it vindictive and personally punitive.

Thompson discusses a wide range of procedures intended to make bureaucratic systems more compassionate and more sensitive to the needs of individuals, including compassionate personnel administration, organization development, sensitivity training, small units, combined roles, "corrupt" political machines and prefectural administration, the ombudsman, and egalitarian ("new left") administration. In the end Thompson rejects all of these as mere gimmicks.

The ultimate solution is an evolution of organizational structures and individual personalities to the point where they are mutually adjusted. Individuals must grow to the point where they can delay gratification and recognize the social dysfunctions of personal favors. Organizations must adapt, with an assist from an advancing technology, to individual needs. As in other instances, Thompson is more persuasive and specific about techniques that will not work than in outlining solutions that will work. He makes the point that in today's world bureaucracy generates considerable resentment.

Bureaucracy and the Modern World. In his most recent book Thompson (1976) distinguishes more fully between natural (informal) and artificial (bureaucratic) systems. In particular he is concerned with the relations of each to innovation and change. Following Weber, Thompson develops the idea that artificial systems are tools to carry out the goals of their owners (the charismatic leader, the electorate, etc.). As tools, they are subject to evaluation and control in light of the goals. Artificial systems are monocratic in that only owner goals are relevant, not the goals of other possible claimants such as employees. Norms of rationality prevail.

Natural systems exist alongside the artificial and are an inevitable concomitant of bureaucracy. They are not tools of the owner, but spontaneously emergent entities serving only themselves. They are not rational systems, and their referent is internal—their members. Thus, a bureaucratic *organization* is pluralistic, even though the bureaucratic system per se is monocratic. The natural and artificial systems have inherent conflicting interests, though on occasion the natural system may complement the artificial in certain respects. Thus the natural system may provide needed redundancy and reliability, flexibility and innovation, and under certain circumstances additional rewards and motivation. At the same time it is primarily devoted to "survival-oriented adaptation to the artificial system," and norms of rationality are not relevant for it.

Thompson (1976) states in a number of places that the natural system, not the artificial, is the source of innovation, flexibility, and change in bureaucratic organizations:

> Innovative adaptations, if they occur, are largely products of natural system conditions (p. 19).
>
> The more organizations are rationalized, the more scientific management is applied to them, the "tauter the ship," and the more romanticism and falsified or erroneous calculations are needed, if there are to be any innovations at all (p. 90).
>
> Because the artificial system, or plan, of the organization can only provide extrinsic rewards, it cannot motivate to innovation. (In fact, innovations cannot even be legitimate,

because their actual relation to the owner's goal cannot be known in advance.) Innovation for the most part, therefore, must occur outside the formal artificial system (p. 95).

Yet the theoretical role of natural systems is muddied by statements such as the following:

An example of a natural system claim is the almost universal resistance to innovation found in bureaucracy. . . . A dynamic artificial system (for example one associated with a dynamic technology) will be associated with a dynamic natural system, and *vice versa*. Where technological change is minimal, as in education, natural systematic development is so strong as to render the organization unchangeable (Thompson, 1976, p. 24).

Given the above, it becomes difficult to identify the hypothesized source of innovation in bureaucratic organizations. Thompson does not draw upon the research in this area in developing his theory. He does, however, favor project teams and venture teams for this purpose.

Specifications in Terms of Types

Blau (1970) differentiates older bureaucracies that emphasize direct controls from more modern bureaucracies that focus on indirect controls. In Chapter 8 Perrow's typology was considered. A number of other theorists have proposed various types of bureaucracies, either lying within the Weber framework or extending beyond it to aspects of professional systems; the mechanistic-organic distinction of Burns and Stalker (Chapter 8) is a typical professional extension on bureaucratic theory. Though some of these typologies deal with organizational forms lying completely outside the bureaucratic model, a number restrict themselves explicitly or implicitly to an overall bureaucratic framework (Carper and Snizek, 1980). In these latter instances Weber's theory of a unitary bureaucratic type is clearly seen as inadequate.

One well-known example of a theory developed in opposition to Weber's concept of a single, pure type is that of the Aston researchers (Chapter 8). They developed a complex taxonomy for bureaucracies based on empirical analyses of data from the original study and on factor analysis (Pugh, 1976; Pugh and Hickson, 1976: Pugh, Hickson, and Hinings, 1969). The three dimensions defining the various bureaucratic forms are noted in Table 8–6. Briefly they are:

1. The structuring of activities—the degree to which the behavior of employees was overtly defined, incorporating the degree of role specialization in task allocation, the degree of

standardization of organizational routines, and the degree of formalization of written procedures.

2. The concentration of authority—the degree to which authority for decisions rested in controlling units outside the organization and was centralized at the higher hierarchical levels within it.

3. The line control of workflow—the degree to which control was exercised by line personnel as against its exercise through impersonal procedures (a smaller number of subordinates per supervisor, as against impersonal control of workflow through formalization of recording of role performance) (Pugh, Hickson, and Hinings, 1969, p. 116).

The ways in which these three dimensions interact to produce seven different forms are noted in Figure 13–1. Potentially there are twelve types, but empirically only seven cells are occupied by clusters of organizations. Elsewhere the implicitly structured organizations are labeled nonbureaucracies (Pugh and Hickson, 1976). Nonbureaucracies are typically rather small firms, whereas workflow

Figure 13–1
The Aston Taxonomy

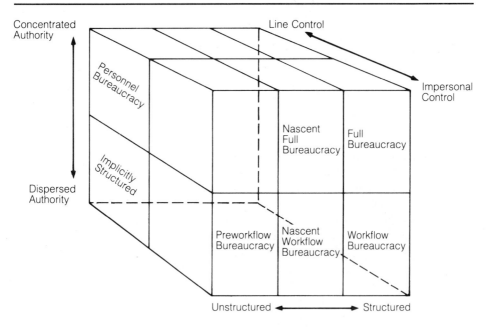

NOTE: Reprinted by permission of the publisher from Derek S. Pugh, David J. Hickson, and C. R. Hinings, "An Empirical Taxonomy of Structures of Work Organizations," *Administrative Science Quarterly*, 14 (1969), p. 123.

bureaucracies tend to be large. The classifications based on the line to impersonal control dimension are conceptually similar to those proposed by Blau. The authors recognize that the theory might be influenced by its empirical base; there was only one full bureaucracy, for instance, in the original sample.

Research on Bureaucratic Structure and Process

Research dealing with the hypotheses of bureaucratic theory was slow to develop, but abundant in the last two decades. The theory has played a central role in sociological thinking and has spawned a wide range of investigations.

Blau's Comparative Studies

Blau's (1955) early research focused on informal relationships within individual bureaucracies, such as consultations between federal enforcement agents on different problems, even when this practice was officially proscribed. However, his most important contributions to the theory of bureaucracy are comparative analyses across multiple organizations (Blau, 1974; Blau and Schoenherr, 1971; Blau, Falbe, McKinley, and Tracy, 1976). Blau assumed that bureaucratic characteristics are actually variables and that therefore real-world (as contrasted with ideal type) bureaucracies are bureaucratic to varying degrees.

Differentiation. Blau's theory of organizational differentiation evolved from a study of employment security units, so that study cannot be used to test the theory. However, subsequent research on samples drawn from government finance departments, department stores, universities and colleges, teaching hospitals (Blau, 1974), and manufacturing plants (Blau et al., 1976) consistently supports the theoretical hypotheses across all types of differentiation. The role of size in organizational structure appears to be important, and correlations with differentiation are substantial, rising as high as the .80s in certain instances.

Decentralization. Clearly, Weber viewed size as a major correlate of bureaucracy, though he did not rule out bureaucratization of small organizations. Weber's predominant position on centralization appears to be that it occurs in conjunction with bureaucracy; yet some of Weber's statements may be and have been interpreted differently on occasion (Child, 1972). This makes the relationship between centralization and other indexes of bureaucratization such as formalization and control particularly important. Blau and Schoenherr's (1971) research has addressed this issue.

Table 13–1

Correlations Between Various Indexes of Formalization or Control and Indexes of Centralization in State Employment Agencies

	Centralization			
Formalization or Control	Of Hiring Decisions	Of Budget Proposals	Of Organization Change Decisions	Of Other Decisions
Extent of personnel rules and regulations	−.18	(−.34)	−.10	−.19
Number of civil service appointments	−.02	.05	−.18	(−.33)
Extent of computerization	(−.34)	(−.29)	−.22	−.12
Degree of standardization of performance ratings	(.27)	.07	−.09	(−.28)
Proportion of managers	(.29)	.22	.07	(−.29)

( ) Correlations statistically significant.

SOURCE: Adapted from Peter M. Blau and Richard A. Schoenherr. *The Structure of Organizations*. New York: Basic Books, 1971, pp. 416–17.

The data from state employment agencies shown in Table 13–1 indicate a generally negative relationship in that increases in formalization are accompanied by *less* centralization. The only meaningful exceptions relate to hiring decisions in which there is a tendency for more standardized performance ratings and more managers (more control) to be associated with more centralization. Blau and Schoenherr (1971) conclude that top management needs to decentralize decisions as the organization grows and the levels of hierarchy increase, but that top management actually does this only when the risks of decentralization can be minimized. The indirect control made possible by standardized procedures, rules, computerized systems, and the like becomes a necessary condition for moving decisions downward. These results certainly go beyond Weber and seem to run counter to his hypothesis that rationalization and centralization increase in tandem.

The Aston Research and Subsequent Extensions

The original Aston research and numerous outgrowths of it have dealt with many variables considered by Blau. Moving through this labyrinth of research is confusing at times, but the results are extremely important to an informed evaluation of bureaucratic theory.

The British Research. Analysis of the original data on forty-six diverse organizations in the Birmingham area of England yields only limited support for the bureaucratic concept (Pugh and Hickson,

1976). Specialization, standardization, and formalization are highly correlated with each other, though the particular measure dealing with standardization of selection procedures, advancement, and the like does not always follow the expected pattern (see Table 13–2). However, centralization is, if anything, negatively related to the other criteria, again with the exception of the index of standardization of personnel procedures. Size of organization tends to reinforce these patterns. Larger size is associated with more specialization, standardization, and formalization, but less centralization. Much the same findings emerged from a subsequent study of comparable manufacturing firms in Great Britain and the United States (Inkson, Schwitter, Pheysey, and Hickson, 1970).

Findings from two other major British studies are summarized in Table 13–3. The variables considered are those hypothesized as characteristics of bureaucracy by Grinyer and Yasai-Ardekani (1980) in their study of forty-five companies located in southeast England. Data are also given in Table 13–3 for Child's (1972) national study of eighty-two manufacturing concerns (see Chapter 8). With the exception of the proportion of managers, the variables are all consistently intercorrelated, but in contrast to the data of Table 13–2, the overall centralization results are not only all negative, but also all statistically significant. Further breakdown of the centralization variable indicates that this departure from bureaucratic theory occurs

Table 13–2

Correlations Among Bureaucratic Criteria—The Aston Study

	Specialization		Standardization		Formalization	
	Functional	Overall	Personnel Procedures	Overall	Performance Recording	Overall
Specialization Functional Overall	(.87)					
Standardization Personnel procedures	−.15	.09				
Overall	(.76)	(.80)	.23			
Formalization Performance recording	(.66)	(.54)	−.12	(.72)		
Overall	(.57)	(.68)	(.38)	(.83)	(.75)	
Centralization	(−.64)	(−.53)	(.30)	−.27	−.27	−.20

( ) Correlations statistically significant.

SOURCE: Adapted from Derek S. Pugh and David J. Hickson. *Organizational Structure in Its Context: The Aston Programme I.* Lexington, Mass.: D. C. Heath, 1976, p. 57.

Table 13–3

Significant Correlations Among Bureaucratic Criteria—National and Southeast England Studies

	Functional Specialization	Formalization	Proportion of Managers	Levels of Hierarchy
Formalization				
National	.69			
Southeast	.70			
Proportion of managers				
National	—	—		
Southeast	.31	.28		
Levels of hierarchy				
National	.51	.48	—	
Southeast	.63	.56	—	
Centralization—overall				
National	−.28	−.53	—	−.41
Southeast	−.63	−.43	—	−.46
By decision type (all Southeast)				
Production	−.63	−.46	—	−.52
Marketing	−.30	—	—	—
Budget change	—	—	—	—
Personnel and buying	−.58	−.48	—	−.63
Organizational change	−.42	−.34	—	—

SOURCE: Adapted from John Child, "Organization Structure and Strategies of Control: A Replication of the Aston Study," *Administrative Science Quarterly*, 17 (1972), p. 169. Peter H. Grinyer and Masoud Yasai-Ardekani, "Dimensions of Organizational Structure: A Critical Replication," *Academy of Management Journal*, 23 (1980), pp. 412–13.

in production, personnel, buying, and organizing decisions. The departure from theory is much less for marketing and financial decisions, though these correlations are not significantly positive either.

In the national study the stability of the factor structure underlying the theory reflected in Figure 13–1 was analyzed. Primarily because of the centralization findings, the structure did not remain stable. The data bring the concentration of authority dimension into question and suggest that decentralization is a component of structuring. "The solution whereby structuring of activities and concentration of authority represent underlying dimensions of organization structure requires further empirical examination. . . . the taxonomy . . . should be utilized with caution" (Child, 1972, p. 174). Based on his analysis of the national study data, Mansfield (1973) goes so far as to suggest that the Weberian concept of a single bureaucratic type not be abandoned in favor of the empirical taxonomy.

Finally, the somewhat different results on centralization between the Aston and national studies—and now the Southeast England study—have been the subject of considerable discussion (Donaldson, Child, and Aldrich, 1975). Random fluctuations and differences in degree of organizational diversity likely have combined to produce the disparity.

The findings on size in the national study parallel those of the original Aston research (Child, 1973). Larger organizations are more bureaucratized in numerous respects and less centralized. These relationships tend toward curvilinearity with decelerating effects. In addition, size is positively related to various indexes of differentiation and complexity. Overall these data tend to support the formulations of Blau.

Less Comprehensive Studies. A further "replication" of the Aston research was carried out in twenty-three Canadian colleges. The findings on bureaucratic variables such as specialization, formalization, and standardization were much the same as before, with sizable positive intercorrelations (Holdaway, Newberry, Hickson, and Heron, 1975). However, now centralization is *positively* and often significantly related to these factors. Furthermore, the factor structure of the data once again failed to match with the Figure 13–1 pattern. These divergences appear to reflect the fact that the colleges contained major professional components and were small in size. They were not bureaucracies overall, but in large part professional systems. Thus, the Canadian research was not a true test of bureaucratic theory.

Perhaps the diversity of the Aston sample permitted a degree of nonbureaucratic contamination, thus influencing the centralization results. In any event the finding that variables do not relate in the same manner in professional and semiprofessional organizations as they do in bureaucracies appears characteristic (Hage and Aiken, 1967). Within bureaucracies, data reviewed previously and other findings (Meyer, 1968; Reimann and Negandhi, 1975) indicate that decentralization tends to occur in conjunction with bureaucratization; in professional systems this pattern does not emerge. Furthermore, in industrial bureaucracies larger size appears to foster this emphasis on decentralization and indirect control (Mahoney, Frost, Crandall, and Weitzel, 1972). Yet there are findings in manufacturing industry that establish decentralization as a separate factor from specialization and formalization, which in turn are separate from each other (Reimann, 1974). In this instance bureaucracy was not consonant with the interrelationships proposed by Weber, but neither was the resulting taxonomy the one the Aston researchers proposed (Pugh, Hickson, and Hinings, 1969). However, a small sample size (N = 19) in the Reimann (1974) study militates against significant relationships between variables and may have contributed to the results.

The Knowledge Factor

For Weber, knowledge was the key to power in bureaucracies and should be positively related to the other indexes. Those who question that conclusion have focused on professional knowledge, not the kind of knowledge that is indigenous to the organization itself. Within the professional domain, however, a good case can be made that knowledge does not follow the path Weber proposed. Not only are organizations in which professional components predominate structured differently than bureaucracies, but within bureaucracies themselves professionalization, like centralization, often does not exhibit the expected relationships.

The early research dealt only with certain forms of rationality and found them unrelated, or in a few instances negatively related, to other bureaucratic variables (Hall, 1963; Udy, 1959). This appears to be somewhat inconsistent with Weber's expectations, but is not directly focused on the professional knowledge issue. Rational approaches may well transcend the bureaucratic context and appear in other types of organizational systems as well.

An extensive review of the research by Hall (1977) emphasizes the incompatibility of bureaucratic and professional systems. There clearly are instances in which bureaucracy incorporates professional components effectively, but that does not mean that the two are part of the same process. Also educational attainment, especially when the bachelor's degree is the highest degree earned, is not an adequate surrogate for professionalism. The point that is being made is well illustrated in Table 13–4. Professionalism and the characteristics of bureaucracy are either unrelated, or perhaps negatively related, depending on how one interprets the data. In large accounting firms for instance bureaucracy and a professional orientation represent an antithesis (Sorensen and Sorensen, 1974). Oliver (1981) has shown that professional systems may be identified as separate entities, even though on occasion they may be incorporated within bureaucracies. These findings regarding professional knowledge do not support Weber, but they do not rule out the possibility that other kinds of knowledge may well follow the pattern Weber indicated—probably they do.

Personality Considerations

Thompson (1961) has discussed the problem of individual adaptation to bureaucracy. Stinchcombe (1974) and others going back to

Table 13–4

Correlations Between Indexes of Professionalism and Bureaucracy

Bureaucratic Criteria	Professional Indexes			
	Degree of Commitment to Professional Organizations	Belief in Service	Belief in Self-regulation	Sense of Professional Calling
Hierarchy of authority	−.03	−.26	−.15	−.15
Division of labor	−.24	−.26	−.23	−.12
Rules	−.14	−.12	−.11	.11
Procedures	(−.36)	−.21	−.10	.00
Impersonality	−.26	−.10	−.02	(−.34)

( ) Correlations statistically significant.
SOURCE: Adapted from Richard H. Hall, *Organizations: Structure and Process.* Englewood Cliffs, N.J. Prentice-Hall, Inc., 1977, p. 169.

Weber have maintained that an effective bureaucracy requires certain motivational patterns. The research data indicate that there are people who can and cannot adjust to bureaucratic systems in various roles. Furthermore, based on the personality data bureaucratic systems differ significantly from professional systems.

Baker, Etzioni, Hansen, and Sontag (1973) have developed a measure of worker tolerance for bureaucratic structure based on attitudes toward rules and regulations, attitudes toward the legitimacy of authority, attitudes toward performing limited and structured tasks, and the capacity to delay gratification. This measure differentiates among organizational contexts in a manner that appears to be positively related to their degree of bureaucratization. It also predicts turnover within bureaucracies and performance ratings.

Gordon (1970) developed a similar instrument that tapped willingness to comply with a superior's wishes, confidence in expert judgment, preference for impersonal relationships, a desire for the security provided by rules and standard procedures, and a desire for the security of organizational identification. Correlations with other measures suggest considerable construct validity. This measure also differentiates among contexts with varying degrees of bureaucratization and predicts turnover in bureaucracies.

A somewhat different approach developed by the author (Miner, 1965; 1977) focuses on the personality characteristics required of managers in bureaucratic systems. Included are measures of characteristics related to functioning within the hierarchy—positive attitudes upward, competitiveness horizontally with peers, and the exercise of power downward; characteristics related to size of organization—assertiveness, and desire to stand out from the group, or be visible; and characteristics related to carrying out the functions of management.

The findings given in Table 13–5, as well as a number of other research results, indicate that these personality characteristics are a source of behavior and decisions appropriate to the bureaucratic managerial context (Berman, 1979; Lardent, 1979; Miner, 1965; 1977). On the other hand these results do not mesh nearly as well with nonmanagerial work and nonbureaucratic systems. Apparently there are people who cannot adapt to and experience considerable anxiety in bureaucratic managerial roles. Furthermore, the kinds of characteristics that make for managerial effectiveness in bureaucracies are generally distinct from those making for professional effectiveness, at least among university professors (Miner, 1980), as indicated in the latter part of Table 13–5. Again, bureaucratic and professional systems appear to be separate, in contradistinction to Weber's hypothesis.

Normative Research

Weber considered monocratic bureaucracy superior to other organizational forms. To test this position would require comparisons pitting bureaucracy against various other types of organizations. In such studies the influence of factors other than the organizational system, such as resource inputs and environmental forces would have to be controlled. Thus, for example, the influences of human resource inputs such as intellectual abilities and appropriate personality characteristics (bureaucratic and professional motivation, for instance, each in its own context) would have to be removed. The difficulty of conducting such comparative research is obvious, and accordingly data of this kind are lacking. On the other hand there are studies in which variations along some dimension of bureaucracy are related to success. Research of this type does not really test Weber's superiority hypothesis, but it does provide insights into the effectiveness of bureaucracy in attaining desired goals.

Research Reviews. A review of research dealing with relationships between organization size, hierarchical levels, administrative proportion, specialization, formalization, and centralization and effectiveness yields consistently inconsistent results, as noted in Chapter 12 (Dalton, Todor, Spendolini, Fielding, and Porter, 1980). However, classical management theory aspires to address all forms of organization, and this review is similarly unrestricted. The review appears most applicable to the theory of Chapter 12. It is not clear what would have been the result if the review had been limited to bureaucratic forms. Furthermore, the review draws on certain measures not implied by bureaucratic theory. Overall the Dalton et al.

Table 13–5
Findings Involving Characteristics Required to Manage in Bureaucracies

Indexes of Bureaucratic Behavior, Choice, and Success	Bureaucratic Characteristics					
	Favorable Attitude toward Authority	Competitiveness	Power Motivation	Assertiveness	Desire to Stand Out	Desire to Carry Out Management Functions
	Means (on a scale from −5 to +5)					
Performance ratings of oil company managers						
Positive	(2.0	(1.9	(1.4	(1.2	1.2	.8
Negative	1.0)	1.1)	.4)	.2)	.8	.3
Level of department store managers						
Department managers	2.0	(−.2	(.8	.4	.8	(1.4
Selling supervisor	2.0	−.8)	−.2)	.2	.2	.7)
Student participants in a bureaucratic simulation						
Managers	0	(−.8	.6	−.3	.6	(.2
Nonmanagers	.1	−1.4)	.6	−.6	.3	−.6)
Company personnel managers						
Vice-presidents	(1.6	(.3	(1.1	(−.1	.9	.6
Below vice-president	.8)	−.6)	.6)	−.7)	1.0	.2
Career aspirations of MBA students						
Managerial	(1.5	(.5	(1.4	(1.1	(.8	(1.2
Nonmanagerial	.4)	−.8)	.4)	.1)	0)	.5)
Army officer candidate school students						
Graduated	1.5	(1.3	.2	(1.4	(1.8	1.4
Failed to graduate	1.2	.7)	.1	.9)	1.4)	1.3
Corporate managers						
Top executive officers	(1.9	(−.3	(1.3	−.1	(1.9	(1.0
Lower level/same age	.9)	−1.2)	.2)	−.2	.4)	0)
Professional Characteristics	Correlations					
Desire to acquire knowledge	.04	.02	.05	.06	0	.05
Preference for independent action	−.02	.14	.03	.04	.09	.01
Status motivation	−.05	.05	.14	(.27)	(.19)	(.20)
Desire to provide help to others	.04	0	(.22)	(.20)	(.21)	(.23)
Feeling of professional commitment	.07	−.05	.15	.15	.14	.10

( ) Mean differences and correlations statistically significant

SOURCES: Adapted from John B. Miner, *Studies in Management Education,* Atlanta, Ga.: Organizational Measurement Systems Press, 1965, pp. 70–71, 76; John B. Miner, *Motivation to Manage: A Ten Year Update on the "Studies in Management Education," Research,* Atlanta, Ga.: Organizational Measurement Systems Press, 1977, pp. 47, 75, 98; Charles L. Lardent, "An Assessment of the Motivation to Command Among U.S. Army Officer Candidates," Ph.D. dissertation, Georgia State University, 1979, p. 121; Fred Berman, "Managerial Role Motivation Among Top Executives," Ph.D. dissertation, Georgia State University, 1979, p. 52; John B. Miner, "The Role of Managerial and Professional Motivation in the Career Success of Management Professors," *Academy of Management Journal,* 23 (1980), p. 493.

(1980) analysis appears more applicable to classical than to bureaucratic theory.

Earlier, Price (1968) considered fifty studies, many of which represent expanded case reports. The findings most relevant to bureaucratic theory are as follows:

1. Organizations which have a high degree of division of labor are more likely to have a high degree of effectiveness than organizations which have a low division of labor (p. 16).

2. Organizations which have a high degree of legitimacy are more likely to have a degree of effectiveness than organizations which have a low degree of legitimacy (p. 49).

3. Organizations which have a rational-legal type of decision making are more likely to have a high degree of effectiveness than organizations which primarily have a charismatic type of decision making (p. 55).

4. Organizations (other than those which are diversified or professionalized) which have a high degree of centralization with respect to tactical decisions are more likely to have a high degree of effectiveness than organizations which have a low degree of centralization with respect to tactical decisions (p. 60). The same applies to all organizations having centralization of strategic decisions.

5. Organizations which have sanction systems with a high degree of grade (related to merit and careers) are more likely to have a high degree of effectiveness than organizations which have sanction systems with a low degree of grade (p. 152).

6. Organizations whose systems of communication are primarily personal (not related to records) are more likely to have a high degree of effectiveness than organizations whose systems of communications are primarily impersonal (p. 175).

All except number 6 above are consistent with bureaucratic theory. In number 4 the construct validity problems surrounding centralization become evident, with considerable confounding of centralization and formalization; in fact, Price's (1968) review appears to treat the two concepts as one.

Selected Studies. There are several publications not included in the preceding reviews that contain data bearing on the normative question. Paulson (1974) studied a large number of health-related organizations, many of which were clearly nonbureaucratic in nature. Though public agencies were analyzed separately from voluntary and professional organizations, it is still not clear that a purified bureaucratic sample was obtained. Nevertheless, high formalization and low centralization are most likely to relate to effectiveness, and structural factors in any event are generally rather weak predictors of organizational outcomes in this health-related context.

However, a study by Becker and Neuhauser (1975) of thirty community hospitals yields somewhat stronger conclusions. Standardization or formalization of procedures and a variable referred to as visibility of consequences, which appears to reflect organizational rationality, both showed substantial positive relationships to various effectiveness indexes in the administrative (bureaucratic) components of the hospitals. In the medical (professional) components, standarization related negatively to effectiveness, but the rationality variable remained positively correlated; once again the disparity between bureaucratic and professional systems is emphasized. In a subsequent study of insurance companies that focused only on the visibility of consequences concept, positive relationships with efficiency measures were obtained.

Reimann and Negandhi (1975) found in a study in India that formalized process (manufacturing) and particularly personnel controls, coupled with decentralization, promoted organizational effectiveness. The combination of high formalization in the form of controls and low centralization is associated with greater effectiveness than either alone (Negandhi, 1975). Also the existence of comprehensive formal planning systems suggestive of greater organizational rationality was related to success.

Greater bureaucratization appears to be associated with increased effectiveness, though there are practically no data on the causal relationships. Centralization typically operates in a manner the reverse of that specified by the theory, and impersonality requires further study. Evidence that bureaucracy is more effective than other methods of organizing human work or that charismatic leadership at the top of a bureaucratic organization creates an ideal structure is completely lacking.

Innovation and Bureaucracy

Contrary to Thompson's (1969) assumptions, bureaucracies can innovate under appropriate circumstances; in particular, they are effective in the implementation of change. A major factor involved is the existence of an innovative climate that expects creativity and originality and a system of supervision that emphasizes freedom of means coupled with accountability for results (Frederiksen, Jensen, and Beaton, 1972). Under such circumstances overall productivity in formalized bureaucratic contexts is the same as that in a more rules-oriented, standardized climate under detailed, close supervision. When climate and supervision are less congruent, productivity drops sharply, but the main pc 'nt is that there are circumstances in a formal bureaucracy under which innovation can be highly effective.

It all depends on how bureaucracy is utilized. The relationships involved are complex, but even the initiation phase of innovations, as distinguished from implementation, can be at a high level in bureaucracies under certain circumstances (Aiken, Bacharach, and French, 1980).

Innovation and change are not inevitable in bureaucracies; clearly circumstances must foster their development. Furthermore, organizational forms that incorporate sizable nonbureaucratic systems also can produce innovations (Daft and Becker, 1978). Innovation appears to vary across organizational types as a function of values and norms quite independent of structural characteristics. At least this hypothesis is as feasible as the expectation that bureaucracy will inevitably constrict innovation.

Dual Hierarchies. Thompson (1961) recommends dealing with problems created by the presence of professional specialists in bureaucracies by creating a dual hierarchy with separate salary scales for the specialists. A review by Schriesheim, Von Glinow, and Kerr (1977) raises serious questions about dual hierarchies. Most applications have been within the research and development context. In practice many anticipated advantages do not materialize. The professionals may experience a lack of power, they may view their position as indicative of failure, there may be a lack of equity with the managerial hierarchy, professional hierarchy positions may be too few in number, and evaluative criteria may be inequitable.

One alternative is a triple hierarchy incorporating liaison personnel with circumscribed areas of authority closely related to professional matters. Another approach is the separation of professional and hierarchical systems, as found in many universities where the spheres of influence of faculty and central administration are clearly differentiated. In any event Thompson's dual hierarchy concept is very difficult to operationalize effectively in primarily bureaucratic organizations.

Venture Teams. Thompson (1976) also advocates the incorporation of an entrepreneurial system within the broad confines of bureaucracy. Such venture efforts have been the subject of some research on his part (Hlavacek and Thompson, 1973; 1975; 1978). The objective is to graft innovation onto a bureaucratic structure that is assumed to be noninnovative by its very nature.

Evidence presented in Table 13–6 indicates that venture teams can be less bureaucratized than personnel carrying out similar efforts totally within the firm, as is the case with product management (Hlavacek and Thompson, 1973). Yet venture teams, like dual hierarchies, are hard to implement well. They typically exist in a

Table 13-6

Comparison of Staff Product Managers and Venture Team Managers in the Same Company on Indexes of Bureaucracy

Indexes of Bureaucracy	Staff Product Managers	Venture Team Managers
	Mean Scores (Larger values indicate a lesser degree of bureaucracy)	
Division of labor	4.1	4.2
Hierarchy of authority	(3.3	4.2)
Procedural specifications	(3.4	4.6)
Rules	(3.1	4.4)
Impersonality	3.8	3.7

( ) Difference statistically significant.

SOURCE: Adapted from James D. Hlavacek and Victor A. Thompson, "Bureaucracy and New Product Innovation," *Academy of Management Journal,* 16 (1973), p. 370.

highly unstable state and end in termination by the parent company (Steiner and Miner, 1982). There are major problems at the interface between the entrepreneurial and bureaucratic systems and conflict between the two is frequent. Knowledge of how to manage this boundary effectively is practically nonexistent.

An analysis of twenty-one venture efforts that did not survive into profitability yielded the following conclusions:

Venture teams do not easily fit into going concerns. They frequently fail, for multiple reasons, including:
(a) increased costs, uncertainty, or underfinancing;
(b) failure to win acceptance within the firm;
(c) insufficient operating freedom for the venture team;
(d) internal power struggles;
(e) a short-term top management perspective;
(f) technically rather than commercially oriented venture managers;
(g) lack of financial or organizational resources for commercial success; and
(h) the established divisions' neglect or resistance to them (Hlavacek and Thompson, 1978, p. 248).

Given current evidence that innovation within bureaucracies is possible, such hybrid forms may not be necessary.

Problems of Measurement

Measures of both technological and structural variables appear to suffer from low levels of construct validity; variables that seem conceptually similar do not relate to each other empirically in the manner expected (Pennings, 1973; Sathe, 1978; Ford, 1979). Low scale reliability cannot account for these results.

Of the three studies noted, the one carried out by Pennings (1973) seems least suited to the present purposes. The sample size is small, and variables, particularly those intended to measure centralization, often are not classified in a manner consistent with that of other investigators or with the criteria of bureaucratic theory (Walton, 1981). The Sathe (1978) research utilized twenty-two departments within a single insurance company, many of which were quite small. Generalization of the results to total organizations of varied types can be questioned, and Ford (1979) provides data suggesting the Sathe findings may be specific to the industry involved. Ford (1979) also used a departmental level of analysis, but drew upon eight different organizations. Again, the units tend to be small and the bureaucratic and professional systems somewhat confounded. Overall, however, the Ford study is the best test of construct validity available to date. Findings are given in Table 13–7.

Of the thirteen correlations, four are significant in the expected direction and one is significant in the reverse direction. Though findings such as these are typically interpreted as reflecting divergence between institutional measures such as those used in the Aston studies and questionnaire data, in the one instance in which two questionnaire measures of the same type of construct were obtained the two were completely unrelated. Overall, adequate construct validity for measures has not been demonstrated, but there are numerous deficiencies in the research undertaken for this purpose (Walton, 1981). Accordingly, one can only look for consistent patterns in the research, with full knowledge that underlying patterns may be masked by problems of conceptualization and measurement. Given the great diversity of measures used in different studies, consistent patterns of results are unlikely to emerge as a consequence of the repetition of errors that are inherent in the measurement process itself.

Conclusions

While bureaucratic theory has been the subject of much discussion, criticism, and debate, relatively little attention has been given to relevant research on the theory. Writer after writer has attacked or defended Weber's theory, and the theories of those who have followed him, without giving any attention to the very sizable body of research evidence that has accumulated. Consonant with the treatments of other theories in previous chapters, the present critique does hold closely to the evidence.

Table 13–7

Correlations Among Various Measures Considered to Reflect Formalization, Specialization, and Centralization

Formalization	Aston Index of Written Documentation		
Questionnaire data on rules and procedures	(.32)		

Specialization	Degree of Functional Specialization	Number of Functions Performed	Number of Job Titles
Questionnaire data on division of labor	.11	−.13	−.01
Degree of functional specialization		(.45)	.19
Number of functions performed			(.29)

Centralization	Degree of Hierarchical Control	Number of Hierarchical Levels	Questionnaire Data on Centralization
Questionnaire data on participation	.00	(−.38)	−.03
Degree of hierarchical control		.23	−.16
Number of hierarchical levels			(−.35)

( ) Correlation statistically significant.

SOURCE: Adapted from Jeffrey D. Ford, "Institutional Versus Questionnaire Measures of Organizational Structure: A Reexamination," *Academy of Management Journal,* 22 (1979), p. 605.

Scientific Goals

Weber's Theory. One reason for the extensive discussion of Weber's ideas is the uncertainty as to what he said. Numerous interpretive essays have quoted various statements to one effect or another. These differences are based only in part on difficulties of translation. Weber often returned to the same subjects, approaching them from different angles and providing fuel for numerous interpretive debates. Thus, Weber's statements are conflicting and ambiguous on the role of collegiality vis à vis bureaucracy; the extent to which bureaucracy may be defined as a self-contained and self-perpetuating entity as opposed to a tool of the user; the relationship of centralization to bureaucracy; the power of bureaucracy; the degree of voluntary versus imperative control inherent in rational-legal authority; and the distinction between the concept of organization as a whole and its bureaucratic subtype. Weber strove for clarity of definition but conveyed a message of considerable fuzziness on certain issues (Abrahamsson, 1977). Scientifically, the theory is logically inconsistent to a degree.

Weber was not totally unaware of the dysfunctions and unanticipated consequences of bureaucracy. Such matters were considered, though they were not his major concern. Thus, the existence and activities of the informal organization (the natural system, to use Thompson's term) represent departures from the ideal type. That Weber did not deal with such matters at length reflects the nature of his domain choice. He wanted to establish how and why bureaucracy works under ideal conditions. This in itself is a massive undertaking, and one cannot legitimately find fault with Weber for not extending his theory with the same detail into new domains. Yet, others have done so, and the theoretical contributions of such individuals as Blau and Thompson, Selznick, Gouldner, and Merton are significant.

Much the same argument applies to the contention that Weber failed to consider organization-environment interactions and produced an overly limited, closed-system theory. As Aldrich and Pfeffer (1976) point out, Weber's historical and comparative analyses dealt at length with the impact of social structure on bureaucracy. And McNeil (1978) has drawn upon Weber's views as a frame of reference for describing how organizations gain power over their environments. Certainly, Weber's formulations regarding external forces are incomplete, relative to his theory of internal factors. Nevertheless, significant theory construction almost inevitably requires focusing on some one domain at the expense of others.

Research on the theory, to the extent it has been conducted with appropriate samples and measures, has in general supported the descriptive theory, though more as a composite of variables than as a single type. Formalization, standardization, and specialization do tend to be highly correlated, and thus to vary together, as the theory would predict.

A considerable body of research relates large size in both composite units and total organizations to the bureaucratic nexus. There are studies that find only a weak relationship here, and there is reason to question whether size is necessarily a cause of the structure (Hall, 1977), but size typically has something to do with bureaucracy. Though small bureaucracies are possible, small organizations are more likely to take some other form. Furthermore, bureaucratization seems unlikely to continue unabated beyond some level of growth. Indeed, the findings of Blau and others suggest a degree of curvilinearity. Nevertheless, bureaucracy appears to be the preferred method of structuring large organizations of any type; in a very real sense it is the *only* method currently in widespread use in the Western world. Thus, the overall data support Weber on this point, though it is possible to sample the total size distribution in such a way as to obtain negligible linear correlations.

The centralization-decentralization variable and results related to it have been the subject of major controversy. Some view Weber's bureaucracy as incorporating centralization, while others think just the opposite. There is considerable confusion regarding how centralization should be operationalized and what the limits of the construct are. This is only part but a very important part, of the construct validity problem that plagues the theory as a whole.

For present purposes it seems appropriate to view formalization and standardization as methods of indirect control that are separate and distinct from centralization of decision making. Though strategic decisions with regard to financial resources and product market position may not follow the same pattern, movement to greater bureaucratization and growth can, and frequently do, call forth greater decentralization of other types of decisions. This has not been a universal finding, but it has been a frequent finding in studies limited to bureaucratic organizations of some size and a relatively narrow definition of the centralization-decentralization variable. Such a conceptualization is supported by strategy and structure theory (Chapter 10). Clearly, inverse relationships between bureaucratization and centralization occur frequently enough to consider Weber's theory inadequate in this area.

With regard to the role of rationality and knowledge in bureaucracy Weber appears to have been both right and wrong. Knowledge related to strategic decision making and policy implementation for the specific organization does concentrate at the top of the hierarchy and greater rationality tends to accrue with it (Steiner and Miner, 1982). However, knowledge that is less organization-specific does not relate to the bureaucratic hierarchy in the manner Weber proposed. This latter, professional knowledge is a source of power, and in a general sense Weber was correct in equating authority and knowledge. But he did not differentiate rational-legal authority from the value-rational type that underlies professional systems (Satow, 1975). Not only does Weber's theory fail to comprehend professional organizations, which appear to fall outside its domain, but it also fails to deal with professional systems, knowledge, and authority lying predominantly within bureaucratic organizations. To this latter extent it is deficient within its own domain. Such professional components within bureaucratic organizations do not appear to be mere deviant cases, but rather separate, distinct systems with their own characteristics and sources of authority.

We know little about Weber's normative theory of bureaucratic superiority. Whether a bureaucratic system at its best is superior to a professional system at its best, for instance, is a completely unanswered question. Furthermore, the significance and role of charismatic leaders at the top of bureaucratic organizations remains highly uncertain. On the other hand there is evidence that increases in various bureaucratic characteristics, as organizations approach the ideal type, are associated with more positive organizational outcomes. What causes what has not been definitely established, but there is no reason to doubt that, within bureaucratic systems, increasing bureaucratization yields the results Weber anticipated. This may not be true for all components of bureaucracy, but it does appear to hold for a basic core.

Finally, there are the bureaucratic subtypes. In this area it is important to distinguish between taxonomies of forms within the overall bureaucratic concept and taxonomies that extend beyond bureaucracy. The Aston formulations lack theoretical precision in this regard. Furthermore, like so many theories based on factor analysis, they do not hold up in subsequent investigations. Accepting the Aston theory as an alternative to Weberian bureaucracy does not seem warranted. On the other hand, nothing in what Weber said would preclude the existence of subtypes within the ideal concept of bureaucracy; he simply did not deal with this issue. Typologies other than the Aston ones remain essentially untested. If any of these should prove valid, the result would seem to be an extension rather than a repudiation of bureaucratic theory. The issue of alternative organizational forms beyond bureaucracy will be discussed in a later section.

Blau's Theory. As noted in the preceding discussion, Blau's views of professional knowledge and decentralization have received considerable support. There is also reason, based on the research, to favor his concept of bureaucratic theory as a set of interrelated hypotheses over the ideal type construction proposed by Weber. Blau raises certain questions regarding Weber's handling of democratic or collegial systems as opposed to bureaucracy. Such systems, like the professional, appear to be different and the sociotechnical research considered in Chapter 4, as well as other findings, indicate that they are.

Rather surprisingly, Blau's theory of differentiation has come under the greatest attack, perhaps because being precisely stated it is easily analyzed and tested empirically. Yet, except in the case of some research carried out by Hall (1977), which only partially supports the Blau findings, the attacks have not been empirically based. In general they have ignored the various studies conducted by Blau and his associates since the original employment security agency work. Furthermore, the Hall (1977) research preceded the formal statement of Blau's theory and thus was not undertaken as a direct test of it.

Argyris's (1972) criticisms follow generally his theoretical position as considered in Chapter 5. He emphasizes Blau's failure to consider the informal organization and certain potential problems of operationalization and construct validity inherent in his measures. These considerations do not invalidate Blau's theory so much as they raise questions for future research. To some extent Blau has answered Argyris's arguments with his research outside the civil service context. On one point, however, this is clearly not the case. Blau's theory of differentiation specifies causal influences from size to the structural variables. However, the tests of the theory are cross-sectional, rather than longitudinal, and thus do not bear directly on the causal hypotheses. Clearly, additional research is needed that considers what organizations do as they increase in size and what temporal relationships are involved. Path-analytic techniques, which have been applied to this problem, are probably not adequate to the task of describing the consequences of changes in size over time.

Turner (1977) takes Blau to task on philosophical grounds, questioning the role of explanation and Blau's claim to deductive rigor. This critique is aimed as much at all the theoretical approaches of modern sociology as at Blau's theory specifically. It fails to deal with the argument that, irrespective of its construction or its level of explanation, a theory that generates empirical support and deals with important questions may be valuable as a source of understanding, prediction, and/or control.

Victor Thompson's Theory. Thompson's views on creativity and innovation in bureaucracy have not always been stated in a consistent manner and lack empirical support, but they were for some time accepted uncritically, as were similar views of other theorists (see Chapter 5). Now it seems other types of organizations that Thompson usually considered to be more capable of innovation—professional and entrepreneurial organizations—can be just as devoid of innovation as bureaucracies, and just as prone to it also. Nevertheless, Thompson's theory does distinguish between bureaucratic systems and both professional and entrepreneurial systems.

Thompson has also identified the problems of adjusting to bureaucracy and the insecurities inherent in bureaucratic management. These appear to be real problems, and the research supports their existence. In fact, this type of reaction to bureaucracy has increased among college students over the period since the mid-1960s (Miner, 1977). Bureaucracies not only can produce anxiety and insecurity in their members, but they also can arouse a great deal of resentment and anger in certain individuals.

That these personality phenomena may amount to a sickness or emotional pathology, as Thompson indicates, is supported by the findings of Table 13–8. The theory states that many such individuals

Table 13–8

Proportion of Emotionally Disturbed Individuals (Discharged from the Armed Forces as Neurotic or Psychotic) Last Working at Upper and Lower Occupational Levels

	Upper-Level Employment, Including Managerial and Professional	Lower-Level Employment, Including Semiskilled and Unskilled
Employed population as a whole	44%	56%
Discharged as neurotic	24	76
Discharged as psychotic	21	79

Source: Adapted from John B. Miner and James K. Anderson, "The Postwar Occupational Adjustment of Emotionally Disturbed Soldiers," *Journal of Applied Psychology*, 42 (1958), p. 320.

cannot adjust to positions in the bureaucratic hierarchy and thus are restricted to lower-level bureaucratic employment or employment outside of bureaucracies. Most of the neurotics and psychotics considered in Table 13–8 became emotionally ill while serving in a military bureaucracy. As a group, they did not achieve nearly the same levels of employment as would have been anticipated from population data over the ten years subsequent to discharge (Miner and Anderson, 1958). Though this downward shift in employment level cannot be attributed entirely to failures of bureaucratic adjustment, a sizable proportion of the differential probably was caused by such factors (Kornhauser, 1965). These data provide a strong argument for a differentiated organizational context in which varied organizational systems are available to match the personality needs of a wide range of individuals.

Bureaucratic and Nonbureaucratic Systems. Blau and Thompson have argued for the existence of nonbureaucratic systems, variously described as professional, collegial or democratic, and entrepreneurial. Weber, on the other hand, contrasts bureaucracy with patrimonial organizations, of which feudalism is a subtype, and with charismatic communities. Insofar as the Western world is concerned Weber's alternatives are primarily of historical interest, though instances of each appear in the news on occasion.

The professional, group (collegial), and task (entrepreneurial) alternatives are widespread in current society and have been established in the research as separate and distinct entities. Their differentiating characteristics are shown in Table 13–9. Clearly, distinct organizational systems other than those envisaged by Weber exist (Oliver, 1980; 1981). Thus, Weber's theory appears to be culturally and temporally bounded. The statements of Table 13–9 are those that clearly distinguish inhabitants of the various organizational systems one from another.

Table 13–9
Empirically Established Characteristics of Bureaucratic, Professional, Task, and Group Systems

Differentiating Characteristics of Bureaucratic or Hierarchical Systems
Work rules and regulations established by management
Job results evaluated by superiors
Organizational changes carried out by management
Individual competence judged by management
Pay levels based on seniority or hierarchical position
Freedom of action limited by organizational guidelines
Organizational leaders appointed by management
Punishments established by management
Screening and selecting new employees accomplished by a personnel unit
Counseling of problem employees carried out by superiors
Replacement of absent employees accomplished by superiors
Job changes initiated by management
Risk of failure assumed by top-level managers
Resources for work accomplishment allocated by management
Meetings called and conducted by management

Differentiating Characteristics of Professional Systems
A large number of jobs classified as professions
Work satisfaction based on enjoyment of one's profession
Learning of a job based essentially on professional training
On-the-job training intended primarily for professional development
Long hours due to professional commitment
Important day-to-day communication, always with fellow professionals and clients
Individual efforts devoted to professional goals
The benefits of work go to clients or colleagues
Relationships with clients based on professional knowledge and trust
Career development oriented toward professional development
Primary loyalty to the profession
Leaders selected on the basis of professional competence
The job is central to one's life and part of one's individual identity
Professional knowledge more important than any other type
Status based on professional and occupational competence

Differentiating Characteristics of Task or Entrepreneurial Systems
Work rules and regulations established by oneself to ensure goal accomplishment
Rewards accrue consequent to effective task accomplishment
Responsibility for daily work loads belongs to the individual
Job results evaluated by the individual
Competence judged by the individual
Long hours accepted to gain personal rewards and achievement
Day-to-day work decisions determined by personal job goals

Table 13–9 (Continued)

Job changes made by the individual without permission from anyone
Personal drive is the most valued characteristic of workers
Risk taking considered necessary for personal achievement
Pay based on successful task completion
Daily work judgments determined largely by personal goals
Personal drive directed to achievement of personal goals
Punishments directly related to failure to achieve personal goals
Advancement based on goal accomplishment

Differentiating Characteristics of Group or Collegial or Democratic Systems

Job learning a consequence of group efforts to share skills and knowledge
Responsibility for daily workloads shared by group members
Individual job results evaluated by the work group
Competence judged by the work group
Important day-to-day communications are with work group members
Job rotation within the group encouraged
New worker selection based on work group evaluations
Individual daily work problems a responsibility of the work group
Sacrifices made for the good of the work group
Incompetence judged by the work group
Screening and selection of new employees a responsibility of the work group
Conflicts within the group resolved by discussion and compromise
Counseling of problem employees a responsibility of the work group
Replacement of absent employees is accomplished by the work group
Housekeeping duties performed by all work group members

Source: Based on two contributions by John E. Oliver, "The Development of an Instrument for Describing Organizational Energy Domains," Ph.D. dissertation, Georgia State University, 1980. *Scoring Guide for the Oliver Organization Description Questionnaire.* Atlanta, Ga.: Organizational Measurement Systems Press, 1981.

Goals of Application

Applications of bureaucratic theory are difficult to discuss, given their widespread nature, though perhaps it is best to consider the current scene more a demonstration of this particular organizational phenomenon than an outgrowth of the theory itself. Probably our organizational world would be much the same had Weber never written, but we would understand it much less well.

Perhaps the major strength of bureaucracy is its capacity to structure large systems. Through Weber's law of the small number, coupled with hierarchy, it is possible for what would otherwise be small group processes to be expanded throughout huge organizations. The individual units and subunits serve partial goals that become their own total goals, but the composite result is an effective organization. The processes involved are not unlike those of regulated capitalism. Each component seeks its own ends, but the overall result redounds to the benefit of the whole.

Given our current knowledge, bureaucracy becomes the structure of choice for large organizations, and the greater the rationality, formalization, standardization, specialization, and decentralization, the more effective it will be. This does not mean there will not be negative side effects for individuals, but these can combine to subvert the structure only where the bureaucratic system was improperly designed and operated in the first place.

The choice of bureaucracy is made easy for large systems because few alternatives are available. One could draw on patrimonial and charismatic forms, but they seem ill adapted to the needs of the modern world, as Weber so effectively argued. The nonbureaucratic forms that do appear appropriate to current needs—professional, task, and group systems—are primarily suited to small organizations. With the exception of representative democracy for group systems, we have not devised methods of applying these systems to large numbers of people. Typically, as organizations grow, bureaucracy is superimposed on the existing system to deal with the expanded size. In such cases, the original professional, task, or group system that is not sufficiently robust can easily disappear under the onslaught of the new bureaucracy.

If organizations are to grow and achieve economies of scale and speed, some degree of bureaucratization appears inevitable, at least until other methods of handling large organizations can be created.

With the exception of bureaucracy itself, most bureaucracy theorists have not spawned or endorsed other organizational forms. The major exception is Victor Thompson. However, Thompson has uncovered more potential problems of bureaucracies than he has solved. No doubt dual hierarchies for professionals in bureaucratic organizations and venture teams for entrepreneurs can be made to work, but before this can happen the integrity of the nonbureaucratic system must be protected. Experience indicates that this does not happen spontaneously. A nonbureaucratic system is more likely to survive when it is the basis for organization to begin with than when it is added as an appendage to an existing bureaucracy. Clearly, there are major challenges to both practice and research inherent in combining multiple systems in a single organization.

References

Abrahamsson, Bengt. *Bureaucracy or Participation: The Logic of Organization.* Beverly Hills, Calif.: Sage, 1977.

Aiken, Michael, Samuel B. Bacharach, and J. Lawrence French. "Organizational Structure, Work Process, and Proposal Making in Administrative Bureaucracies," *Academy of Management Journal,* 23 (1980), 631–52.

Aldrich, Howard E., and Jeffrey Pfeffer. "Environments of Organizations," *Annual Review of Sociology,* 2 (1976), 79–105.

Argyris, Chris. *The Applicability of Organizational Sociology*. Cambridge, England: Cambridge University Press, 1972.

Baker, Sally H., Amitai Etzioni, Richard A. Hansen, and Marvin Sontag. "Tolerance for Bureaucratic Structure: Theory and Measurement," *Human Relations*, 26 (1973), 775–86.

Becker, Selwyn W., and Duncan Neuhauser. *The Efficient Organization*. New York: Elsevier, 1975.

Berman, Fred. "Managerial Role Motivation Among Top Executives," Ph.D. dissertation, Georgia State University, 1979.

Blau, Peter M. *The Dynamics of Bureaucracy: A Study of Interpersonal Relations in Two Government Agencies*. Chicago: University of Chicago Press, 1955.

———. "Decentralization in Bureaucracies." In Mayer N. Zald (ed.), *Power in Organizations*. Nashville, Tenn.: Vanderbilt University Press, 1970, pp. 150–74.

———. *On the Nature of Organizations*. New York: Wiley, 1974.

Blau, Peter M., Cecilia M. Falbe, William McKinley, and Phelps K. Tracy. "Technology and Organization in Manufacturing," *Administrative Science Quarterly*, 21 (1976), 20–40.

Blau, Peter M., and Richard A. Schoenherr. *The Structure of Organizations*. New York: Basic Books, 1971.

Carper, William B., and William E. Snizek. "The Nature and Types of Organizational Taxonomies: An Overview," *Academy of Management Review*, 5 (1980), 65–75.

Child, John. "Organization Structures and Strategies of Control: A Replication of the Aston Study," *Administrative Science Quarterly*, 17 (1972), 163–77.

———. "Predicting and Understanding Organization Structure," *Administrative Science Quarterly*, 18 (1973), 168–85.

Daft, Richard L., and Selwyn W. Becker. *Innovation in Organizations*. New York: Elsevier, 1978.

Dalton, Dan R., William D. Todor, Michael J. Spendolini, Gordon J. Fielding, and Lyman W. Porter. "Organization Structure and Performance: A Critical Review," *Academy of Management Review*, 5 (1980), 49–64.

Donaldson, Lex, John Child, and Howard Aldrich. "The Aston Findings on Centralization: Further Discussion," *Administrative Science Quarterly*, 20 (1975) 453–60.

Ford, Jeffrey D. "Institutional Versus Questionnaire Measures of Organizational Structure: A Reexamination," *Academy of Management Journal*, 22 (1979), 601–10.

Frederiksen, Norman, Ollie Jensen, and Albert E. Beaton. *Prediction of Organizational Behavior*. New York: Pergamon, 1972.

Gordon, Leonard V. "Measurement of Bureaucratic Orientation," *Personnel Psychology*, 23 (1970), 1–11.

Gouldner, Alvin. *Patterns of Industrial Bureaucracy*. New York: Free Press, 1954.

Grinyer, Peter H., and Masoud Yasai-Ardekani. "Dimensions of Organizational Structure: A Critical Replication," *Academy of Management Journal*, 23 (1980), 405–21.

Hage, Jerald, and Michael Aiken. "Relationship of Centralization to Other Structural Properties," *Administrative Science Quarterly*, 12 (1967), 72–92.

Hall, Richard H. "The Concept of Bureaucracy: An Empirical Assessment," *American Journal of Sociology*, 69 (1963), 32–40.

———. *Organizations: Structure and Process*. Englewood Cliffs, N.J.: Prentice-Hall, 1977.

Hlavacek, James D., and Victor A. Thompson. "Bureaucracy and New Product Innovation," *Academy of Management Journal*, 16 (1973), 361–72.

———. "The Joint Venture Approach to Technology Utilization," *IEEE Transactions on Engineering Management*, 23, no. 1 (1975), 35–41.

———. "Bureaucracy and Venture Failures," *Academy of Management Review*, 3 (1978), 242–48.

Holdaway, Edward A., John F. Newberry, David J. Hickson, and R. Peter Heron. "Dimensions of Organizations in Complex Societies: The Educational Sector," *Administrative Science Quarterly*, 20 (1975), 37–58.

Inkson, J. H. K., J. P. Schwitter, D. C. Pheysey, and D. J. Hickson. "A Comparison of Organization Structure and Managerial Roles: Ohio, U.S.A., and the Midlands, England," *Journal of Management Studies*, 7 (1970), 347–63.

Kornhauser, Arthur. *Mental Health of the Industrial Worker: A Detroit Study*. New York: Wiley, 1965.

Lardent, Charles L. "An Assessment of the Motivation to Command Among U.S. Army Officer Candidates," Ph.D. dissertation, Georgia State University, 1979.

McNeil, Kenneth. "Understanding Organizational Power: Building on the Weberian Legacy," *Administrative Science Quarterly*, 23 (1978), 65–90.

Mahoney, Thomas A., Peter Frost, Norman F. Crandall, and William Weitzel. "The Conditioning Influence of Organizational Size Upon Managerial Practice," *Organizational Behavior and Human Performance*, 8 (1972), 230–41.

Mansfield, Roger. "Bureaucracy and Centralization: An Examination of Organizational Structure," *Administrative Science Quarterly*, 18 (1973), 477–88.

March, James G., and Herbert A. Simon. *Organizations*. New York: Wiley, 1958.

Merton, Robert K. "Bureaucratic Structure and Personality," *Social Forces*, 18 (1940), 560–68.

Meyer, Marshall W. "The Two Authority Structures of Bureaucratic Organizations," *Administrative Science Quarterly*, 13 (1968), 211–28.

Miner, John B. *Studies in Management Education*. Atlanta, Ga.: Organizational Measurement Systems Press, 1965.

———. *Motivation to Manage: A Ten Year Update on the "Studies in Management Education" Research*. Atlanta, Ga.: Organizational Measurement Systems Press, 1977.

———. "The Role of Managerial and Professional Motivation in the Career Success of Management Professors," *Academy of Management Journal*, 23 (1980), 487–508.

Miner, John B., and James K. Anderson. "The Postwar Occupational Adjustment of Emotionally Disturbed Soldiers," *Journal of Applied Psychology*, 42 (1958), 317–22.

Negandhi, Anant R. *Organization Theory in an Open System*. New York: Dunellen, 1975.

Oliver, John E. "The Development of an Instrument for Describing Organizational Energy Domains," Ph.D. dissertation, Georgia State University, 1980.

———. *Scoring Guide for the Oliver Organization Description Questionnaire*. Atlanta, Ga.: Organizational Measurement Systems Press, 1981.

Paulson, Steven K. "Causal Analysis of Interorganizational Relations. An Axiomatic Theory Revised," *Administrative Science Quarterly*, 19 (1974), 319–37.

Pennings, Johannes. "Measures of Organizational Structure: A Methodological Note," *American Journal of Sociology*, 79 (1973), 686–704.

Price, James L. *Organizational Effectiveness: An Inventory of Propositions*. Homewood, Ill.: Irwin, 1968.

Pugh, Derek S. "The Aston Approach to the Study of Organizations." In Geert Hofstede and M. Sami Kassem (eds.), *European Contributions to Organization Theory*. Amsterdam, the Netherlands: Van Gorcum, 1976, pp. 62–78.

Pugh, Derek S., and David J. Hickson. *Organizational Structure in Its Context: The Aston Programme I*. Lexington, Mass.: D. C. Heath, 1976.

Pugh, Derek S., David J. Hickson, and C. R. Hinings. "An Empirical Taxonomy of Structures of Work Organizations," *Administrative Science Quarterly*, 14 (1969), 115–26.

Reimann, Bernard C. "Dimensions of Structure in Effective Organizations: Some Empirical Evidence," *Academy of Management Journal*, 17 (1974), 693–708.

Reimann, Bernard C., and Anant R. Negandhi. "Strategies of Administrative Control and Organizational Effectiveness," *Human Relations,* 28 (1975), 475–86.

Sathe, Vijay. "Institutional Versus Questionnaire Measures of Organizational Structure," *Academy of Management Journal,* 21 (1978), 227–38.

Satow, Roberta L. "Value-Rational Authority and Professional Organizations: Weber's Missing Type," *Administrative Science Quarterly,* 20 (1975), 526–31.

Schriesheim, Janet, Mary Ann Von Glinow, and Steven Kerr. "Professionals in Bureaucracies: A Structural Alternative." In Paul C. Nystrom and William H. Starbuck (eds.), *Prescriptive Models of Organizations.* Amsterdam, the Netherlands: North-Holland, 1977, pp. 55–69.

Selznick, Philip. *TVA and the Grass Roots.* Berkeley, Calif.: University of California Press, 1949.

Simon, Herbert A., Donald W. Smithburg, and Victor A. Thompson. *Public Administration.* New York: Knopf, 1950.

Sorensen, James E., and Thomas L. Sorensen. "The Conflict of Professionals in Bureaucratic Organizations," *Administrative Science Quarterly,* 19 (1974), 98–106.

Steiner, George A., and John B. Miner. *Management Policy and Strategy.* New York: Macmillan, 1982.

Stinchcombe, Arthur L. *Creating Efficient Industrial Administrations.* New York: Academic Press, 1974.

Thompson, Victor A. *Modern Organization.* New York: Knopf, 1961.

———. "Bureaucracy and Innovation," *Administrative Science Quarterly,* 10 (1965), 1–20.

———. *Bureaucracy and Innovation.* University, Ala.: University of Alabama Press, 1969.

———. *Without Sympathy or Enthusiasm: The Problem of Administrative Compassion.* University, Ala.: University of Alabama Press, 1975.

———. *Bureaucracy and the Modern World.* Morristown, N.J.: General Learning Press, 1976.

Turner, Stephen P. "Blau's Theory of Differentiation: Is It Explanatory?" In J. Kenneth Benson (ed.), *Organizational Analysis: Critique and Innovation.* Beverly Hills, Calif.: Sage, 1977, pp. 19–34.

Udy, Stanley H. "Bureaucracy and Rationality in Weber's Organization Theory: An Empirical Study," *American Sociological Review,* 24 (1959), 791–95.

Walton, Eric J. "The Comparison of Measures of Organizational Structure," *Academy of Management Review,* 6 (1981), 155–60.

Weber, Marianne. *Max Weber: A Biography.* Translated and edited by Harry Zohn. New York: Wiley, 1975.

Weber, Max. *From Max Weber: Essays in Sociology.* Translated and edited by H. H. Gerth and C. Wright Mills. New York: Oxford University Press, 1946.

———. *Max Weber: The Theory of Social and Economic Organization.* Translated and edited by Talcott Parsons and A. M. Henderson. New York: Free Press, 1947.

———. *Economy and Society.* Vols. I–III. Translated and edited by Guenther Roth and Claus Wittich. New York: Bedminster Press, 1968.

14

Contributions of Theory in Organizational Structure and Process

In previous chapters various theories of organizational structure and process have been individually evaluated against the criteria of theoretical soundness, research support, and practical utility. In this chapter the theories will be compared with each other in certain topic areas. Which theories have produced the greatest yields, and in what respects? In what ways have theories of organizational structure and process truly advanced understanding, prediction, and practice? Where are the greatest gaps in existing knowledge, and what can be learned from past theoretical failures?

A major question relates to the mapping of domains. Theorists typically establish certain boundaries for their formulations, either explicitly or implicitly by the range of their discussions. But subsequent research does not always position the theory in exactly the same manner as the theorist indicated. Some theories work in smaller domains, and occasionally a theory works in a broader domain. What domains have been studied well? What gaps exist? What areas have failed to attract theoretical exploration or have consistently been scenes of theoretical failure?

A second question involves the development of theoretical constructs in the field of organizational structure and process. To be valid and useful, constructs need to be unambiguously defined, and they need to deal with significant factors. Which constructs appear most promising?

Closely related to establishing constructs is measuring constructs. Measurement of some kind is a necessary condition for research and for that reason theories do not generate research until their major constructs have been operationalized. Many theories that are put forth without adequate attention to measurement drop rapidly into oblivion, but some theories that apparently strike important value chords in the scientific or managerial communities win widespread, uncritical acceptance. In either case real knowledge becomes possible only with reliable and valid measures. We must look at our theories to determine to what degree this measurement has been achieved.

Then, there is the key issue of predicting outcomes. To what extent have theories predicted their dependent variables? The most important variable is organizational effectiveness, as defined in relation to operative goals. However, other outcomes are of theoretical significance—innovation, turnover, organizational decisions, and the like. In their prediction of different outcomes, to what do the various theories aspire and in what do they succeed?

What procedures for changing organizations have been developed? Has theory created new, effective, and useful organizational forms? Have methods for introducing and stabilizing such forms been devised? The concern here is essentially goals of application and the objectives of management. However, to the extent that professional, group, or task systems are involved, management is not the key factor in change, nor is management the organizational component concerned with applications. It becomes necessary to consider changes that are consonant with any goals of application, not just with managerial goals.

Finally, there is the overarching matter of understanding. What have the theories really done to advance understanding of organizations and their functioning? What have been the blind alleys and the major breakthroughs? How well have theories of organizational structure and process performed in relation to theories in organizational behavior? In short, what is the overall state of knowledge in the macro study of organizations, and what does the current state imply for the future?

Mapping Domains

Only relatively few theories of organizational structure and process give detailed attention to their boundaries. The typical theory deals with *organizations in general*, including both their micro and macro levels. However, specific theoretical statements make it evident that domain limitations exist. Some theories give primary attention to work group dynamics and only cursory attention to macro structure. At the other extreme are theories that give practically no attention to motivation, leadership, and other intragroup relationships. Organizational environments are stressed to varying degrees. Within organizations the focus falls on certain variables and not on others. Some theories treat only hierarchical organizations and even seem to assume that hierarchical forms are the only forms existing in the organizational world; others clearly extend beyond the hierarchical domain in various respects.

The degree of differentiation of the various theories in terms of their actual domains turns out to be much greater than initial statements might lead one to expect. The loose commitment to organizations in general rapidly breaks down as theorists move off in different directions. The research evidence often disconfirms a theory's applicability in certain areas, limiting it more than originally anticipated. On occasion, research suggests an entirely new domain for the theory. The cumulative effect is a set of theories that in fact address themselves to widely differing issues.

Macro Aspirations and Micro Performance

Some theories lie on the borderline between organizational behavior and organizational structure and performance. This is particularly true of those theories that arose out of the early leadership and group dynamics research at the University of Michigan and Ohio State University. Clearly, these theories build upward from the work group, but often they build relatively little. Intergroup or organizationwide constructs tend to be few and/or imprecise. Research at the macro level is nonexistent, minimal, or disconfirming.

Both system 4 theory and psychological open systems theory fall into this category. Whatever strengths system 4 theory has are found at the work group level. The linking pin concept that extends beyond the work group shows some promise, but it is hardly a broad enough base on which to build a total theory of organizational structure and process; too much is left unconsidered. Several applications of system 4 theory, including human resource accounting and survey feedback, also extend beyond the work group, but they do not provide a comprehensive theory of organization and their objective is to promote work group change. Likert aspires to a macro theory that dispenses with hierarchy, but he has not devised anything to replace hierarchy and has only a rudimentary theory above the work group level.

Among the psychological open systems theorists, Stogdill has most consistently held to the micro level. For many years he merely contended that larger organizations operate in the mode of the small group. This concept fails to consider that the units within an organization may have widely differing goals, as they do in bureaucracy. Thus the units take on quite disparate characteristics, while combining to serve the goals of the total organization. To know how the units in a large organization function individually is no more likely to lead to an understanding of the whole than is knowledge of individual business enterprises likely to lead to understanding of the capitalistic system. Ultimately, Stogdill recognized these problems and moved toward a distinct macro theory, which has not been tested as yet. The Stogdill theory that has been tested is basically one of organizational behavior.

The Katz and Kahn open systems theory is clearly aimed at a comprehensive goal and contains a wide range of distinctive constructs to prove it. Yet the really testable and tested hypotheses arise out of concepts such as role prescriptions and leadership, which fall within the domain of organizational behavior. Almost all the relevant research is focused at the micro level. The theory is organizationwide in its formulations, but only specific and testable at the level of motivations, leadership, the work group, the job, and the like. The theory's origins have prevailed to the point where its true domain appears to be more circumscribed than the basic statements indicate.

Sociotechnical systems theory, though not a direct descendant of either the Michigan or Ohio State leadership studies, shows similar symptoms. Management above the work group level is posited, but only to deal with external forces. The mediation of external and internal variances is handled weakly—through the concept of directive correlations via common values. Again, the alternatives to hierarchy above the lowest level are insufficiently explicated. The theory does blossom again in depicting various types of environments. But these latter formulations present numerous problems in terms of their logical arguments and their lack of research support. At present, sociotechnical systems theory appears to be thrust back into the group dynamics domain—especially in its key formulations regarding autonomous work groups, where it has achieved its greatest successes.

Goal congruence theory, though it aspires on occasion to macro status, tends to concentrate on matters related to employee personality, and in this area it makes its original theoretical contributions. Conceptualizations dealing with structural variables, such as the mix model, draw heavily on the theorizing of others, including Likert, Weber, and Fayol. The relevant research also focuses on individual personality variables—self-actualization and similar motives, anxiety, and the like. In the early period organizational variables seemed of greatest concern to Argyris, but over time they have tended to disappear from both his research and his theorizing. Thus, goal congruence theory, insofar as it makes an original contribution, seems to be essentially a theory of organizational behavior. The major exception to this would be its application to the domain of scientific research itself.

These theories as a group were all authored by individuals with a background in psychology. Furthermore, psychology is the predominant orientation within the field of organizational behavior in general (Miner, 1980). It is not surprising that psychologists gravitate toward micro-level formulations even when they intend to create more comprehensive theory. On the other hand, at least one theory developed by a sociologist has ended in a similar domain.

Perrow's concept of technology appears to be allied in numerous respects with theories of job characteristics and design. Furthermore, the research evidence strongly reinforces this interpretation. Certainly, Perrow attempts to develop constructs and hypotheses of a macro nature, but as he moves away from the actual productive work of the organization, his formulations become more tentative and less precise. To the extent the theory possesses the power of understanding and prediction, it does so within the confines of organizational behavior.

True Limited Domain Theories

It may be extremely difficult to construct theories that operate effectively within the confines established for the study of organizational structure and process. Theories tend to move toward a primary locus in organizational behavior, regardless of the theorists' intent. One solution to this problem appears to be to focus on a narrow set of organizational variables and thus carve out only a limited domain in the macro sphere.

The theories that have limited their focus typically have been rather successful. Control theory is probably the most restricted of the theories considered. Yet it deals with an important area and has stimulated considerable research that confirms a significant segment of the theory. Much the same holds for strategy and structure theory, which deals with a particular type of top-level decision and the operation of a limited set of structural alternatives within a certain organizational environment involving competition. Strategy and structure theory has not spawned a large body of research, but within the area of strategy formulation as a whole, its research is impressive. A number of the theory's hypotheses have been supported, though others have failed of confirmation.

The third theory that takes a limited set of variables as its domain of inquiry is the decision-making work of Simon, March, and Cyert. Actually, their formulations cannot be considered a single theory, and the research treatment received by the subtheories has not been the same for each. Nevertheless, the subtheories have consistently focused on decision making and primarily on programmable decisions. That is the starting point from which one approaches any organizational issue—structuring, membership, goals, conflict, and so on. In this regard there is a distinct limitation of domain. Overall, in spite of certain other research restrictions, the limited domain approach has been successful here. Perhaps it is relevant that such an approach itself bounds rationality.

Comprehensive Theories

More comprehensive theories of organizational structure and process take various approaches and carve out differing domains. One theoretical strategy has been to contrast two categories of organization, one of which is viewed as normatively superior under most existing or future circumstances. Thus, Weber contrasted prebureaucratic forms of organizations with bureaucratic organizations as an ideal type, but failed to differentiate professional and group or collegial systems as separate entities. His theory of bureaucracy was somewhat culturally and temporally bounded, and it has remained for more recent theorists to separate out the organizational forms that Weber confounded with bureaucracy.

Bennis also considers a bureaucratic and a nonbureaucratic form, but in this instance it is the nonbureaucratic, professional organization that is normatively superior. Two other theories take a parallel approach. Burns and Stalker cite mechanistic (bureaucratic) and organic (nonbureaucratic) forms and endorse the latter as appropriate to rapidly changing technologies and markets of the future. Lawrence and Lorsch stress the superiority of the high-differentiation and high-integration organization, as reflected in the matrix structure, for coping with uncertainty. To some degree other human relations oriented theorists, such as Likert, Trist, and Argyris, outline dual-form domains and endorse one form as more effective.

Overall, creating and contrasting two categories of organization has not been too successful. The domains created often constrain the theorists from considering crucial, related issues. Though potentially rewarding, the comparative approach has focused on the normatively superior component of the domain to such a degree that little else has been learned. Size of the domains does not appear to be as great a problem as configuration. Weber considered organizational but not professional knowledge; Lawrence and Lorsch utilized a global concept of environmental uncertainty to establish boundaries; Bennis and others assumed a particular model of organizational innovation that served to circumscribe the domain; and so on. These domains, once established, made it difficult to expand the theories into other areas where more fruitful hypotheses could have been developed.

Each of the remaining theories presents certain special problems. Classical management theory comes closest to a grand theory of all those considered, at least in its aspirations, and like most such theories, fails to achieve its goals (Miner, 1980). It simply is not a theory for all organizational forms, which Fayol seems to have recognized toward the end of his life. Sociological systems theory also covers a wide domain, though it excludes voluntary organizations. However, within this domain it concentrates on a number of well-defined conceptual islands where James Thompson saw the possibility for theoretical breakthroughs. One wonders what would have happened if Thompson had restricted himself to even fewer conceptual islands and developed really specific, testable hypotheses in each limited domain. In spite of the existing theory's partial success, it is clearly spread too thinly over its domain.

The technological imperative as developed by Woodward was originally a theory for manufacturing organizations, though it has since been expanded. Given the research results and the conceptual problems with the technology variable, it is difficult to say what the theory's boundaries are at present. They are almost certainly much narrower than originally envisaged, but how much narrower remains unclear. It is apparent now that core technology is not *the* determinant of the total structure of large organizations. So, once again, a macro theory is found to occupy a smaller domain than initially anticipated.

Establishing Constructs

Not a single theory among those considered in this volume does not suffer from some construct-related problem. Ambiguity of statement, conflicting formulations, lack of anticipated relationships to other variables, failure to specify significant aspects, logical inconsistencies—these and other shortcomings abound. No other factor has done more to impede the development of theory in organizational structure and process than the theorists' seeming inability to formulate sufficiently valid constructs. Even the more powerful constructs function more as blunt instruments than as sharp knives in opening a path through ignorance.

A number of factors seem to contribute to the lack of valid constructs in theories of organizational structure and process. For one thing, the subject is new in scientific theorizing and research. Ties to value-laden philosophies still abound, and precise construct definitions and testability have not always been of prime concern. Theorists often introduce new constructs and related formulations without saying how these additions affect past constructs. Overly global specification of constructs permits them to absorb a wide range of phenomena having little relationship to each other. The subject matter itself seems to invite difficult, abstruse treatment. Several preceding chapters require very close reading, reflecting in large part the difficult nature of the original statements. Consequently much organizational planning, even that of a formal nature, is carried out without benefit of theory.

Contingency Constructs

Theories that are essentially contingent suffer almost irreparable damage if their underlying contingency constructs run into difficulty, and this is what happened to these theories with considerable regularity. Sociotechnical theory is a good example. In its most recent versions it contains two types of contingency variables, the internal technical type from which it draws its name and an environmental variable related to turbulent change. Obviously, under certain circumstances these two provide conflicting guides to organizational structuring. Yet, the theory does not deal with this issue and does not have to, because its two contingency constructs are so loosely defined that the use of an autonomous work group can be advocated in practically any situation. What this means is that the contingency constructs, though major components of the theory, actually are not related to structure.

Every theorist who has introduced some technology construct as a contingency variable has faced construct difficulties. This problem extends from Trist and James Thompson, to Woodward, to Burns and Stalker, to Perrow, and even to Lawrence and Lorsch, who treated technology as a component of environmental contingency. Inevitably, technology becomes confounded with other variables—control, macro structure, and job design, among others. No one has maintained clear distinctions among types of technologies, and between technology and other constructs. Even technological change becomes muddy. Is technological change defined by scientific advance of a kind that permits the adoption of new technologies or by such events as actual change in the machinery on the shop floor?

Technology probably can be defined unambiguously and narrowly enough to be utilized effectively as a theoretical construct, but the history of attempts to do so should be enough to give pause. Furthermore, the farther away one gets from the particular technology that is the focus of theoretical concern, the more difficult it becomes to specify logical hypotheses in contingency form. This is why Perrow became so tentative in discussing top management, goals, social structure, and the like. In short, technology as construct does not look powerful enough to advance knowledge of organizational structure and process, even if construct validity could be assured.

Similar problems have arisen with environment-derived contingency variables—primarily uncertainty, but also change, heterogeneity, and the like. Here, the global definition of variables appears to be wholly self-defeating. Even if one resolves all the difficult conceptual problems related to the locus of uncertainty, what creates it, and what reduces it, each single organizational decision still has its own context of certainties and uncertainties. Certainty may prevail in almost every area, but if it is not clear whether or how quickly competitors might enter the market to counter a potential new product introduction, *that* decision is surrounded with uncertainty. Whether uncertainty can be differentiated as a construct to the point of dealing with individual decisions in this manner is questionable, but if it cannot, contingency theories predicated on such an environment-derived contingency construct are unlikely to prove viable. Construct validity problems in this area have plagued the Lawrence and Lorsch theory primarily, in large part because it is stated precisely enough to be tested, but such problems pose a similar threat to other theories such as open systems.

Systems Constructs

The pervasive problem of the various systems theories is the looseness, ambiguity, and abstractness of the definition of their constructs. This problem has important implications for measurement and, ultimately, for research, but even at the level of theory construction, it represents a source of difficulty, as James Thompson recognized.

Many of Stogdill's constructs are not clear, either because he failed to operationalize them, as with the input variables, or because he endorsed multiple operationalizations with low correlations, as with the output variables. In later versions of the theory numerous constructs were introduced without their position being firmly fixed within the body of the theory. Many such constructs were extracted from other theoretical contexts. It is the essence of the systems approach that everything interacts with everything else, and accordingly these theories attract large numbers of variables, often to the point of threatening parsimony. Stogdill recognized this and attempted to deal with the problem in his very latest theoretical statements. Indeed, his final, mathematical formulations represent the most precise of any systems statements. It is noteworthy that these formulations are much less far-ranging than his own previous theorizing or the work of other systems theorists such as Katz and Kahn, and James Thompson.

What appears to come easily for systems theories is the construction of a broad framework. What comes with much more effort is the definition of salient constructs that are readily operationalized and stated precisely enough to avoid basic problems of construct validity. Neither Katz and Kahn, at the level of organizational structure and process, nor James Thompson appears to have surmounted this hurdle. Stogdill may have done so, but only very late in his career, and the supporting research has not yet emerged.

Additional Construct Problems

In the field of organizational structure and process, construct validity problems are less evident because of the results of empirical investigation than because of obviously conflicting or insufficient statements. There are instances where empirical study has raised questions, however. This is most manifest in the case of the various technological and environmental contingency constructs. It also occurs to some degree with regard to Tannenbaum's key control construct. What is assumed to be one construct measured at various levels and by various means may in fact be a set of somewhat different constructs. The theory is powerful enough to yield significant results in any event, but this seems to be another case of having a blunt instrument rather than a sharp knife. The same is true of Chandler's strategy and structure constructs. They have not been as easy to operationalize consistently as it might appear. The boundaries between the various structural forms appear to be fuzzy, and the empirical studies have revealed a need for more precise definitions. Furthermore, there have been some problems in obtaining the expected correlations among different measures of key bureaucratic theory constructs. This, however, is probably as much a measurement as a construct validity problem.

The system 4 and 4T formulations suffer most from inconsistent treatment of the hierarchy construct. The theory cannot really handle a lack of hierarchy, as reflected in the rather vague system 5 statements, but hierarchy by its very nature is conceptually opposed to much of the theory. Problems are also inherent in the cultural variation and lag constructs. Neither construct is specified precisely enough to predict when and in what manner it can be expected to operate. As a result, both constructs act as tempting escape hatches for the theory.

Goal congruence theory faces the greatest construct validity problems with regard to self-actualization and the infancy-maturity dimension. This problem has plagued other theories as well (Miner, 1980). Argyris has obviously struggled with it at length, but his statements remain conflicting and imprecise. There is also some confusion of objective and subjective dependency; the employee dependency construct needs further development and differentiation.

The theory of bureaucratic demise also suffers from internal inconsistency and conflicting statement. What is the nature of the bureaucracy construct at present? Is it inherently self-defeating or not? Can bureaucracies innovate and thus adapt to change or not? Do bureaucracies have the means to handle conflicts that might destroy them internally or not? The theory is currently unclear on such matters.

Among the Carnegie theorists, Simon and Cyert have steered clear of most construct problems, though the role of satisficing within the inducements-contributions decision has not been adequately elaborated. The March theory dealing with organized anarchies is both original and inadequately developed—a not infrequent state of affairs. Clearly, more precise constructs are needed to facilitate the development of measures. These needs are particularly great in the areas of organizational attention and learning under ambiguity.

Classical management theory faces two construct problems that together threaten the future usefulness of the theory. One is the ambiguity and logical inconsistency that Simon noted many years ago. These difficulties have not been overcome by those who have worked with the theory after Fayol. Second, the existing constructs, which are closely tied to practice in a particular place and time, cannot handle many current organizational phenomena.

Bureaucratic theory, though a product of much the same circumstances as classical theory, seems more capable of being updated. At least, it has been modified by such theorists as Blau and Victor Thompson. Yet there are the usual construct problems. Weber leaves the reader uncertain about the nature of voluntary and imperative processes in rational-legal authority, the role of professional knowledge in bureaucracy, the relationships between collegial and bureaucratic systems, and the role of centralization in bureaucracy. Those who have followed Weber often have corrected such ambiguities, uncertainties, and conflicts in their own versions of the theory, but they have introduced new problems as well, such as Victor Thompson's formulation of the innovation construct as it relates to natural systems.

Powerful Constructs

In the literature of organizational structure and process the number of seemingly good ideas that have not worked out well is overwhelming. In large part this is because of problems inherent in the original constructs. Yet some constructs have held up well and appear to hold clues to the direction of future theory and research in the field.

One construct that has worked is that of bureaucracy, though all of its component variables have not been identified as yet. Within the framework of bureaucracy, formalization, standardization, specialization, and size are clearly important. So, too, is rationality, and this has been reinforced by the work of the Carnegie theorists and by Lawrence and Lorsch's formulations on confrontation. At the center, of course, is the key concept of hierarchy.

Outside of bureaucracy, it is now apparent that separate organizational system constructs are viable. The group or collegial systems considered by sociotechnical systems theorists and by Blau are one alternative. Professional systems set forth by post-Weberian sociologists are another. Entrepreneurial or task systems, which have their primary theoretical grounding in organizational behavior, have been introduced into macro theory by Victor Thompson and others. These organizational system constructs can be established as separate variables, and without them, the bureaucratic concept becomes much more clearly recognizable.

Integration appears to be a powerful construct for understanding organizations. It is a major component in the theories of Argyris, Stogdill, Katz and Kahn, Lawrence and Lorsch, and (as concordance) in a variation on Tannenbaum's control theory. Though these theorists describe and utilize the construct somewhat differently, integration appears to be a core concept and has proved productive in research.

A related construct is that of control, as utilized by Tannenbaum. Less has been done to relate this factor to other important constructs of the field than might be desired, but there are almost certainly overlaps. One is immediately reminded of Weber's types of authority and of the different forms of power. This bundle of constructs surrounding control is important, but much more work is needed. Control theory has led the way in this endeavor.

The central role of decision processes in organizations has been demonstrated most extensively by the Carnegie theorists, but it is evident in Chandler's strategy-structure formulations as well. It now appears that the greatest potential for pulling together the disparate strands of research on organizational structure and process lies in studying organizational decisions and strategies at whatever point they are created. We need to know how various structures come about and what other things such as technological changes happen in the organization in conjunction with them. A set of constructs exists, primarily as a result of the work of Simon, March, and Cyert, that has considerable potential for yielding an understanding of these matters. In utilizing these constructs, however, one must distinguish between individual decision making and organizational decision making; the two do not appear to be the same.

This discussion of powerful constructs is by no means complete, but it points up some potential building blocks that have held up under research investigation with some consistency. In spite of frequent dead ends, there have been stretches of open highway, too.

Creating Measures

Theories that do not generate measures of their key constructs at an early point tend to yield little research. Ideally, the measures are developed by the theorists themselves, because these provide additional evidence of what the theorists meant. In a field characterized by fuzzy constructs, this is important. When theoretical constructs are adequately and precisely defined and illustrated, it should not matter who devises the measures. Unfortunately, in the field of organizational structure and process, it matters.

Measures Devised by the Theorists

Conceptually, the measures developed by the theorists themselves reflect the underlying constructs quite well, as might be expected.

Major difficulties have tended to arise in connection with psychometric properties of measurement such as reliability and validity.

Some of the best measures, as one might expect, have been developed at the Survey Research Center of the University of Michigan. Research on the Likert theory has benefited from the early development of the "Profile of Organizational Characteristics" and the "Survey of Organizations."

Both of the Michigan research center's basic survey measures have changed substantially over time. Though the net effect has been improvement, comparability of data from study to study has suffered. Reliability appears adequate, though more test-retest information is needed. The greatest difficulties occur in repeated measurements. Like most survey instruments, these measures offer organization members an opportunity to report on their organization. If members have been taught that some organizational forms are "better" than others, this can easily influence the results, and the various organizational development interventions involving systems 4 and 4T do just that. The self-reports may change, not because the organization has really changed, but because the individual's concept of a good organization has changed. The responses are different because the respondents now know what the researchers want to hear. There are methods of dealing with this problem, but the Michigan researchers have not used them. Reports of organizational change based on these instruments must be accepted only with considerable caution; the measurements may not be valid.

Another derivative of the Survey Research Center is Tannenbaum's control theory. Again, the basic instrument has not remained exactly the same over time. Furthermore, there are some questions regarding reliability. No doubt the theory would benefit from a better measure, and the whole matter of concordance needs amplification. Yet, given the existing context, the present measure, in spite of its imperfections, has value. Ideally, a new instrument would reduce the existing "noise," to borrow a term from information theory. What we have now is a construct so powerful that it works to some degree in spite of measurement imperfections.

Other Michigan-based theories do not show the same degree of measurement support as the Likert and Tannenbaum formulations. The psychological systems theory of Katz and Kahn consistently has produced measures only in the role theory area. Overall, this theory with its wide-ranging systems perspective has elicited few measurement efforts from its authors. Others have attempted to fill this void, but there are questions about the degree of match between measures and constructs. Without question, many constructs such as negative entropy are difficult to operationalize. Yet the net effect of difficult constructs and few measures has, as usual, stifled research.

Goal congruence theory and Stogdill's open systems theory both have produced author-developed measures. Argyris utilized interview-scoring procedures at an early point that suffered from low reliability but served as the basis for the creation of more effective instruments by others later. Unfortunately, however, the anticipated research has not been forthcoming. Argyris stopped doing research on his theory, and his negative views toward traditional research no doubt discouraged others.

Stogdill contributed to the development of a number of instruments, only some of which were related to the constructs of his theory. The major focus was on output variables, but he helped develop measures of authority and responsibility as well. In general, the reliabilities appear to be acceptable. However, the global nature of the input variables as originally stated seems to have discouraged measurement, and for this reason it has not been possible to test the total theory. The latest version of the theory calls for a number of measures that currently do not exist. Thus, in spite of Stogdill's sizable efforts in the measurement area, the fact that his instruments do not focus directly on the theory or on all of its key constructs has dampened research output.

Among the technological imperative theorists, both Woodward and Perrow developed measures. Both encountered major difficulties in measuring technology, as they defined the construct. These difficulties appear to have been a major factor in the subsequent disillusionment experienced by both theorists with regard to the power of the technological imperative. Nevertheless, the fact that measurement was undertaken in this area is directly attributable to these theorists, and a number of other instruments such as those developed by the Aston researchers have appeared subsequently. Clearly, the fact that measures of some kind were created, irrespective of the underlying construct problems, served to stimulate a great deal of research.

Much the same conclusion holds for the Lawrence and Lorsch contingency theory. It is to the theorists' credit that they developed measures in the beginning. In doing so, they stimulated considerable research. However, unreliability in the measurement of uncertainty has occurred so frequently that the problems must be inherent in the underlying construct. Unfortunately, the other measures developed by these theorists have not been subjected to similar scrutiny.

The Measurement Lag

Though theorists who do not develop measures of their constructs typically experience some lag before research on their ideas begins, measures often do appear eventually and study is begun. Sometimes students create measures to test the theory for dissertations. The prime example of this is strategy and structure theory. In this particular instance the results to date have not been entirely satisfactory. Much more research on reliability is needed, but what has been done makes it apparent that existing strategy and structure schemas do not always yield reliable results.

The older theories such as classical management and bureaucracy experienced long delays before measures began to emerge. Only a limited number of key constructs of classical management theory have been the target of intentionally developed measures even now, though certain measures developed for other purposes may serve classical theory, too. Vague constructs tend to give birth to poor measures, as in the case of contingency theory, or to no measures at all, as in the case of classical management theory.

The theory of bureaucracy, on the other hand, was widely researched during the 1960s and 1970s, primarily because Blau, the Aston researchers, and others began to develop measures of key variables. In general, these measurement efforts have been successful, at least relative to what has happened with other theories. The major questions are does a particular measure actually tap Weber's construct, and what really was Weber's construct. One approach seeks to deal with these problems by differentiating questionnaire and institutional measures, but it now seems that there are construct problems as well as measurement problems. Weber's theory remains unusual in the amount of attention given to measurement of its variables, considering the nature and time of its origin.

The remaining theories have suffered badly from measurement failures that remain to this day. Sociotechnical research has focused almost entirely on existing output measures. There has been a continuing need for measures of dependent variables, though what few instruments have been available have not been used in the research. Measures of relevant individual differences also are needed to determine if such factors might operate as contingency variables in explaining the uneven nature of the research outcomes.

The theory of bureaucratic decline has similarly failed to generate the necessary measures, though in some key areas such as innovation and professionalism certain measures have been created independent of the theory. These measures owe a much greater debt to bureaucratic theory than to Bennis's hypotheses. In addition, a number of these measures do not have the same focus as Bennis's constructs. Given the current status of the theory, it is unlikely that measures will be introduced, but should this happen, the measures should reflect the science-oriented nature of the theory's constructs.

The Burns and Stalker theory has attracted measures of technological or product change, but not of market change. Certain proxy variables have been utilized to fill this void, but the need for direct measurement of market change is obvious. The limited amount of research on the mechanistic-organic formulations can be traced directly to the lack of appropriate measures. For much the same reason, sociological open systems theory has produced only a dribble of research in comparison with what might have been anticipated and desired from such a creative piece of work. For lack of measures, researchers have either gone elsewhere or guessed at appropriate measures. Some of these guesses were probably strongly influenced by the availability of data and did not match what James Thompson had in mind. On the other hand, given the abstractness of the constructs, it is very difficult to reject any contender as unsuitable.

The final set of theories affected by measurement lag and reduced research output is the Simon, March, and Cyert group. Much of the work related to these theories has utilized computer simulations that do not require measurements of real-world variables. This can be a drawback. Some measures have been developed in connection with the research on satisficing, but little is known about their psychometric properties. In other key areas such as slack, measures now are beginning to appear, and there is reason to hope that the measurement lag will end for other constructs as well. The very promising ideas of Simon, March, and Cyert have been left in limbo much too long for lack of adequate attention to measurement issues.

Predicting Outcomes

In spite of a host of conceptual and measurement problems, theories of organizational structure and process have predicted some outcomes successfully. It is rare for a theory to predict in all of its aspects, but in a number of instances one or two key hypotheses have been confirmed consistently by the research. In addition, several theories that work on occasion, but not with the consistency needed to consider them truly supported, need further refinement if they are to predict more consistently. In contrast to the above theories, there is an almost equal number of theories that either do not yield valid predictions with any frequency or cannot be evaluated for lack of necessary research. There often is reason to believe that the unresearched theories may never be studied.

Theories That Do Predict

Control theory has been consistently successful in predictions involving total control, and there is evidence of a causal effect from control to performance. Whether control causes satisfaction is uncertain because measures of the two variables lack independence.

On the other hand the results related to slope as a predictor are much less convincing. Perhaps the early theory was correct in avoiding this type of hypothesis. There is a clear need to separate bureaucratic systems from other types of systems, and the theory has not yet provided guidance on such matters. Conflict and trust appear to be important moderators. In certain respects research has already gone beyond the basic theory. This is also true in the analysis of concordance. Whether overcontrol can occur and cause outcomes to turn downward has not yet been determined. Nor is it clear when the control pie may be expandable or reciprocal. Yet the results involving total control stand as a major finding of organizational science.

The data on the basic proposition of goal congruence theory that a fit or integration between individual and organization fosters effectiveness have been consistently positive. Argyris's views on this matter, though relatively undifferentiated, were ground-breaking. Research makes it increasingly apparent that each organizational form has its own personality constellation that fosters integration and that, as Victor Thompson surmised, a lack of fit can lead to negative consequences for any individual who is unsuited to the particular organizational system. Other aspects of Argyris's theory have not fared well or have not been tested. Thus, hypotheses from the mix model, such as authoritarian systems can be effective if authorized by democratic processes, simply have not been studied adequately.

The Katz and Kahn theory basically lacks testable constructs, measures, and research of the kind needed to provide support. But the theory has proven quite effective in the prediction of outcomes from role constructs. Indexes of role conflict and ambiguity relate negatively to a wide range of outcome indexes. Individual moderators influence these results, but the findings often hold up even without consideration of individual differences. Other research related to theoretical predictions is too sketchy to produce firm conclusions.

Another theory that has produced stable results is that of strategy and structure. Strategy predicts structure with a frequency well above chance. Lag plays a definite role here, and the theory anticipates it. On the other hand, formulations of the lag concept precise enough to permit accurate predictions in time are lacking, just as they are from other theories. Strategy-structure fit also seems to predict to growth, but not to extend beyond this to profits, perhaps because of a failure to control for industry variance, or inadequacies of measurement, or inadequacies of the theory itself. At this point it is not possible to say.

March's views on garbage can decisions have not been researched as adequately as have some earlier Carnegie hypotheses, especially those dealing with programmed decisions, satisficing, and the like. Here the descriptive theory performs quite well, though individual differences in decision-making styles clearly introduce considerations beyond the basic theory. Other problems include the finding that organizational decisions may indeed correct for satisficing bias and that unprogrammed decisions may in fact be programmed within a larger, extraorganizational set of constraints. Though the theory is not explicitly normative, the desirability of rationality is frequently indicated. Research in other contexts tends to support this conclusion. Thus, certain core ideas on decision making in this body of theory have been researched and with positive results.

Bureaucratic theory has not been evaluated by pitting bureaucratic systems against other systems and controlling the relevant variables. However, the more bureaucratized a system is in terms of its key variables, the more effective it is likely to be. In this constellation of variables the role of size tends to taper off rather quickly, and decentralization, rather than centralization, appears to join the core constructs most frequently. In numerous respects bureaucratic theory especially in its more recent extensions, does have predictive power. Yet, one must question Victor Thompson's views on innovation, and Weber's concept of the normative superiority of bureaucracy headed by a charismatic leader has not been tested.

Theories That May Predict

System 4 and sociotechnical theory both possess many similarities, among them unusually mixed outcomes from research; sometimes prediction is achieved and sometimes it is not. Explanations for the failures include lag and a lack of cultural fit. However, the research suggests that certain kinds of people are more responsive to a participative approach than others; yet both theories have failed to incorporate such individual differences in the past. The inclusion of the personality characteristics and motives of organization members should yield a more stable pattern of prediction.

In the case of system 4 theory in particular, a major question of confounding makes even positive results difficult to interpret. As Weber emphasized, managers often are more knowledgeable on job-related subjects, and many instances of apparent participation may only be a further demonstration of the rational use of hierarchy. Also in system 4T a number of other factors known to predict positive outcomes, such as goal setting, are included. It is questionable in any given instance whether participation can be singled out as the causal agent.

Sociotechnical theory tends to remove the workers farther from hierarchy and give them more job knowledge. The potential for confounding is reduced, and such actions may be a necessary condition for positive results. There is a developing body of evidence from professional systems and venture teams, as well as autonomous work groups, that infusing such systems with too much hierarchy can lead to failures. In any event, there is no basis for the hypothesis that sociotechnical systems will invariably produce more creative outcomes than other structures.

Another theory that may predict is classical management theory. There are areas in which its predictive power has been demonstrated, though typically similar predictions would be made from other theories. Unity of command yields positive outcomes, but role theory would have predicted the same thing, and at the same time provided more comprehensive understanding. Similarly, formal planning has been found to yield favorable results, but the same outcomes can be predicted from theories that emphasize the normative value of rationality. The results of research on bureaucratic theory suggest that if classical theory is restricted to the domain of hierarchical systems, certain other effective predictions would result; the two theories are overlapping at certain points. However, classical management theory continues to assert the generality of management, and bureaucratic theory accordingly provides the more precise predictions.

Theories That Appear Not to Predict

The various concepts of the technological imperative have been the subject of a good deal of research. Typically, those studies that have attempted to carry through to variables such as organizational or unit effectiveness have not produced evidence to support the theories. There may be ways of matching technology and structure that yield positive outcomes, but there is no basis for concluding that theorists have found them. Furthermore, even the correlations between technology and structure that have been found are in all likelihood a consequence of the influence of a third variable—choice by the decision maker.

Contingency theory of organization also has been investigated often enough to lead to some conclusions. Differentiation as formulated has shown no consistent relationship to success indexes. Integration yields much more positive results, but not on the contingent basis posited by the theory. Rather integration is related consistently to success, irrespective of uncertainty, which fits with the conclusions from various other theories. If the research on which these conclusions are based had taken into account a time lag factor and assumed movement toward uncertainty reduction under conditions of theoretical fit, more positive results for the theory might have been obtained. However, the theory does not contain this kind of variable, and its authors conducted their research without reference to it.

Where Evidence Is Lacking

The Bennis theory does not receive support for its statements about adaptive, innovative output from bureaucracies. In this respect it faces the same problems as do the theories of Argyris and Victor Thompson. But the Bennis theory also posits the superiority of certain temporary and professional systems under environmental conditions that are said to be rapidly advancing in frequency. Later, there was some equivocation on the rate and extent of these changes, but the basic ideas regarding professional systems remain. They appear to be useful and have some validity. However, practically nothing is known about the relative effectiveness of such professional systems, let alone how effective they are in different environments. Thus this aspect of the theory has not been evaluated, and since it is probably the key aspect, it seems wise to withhold judgment at this point.

Stogdill's open systems theory presents a somewhat similar problem. Research on the early versions of the theory focused on relationships among outputs rather than the prediction of outputs and often failed to support the theoretical propositions. However, the newer theory provides much more precise statements of constructs and indicates a need for new measures. This theory has not even been formally published, let alone tested. With Stogdill's death further research on the theory may not be conducted. Yet, without it, the theory cannot be evaluated.

Finally, there is another system theory, that of James Thompson. Though there has been some research related to the theory, the number of studies dealing with organizational outcomes is miniscule, and many of the theory's numerous propositions have not been the subject of research at all. The formulations dealing with the role of the environment have not been supported, but because the theory's propositions tend to be stated separately, this has little implication for the rest of the theory. In spite of the time that has elapsed since Thompson first stated the theory, we know little about the theory's predictive power.

Changing Organizations

A number of theories in the organizational structure and process field carry no special implications for changing organizations, other than the suggestion that organizations should operate in accordance with the theory's normative propositions. Purely descriptive theories do not even suggest that. Theories of this kind have not produced their own change methods or technologies, nor have they endorsed existing techniques that are particularly theoretically relevant. They offer few guidelines as to how best to achieve the organizational states they advocate.

Perhaps the most notable of these are the systems theories, both psychological and sociological. Among these theories, only the Katz and Kahn approach deals with change procedures at all and that is an endorsement of democratization technologies borrowed from other theories, which have no particular relevance to psychological open systems theory itself. Similarly, all theories rooted in the technological imperative fail to deal with problems of change, though some authors recognize the need to do so. Control theory implies that changes should be introduced to increase the total amount of control, but it does not say how this should be done, nor are there demonstrations of any such technology. One might guess that decentralization, coupled with indirect controls, might contribute to such a result. The Carnegie theorists, too, have failed to suggest a technology for change. In fact, much of the theory is descriptive. The authors imply that computers should increasingly be inserted into the decision process, but they do not demonstrate that doing so yields or does not yield the anticipated results.

Organization Development

As is evident from reading the preceding chapters, organization development comes in a variety of forms. All forms seek to change organizations toward a new set of values that are essentially democratic in nature and frequently toward a structure that is consonant with those values. Coming from somewhat different theoretical orientations, however, the various organization development approaches utilize different techniques in seeking their ends. Thus, a change effort undertaken out of system 4 theory is not the same as one out of sociotechnical theory, or goal congruence theory, or bureaucratic demise theory, or contingency theory.

The distinguishing characteristic of the system 4 approach is survey feedback. Other aspects characteristic of system 4 are the use of cross-functional teams and management by group objectives, but these originate, at least in part, outside system 4 theory. Human resource accounting is closely allied to organization development, especially as it may be applied as an agent of organizational change, but it is not actually part of the process.

Evidence on the effectiveness of system 4 organization development is mixed, and once again the contingency factors that might help identify specific areas of applications are unknown. Certainly, the approach has potential, but whether it has as yet moved from an experimental procedure to a true applied technology is questionable. Furthermore, the long lag times between the introduction of change and results make such participative approaches less attractive; sometimes it is not possible to wait that long. The risks inherent in this approach have not been fully evaluated either. If any vestige of hierarchy remains so that those at the top may be held accountable by stockholders and society as a whole, creating highly cohesive work groups at the bottom and decentralizing authority down to them when they are not responsible for results can be very risky. The linking pin concept does not appear to eliminate this risk.

Obviously, the creation of autonomous work groups involves the same type of risk. On the other hand, this approach to organization development appears to work best if there is a sizable separation between bureaucratic and group systems. It is not just company bureaucracy that is involved; union bureaucracy can be just as damaging. Furthermore, the approach needs to be supported by existing work traditions, the surrounding culture, or consultant activities. Perhaps these elements keep the groups in tune with organizational goals as a whole. In any event autonomous work groups appear to be very vulnerable in that the system can easily break down and revert to bureaucracy. Yet, if this can be avoided, the approach can result in considerable efficiency. It can yield high productivity and sizable reductions in manpower costs.

Approaches such as those based on the Argyris and Bennis theories do not appear to work very well to the extent they continue to draw heavily on T-group or sensitivity training procedures. Even when they do not, they tend to move only as far as value or climate change, not on into structural change. On the evidence, however, the Argyris and Bennis theories can yield positive results for an organization within some boundaries that as yet are not clearly established. Also the exact area in which these positive outcomes will occur is difficult to predict. It may be productivity, but it may just as well be something else. There is very little comparative research to tell us whether other change procedures, including those outside the area of organization development that make greater use of hierarchical authority, might not yield equal or even better results.

Organization development based on a contingency theory orientation is more structural than other approaches in the early period, and more often comprehensive within the organization as well. Contingency theory seeks to achieve highly differentiated and at the same time integrated structures such as matrix organization and must assume considerable environmental uncertainty by the standards of the theory. Yet, according to the theory, there might also be a need to reduce differentiation and integration on occasion. At least, such a technique ought to be considered, in case it should ever be needed. The fact that the authors do not outline an alternative procedure makes their commitment to a true contingency approach to organization somewhat questionable. In any event there is little direct evidence of the effectiveness of the approach. Of the various organization development approaches, that of Lawrence and Lorsch has attracted the least research.

Overall the various organization development technologies demonstrate considerable capacity to change organizations and on occasion to yield greater effectiveness, too. Still there is a great deal that is not known. Further advances in this area seem to await the development of some new theory. At the moment organization development practice appears to have outstripped its theoretical origins.

Structural Change

The remaining theories all endorse a hierarchical system of authority. Thus change can be assumed to occur as a result of communication down through the hierarchy of policies and procedures formulated at the top. This is true of strategy and structure theory, of classical management theory, and of the theory of bureaucracy. Each espouses a particular constellation of structural and process variables. In none of these instances did the theory invent the organizational form; the theoretical contribution was to codify and explain what had already occurred in practice.

The Chandler theory has spread the multidivisional forms identified as a result of historical study. Whether adopting these forms to implement a diversification strategy is in the best interests of the company has not been demonstrated fully. Certainly, doing so appears not to hurt profits and to facilitate growth, but further research with better measures and better controls is needed before the question of profitability effects can be answered. Given the widespread adoption of multidivisional forms, however, a firm might do well to follow suit, simply to avoid the risks of competitive disadvantage.

Classical management theory no doubt influenced practice in the past. Organizations were structured and operated in a manner intended to duplicate the ideas of Fayol and those who followed him. Guides were developed for use by certain major management consulting firms to facilitate the implementation of classical theory. However, such guides are rarely, if ever, consulted today. Practice has moved on, and it seems unlikely that many reorganizations now are modeled after classical theory in anything but the most general sense. With a few exceptions such as the introduction of formal, long-range planning there is no solid basis for believing that they should follow classical theory. One can force the theory's constructs and contend that much of what is done in the business world, for instance, fits one or more of Fayol's formulations. However, line-staff and project structures, profit centers, an office of the president containing several coequals, venture teams, dual hierarchies, even multidivisional forms, and many other aspects of the current organizational scene, really are not part of classical theory.

Bureaucratic theory appears to be more adequately reflected in today's organizational forms, primarily because of the nature of its variables and the level of abstraction of its propositions. Our large organizations tend to be bureaucracies almost without exception. To the extent these organizations are formalized, standardized, specialized, rationalized, and decentralized, they tend to be more effective. In other words, if one is going to use a bureaucratic system, one should go all the way, and also staff it with managers whose motives are appropriate to that context. But there is nothing that says that bureaucratic systems per se are more effective than other types of systems. They may be, as Weber hypothesized, but we do not know that for sure, because the kind of research that takes pure samples of various systems and controls them for all possible effects from sources other than the organizational form itself has not yet been carried out.

Understanding Organizations

Ideally, it would be possible at this point to rank the theories of organizational structure and process on various factors and choose the ones to follow. Such an exercise would, in fact, be meaningless. The theories are spread over a number of domains dealing with different aspects of the total problem. Some not very powerful theories would have to be endorsed, at least temporarily, simply because they occupy domains alone, while other theories that are more powerful might have to be rejected because there are even better formulations within the same theoretical space. Tying the best available theories in the various domains together into a unified, super-theory also would serve the goals of science and application alike. Unfortunately, that too would be premature. Overlapping domains, uncharted areas, and numerous constructs with unknown relationships to each other assure the failure of any such unifying effort at the present time.

Clearly, the theory of organizational structure and process has not as yet achieved what we would like from it. At the same time the various theories have generated a considerable body of knowledge. Understanding, prediction, and the capacity to manage the future have been advanced in numerous ways. Without question, the major portion of existing knowledge in the macro organizational field derives from theories and theory-related research. Contributions to this body of knowledge have been uneven, however. Some theoretical approaches seem to have been much less fruitful than others.

Grand theories covering a wide landscape have characteristically not done as well as theories of more limited scope. Contingency theories that stress a single contingency variable such as technology or uncertainty have not done well, either. One suspects that a more effective theoretical approach would utilize multiple contingencies, applying different factors to the various aspects of structure and process. The existing theories in this area have sought to cope with this need by defining a single contingency variable in very broad terms, apparently in the hope that most of the important multiple contingencies could be accommodated within the one construct. The results have been serious problems in the area of construct validity that make measurement difficult and clear interpretation of the findings impossible.

Systems theories, too, are unlikely to contribute a great deal in years to come. One difficulty is the broad domain to which they typically aspire; they may well be attempting too much and accordingly end by spreading their propositions too thinly. A second problem is that systems theory is based on highly abstract and abstruse constructs that are difficult to operationalize. As a result, research is not forthcoming and little is actually learned.

Perhaps more important than either of the preceding problems is the systems theory assumption that any variable may be related to any other. This is a basic article of faith. The theory anticipates all kinds of reciprocal interactions, feedback loops, and causal relationships. Even domain limitation is hardly justified for open systems theory, with the result that theorists do not know where to stop. Good theory needs to separate the wheat from the chaff and settle on a limited set of directional, causal hypotheses of maximum explanatory and/or predictive power. The very nature of systems theory tends to thwart the attainment of such goals. As a result, truly researchable hypotheses dealing with relationships between variables tend to be few in number.

Systems theories to date have provided a framework for thinking about organizations but have not stimulated research. The framework has been useful, but it is unlikely to encourage further progress. The current need is to free these constructs from the shackles of systems thinking, refine them, posit hypotheses regarding the causal processes involved, and do research.

In the time-long controversy between theories of a human relations bent and those of a hierarchical nature neither appears to be right or wrong. The human relations theorists have been struggling toward a theory of group or collegial systems, though at times they have confounded these with professional systems, and even with task or entrepreneurial systems. They have apparently come close to isolating pure cases in some of the autonomous work group studies. The bureaucratic or hierarchical systems theorists have focused on a different system that operates in a quite different manner and is effective when staffed with different kinds of people.

Both systems *can* be effective. One appears more suited to larger organizations; the other, to smaller organizations or to relatively isolated cells within a larger context. To the extent a society consists of all kinds of people with wide individual differences, both systems are needed (and others, too) to capitalize on the varied strengths of its members. In this context it matters very little whether hierarchical systems are somewhat superior to group systems or vice versa. On the other hand, were the society to homogenize its membership in some manner, such issues could have considerable practical significance.

Conclusions

In its objectives and approach the present volume closely parallels *Theories of Organizational Behavior* (Miner, 1980). One might ask, which aspect of organizational science, the micro or the macro, has produced the more effective body of theory. Based on intensive study of some thirty separate theories, the highly subjective conclusion appears to be that the field of organizational behavior has a larger number of better theories judged against criteria of scientific and practical value. Organizational structure and process is not devoid of theories of comparable worth, but it appears to have fewer of them.

It is hard to explain this difference. If anything, the macro theories tend to be older, but because a theory is older does not mean that it performs poorly. As noted at the end of Chapter 1, the selection of theories to consider in the two books was preceded by a survey of a panel of thirty-five knowledgeable individuals who nominated theories for inclusion on the basis of the criteria of scientific value, amount of research generated, and practical application. One might expect that the organizational behavior theories would have received more nominations, but the difference was slight (an average of 13.0 to 11.5). There is little evidence of a relation between frequency of nomination and judged contribution in either field.

In disciplinary origin the organizational behavior theorists tend overwhelmingly to have backgrounds in psychology. A number of the organizational structure and process theorists do also, but they are joined by another large group from sociology and a smattering from each of a number of other social sciences. When psychologists get into the macro field, they do less well as theorists than the psychologists in the micro field. This is surprising because psychologists in the macro area tend to develop primarily micro-domain theories. The sociologists as a group have not been highly effective in creating structure and process theories, but their relative position is essentially attributable to their preoccupation with the technological imperative. It seems unlikely that disciplinary origin can account for the micro-macro theory differential either. It may well be that a difference in the resistance of the subject matter to theoretical penetration constitutes the major factor.

It is significant that psychologists are stimulated to produce organizational behavior theories or, if they enter the structure and process field, to focus their primary efforts at the micro level. Sociologists, political scientists, economists, historians, and those in the management field develop theories that are almost always of a macro nature. The result tends to be a somewhat artificial, discipline-related segmenting of the field of organizational science.

The potential advantages of linking motivational and leadership theories of organizational behavior more closely have already been noted (Miner, 1980). Now it appears that tying these theories into constructs from organizational structure and process theory might prove equally fruitful. Apparently because of disciplinary boundaries, this has been done effectively only on a very limited basis, in the case of Argyris's goal congruence concept of integration, for instance, or Victor Thompson's bureaupathology. Further efforts of this kind might join together what tend now to be two separate areas of study, to the mutual advantage of both.

References

Miner, John B. *Theories of Organizational Behavior*. Hinsdale, Ill.: Dryden Press, 1980.

Name Index

Page numbers followed by *t* indicate tables. Page numbers followed by *f* indicate figures.

Subject Index

Page numbers followed by *t* indicate tables. Pages numbers followed by *f* indicate figures.